Safdar Ahmed is Lecturer and Tutor in the Department of Islamic and Arabic Studies at the University of Sydney, where he also obtained his PhD.

REFORM AND MODERNITY IN ISLAM

The Philosophical, Cultural and Political
Discourses among Muslim Reformers

SAFDAR AHMED

I.B. TAURIS
LONDON · NEW YORK

Published in 2013 by I.B.Tauris & Co Ltd
6 Salem Road, London W2 4BU
175 Fifth Avenue, New York NY 10010
www.ibtauris.com

Distributed in the United States and Canada
Exclusively by Palgrave Macmillan
175 Fifth Avenue, New York NY 10010

Copyright © 2013 Safdar Ahmed

The right of Safdar Ahmed to be identified as the author of this work has been asserted by the author in accordance with the Copyright, Designs and Patent Act 1988.

All rights reserved. Except for brief quotations in a review, this book, or any part thereof, may not be reproduced, stored in or introduced into a retrieval system, or transmitted, in any form or by any means, electronic, mechanical, photocopying, recording or otherwise, without the prior written permission of the publisher.

Library of Modern Religion 26

ISBN 978 1 84885 735 3

A full CIP record for this book is available from the British Library
A full CIP record for this book is available from the Library of Congress

Library of Congress catalog card: available

Typeset by Newgen Publishers, Chennai
Printed and bound by CPI Group (UK) Ltd, Croydon, CR0 4YY

CONTENTS

Acknowledgements	vi
Introduction: Islam, Postcolonialism and Modernity	1
1. Islamic Modernism and the Reification of Religion	43
2. Literary Romanticism and Islamic Modernity: The Case of Urdu Poetry	75
3. Education and the Status of Women	100
4. Muhammad Iqbal, Islam and Modern Nationalism	120
5. The Theory of Divine Sovereignty	148
6. Maududi and the Gendering of Muslim Identity	176
7. Progressive Islam: The Hermeneutical Turn	200
Conclusion	224
Notes	229
Bibliography	272
Index	291

ACKNOWLEDGEMENTS

The idea for this book began as part of my doctoral research with the Department of Islamic and Arabic Studies at the University of Sydney. I would specially like to thank my supervisor, Ahmad Shboul, for his generosity of spirit and high standards of scholarship. What might have seemed like difficult work was made pleasurable thanks to the many informative and stimulating discussions which enabled me to find my own perspective, and which assisted me at every stage of the writing process. I am grateful to Nijmeh Hajjar, who was my teacher in Arabic at the University of Sydney and to Hashim Durrani, who assisted me in the translation of Urdu texts. I am also deeply indebted to James Piscatori, Ali Mahafzah and Youssef Choueiri who provided thoughtful and considered feedback on the entire manuscript, and to Jim Masselos, who gave valuable support in the production of its second chapter. For their patient editing, which gave greater concision and clarity to the text than I was able to achieve, I thank Emma Wise and Hannah Wilks. I am also grateful to the staff of Fisher Library at the University of Sydney and their inter-loan department. I have been fortunate to teach and learn alongside some very bright students at the University of Sydney, who have also been an important and inspiring sounding board for new ideas.

For supporting me in other spheres of life, and for providing important feedback on particular chapters and themes which were then under consideration, I am indebted to a number of cherished friends.

Acknowledgements

These including Briony Denver, Robin Denver, Anton Pulvirenti, Ted McKinlay, Chris Matos, Renata Hoare, Chrissie Ianssen, Arthur Lawrence, Lisa Worthington, Stephen Buckle and Heather and Ellen McIlwain. Special mention must go to Jillian McIlwain for supporting me during times of ill-health. In the requisition of books, I am grateful to my stepmother, Farrukh Ahmed, and those family members in Pakistan who purchased and sent books to Australia. Bilquis Ghani and Omid Tofighian provided me with the sort of friendship that will only grow as the years roll on, and which developed around our support of asylum seekers at Sydney's Villawood Detention Centre. Their companionship has been precious to me. And lastly, this book would have been impossible to write were it not for the encouragement, patience and unconditional love of my family: Anna Broom, Nazeer Ahmed, Iqbal Ahmed and Zehra Ahmed.

INTRODUCTION

ISLAM, POSTCOLONIALISM AND MODERNITY

The overarching theme of this book is that there is no singular or transcendental definition of modernity next to which other variant or lesser modernities are compared. This is not to claim that modernity is so diffuse as to bear no meaning or that it connotes different things to different people. Rather, modernity must be placed in its historical setting, which is to release it from the exclusionary Eurocentric paradigms by which it is commonly defined. Whilst modern ideas, movements and ideologies properly begin in Western Europe during the time of the Enlightenment, their historical paths (under the engines of colonialism, global capitalism, nationalism and globalisation) are so fractured and complex as to exceed any particular doctrine, culture or essence. To speak of modernity in historical terms, therefore, is to invoke a cluster of contested philosophical ideas and practices which provide the conditions, or common ground, for the generation of diverse ideologies both in and outside Europe.

Yet, too often, when historians, media pundits and policy analysts sit down to interpret modernity in the context of contemporary Islamic thought, a homogeneous, flat and hackneyed conception of the modern world emerges. This is not a consequence of Islam's own encounter with modernity, but of its being placed in an anterior historical and chronological position to that of the modern West. Islam, we are told, must get through its religious wars, find its Martin Luther and learn to separate the powers of church and state if we are to see the arrival of such things as democracy, human rights and women's freedoms in the Muslim world. This claim gets co-opted by secular political discourses in which modernity or a modern 'way of life' is opposed to Islamic revivalism – or Muslim culture more generally – in tones reminiscent of the Cold War. At its most distorted, this dichotomy simplistically conflates modernity with all that is rational, forward-looking and civilised, to be defended from an Islam cast as irrational, totalitarian and atavistic.

In the reactive and often shallow political commentary of policy analysts, media pundits, journalists and opinion-piece writers, Islam or Islamist movements are placed against a normative definition of secular modernity. Francis Fukuyama, for one, has likened the reactionary or anti-modern character of contemporary Islam to the worst strains of totalitarian thought, using the pejorative term: 'Islamo-fascism'.[1] Likewise, one often hears contemporary Islamist groups, such as the Muslim Brothers in Egypt or the Islamic regime in Iran, described as 'anti-modern' or 'un-modern' for purportedly opposing the tenets of political liberalism: a stance which constitutes them as walking anachronisms, or relics of another time.[2] Yet in the use of terms such as 'Islamic terrorism', as Alain Badiou points out, 'the predicate "Islamic" has no other function except that of supplying an apparent content to the word "terrorism", which is itself devoid of all content'.[3] In this sense, 'terrorism' (like 'fundamentalism' and 'fascism') is conflated with the adjective which precedes it, becoming, in turn, a part (the 'problem') of Islam itself.

Alas, rhetorical cues such as the 'war on modernity' and the 'threat to the Enlightenment' cannot accommodate Islamic reformism's complex and sustained entanglement in the historical and political conditions of modernity. The implication that Islam simply needs to 'catch up' with the West involves a one-dimensional image of both Islam and the West which reduces their internal complexities whilst overlooking the histories they share. One cannot understand the contemporary societies of the Muslim Middle East, for instance, without accounting for the communications, differences and interactions which have occurred amongst and between European powers and indigenous peoples since the colonial period. Before I explore the implications of this (over and above the inaccuracy of attributing to Islam a variation upon the ideology of European fascism), it is important to underscore the different conceptions of modernity to which Muslim societies have been exposed, and from which their own modernity is shaped.

Defining Modernity

By way of a definition, there are two general though often opposed philosophical conceptions of modernity which chart a wide and tangled path in global history from the eighteenth century onwards. The one I will address first is understood, according to the tenets of Enlightenment thinkers such as Immanuel Kant and David Hume, as a project for the liberation of human beings from the self-incurred bonds of irrationality and superstition through the application of reason-centred ideas and institutions. This point of view circumscribes a teleological scheme, in which history's dialectical turns and negations are streamlined towards the realisation of a singular truth, spirit or historical destination. This conception of history as an ends-driven process, which aims towards a particular outcome premised upon notions of human happiness or improvement, underpins such twentieth-century ideologies as Marxism and neo-liberal capitalism. In traditional Marxism, for instance, this takes the form of a particular class, the proletariat, which has not yet become sufficiently conscious of itself to forge a society in which abilities and needs are balanced equitably. In the case of economic neo-liberalism, it takes the form of a society guided by benign market forces which purportedly increase individual freedoms and loosen the grip of authoritarian governments. These ideologies, whose opposition became a feature of Cold War politicking, are universal in their scope. They propose to resolve the dialectical oppositions and disintegrating forces which assail the political, economic and existential development predicted for all (post-capitalist or post-industrial) societies. (The other conception of modernity, whose development cannot be subsumed beneath an overarching historical theme or essence, will be described shortly.)

A singular and trans-historical conception of modern thought came into its own during the late eighteenth and nineteenth centuries when liberal notions of 'development' and 'progress', exhorting the supremacy of European statecraft, science, politics and culture, were promoted as a part of imperial ideology and accepted amongst indigenous elites. In colonial India, for example, liberal imperialists such as John Stuart and James Mill, Lord Macaulay and Jeremy Bentham, bestowed ideological legitimacy upon British rule by claiming that its mission would be to help the societies under its administration achieve the levels of political maturity and 'civilisation' required to take on the mantle of representative democracy. Because all societies cannot be graded equally, and those under British administration had not yet satisfied the requisites for representative government, liberal thinkers endorsed colonial rule – which they conceived as a form of tutelage – for those who existed at a lower point on the linear gradient of historical progress. Through education and training, Indians were to acquire a model of bourgeois civility which enforced the modern state's distinction between public (civil) and private spheres of life, and which accompanied bureaucratic types of industry, science, medicine and so forth, organised beneath the arch of reason.[4] This pedagogical aspect of imperial ideology is reflected in statements advocating the need to lift indigenous peoples to a higher rung of the civilisational ladder (as conceived in James Mill's *History of British India*) or to drag them out from a position analogous to Europe's past, into the present.[5]

However, this discourse towards indigenous improvement bore a fundamental ambivalence which (as historians aligned with the *Subaltern Studies* project of Indian historiography have pointed out) impacted upon the thinking of anti-colonial and nationalist elites.[6] Because Europe represented the final realisation of the ideological forms of modern life, it is an ironic truism that the deficiencies attributed to colonial or postcolonial societies could not be understood except from within a universalised European historical narrative from which they were simultaneously excluded. Non-European societies were seen as mired in an elementary, or less fulfilled, stage of the West's epistemological development until such time as they were able to catch up with and so make themselves a tropical extension of the West. But how can societies which exist in an anterior position to the modern world be brought up to it? Moreover, how could one become authentically modern when the vision of historical progress imposed onto the colonised world simultaneously constituted it as a belated replication of the West? As Homi Bhabha points out, in his reading of Macaulay's *Minute on Education* (1835), the education of Britain's Indian subjects to European standards of bourgeois civility deferred the promise of liberal citizenship by presenting them as the objects of 'mimicry', 'lack' or 'failure'.[7]

This ambivalent aspect of colonial discourses, which enjoined Indians to embrace a model of bourgeois civility whilst establishing the conditions for their failure to do so, is disparagingly ironised in a journal entry by the influential Muslim modernist and popular historian, Sayyid Amir 'Ali (1849–1928):

> The superimposition of the utilitarian and not very altruistic civilisation of the West on the Indian civilisations has produced some anomalous features. For years past Englishmen have been engaged in diffusing Western ideas among the people. The effort has been to Christianise, Europeanise, modernise Indian thought and Indian life, to break down old customs and habits, to alter social institutions and family conditions, to develop a national sentiment. In some directions the effort has met with success, in others with hopeless failure. And now that after several generations of continuous labour it has begun to bear fruit, the result is viewed with surprise mixed with resentment.[8]

For Amir 'Ali, this 'surprise mixed with resentment' speaks for the predicament of colonial institutions, in which:

> ... the failings which every virile race despises were stigmatised as 'Oriental attributes', and Indians were advised to cultivate self-respect, independence of character, manliness and originality of thought – qualities they were supposed to be wanting in. It is an extraordinary circumstance, however, that the possession of these very qualities is a serious handicap to those who have them; whilst servility and sycophancy, despised in theory, receive encouragement in practice. The effect of this cynicism is disastrous on the national character of Hindus and Muslims.[9]

So it is that discourses committed to the improvement of indigenous lives betrayed an internal ambivalence which impacted on local efforts towards reform and 'self-improvement'.

Whilst Amir 'Ali rebukes the British Empire for not being as civilised as it claimed to be – a charge echoed in the numerous complaints of anti-colonial nationalist leaders and nativists for whom the empire had stalled on promises of liberal equality – he also connects the motif of indigenous 'failure' to those ambivalences, contradictions, and ironies which befog such terms as national 'improvement' in the first place. This discursive strategy was to be reproduced by the celebrated Algerian anti-colonialist, Frantz Fanon, who urged his compatriots to reject a Europe which is 'never done talking of Man, yet murder men everywhere they find them'.[10] Whilst such sentiments may be misconstrued, in the wrong hands, as a type of ideological nativism, they also point to an ambiguity which, as Homi Bhabha claims, is 'not necessarily an act of political intention, nor is it the single negation and exclusion of the "content" of another culture'. Rather:

> It is the effect of an ambivalence produced within the rules of recognition of dominating discourses as they articulate the signs of cultural difference and reimplicate them within the differential relations of colonial power – hierarchy, normalization, marginalization, and so forth. For colonial domination is achieved through a process of disavowal that denies the chaos of its intervention. . .[and] dislocatory presence in order to preserve the authority of its identity in the teleological narratives of historical and political evolutionism.[11]

Modern civilisation's 'anomalous features' (as described by Amir 'Ali) must be attributed more to those Oriental 'failings' which the colonial discourse instantiates, and simultaneously combats, than to any real deficiency (however that is to be judged) on the part of indigenous actors. In the context of nineteenth-century colonialism, this ambivalence disrupts such ideas as civilisation, progress and modernity, which are inscribed by the strategies of cultural authority and resistance these themes enact.

This refers us to the historical discourses of Orientalism and modernisation, in which the theme of mimicking Europe and lacking the means to emulate it has continued to influence the appraisal of colonial and postcolonial societies. Whilst I will examine these approaches in more detail shortly, a problem arises when the historicist image of Europe's (and the world's) modernity is contrasted with the 'non-modern', collective, irrational or 'mythical' mentalities of formerly colonised peoples, who are then benighted with a lesser or unfulfilled version of the West's intellectual history.[12] The theoretical implications of this are highlighted in Abdallah Laroui's observation that whilst modern intellectual paradigms have irrevocably distorted the way historians approach the Third World, contemporary Arab intellectuals nonetheless have no option but to work within such paradigms if they are to resolve the problems of development and modernity. For Laroui, the 'crisis' of the Arab intellectual – which is the crisis of Arab society as a whole – can only be remedied through a historicist critique of those contemporary ideological trends (the atavistic traditionalism of *salafist* intellectuals or the ideological eclecticism of modern leftists) which have distorted the way Arabs view their society and their past.[13] Whilst Laroui's move towards a critical and self-reflexive historicism is salutary, the question remains as to whether Third World societies can indeed negotiate a post-liberal Western culture which embraces them as modernity's latecomers – just as it concedes their 'cultural retardation'.[14]

Against the trans-historical claims of modern liberal thought to a singular philosophical viewpoint, then, I would point to the usefulness of another paradigm with which to theorise the recalcitrance of supposedly 'non-modern' cultures and societies. This does not conceive of modernity in singular terms but as an open-ended dialectic of movement, change, self-criticism and reinvention unconstrained by a unitary historical premise. This paradigm cannot be described as a continuous tradition and I do not have the space to explore it in all its dimensions here, except to point out that it develops the notion, familiar to such eighteenth-century thinkers as Vico and Herder, that human history does not move along a straight line and cannot be associated with the triumph of a particular culture, religion or nation. Whilst Arthur Strum attributes this to the Enlightenment penchant for self-criticism, encapsulated in Kant's imperative to rebel against the illegitimate guardians of philosophical and theological despotism, others have located it in the thought of the Romantic counter-Enlightenment.[15] Yet whichever factor is more determinative is of secondary importance to that dialectical scheme from which particular philosophers and historians have been able to resist the singularisation of European intellectual history.[16] A conflictual notion of modern thought also means that no single phenomenon, least of all the premise of a pure and distanced rationality, can be used to define the present age.

This paradigm is eminently useful for opening modernity out to the complexities, paradoxes and ambivalences which have marked its ideological and political projects since the eighteenth century. By refusing to conceive of history as a teleologically-motivated or ends-driven process, one allows for modernity's exchange, reconstitution and entanglement across and between disparate cultures and geographies under the aegis of colonialism, capitalism and globalisation. History no longer embodies the unfurling of a transcendent truth or 'grand narrative' but is the product of human activities which are irrevocably contingent, fickle and changeable. And because colonialism was not peripheral but central to the universalist projects of empire and capitalism, I hold the view, in agreement with Robert Young, that colonial discourse analysis is uniquely placed to critique the conditions, languages and cultures of modernity.[17] By overseeing the formulation and application of modern liberal paradigms in a society made up of both colonisers and their indigenous subjects, the colonial project clears a space for the criticism of modern thought which extends far beyond the theoretical exemplars of European liberalism.

Moreover, the technological scope of Europe's nineteenth-century colonial regimes – encompassing developments in industry, global trade, travel and communications networks – produced an environment in which otherwise disparate cultural pasts and historical patterns would converge.[18] One might point out that big empires have always done this. Of course, the pre-modern empires of the Habsburgs, Ottomans, Mughals, Manchus and Tsars created their own world economies (and intellectual hegemony) into which exterior societies were drawn. Yet, unlike these dynasties, modern imperialism is uniquely relevant to a discussion of contemporary political exigencies for the way it incorporated its colonial satrapies into the global capitalist system and subsequent ordering of nation-states. Modern imperialism can thus be distinguished from its ancient and medieval forerunners precisely in its ability to draw the cultures and societies of diverse geographical regions together within an expanding capitalist economy, which then catalysed the present global order. As sound studies of imperial thought and the construction of Victorian identities have concluded, the ideological forms which came to define European colonial power were not created exclusively within Europe's metropolitan and cultural centres *before* they were exported to the colonies, as is commonly assumed. Colonialism instead provided the context and environment in which ideas of civilisation, progress and modernity took shape, which is to say that the identities of both the coloniser and colonised emerged alongside, against and in counterpoint to one another.[19]

Here I am instructed by the claim of the anthropologist historian, Peter van der Veer, that the imperial context enables us to critique those conventional colonial and nationalist frameworks in which the coloniser and colonised are held at arm's length.[20] It would certainly be wrong to conceive – as anti-colonial nationalists often have – of the colonial relationship as a meeting point between all-powerful European imperialists (bearing a pre-formed European identity) and indigenous populations, in which the former's domination over the latter laid the ground for the eventual and belated reclamation of a pure, native identity. Instead we must attend to the manner in which the ideological projects of anti-colonial and nationalist elites overlapped, in aim and content, with the modernising aspirations of colonial authorities. This is not to posit a betrayal of the emancipatory themes propagated by postcolonial nationalists since the early twentieth century, but to point out that theirs was also a modernising agenda which was contingent upon notions of bureaucratic citizenship, secular-linear time and the separation of public and private spheres. Nor is it to slight the undeniable political, economic and military superiority arrogated by the imperial powers. It is to affirm, rather, that modern imperial-metropolitan identities were as influenced by, and sustained through, the conditions of colonialism as those they exploited.

So begins the story of our mutually entangled modernities. Since the colonial era, it is no exaggeration to assert that the modern age has witnessed unprecedented levels of migration, displacement, communication and the globalisation of goods and cultures across vast geographies and at unprecedented speeds. Today, new diasporas and patterns in migration are closely linked to the global autonomy of commerce and financial capital, which coincides with such problems as human and drugs trafficking, prostitution, the spread of diseases, organised crime and international terrorism. Likewise, the globalisation and spread of popular cultural forms and organisations through the internet and electronic media provides new spaces for the forging of communities. Indeed, the fluid and immediate nature of internet communications has allowed trans-global organisations committed to issues such as human rights, freedom of speech and the conservation of the environment (amongst a host of less serious or commendable online communities) to bypass the intellectual hegemony of the state in countries in which ruling elites have hitherto exerted a censorial influence over media and information. The functional role played by information-sharing and social networking websites, such as YouTube and Facebook, in the democratic uprisings in Tunisia and Egypt of 2011 are a testimony to this. By the same token, processes of globalisation have provided a space for the de-territorialisation of ethnic nationalisms and religious movements whose survival was formerly dependent upon the classical sociological locus of the nation-state.[21] None of this means that the nation-state will disappear. Rather, the proliferation and speed of modern communications only increases the fluidity with which national and trans-national social imaginaries are formed.

Contrary to the notion that 'advanced' Western societies are the eternal harbinger of a self-fulfilling modernity which it is the rest of the world's destiny to emulate if they are so able, this thesis will focus on the common ground, or shared problem-space (alongside and in counterpoint to the West), which has informed the discourses and presumptions of Muslim reformist thought from the second half of the nineteenth century. My purpose is clearly not to 'update' Islamic history by showing that it compares to, or mimics, a simplified version of the West's own development. Instead it is to show that modern

Muslim reformist ideologies relate to, and are instructed by, those global conditions in which the West's and all other modernities are grounded. This is a largely un-thought or unexamined history, I argue, due primarily to those positivistic, Eurocentric historical paradigms which have influenced social science theories of modernisation and a great deal of independent scholarly analysis.

Whilst the search for a proper historical theory of modernity is first and foremost an intellectual endeavour, certain aspects of the global discourse surrounding Muslim terrorism, and Islam in general, since the attacks on New York and Washington in 2001 have given this task a contemporary urgency. Now more than ever, it seems, there is no alternative to a rhetorical style which constructs Islam against everything that proposes itself to be 'modern' in the sense of being humane, rational and secular. Yet this dichotomy is inherently unstable, if not untrue, because it elides those intellectual histories which are both contested and shared between the worlds of Islam and the West (if one may speak of them, in shorthand, as separate worlds and not as an agglomeration of heterogeneous cultures and peoples).[22] In what follows, I will set out to critique those historical models which impede our understanding of modern Muslim thought by contrasting it with a singularly conceived notion of European modernity. In their place, I shall restate the need for a more complex idea of modernity with which to properly historicise the phenomenon of Islamic reform.

Modernisation Theory as Enlightenment Universalism

The dominant theory of modernisation, which is derived from the sociological analysis of thinkers such as Marx, Durkheim and Weber, proposed that modernity accompanied the ideas and attitudes which attended the development of capitalist political economies and the secular nation-state as they arose in the West. The assumption was that processes of modernisation (the structural processes of urbanisation, industrialisation, bureaucratisation and so forth) would inevitably lead to the relative convergence of societies everywhere, resulting in a condition of global technological and economic parity. This convergence was guaranteed by modernity's superseding of 'tradition' in which pre-modern religions, metaphysical systems and superstitions were to adapt to (or make way for) processes of rationalisation, secularisation and technological development. Whilst modernisation theorists often stressed different types of change, spanning the economic, cultural, psychological and political spheres, a mainstay of sociological theory after Max Weber holds that modern capitalist societies are characterised by a process of 'rationalisation', or instrumental reason, amongst institutions which work towards liberating individuals from the collectivising hold of 'primitive' or pre-modern cultures, dispositions and rituals.[23]

For modernisation theorists, this emphasis on modernity as the promise and condition for human freedom premised the individual, unencumbered self as the creator and purveyor of all meaning. After Max Weber's *Capitalism and the Protestant Ethic*, which stressed the influence of personal values on the rise of capitalism, modern ideas and institutions were conceived as reflecting the cultural beliefs and agency of worldly, self-creating individuals.[24] According to this notion, modernisation is not a by-product of largely impersonal historical or economic forces, but realises itself as the fulfilment of a universal, or extra-historical, human condition. It cannot be linked to a propitious moment in time, in which the right psychological and material conditions arose within the societies of Western Europe and the US, but must be attributed to the psychological orientation of those peoples. Because modernity entails the scientific demystification or 'disenchantment' of irrational religious beliefs and rituals, its structural transformations would foster a forward-looking, deliberative, and rational notion of the self. To this end, modernisation theory reproduced the teleological premise of liberal European schemes for the improvement of human history and realisation of a global common good.

This teleological aspect of modernisation was acted out, during the 1950s and 1960s, on the back of American liberal ideology in the bipolar political order of the Cold War.[25] Because the exponents of modernisation in the United States presented it as a scientific model for the formation of democratic states within the capitalist world system (of which communist states were a 'deviant' and distorted form), modernisation supplied a blueprint to be emulated by the decolonising countries of Asia, Africa, the Middle East, and Latin America. Whilst modernisation theorists now and then made room for the necessary adaptation of 'traditional' cultures, forms and institutions, these were ultimately devalued as obsolete entities on the path of technological and political progress. Because traditional religious institutions were deemed out of step with the ideas and functions of the modern state, modernisation would, of its own accord, vitiate such institutions and their founding visions. Such assumptions informed the modernising projects of newly liberated postcolonial states and played a significant role in the formulation of American foreign policy towards the countries of the 'developing world'.

An early though paradigmatic account of this organising myth was presented in Daniel Lerner's *The Passing of a Traditional Society* (first published in 1958), which sought to evaluate the prospects of political and economic development in the Arab Middle East.[26] Positing a linear path of development, from a 'traditional' to a 'modern' society, Lerner associated modernity with a forward-looking, altruistic, 'mobile' type of personality, which accompanied processes of urbanisation, increased literacy, access to news media and political participation in the Middle East. Because modern democratic states foster a notion of citizenship which is facilitated by participation in elections, increased levels of literacy, and access to electronic and print media, they engender forward-looking individuals who are required to take an interest in matters extending beyond the traditional spheres of their family circle and tribe. Following the work of the modernisation theorist David Reisman, Lerner described the emotion of empathy, or 'capacity to see oneself in the other fellow's situation', as a defining psychological feature of those who live in modern societies.[27] Indigenous cultural and religious traditions, on the other hand, were felt to work against the formation of the modern self. Because such pre-modern traditions are collectivist and doctrinaire, they cannot accommodate the needs of autonomous individuals within a democratic society. Those considered modern, then, are those that have realised a normative pattern of behaviour which is based on the emotion of empathy, and which arises through participation in mass media and democratic elections. The dichotomy established between tradition and change, evoked by

Lerner as a choice between 'Mecca and mechanization', provided a lens through which issues of development within the Arab world were to be analysed and understood.[28]

However, this paradigm for the development of the region came under revision during the 1970s, when it became obvious that the forces of 'culture' and 'tradition' were not going to disappear under the influence of modernisation and may just as easily act as a vehicle for it. At the outset, Lerner's optimism surrounding technological modernisation and a spirit of empathy begetting the growth of democratic institutions fell out of step with the consolidation of one-party dictatorships across the Middle East. Moreover, the rise of new or rejuvenated political-religious movements, the most dramatic of which was the 1979 Islamic revolution in Iran, prompted modernisation theorists to attempt to account for the seemingly inexplicable presence of pre-modern cultural and religious dispositions in the formation of nation-states. That such political theologies were not restricted to the Muslim Middle East but emerged on a global scale (including the Zionist settler movement of Israel, Hindu nationalists in India, Sinhalese Buddhists in Sri Lanka and the Christian right in the US) further challenged the validity of modernisation theory's universalist claims to the rationalisation, or secularisation, of the world. Area specialists who had long been comfortable with the transposition of a European historical frame to their area of expertise were discovering the shortcomings of a theory which could no longer claim to understand local developments.

In its place, various historians found a productive alternative in Marxist-inspired 'dependency theory' and its account of the initial and ongoing economic disparities which separated imperial from colonised societies. Breaking with the convergence hypothesis at the heart of modernisation theory, in which development was relegated to independent nation-states whose eventual success would purportedly lead to a condition of universal parity, dependency theorists posited that all nations belonged to a single, global economic system whose outcomes were not the same for everyone. Samir Amin's examination of the historical integration of the Arab Middle East under imperialism into the world economy, in *The Arab Nation*, did not frame modernity as a benign or transparent process contingent only upon Arab countries' individual levels and speeds of 'development', as modernisation theorists had presumed. The Arab world was instead reconstituted under imperialism as a 'dominated periphery' of the capitalist system, which made it subsidiary to the economic and political fruits of global capitalism.[29] Whilst dependency theory supplied a persuasive theoretical model and explanation for the economic disparity between developed and less (or 'under-') developed countries, it nonetheless reproduced modernisation theory's penchant for contrasting tradition and change within an overarching metanarrative of structural and economic progress.

Alternatively, social scientists associated with the work of S. N. Eisenstadt have sought to encompass the diverse and often paradoxical political, economic, institutional and cultural programmes of modernity throughout the world with the theory of 'multiple modernities'.[30] From the premise that Westernisation, or a narrow interpretation of what the West is meant to represent, cannot be taken as the normative model for modernising societies everywhere, the notion of multiple modernities supplies a framework for sociological analysis which is less dismissive of the modernising projects of ethnic nationalists and religious revivalists. For Eisenstadt, the expansion of modernity represents the formation of a new type of civilisation, going back to the Axial Age, which is defined by common structural and economic patterns, but whose cultural manifestations are as diverse and pluralistic as the human societies it encompasses. Whilst Eisenstadt's thesis represents a useful point of departure for thinking about modernisation, the notion of multiple modernities still posits the equal stake of different societies to become modern whilst overemphasising the primacy of essentialised cultural units to negotiate modern ideas on their own terms.

Because modernisation theory provided no theoretical alternative to the overarching scheme of a world made over in the shape of the West, its passing should not be mourned.[31] And yet, no alternative emerged which was not already implicit in the theme of 'multiple modernities'. Instead, the notion that processes of modernisation would transform local cultures into one global culture was substituted for an equally reductive theory in which Muslim culture and faith are seen to influence, and in some cases determine, the changing (modernising) social and political conditions of the Arab Muslim world. This spelled a rejection of the cultural relativism of modernisation theorists such as Daniel Lerner who (to the extent that they thought about culture at all) had presumed the equal ability of different societies to throw off past traditions and converge in the way of 'developed' Western countries. In its place, a more rigid and essentialising view of Arab society, which emphasised the stasis of tradition over change and which had long defined the position of Orientalist scholars in America and Europe, came to wield the prestige and explanatory power modernisation theory once enjoyed.

Orientalism and the 'Clash of Civilisations'

For Orientalist historians, the Muslim world's apparent unwillingness to embrace the changes of modernisation was a reflection on the static nature of Islam. After the World War II, the German-American cultural anthropologist and historian Gustave von Grunebaum claimed that whilst 'few culture areas have been subjected to so much and so violent change as that of Islam' in the modern period, perhaps none had 'so consistently refused to accept the ontological reality of change'. For von Grunebaum:

> The truth of Islam... is not only one and indivisible, it is also immutable; it is neither growing nor shrinking; its understanding may vary in adequacy but it has been changelessly available since it was vouchsafed [to] mankind through the Seal of the Prophets. This goes for doctrine and conduct as well as for their institutionalization.[32]

Von Grunebaum's statement, which ties Islam to a 'truth' distinguished by its immutability, is representative of a great deal of Orientalist scholarship in the twentieth century. When Islam is treated as a coherent and self-explanatory category of analysis, as a 'culture' or 'civilisation' whose external forms can always be distilled into a stable and timeless religious essence, the historian need only identify a correspondence between the social forms and structures of a given moment in Islamic history and the concepts of religious ideology which are assumed to have shaped and defined those structures. This then legitimates attempts to evaluate or compare Islam to other (homogeneously conceived) cultures and civilisations. Such an approach reflects the tendency amongst Orientalist historians of the nineteenth century to understand 'culture' through the narrow study of canonical religious texts, to the exclusion of the variant and diverse interpretations, doctrines and practices so often encountered in continuing legal and theological traditions. The notion that religious thought is complex, that it is born of different and contradictory influences, was less meaningful than the determinative and overwhelming agency of Islam conceived as both a religion and culture.

For those who subscribe to a rigid and unchanging view of Muslim 'tradition', the modernisation of the Muslim world was superficial, distorted or at best incomplete. Frequently, this is attributed to the notion that Muslims accepted modernisation on restricted terms so as not to jeopardise the stasis of essentially *pre-modern* ('Islamic') beliefs and dispositions. According to this view, the modernising leaders and technocrats of the Arab world wholeheartedly embraced the technological and material innovations of the West, which included the infrastructure, amenities and services of the modern state, whilst averting their gaze from the cultural and philosophical content of Western modernity. Planes, cars, defence systems, microchips and mobile phones were welcomed for their utility whilst the Western European or Atlantic American cultures from which these originated were to be resisted or adopted only partially. This no doubt undermined the status of 'progress' in the Arab world, becoming an explanatory factor in its lack of 'development'. Thus, the same generalisations derived from Western historical and political experience once found in modernisation paradigms remain, but are now given the retrospectively legitimising air of cultural and religious explanation.[33] The study of 'culture', which was once a rarified category amongst political scientists, entered the analysis of contemporary politics under the more determinative and portentous rubric of 'tradition'.

An important historian in this regard is Bernard Lewis, who is often praised by his admirers for having correctly 'interpreted' Islam and the Arab world for a Western audience.[34] According to Lewis, Middle Eastern politics, the so-called 'war against terrorism' and the circumstances surrounding the Arab-Israeli conflict must all be understood in the context of Islam as a civilisation-shaping force and that civilisation's present state of decline vis-à-vis an ascendant West. This condition of decline, according to Lewis, represents the 'failure' of Arab Muslim civilisation, and is crucial in explaining the current unhappiness and anti-Western sentiment on the part of contemporary Muslims. In this instance, a psycho-historical theory of rival civilisations, which witnesses the flourishing of one and subsequent frustration of the other, is used to make sense of recent political and historical circumstances.

In his bestseller of 2001, entitled *What Went Wrong?*, Lewis addresses the question of why the political and intellectual culture of the Ottoman Empire could not compete with, or defend itself from, European knowledge and technology.[35] How this subject relates to the present or post-Ottoman period of Middle Eastern history is made clear in both the conclusion and preface to the book, where Lewis states that his thesis covers the 'larger pattern of events, ideas and attitudes that preceded and in some measure produced' the terrorist attacks on New York and Washington of September 2001.[36] In his asking 'what went wrong?' for Islam and the Ottomans, Lewis pays little attention to the clear imbalance of power that prevailed amongst European colonialists and local actors in the Middle East throughout the nineteenth and twentieth centuries. There is little account taken, for instance, of the control exerted over Middle Eastern societies by European armies, trading companies and banks during this time. Nor does Lewis stop to consider the ambiguous legacy of colonial ideas and institutions in the trajectory of postcolonial Arab Muslim societies. Such would include a complex mix of international and domestic (sectarian) alignments and rivalries, the large-scale production of oil and assumption of American political patronage in the bipolar order of the Cold War, not to mention the founding of Israel and its military dominance over the indigenous inhabitants of Palestine and the region. In fact, little causal importance is given at all to the historical context of the colonial and postcolonial Arab world and the political forms which emerged from this time. Instead, Lewis focuses upon those ingrained cultural and religious factors which supposedly pre-date the colonial period, but which have since determined Islam's intellectual and political stagnation.

A central premise of Lewis' thesis hinges on the claim that political secularism grew out of tendencies inherent in Christian doctrine and Western European history, tendencies which are wholly alien to Islam. According to Lewis, Christianity's endorsement of secularism (present in Christ's advice to 'Render unto Caesar the things that are Caesar's and unto God the things that are God's' – Matthew 22:21) paved the way for a secular sensibility which emerged first in the adoption of Roman law and, latterly, in the separation of church and state power after Europe's religious wars of the sixteenth and seventeenth centuries.[37] In Islam, by comparison, a clear separation of the powers of church and state, appropriate to the distinction between domains labelled secular and religious, did not take root. In an essay titled 'Islam and liberal democracy', Lewis asserts that the state in Islam was theoretically: 'God's state, ruling over God's people; the law was God's law; the army was God's army; and the enemy, of course, was God's enemy'.[38] Because the state is here conceived as 'God's polity', 'legitimate authority comes from God alone, and the ruler derives his power not from the people, nor yet from his ancestors, but from God and the Holy Law'. Thus, according to Lewis, the power of the ruler was a functional one of no distinct importance. The legislative authority of the caliph simply represented 'elaborations or interpretations' of divine law.[39]

Because political authority in pre-modern Islamic societies was theocentric, which is to say that it derived all of its legitimacy from the 'sacred law', it tended to produce strongly autocratic forms of government which stratified the communities under its sovereignty and prevented the emergence of civil society.[40] So long as Islamic societies did not recognise secular, or civic, sources of authority, Lewis posits, they were unable to develop or embrace the sorts of independent corporate bodies and institutions which were an important prelude to the rise of capitalism and subsequent development of democracy in the West. Due to the arbitrariness of law, land rights, property and civic relations under Ottoman authority, there was little investment in the trade and craft industries and no firm ground for the development of a capitalist, urban bourgeoisie.[41] Thus, individual wealth and rights to private property were arrested in the absence of those personal securities which derive from a faith in corporate, commercial and political bodies.[42]

Here, I disagree with some of Lewis' historical generalisations. For instance, his picture of a theocratic system in which 'there was no distinction between the law of the church and the law of the state' does not account for the tensions and rifts which existed between various religious and secular sources of authority in Islamic history.[43] Under the Umayyad dynasty, there was a pronounced and obvious tension between the political ideal of an Islamic state and the reality, which saw the *fuqaha* (legal scholars of Islam) ensuring that their institutional and legislative authority remained independent of political power. Indeed, from this time onwards, Islamic law was never in cahoots with state institutions and was rarely subjected to, or conflated with, the latter's hegemony. Commonly, the holders and interpreters of Islamic law exercised little sway over matters of state policy and were superseded by a higher source of authority, the *mazalim* courts, whose pronouncements were an expression of the judicial powers of the caliph. Thus, the caliph's authority existed supplementary to, and independent of, the legal jurisdiction of religious scholars. Muslim jurists accepted this arrangement on the precedent that it is optimal to live under a regime which, even if it is not based on religious precepts, is nonetheless strong enough to ensure the general protection and welfare of the community.[44] This separation of functions became a de facto feature of political life from the eighth and ninth centuries and was often characterised by an asymmetry of power between religious institutions and the state in pre-modern Islamic societies.[45]

Whilst Lewis' argument for the structural deficiencies of a patrimonial system of authority has some basis in historical research regarding the weakening of the Ottoman Empire,[46] his thesis is notable for attributing such causes to the ideological and cultural agency of Islam. A manifestation of this agency can be found in the supposed Arab Ottoman disregard for secular time and the material benefits derived from this concept. Pointing to the Qur'anic description of non-believers as those who trust only in 'the passage of time' (*dahr*), from which classical Muslim theologians derived the term *dahriyyah* (pejoratively referring to the sin of 'materialism'), Lewis claims to have uncovered the origins of that disinclination to recognise the worldly importance of secular time, and consequent lack of punctuality, which was often commented upon by European visitors to the Ottoman Empire since the eighteenth century. On account of the Muslim leaning towards an other worldly notion of time, Western cultural art forms and technologies for which the exact measurement of time is essential were largely ignored. One such form is polyphonic music, which not only requires a precise coordination of time, but a cooperative sensibility, in which alternating voices are brought together in a complementary fashion towards the formation of a whole.[47] Expanding upon this theme, Lewis stresses that it is precisely this cooperative, worldly, *time-bound* aspect of Western civilisation – also found in team sports, the modern novel, theatrical plays and parliamentary democracy – which constitutes an 'essential feature of modernity'.[48]

Lewis is certainly not the first to claim that modernity requires a conception of time (and correlative space) which is uniquely linear, homogeneous and emptied of sacred, metaphysical or para-historical references. In his *Imagined Communities: Reflections on the Origins and Spread of Nationalism*, Benedict Anderson claims that a modern conception of homogeneous, empty time, enabled also by new forms of communication such as the newspaper and modern novel, structured new ways of imagining citizenship intrinsic to the emergence of the nation-state.[49] Unlike the diachronic 'simultaneity-along-time' imputed to the medieval Christian world (in which temporal events and occurrences were believed to reveal a notion of divine providence), Anderson points out that modern nations depend upon a conception of themselves as moving along a chronological and homogeneous expanse of calendrical time which is void of extra-historical importance. Nonetheless, there is a clear difference between Lewis' and Anderson's treatment of this theme. Whilst Anderson attempts to historicise secular time within modern processes of production and industry, for Lewis it is inherent in modernity as a European innovation and cannot be replicated easily. According to Lewis, Western culture and religion weights that inherent tendency towards a secular sensibility and ethic of cooperation – against Islam's authoritarian theocentricity – which most successfully defines and circumscribes the condition of modernity.[50]

From the premise of Islam's culturally determined 'failure' or inability to modernise came what was arguably Lewis' most far-reaching contribution to the area of Middle Eastern studies, which is the theory that Islam and the West are currently bound up in a large-scale 'clash of civilisations'. In a now famous essay, titled 'The roots of Muslim rage' (1990), Lewis contends that recent acts of terrorism by Muslim agents against Western targets and the anti-Americanism which accompanies them are but one sally in a long-running 'rivalry' between the civilisations of Islam and the West:

> It should... be clear that we are facing a mood and a movement far transcending the level of issues and policies and the governments that pursue them. This is no less than a clash of civilizations – the perhaps irrational but surely historic reaction of an ancient rival against our Judeo-Christian heritage, our secular present, and the worldwide expansion of both.[51]

Here, the fundamentally incompatible religious, political and cultural doctrines which are presumed to separate the Islamic and Western civilisations find their apotheosis in contemporary politics. And of particular interest are Lewis' efforts to distance this 'rivalry' from the short-term historical and political conditions in which acts of violence (terrorist acts, for instance) occur. Indeed, the notion that this clash of civilisations is somehow primordial, that it transcends the level 'of issues and policies and the governments that pursue them', obviates the reality of contemporary political power. I will develop this insight shortly, but only after commenting upon the way Lewis misconstrues the very forces which can be shown to animate traditions of political thought within the Muslim world.

Primarily, Lewis' portrayal of an Islamic civilisation reacting with hostility to Western dominance does not relate to the ways religious authority and knowledge are redistributed in the contemporary age. To support the claim that terrorism and anti-Americanism are symptomatic of a general Muslim rejection of Western ideas and values, Lewis invokes the survival of a medieval juristic discourse in which Muslim territory, the 'House of Islam' (*dar al-Islam*), is distinguished in moral and political terms from non-Muslim lands, the 'House of War' (*dar al-harb*):

> In the classical Islamic view, to which many Muslims are beginning to return, the world and all mankind are divided into two: the House of Islam, where the Muslim law and faith prevail, and the rest, known as the House of Unbelief or the House of War, which it is the duty of Muslims ultimately to bring to Islam.[52]

But a distinct problem for Lewis' thesis is that this paradigm is not ideologically determinative in the contemporary Muslim world. At the outset he seems unaware that this concept belongs more to the realm of politics than to theology, and thus cannot be attributed to a homogeneous Islam without serious reservations. Moreover, those modern Islamists and political extremists who appropriate the notion of an offensive military jihad against non-Muslims forthrightly reject the juristic guidelines under which such a jihad was conceived to be legitimate. Even if they claim to act in defence of *dar al-Islam*, most contemporary radicals view the corpus of classical Islamic law as an obstacle to the reformation of Islam and have bypassed, or cannibalised, such texts in their critique of modern evil.[53]

And this is not an entirely new development. The rejection of medieval law in favour of a more direct and unmediated interpretation of Islam's sacred sources has been a common aspect of reformist thinking in the Middle East and elsewhere since the nineteenth century. In Egypt, individual reformers associated with the political activist Jamal al-Din al-Afghani (1839–1897) reinvigorated the notion of the 'pious forbears' (*as-Salaf as-Salih*) as the heuristic model by which a truly Islamic life could be realised. By taking the example of the Prophet and his companions as their primary reference for matters of religious interpretation and practice, such reformers were able to bypass or selectively appropriate centuries of traditional legal, theological and mystical exegesis.[54] Moreover, this period witnessed the beginnings of a transition of religious leadership, from traditional religious scholars to lay intellectuals and indigenous elites, in which a direct, individualising hermeneutical method was carried out beneath the juridicial moniker of *ijtihad*, a term which had previously referred to independent legal reasoning amongst Muslim scholars regarding matters upon which there was no consensus, but which now connoted the exercise of free reason in the interpretation of Islam's sacred sources. Such an individual hermeneutical approach, regardless of whether its proponents called it *ijtihad*, was no doubt practised by such prominent Islamists as Sayyid Abul A'la Maududi in India and Sayyid Qutb in Egypt.[55] The imputation, on Lewis' part, of a continuity of thought towards the non-Muslim other (in which a return to the medieval juristic tradition somehow maintains an 'ancient' rivalry between Islamic and Judeo-Christian civilisations) serves only to conceal the very modern upheavals, the break with past precedent, to which much Islamic reform is indebted.

Rather than invoke the presence of timeless cultural and religious essences, one might better attend to how and why the discourses and practices of Islamic law have changed to suit evolving historical contexts and environments. As Sami Zubaida points out, Islamic law has always represented legal and moral leverage for the power claims of various social groups and cannot simply be conflated with the hegemony of the traditional scholars of the classical tradition.[56] In the era of modernisation, for instance, the etatisation of some aspects of Islamic law into a set of codified state laws diminished the legal authority of the *'ulama* (the religious scholars of Islam) and brought an end to the flexibility which had characterised historical traditions of jurisprudence in their ability to encompass a range of accepted methodologies and interpretations. It would be more relevant, then, to analyse continuities and changes in the discursive grammar of Islamic law and the extent to which its views, stipulations and embodied rituals make particular thoughts and actions possible.

Whilst the theory of clashing civilisations cannot account for the historical complexity of Islamic law (in its modern and pre-modern incarnations), Orientalist historians have nonetheless used it – in a simplistic manner – to make sense of the present-day political arena.

In my exposition of this, I'll begin with the historical association that is sometimes made between the political and religious culture of the Muslim Middle East and Europe's ideological nemesis of the middle of the twentieth century: political fascism.

In the wake of the 1967 Arab–Israeli war, particular historians have developed a revisionist interpretation of the Arab world which posits enduring ideological and historical links between Arab nationalism and political Islam on one hand, and the worst strands of European political totalitarianism on the other. In *Semites and Anti-Semites*, Bernard Lewis argues that the political modernisation of the Arab world owed more to the influence of Fascist Italy and Nazi Germany than to the constitutional democracies of Britain and France, which an earlier generation of historians had assumed.[57] According to Lewis, Arab anti-Semitism was successful in joining indigenous sources of animosity towards Jews with the ideology of Nazism, as demonstrated by the alignment of figures such as the Palestinian Arab leader al-Hajj Amin al-Husaiyni (1897–1974) with Hitler's regime during the World War II. Yet here, Lewis fails to account for Arab anti-Semitism's historical causes. Whilst the presence of European anti-Semitism in the Middle East amongst Arab intellectuals since the 1930s and 1940s is undeniable (though the extent of its influence is arguable), Lewis makes little attempt to contextualise this phenomenon within the contemporary political and historical circumstances then affecting the Arab world. The beginnings of Jewish settlement on Palestinian land, the establishment of Israel in 1948, the concurrent expulsion of up to three-quarters of a million indigenous Palestinians and subsequent drive to quell Palestinian, and regional, aspirations are registered not in an effort to understand the causes of Arab anti-Semitism, but as historical vignettes by which the hubris and intolerance already built into Arab Muslim politics is revealed.[58]

The connections and similarities between Arab nationalism, political Islam and European fascism are also developed in Fouad Ajami's interpretation of the irrational and undemocratic nature of modern Arab political regimes. In *The Arab Predicament*, Ajami describes the political culture of the Arab Middle East since the 1967 War according to its weakness for the 'grand schemes and ready made doctrines' of German nationalism, Arab socialism, the Pan-Arabist *nahda* ('renaissance') and, more recently, political Islam.[59] For Ajami, Arab Muslim politicking places romantic, utopian reveries and quick-fix, catch-all solutions ahead of the sobering and much harder tasks of rational self-criticism and analysis. Political Islam is instructive not on the terms which it sets for existing social and historical conditions, nor for what its adherents invest in it, but as a barometer of the Arabs' inherent inability to rationally appraise unpleasant social, political and cultural realities.

After 1993, the conflation of political Islam with totalitarian ideology was significantly popularised by Samuel Huntington's 'clash of civilisations' article (and book of the same name) which transported the political science terminology of the Cold War into the conceptual arena of a new global religious struggle.[60] According to Huntington, nation-states will no longer go to war in the service of historically ambitious political ideologies, as they did during the Cold War and the struggle against fascism. They will revert instead to those larger civilisational identities which have witnessed a much longer, pre-national legacy of historical animosity. Amongst these long-running trans-historical forces, the relationship between Islam and the West has always been, and is destined to remain, a potential flashpoint.[61] To prove as much, Huntington collects an array of data predicting economic, demographic and political instability between the two civilisations. 'The underlying problem for the West', asserts Huntington, 'is not Islamic fundamentalism' but 'a different civilisation whose people are convinced of the superiority of their culture and are obsessed with the inferiority of their power'.[62]

This essentialist view of Arab Muslim society received a considerable boost amongst foreign policy analysts and historians loyal to the administration of George W. Bush in the aftermath of the attacks on the World Trade Centre in 2001 and during the lead-up to the American-led invasion of Iraq in 2003. In its attempts to edify a local and international audience regarding the reasons underlying the 2001 attacks, the Bush administration continually asserted that Islamic terrorists harbour an irrational hatred towards the West, the motives and aims of which cannot be deciphered. Echoing Lewis' conceptualisation of monolithic and incommensurable civilisations, it was explained that terrorist attacks cannot possibly be understood in relation to the foreign policies or actions of past US governments, but must be located in the terrorist's apolitical resentment towards 'our freedoms', which include the freedom of 'religion' and 'speech'.[63] Any consideration of possible historical causes, including America's instrumental role in supporting repressive dictatorships across the Arab Middle East, was substituted for a raft of inaccurate but politically expedient generalisations about Islam and Arab culture.[64]

Bernard Lewis' contribution to this culturalist refrain was significant in the months leading up to the American-led invasions of Afghanistan in 2001 and Iraq in 2003. Echoing those neo-conservatives in the American administration whose sentiments he shared, Lewis published a number of opinion pieces (with breathless headlines such as 'A Time for Toppling') underscoring the need for the United States to intervene in the 'Axis of Evil' countries of Iran and Iraq. Comparing the situation with the threat of Nazism leading up to World War II and of the Soviet Union during the Cold War, Lewis informed his readers that those who live under hostile and oppressive regimes in the Middle East are often the most pro-American, and naturally look to the United States for 'help and liberation'. 'Help and liberation' in this context signalled the option of 'regime change [in Iraq]' which 'may well be dangerous', Lewis cautioned, 'but sometimes the dangers of inaction [for the West] are greater than those of action'.[65] With this warning, he joined the chorus of those supporting a US-led military invasion and occupation of Iraq under the pretext of spreading liberty and freedom. This sentiment became a key line of the Bush administration which, despite its claims that the so-called 'war against terrorism' was not a war against Islam, nonetheless continued to deploy essentialist arguments, vapid cultural clichés and the empty slogans of 'liberation' and 'democracy'. Disappointingly, these slogans were invoked to legitimate doctrines of pre-emptive war, military occupation and the flouting of international laws concerning the human rights of prisoners and permissibility of torture.[66]

The Critique of Orientalism

Since the 1960s, the nexus between Orientalist writing on the Middle East and the political and ideological interests of European or American imperial power has been hotly debated across a broad spectrum of disciplines and areas. This was initiated, during the 1960s, by various Third World and Marxist intellectuals, who objected to what they saw as the ideological biases underlying much of what passed for the scholarly study of non-Western cultures in places such as the Middle East, China and India.[67] Such objections were put within a cohesive theoretical framework in the 1970s and 1980s by such scholars as Talal Asad and Edward Said, who were informed by – though not always located within – the new critical and deconstructive approaches then developing in the areas of philosophy, linguistics and psychoanalysis.[68] These critical interventions questioned the essentialism at work in regnant historical narratives and initiated a much-needed appraisal of the epistemological and methodological stances underpinning scholarship in areas as diverse as history, sociology, philology, literary criticism and anthropology within the field of Middle Eastern studies.

Regarding the West's understanding of Islam, Arab culture and the Middle East, few books would be as influential as Edward Said's significant work of historiographical criticism, *Orientalism* (1978).[69] In *Orientalism*, Said argues that the historical profession, in tandem with the modern sciences of archaeology, anthropology, philology and ethnography, had studied the 'Orient', explained its societies, categorised its people and objectified its past, in the service of imperial interests. Employing the insights of the French poststructuralist, Michel Foucault, Said refers to Orientalism as a 'discursive formation', or set of disciplinary texts, methods and assumptions which form a self-referential body of knowledge about the Orient or, in his example, the Arabs and Islam.[70] Far from creating a monolithic or univocal discourse, Said argues that Orientalist themes circulated freely in many noteworthy literary aesthetic works of European culture on one hand, whilst playing an ideologically durable role amongst colonial institutions and offices, on the other.[71] Thus, the common nineteenth-century themes of patriarchal intolerance, religious fanaticism, irrationality, lethargy and violence associated with Arab Muslim society occurred in various literary and aesthetic guises whilst playing a significant part in the ideological justification of colonial policy. Because the Orientalist canon is self-referential, its practitioners derive their authority more from the exemplary texts of their profession, and the expectations of relevant funding institutions and ideological bodies, than from any correspondence with the 'real' Orient they purport to represent.[72]

Said's work is indebted to a methodology that analyses the languages, discourses and habits of thinking that pertain to a given subject alongside the underlying structures of social and political power that legitimate and authorise them. This approach, which is strikingly exemplified in Michel Foucault's *The Order of Things: An Archaeology of the Human Sciences*, has an important historical value.[73] This is because the sort of 'history of ideas' commonly practised amongst intellectual historians does not include a critical understanding of the historian's own epistemological framework and assumptions. Indeed, this can only arise from a history in which the analyst's own systems of thought are interrogated and laid bare. This, in short, was what Foucault referred to as 'archaeology'.[74] In the context of Orientalist scholarship, this critical attention to the production of knowledge is essential. For whilst 'the Orient' and 'the Occident', or 'Islam' and 'the West', are indeed imaginary entities, they are, nonetheless, entities whose projection onto the historical past *was itself a moment in the making of that history*. The evocative historical and geographical domains of 'Europe' and 'Islam' are not timeless and eternal, but were shaped by, and formative of, the various political nationalisms and empires which came to prominence in the medieval and early modern periods. To reveal the epistemological and culturalist biases in the scholarly study of Islam and the Arab World is useful not as an exercise in theoretical deconstruction but in the service of a more accurate historicising mode.[75]

This task is made more urgent by the way various misconceptions about Islam and Islamist movements are mobilised within global self-representations of the nation-state and the political doctrine of secularism. Over the past few decades, European or Western self-definition has been heightened by fears associated with globalisation, migration, asylum seekers and international terrorism. Furthermore, these fears are manipulated for political advantage by parties on both the right and left side of politics in countries such as Holland, France, and Australia.[76] To cite one example, the Australian Prime Minister in 2006, John Howard, deliberately conflated the threat of international terrorism with concerns about Muslim migration when he asserted that aspects of Muslim culture were 'utterly antagonistic' to Australian society and posed a unique threat to its migration experience. 'You can't find any equivalent in Italian, Greek, or Lebanese, or Chinese or Baltic immigration to Australia,' Howard told *The Australian*. 'There is no equivalent of raving on about jihad... [which] is the major problem.'[77] Such assertions agree with the view that global terrorism somehow represents the exacerbation of a much larger and ongoing culture war between Islam and the West, so conflating the real with the imaginary threat.

Citing Islam, Defending the West

The themes of religious and cultural incommensurability, as presented in the 'clash of civilisations' paradigm, move beyond the need to make sense of our historical past when they suggest normative implications for the relationship between civilisations, states, cultures, societies and individuals in the present. When adopted as a lens through which the world is interpreted and so changed, this theory necessarily impinges on the realm of ethics and how we treat those whose cultural and religious traditions appear incompatible with our own. Moreover, the belief that secular political institutions, ideas and regimes somehow constitute the best or only means for human development makes it possible to construct Islam as a force for all that is dangerous and irrational. As we shall see, this allows little if any ground for consensus between religious (Muslim) and secular (Western) actors by characterising political Islam as a totalising ideological system whose motives and goals are fundamentally incompatible with our own.

I will begin with the theme of incommensurability. Developing the notion that the 'clash' between Islam and the West cannot be reduced merely to 'issues and policies and the governments that pursue them', Bernard Lewis counsels his readers to see beyond the political claims of contemporary Muslims on the understanding that their motivations owe little to the rational calculations imputed to political actors as we recognise them:

> One... gets the impression that the offence of imperialism [for Muslims] is not – as for Western critics – the domination by one

people over another but rather the allocation of roles in this relationship. What is truly evil and unacceptable is the domination of infidels over true believers... For true believers [Muslims] to rule misbelievers is natural, since this provides for the maintenance of the holy law and gives the misbelievers both the opportunity and the incentive to embrace the true faith. But for misbelievers to rule over believers is blasphemous and unnatural, since it leads to the corruption of religion and morality in society, and to the flouting or even the abrogation of God's law. This may help us to understand the current troubles in such diverse places as... Indian Kashmir, Chinese Sinkiang and Yugoslav Kosovo, in all of which Muslim populations are ruled by non-Muslim governments.[78]

Whilst Lewis suggests, at the outset, that the legacy of European colonialism and present disparities of global power are sources of resentment for Muslims, this is not due to their having understood the same rights-based discourse that contemporary Western liberals assume to be universal. No, Muslims resent not that they are dominated per se, but that they are dominated by 'infidels' whom, it is implied, they would dominate if they could. Muslim resentment therefore stems, again, from the political theocentrism inherent in Islam and not from any sense of historical context. Their claims are not the sort that can be understood or justified through rational dialogue, but reflect a self-aggrandising religious conviction which has no basis in intelligible political or social realities. (Nevertheless, one wonders how the hubris of Muslim ethnic minorities might help us to understand the tragedies of Kashmir, Sinkiang and Kosovo. In each case, a religious and/or ethnic community was persecuted or drawn into conflict for falling outside the imaginary parameters of a dominant or more powerful national group. Such examples may prompt us to contemplate the pathological underbelly of modern nationalisms but do not support the notion of a timeless and ongoing clash between Muslim minorities and non-Muslim majorities.) Thus, for Lewis, the 'offence of imperialism' amongst Muslims cannot point to a moral ground delimiting those values or standards which the proponents of inter-civilisational dialogue assume to be universal. It is indicative only of the hostile division and lack of understanding between civilisations.

This apparent lack of commensurability between the civilisations of Islam and the West is reproduced in the work of the Syrian-German anthropologist-historian, Bassam Tibi.[79] Asserting a theoretical notion of modernity as the creation of rational, forward-looking individuals, Tibi identifies the philosophical underpinnings of secularism with Jurgen Habermas' notion of 'cultural modernity': connoting a worldly disposition which is based upon a self-reflexive and reason-oriented 'principle of subjectivity'. According to Habermas, cultural modernity mandates the decoupling of reason from the domains of religion and metaphysics, and allows for it to flourish in the secular disciplines of science, morality and art.[80] Crucially for Tibi, this orientation valorises the individual who is able to maintain a rational and critical distance from the totalising values which religious emotions are seen to inspire.[81]

In Tibi's analysis, this secular aspect of the West's cultural modernity poses a significant difficulty for the Muslim world. 'Islamic fundamentalism', Tibi declares, has become the 'pervasive view of the world now shared by the majority of Muslims'.[82] In Tibi's conception of the term, fundamentalism represents a 'sociopolitical worldview' derived not from internal religious discussions over correct doctrine or belief, but from a 'selective and arbitrary politicisation of religion'.[83] A 'fundamentalist', then, is someone who downplays Islam as an ethical tradition and seeks only to impose its exogenous forms over the public sphere. The privatised metaphysical and ethical doctrines of Islam's legal and mystical traditions have been torn from their element and transformed into a social or political ideology. To address this problem, Tibi proposes that any grounds for dialogue between the civilisations of Islam and the West must be based upon a mutual respect for universal secular values, especially those contained in the political process of democracy and international charter of human rights.[84]

Lest one suppose that Tibi seeks to supplant one cultural system with another, he points out that secular Western values are not universal in an a priori sense but are the best practical means for achieving dialogue under conditions of security and justice. Whilst human rights were a distinct product of the philosophical concepts of the European Enlightenment, and were promulgated after the French and American revolutions, they have since been historically universalised as that international order which is recognised by the modern system of nation-states and international justice. Human rights therefore do not enjoy a trans-historical or metaphysical claim to universality but form the ground upon which the international order of nation-states and civilisations may best find pragmatic and practical solutions in common. Although of Western origin, human rights are now the 'general human heritage' to which Islamic and other non-Western cultures make global theoretical and legal claims.[85] For this reason, the 'morality of human rights', Tibi hopes, may act as 'an element of convergence, a bridge between clashing civilizations', to be accepted 'as international morality'.[86]

The problem with establishing human rights as the basis for cross-cultural consensus, however, is that Muslim cultures favour group rights before those of the individual. 'If Muslims are to embrace human rights', asserts Tibi, 'they need to achieve cultural religious reforms in Islam – not as [a] faith but as a cultural and legal system. In fact, Islam is a distinct cultural system in which the collective, not the individual, lies at the centre of the respective world-view.'[87] For this reason, any meaningful process of reform must bring the cultural and legal structures of the Muslim world into line with a scheme of rights which places the individual at its centre. But if Islam constitutes a 'distinct cultural system' whose very worldview negates the concept of individual rights, as Tibi claims, mightn't its resistance to secular values in fact go deeper than the level of its institutions?

At the conclusion to his thoughts on human rights, Tibi answers this question in the affirmative. The Muslim world's human rights issues, it turns out, cannot be attributed simply to its political or cultural institutions. Rather, it is Islam's theocentric worldview which stifles claims to individual freedom: 'Here lies the problem. It is a conflict between the man(reason)-centered and cosmological theocentric view of the world and also between the related civilizations.'[88] And here Tibi shows his hand. After identifying a lack of human rights in Islam's cultural institutions, he nonetheless traces its beginnings to a cosmological theocentrism which opposes the universal 'reason-centred' ontology upon which human rights are established. Moreover, the value of reason takes the form, in Tibi's discussion, of an ideological commitment: 'I concur fully with Max Weber's view that modern Western science is the only universally valid standard humanity has ever known. From this I infer that it is justifiable to judge Islam in terms emanating from cultural modernity, being a source of modern universal knowledge.'[89]

What interests me at this point is that, for Tibi, Islam's theocentrism is not a postmodern phenomenon insofar as it does not arise from within – or after – the conditions of modernity. Amongst its followers, Islamic fundamentalism mounts a 'defensive cultural response' to secular, Western ideas so this aspect of it *does* represent a reaction to contemporary circumstances. But the theocentric orientation which forms the greater part of it, and which spurs this response, is grounded in fundamentally *pre-modern* emotions and understandings. Like Lewis, Tibi cannot attribute modern 'fundamentalism' to the historical transitions that took place under the conditions of colonialism, because its foundations predate these events, being implanted in the Qur'an and life of the Prophet.[90] The worldview of the Islamic 'fundamentalist' (which Tibi hastily attributes to 'most of the world's Muslims') does not seek to critique, ironise or invert the Western metanarrative of a rationally comprehended universe as the Romantic or postmodern movements within the West have done. The fundamentalist worldview is inherently pre-modern in the sense that its rejection of reason predates the very response to reason already claimed by those cultures which have undergone a more authentic transition to, or through, modernity.

Too often, self-styled defenders of the West adopt this oxymoronic position towards modernity, which emerges in their notion of the relationship between modernity and Islam. This is seen in the notion of dialectical modernity, which is often upheld as an example of the West's intellectual strength and regeneration, just as it is charged with exposing the West to the barbs of external and internal enemies. For thinkers such as Leszek Kolakowski and Paul Berman, for instance, the modern West's tradition of rational self-criticism was the positive legacy of modernity's dialectical drive towards innovation, inquiry and freedom of thought.[91] But although this self-questioning dimension is seen to give the West an undeniable intellectual and technological advantage over other cultures, it simultaneously exposes it to the threat of rival and less internally riven ideologies, such as Islamism, from which the West must be defended.

Roger Scruton's spirited defence of Western notions of democratic citizenship provides a case in point. Whilst modern democracies are founded upon secular sources of authority which require processes of consensus and deliberation, Islam (with its presumption of divine sovereignty) provides 'no scope...for the kinds of purely political developments, through the patient building of institutions and secular laws, that we know in the West'.[92] Yet, instructively, Scruton's argument has less to do with Islam than with his aspirational vision for the West (what it was, is, and must not forget itself to be). For Scruton, the faddist ideologies of multiculturalism and postmodernism have undermined Western civilisation by usurping the corporate political culture (enjoining loyalty to the nation-state and a secular conception of law) upon which modern notions of citizenship are based. In its place, there festers a political correctness and cultural relativism which loathes the status quo, silences the critique of minority cultures and insists on plurality and social fragmentation at the expense of the centre. Western liberal democracies have been hollowed out, encouraging a 'form of apartheid' which would presume to make no integrating claims on the loyalties of its migrant-Muslim communities who (in keeping with their faith) nurture an attitude of hostility towards the system whose rights and protections they simultaneously enjoy. Thus Scruton's notion of the Islamic threat becomes a convenient foil for the admonition of those modern intellectual trends (postmodernism, aspirations to belong in a strengthened European Union, youth culture and postcolonial theory) which would undermine the edifice of Western civilisation.[93] The perceived threat of Islam cuts to the heart of the way secular democracies must define themselves and how they relate to the supposedly non-democratic other in their midst.

Here I concur with Gayanendra Pandey's observation that the concept of secularism in our time is less pertinent to the expansion of secular spaces in the public domain (the secular policing of the sacred) than to 'the recognition and acceptance of difference' between and amongst religious and non-religious communities.[94] One need only look at the legislation in France targeting Muslim women who choose to cover their hair in public spaces, for instance, to realise that the French government's claim to defend universal notions of citizenship connects with deeper, nationalist anxieties surrounding the 'integration' and loyalty of France's Muslim minorities and former colonial subjects. As Joan Scott points out in her analysis of this issue, the insistence that secular values apply to everyone in French society, combined with popular misconceptions regarding the nature of Islam, actively discouraged the symbolic inclusion of France's Muslims.[95] This no doubt reflects a broader trend, in which the terms of a supposedly universal secular disposition, based on abstracted cultural norms and expectations (though of Western origin), are used as a truncheon against supposedly non-integrating religious minorities. To circumvent this bind, as Hent De Vries claims, is to devise a position that accounts for the way religious and non-religious sensibilities are expressed, through civil society and in the political arena, within the fragmentary and reconstituting effects of the global market.[96]

Moreover, any approach to religious thought must account for the fact that our language, notions of justice, autonomy and so forth are born of, and located within, a historical context and community. In other words, there is no transcendent position, no Archimedian rational viewpoint (memorably described by Thomas Nagel as the 'view from nowhere') or empiricist notion of a detached self – standing forever apart from society – to fall back upon.[97] One must instead consider the collective and individual narratives which structure personal action and identity, including practices of rationality, and the way these are socially and historically constructed. Because, as Seyla Benhabib points out, 'reason is the achievement of contingent, linguistically socialised, finite and embodied creatures... the legislative claims of practical reason must be understood in interactionist terms'.[98] Contrary to Tibi's proposal for a 'cross-cultural morality', in which a hackneyed version of modernisation theory is imposed onto Muslim societies, one might build upon a vision of democratic process which is theoretically alive to the problem of incommensurable values as and when they arise.

The Post-secular Point of View

As I hope to have made clear, one cannot reduce the complex reception of European thought in the colonies to a supposed 'failing' on the part of non-Europeans to become truly modern. Nor, to play out another variation on this dichotomy, did the 'resistance' of indigenous elites-cum-nationalist leaders to European domination provide for the liberation of an essential indigenous identity, as nativist ideologues have claimed.[99] Modern colonialism did not represent the convergence and eventual separation of opposed peoples, cultures, religions and civilisations. Instead it brought them within the system of global capitalism and international order of nation-states, whose markets, tariffs, schools, prisons, hospitals, banks, offices and courts have enabled their concurrent – though unequal – processes of national, cultural and religious self-development. What is therefore needed is a historical sensibility that can accommodate the dichotomous assumptions of progress and decline, reason and irrationality, within new ideological and cultural forms.

Throughout this thesis, I will work from a point of view which some theorists have labelled 'post-secular', and which is drawn from Talal Asad's definition of 'secularity'. According to Asad, the secular is a concept which 'brings together certain behaviours, knowledges and sensibilities in modern life' and should not be mistaken for the political doctrine of secularism.[100] It does not supply a teleological version of historical development, contiguous to theories and beliefs about modernisation, in which modern rationality is sought to displace religious beliefs, irrational myths and superstitions. Rather, the concept of 'the secular' holds credence insofar as it *constitutes and works through these oppositions*, including the oppositional arrangement of such things as reason and superstition, rationality and belief, what is sacred and profane, private and public, and so forth.[101] Secularity is, therefore, a global condition which encompasses those things which come to be designated and perceived as either 'religious' on one hand or 'secular' on the other.

On the issue of political secularism, I endorse William Connolly's claim to explore 'layered conceptions of thinking, ethos and public life appropriate to a timely vision of multidimensional pluralism' which is neither wholly secular nor theocentric (when these are often the only choices presented to us).[102] Because modernity is a diverse and complex formation of old and new traditions, sensibilities and doctrines, it cannot be reduced to a caricature of that modern Western rationality against which Islam is usually positioned as a convenient ideological foil.

Of course, the universal precepts of reason, progress and human rights which are so often conflated with notions of modernity are not to be forsaken for a relativist pantheon of equal cultures. It is not the object of this thesis to deny the attainability of truth and give up on the emancipatory or democratic currents of modernist thought. Rather, the desire to weaken the transcendental claims of modernisation, rationality and so forth must be mobilised towards the task of critically understanding modernity's ideological pretensions (its sole identification with the recent history of Europe, for example) as an imposition over the history of others. This is not to dispense with a normative or universalised notion of secular modernity but to balance it against its diverse local and particular forms in such a way that each may historicise (by calling into question) the other. Only by attending to the complexity of such notions as secularism and religion may we analyse their particular manifestations without crassly personalising them into monolithic blocs labelled 'Islam' and 'the West'.

Structure

This book consists of seven chapters – in addition to this introduction – and a conclusion. Chapter 1 will analyse the work of three nineteenth-century intellectuals, Jamal al-Din al-Afghani, Muhammad 'Abduh and Sayyid Ahmad Khan, who attempted to reform Islam according to modern categories of knowledge. Each of these thinkers, it is well known, were impressed by the value of Western science, and sought to prove that Islam was compatible with modern reason. Yet, in the colonial context, science and reason were not value-free, given that they played an integral part in the instrumentalisation of colonial rule. For this reason, modernist reformers sought to separate what they perceived to be the useful from the bad elements of modern knowledge, which generated the notion of entirely separate epistemologies, labelled 'Islamic', on one hand, and 'materialist', on the other. Thus, Islam could be proved a friend to modern thought whilst engaging in a defensive intellectual movement against the worst aspects of colonial knowledge. From this process, we also witness the modern essentialisation of Islam as something which is reified and fixed, and which complements similar changes in the concept of 'religion', or of religious systems, then taking place within Europe.

My second and third chapters analyse the consequences of this for the production of cultural signs and meanings amongst indigenous reformers under colonial rule in the latter part of the nineteenth century. In chapter 2, I examine the efforts of modernist intellectuals associated with the Aligarh movement in northern India to reform the content of Urdu poetry. For these thinkers, a didactic notion of 'progress' motivated efforts to reform the romantic Urdu ghazal, whose imaginative, semi-mystical content was to be replaced with realistic, ideally 'natural' themes. Yet, as I will argue, this movement for 'natural poetry' led, instead, to the construction of a new literary romanticism, in which the idealised trope of the Muslim community, or nation-state, came to replace the conventional poetic figure of the 'beloved'. Chapter 3 is concerned with the discourse towards women of two important educationalists in colonial Egypt and India, Qasim Amin and Ashraf 'Ali Thanawi. These thinkers accepted the premise – implicit in colonial critiques of their culture – that women were the signifiers of a society's moral status, and sought to reform the position of women accordingly. However, I will argue that their attempts to construct the late nineteenth-century Muslim woman as a modern civil subject were marked by ambiguity, and were symptomatic of the expectations and pressures exerted by the newly idealised status of women.

In the first half of the twentieth century, Muslim revivalists struggled to reconcile their religious universalism with the limitations of a territorial or ethnic conception of national identity. Chapter 4 explores the implications of this struggle for the work of the celebrated Indian poet-philosopher, Muhammad Iqbal. In particular, Iqbal's identification of Islam with the themes of modern nationalism (*qaumiyyah*) represents a significant point of ambivalence in his work. This is shown in his adoption of the idea of race, to which Iqbal (and Iqbal's idea of Islam) was nevertheless opposed. Yet far from showing a contradiction or weakness in Iqbal's thought, I argue that his ambivalence towards the themes of race-based nationalism was central to that dualism which contributed to notions of self and other, creation and creator, change and permanence, in his philosophical thought. Iqbal did not envisage Islam as a static national ideology, which no doubt undercuts his posthumously acquired status as a nationalist, or Islamist, figure.

Chapter 5 examines the presence of modern secular understandings in the work of the influential twentieth-century Islamists, Sayyid Abul A'la Maududi and Sayyid Qutb. For instance, Maududi's conception of a religious state attempts to place Islamic themes within the same morally abstract, universalising terms as modern charters, draft constitutions, and so forth. Likewise, for Sayyid Qutb, Islam is realised through a non-rational, literary aesthetic interpretation of the Qur'an, which is equally indebted to modern categories. Whilst Islamism presents itself as a radical alternative – and challenge – to a regnant Western secularist epistemology, I will argue that secular terms and understandings form the premise upon which its themes are contested and defined. This insight is developed further, in chapter 6, through an analysis of Maududi's idealisation of Muslim femininity. By locating the normative Muslim woman within a domain of binarised and conflicting significations, Maududi leads us to the 'Western woman' who is both victim and participant in the exploitation of her femininity. Indeed, I argue that Maududi's understanding of female sexuality is so dependent upon the example of modern gender-types as to be inseparable from the recent history of Western sexual politics and morality in which he becomes embroiled.

Chapter 7 examines the efforts of 'progressive' Muslim intellectuals to address the current impasse of hermeneutical thinking in contemporary Islamic thought. Because modern Muslim reformers have, since the nineteenth century, disaggregated and selectively recombined elements of Islam's intellectual and juristic traditions, the question of how to reform Islam for progressive Muslims mandates an examination of the historical context, circumstances and conditions under which such interpretation becomes possible. In this sense, I will explore how thinkers such as Fazlur Rahman, Amina Wadud, 'Abdolkarim Soroush and Mohammed Arkoun have, in different ways, constructed the terms for a new hermeneutical project.

Far from making a complete survey of every event and thinker pertinent to the field, this book will address certain themes and questions surrounding the subject of Islamic reform and its relationship to the philosophical, cultural and political discourses of modernity. For this reason, my examples are limited to a select number of reformers whose works are representative of the topics to be addressed. In particular, I will focus upon the ways in which Islam has been reformed, rethought, and in some sense reconstituted, as a response to, or means of subsisting within, the various conditions of modern life.

What Becomes of 'Tradition'?

Finally, let me revisit that notion of 'tradition' which modernisation theorists once doomed to extinction and which has since been grossly over-determined in the analysis of contemporary Islam. If the view of modernity as a condition of freedom is not to be taken at face value, nor can it be supposed that what passes under the category of 'tradition' universally opposes human rationality, individuality, and so forth. For historians, this is to remove the overpowering agency of Islam, as Bernard Lewis imagined it, and give some agency back to those Muslims who make Islam a meaningful and practicable religion under modern conditions. This does not mean that Muslims may make of Islam whatever they wish or that the normative content of Islamic thought does not produce its own continuities and constraints. Rather, Islam has only been a relevant force in the lives of individuals and communities to the extent that its internal themes, motives, rituals and practices address, answer to, and provide solutions for, the issues and quandaries of a given age. To register the survival of a tradition, then, is to account for its contestation and re-conceptualisation amongst those who have carried it through the historical changes of colonialism, capitalism and globalisation.

With these considerations in mind, a self-adapting notion of tradition, such as the one developed by Alasdair MacIntyre, is particularly useful. For MacIntyre, living traditions must include 'continuities of conflict' through which their internal values are contested, re-evaluated and made relevant to their time.[103] Because a tradition can exist only if its members play an active part in defining its worth, it must be answerable to, and influenced by, the needs of its time. One cannot thus essentialise a tradition without undermining that which makes it function historically in the first place. To put it another way, an overly rigid, unchanging notion of tradition denies to its practitioners that tradition's historical relevancy. For this reason, I will not nit-pick over whether particular reformist thinkers were 'traditional' or 'modern' in their intellectual orientation or methodology. It is enough to observe that the Muslim reformist tradition in the modern period supplies an important precedent for change and adaptation.

CHAPTER 1

ISLAMIC MODERNISM AND THE REIFICATION OF RELIGION

Introduction

In the modern world, the categories of 'science' and 'religion' are often conceived as opposing one another. However, this dichotomy is not eternal, and is far more usefully placed in its social, political and historical contexts. For instance, the flourishing of scientific reason in the early modern period, far from undermining religious beliefs, in fact gave rise to notions of faith which were founded upon rational knowledge. Furthermore, as Colin Russell points out, the supposed opposition between science and religion did not arise from within the natural sciences, but was the construction of nineteenth-century historiographers, such as John William Draper (1811–1882) and Andrew Dickson White (1832–1918), whose criticisms were directed more against the intellectual hegemony of the Roman Catholic Church than against religion per se.[1] Whilst the 'conflict thesis' (referring to the perceived conflict between science and religion) permeated the history of science for a century and came to influence Whig notions of historical progress, notable Christian theologians, scientists and Deists continued to argue for the rational 'proof' of God's existence on the premise that science and faith were in fact compatible.[2]

This notion of a conflict between religion and science has also been projected, somewhat anachronistically, onto the history of science in the Muslim world. In 1916 Ignaz Goldziher, in an article titled 'The attitude of orthodox Islam towards the "ancient sciences"', posited a tradition of opposition amongst early Muslim scholars towards the 'foreign sciences' of Greek, Persian and Indian intellectual provenance.[3] This was expanded upon by A. J. Arberry's thesis that Abu Hamid al-Ghazali's eleventh-century treatise, *The Incoherence of the Philosophers*, dealt a fatal blow to Aristotle's theory of causality within the rational sciences.[4] However, there are reasonable grounds to argue that Arberry misconstrued al-Ghazali's philosophy. Because the Aristotelian theory of secondary causes seemed to posit a lack of primacy on God's part over the natural world, al-Ghazali promoted the view that all phenomena must be attributed, instead, to God's direct will and immanence.[5] Yet al-Ghazali's occasionalism – which asserted that the laws of causality are a product not of the natural world but of our knowledge of it – furnished no conclusive evidence for why religious dogma should snuff out rational inquiry. Moreover, the historical record shows no diminution of philosophical and scientific activity after the time of al-Ghazali, who is credited with legitimising methodological uses of logic and dialectical argument in his theological and philosophical writings.[6]

Since the time of the Graeco-Arabic translation movement, which spanned the middle of the eighth to the tenth centuries, science was valued within the context of Islamic culture and not against it.[7] This was ensured, in part, through the disciplinary independence afforded to theology and science, so that neither was able to take over the other's theoretical domain.[8] Whilst theologians and natural philosophers disagreed about certain subjects (such as the Aristotelian theory of the eternity of the world), the distinction between science and theology nonetheless fostered significant areas of complementarity. As the modernist reformer Shibli Nu'mani (1857–1914) observed, for classical Muslim theologians the reflection upon God's signs (*ayat*) in the world pointed to the evidence of nature within a theological framework.[9] Such signs were proof of the perfection and comprehensiveness of creation just as they evoked nature's (and God's) beneficence in a moral sense, through the mercy of rain which allows the harvesting of crops and so forth. The purpose of reflecting upon God's signs in nature, then, was not simply to enhance scientific knowledge of the natural world but to strengthen the presence of belief through contemplation. This could not be said, however, of Muslim attitudes in the late nineteenth century, in which the relationship between science and religion had acquired a tone of mutual irreconcilability.

It is the thesis of this chapter that the conflict which arises between religion and science for Muslim modernist reformers was deeply informed by the epistemic conditions of European imperialism.[10] Because science and reason played a significant role in the instrumentalisation of colonial power, and were not the value-neutral fields which liberal imperialists had touted them to be, modernist reformers sought to sift through and identify the best parts of European knowledge, which they then compared to the tenets and values of Islam as they understood it. Thus, modernist reformers could prove that Islam was a friend to contemporary thought whilst simultaneously protecting Islam from modernity's most harmful elements.

Furthermore, I will argue that modernist reformers were significantly influenced by the reification of religion and religious systems amongst European and Orientalist scholars in the late nineteenth century. For instance, the modernist argument that Islam is compatible with reason often deferred to the way Romantic philologists and modern historians then defined religious cultures, by supposing that Islam must conform to the template of its ideal and unsullied scriptural origins. This was influenced by a shift in the Western notion of 'religion' during the nineteenth century: from a collection of subjective acts and beliefs which were bound up in a particular liturgical or ritual tradition to a fixed (ahistorical) system of doctrines and ideas.[11] My focus upon this will encompass the work of three seminal figures of the late nineteenth century: the political activist and reformer, Jamal al-Din al-Afghani; his disciple and successor in the project for theological reform in Egypt, Muhammad 'Abduh; and the founder of the Aligarh movement in northern India, Sayyid Ahmad Khan. But first, I will begin by explaining what the study of religion owed to Orientalist notions of language and race.

Philology and the Study of Religion

For historians in the eighteenth and nineteenth centuries, the discipline of philology — which traced the origin and development of languages and thus oversaw the translation and comparative historical analysis of religious texts — paved the way for the modern study of religious systems.[12] By assuming a transparency of meaning between a religious text and the particular racial or national culture which produced it, Romantic theories of language simplified the way modern scholars of religion approached their subject.[13] This was influenced by the work of Johann Gottfried Herder (1744–1803), who proposed that a language acts to mould and structure the character and nature of the people who employ it and so forms the best source for uncovering that people's cultural history.[14] Language or speech, according to Herder, represented the *Volkstimme* or inner expression of the outward form of a nation or people. Employing this premise, European philologists of the ancient languages of the Middle East and Asia saw in their object of study a historical repository of the national cultures from which such languages arose. J. D. Michaelis summed up this approach to the study of ancient texts when he pronounced language to be 'a kind of archive in which human discoveries are protected against the most harmful accidents, archives that flames cannot destroy and that cannot perish unless an entire nation is ruined'.[15]

Whereas previously the philological study of Middle Eastern languages had been motivated by the desire to uncover the sacred Edenic tongue in which God first spoke to Adam, scholars of the eighteenth and nineteenth centuries took up the alternative view that a language's origins denote the earliest attempts of primitive humans to describe the thoughts or feelings embedded in certain things and their concepts.[16] However, this desire to historicise language as the product of secular history (and not of divine origin) threatened to denude such scholarship of a higher mission. To make of philology an entirely scientific enterprise — divested of theological references — in which language is grounded in the living speech of a particular human community is to say that languages cannot be judged for better or worse. The view that all languages are historically constructed risked undermining the then popular notion that language (given force in art and literature) may fulfil a civilisation's higher mission or calling. For his part, Herder resisted the implications of this secular scientific view by claiming that the evolution of languages – which is also the development of human thought – contained an inner unity, harmony and coherence expressive of a transcendent, immaterial power. For Herder, this higher, providential purpose blocked the move to falsely equate or relativise the production of languages and cultures.

In the early nineteenth century, a comparable notion of the history of languages was attributed by the French philologist and historian, Ernst Renan (1823–1892), to the differences between the Semitic and Aryan races. For Renan, William Jones' (1736–1794) acclaimed discovery of the Indo-European family of languages – which revealed Sanskrit, Greek, Latin and Pahlavi's common linguistic origins – confirmed the formation of a European identity distinguished by its scientific and rational temperament. In Renan's view, the Aryan and Semite bore very different characteristics. The former was associated with the intellectual dynamism and vitality of the European races, whilst the latter was associated with the cultural senescence and fatalism of the 'Orient'. What sustained this approach to the study of ancient languages for Renan is the notion that different cultures can be pinned down and described according to their essential characteristics. Crucial, also, to this pinning down is the notion that Europe's discovery of modern science and 'reason', as the legacy of ancient Greece peculiar to the Aryan or European genius, validated the conquest and tutelage of other, less advanced nations.[17]

Furthermore, the European identity's attachment to science and reason had implications for the way these were received and negotiated by colonised peoples in the nineteenth and twentieth centuries. Gyan Prakash has shown how, in British India for instance, science's claim to universality was simultaneously undermined by its contextual role in the instrumentalisation of British power.[18] If liberal theories touted science's potential to uplift and improve the condition of people everywhere, they also enabled the colonial state to better govern, objectify, order and control those of a less advanced race. Because of this double role, indigenous reformers had to negotiate science's worth at a general, epistemological level and in relation to matters specific to their political, social and cultural circumstances. On the whole, such reformers restaged the reception of science as an opportunity for self-improvement on the premise that knowledge was value-free and that the benefits of its acquisition formed the true lesson that should be taken from colonial rule. Because modern knowledge was crucial to governmental power, and Europe's global supremacy was only guaranteed by its superiority in the fields of science, military technology, medicine and engineering, they rightly concluded that their own political weakness could not be remedied without the wholehearted adoption of the modern sciences. However, the dual role of colonial knowledge, to appear universal whilst undermining the position of indigenous non-Europeans, remained of profound consequence in the latter's reception of it.

Jamal al-Din al-Afghani and the Modern Salafiyyah

In the effort to reform Islam in light of modern science and the authority of reason, the influence of the Iranian-born activist and religious orator Jamal al-Din al-Afghani was substantial.[19] Born in As'adabad in Iran in 1839, al-Afghani was schooled in the intellectual and philosophical discourses of Iranian Shi'ism, which placed the study of *fiqh* (jurisprudence) and rhetoric alongside that of philosophy and mysticism. During a sometimes tumultuous career as a political activist and public intellectual, al-Afghani travelled through the Muslim polities of Central and South Asia, Iran and the former Ottoman Empire, where he involved himself in local struggles for social reform and agitated against the political hegemony of the European powers. In 1855–56 he travelled to India, where the harsh treatment meted out to Indian Muslims by British authorities radicalised him politically, instilling a deep resentment of European imperialism. In Egypt during the late 1870s, al-Afghani denounced French and British influence in the region and was particularly scathing towards the government of the Khedive Ismail, whose maladministration had gravely indebted Egypt to European banks and brought the country to economic near-ruin. A charismatic orator, he attracted a circle of admirers who included the distinguished Christian writer, Adib Ishaq, and the future Egyptian nationalist leader, Sa'd Zaghlul. Of those inspired by al-Afghani's call for religious reform, his closest associate and disciple became the most significant reformer and educationalist in the Arab Middle East around the turn of the century, Muhammad 'Abduh. A point of entry into al-Afghani's ideology is his public speeches and debate with the abovementioned French philologist and historian, Ernst Renan.

During the nineteenth century, no Western scholar did as much as Renan to establish and contrast the opposing characteristics and essences of the Indo-European and Semitic races. For Renan, as we have seen, the Aryan racial family was characterised by a spirit which was at once energetic, dynamic and rational, whereas the Semitic tribes had changed little over thousands of years. Reflecting the common nineteenth-century slippage between the language and race of a particular group, the Aryan and the Semite were to be distinguished by the function, structure and efficacy of their respective languages. It was the Aryan races who, aided by their superior languages, grew and adapted to the flux of history whilst the present-day Semitic tribes (both Jewish and Arab) were bound by the ancient tongues, cultures and mental structures in which their societies originated. Such racial categorisations became a guiding principle of the discipline of philology.

Comparing the Aryan and the Semite as one compares the development of a mature adult to a child, Renan attributed the Indo-Europeans' intellectual sagacity to their superior conjugation of verbs: 'This marvellous instrument, created by the instinct of primitive men, contained the seeds of all the metaphysics that would be developed later on by the Hindus, the Greeks or the Germans.' The same, unfortunately, could not be said of the Semitic tongue, whose 'greatest mistake [because the most irreparable], was to adopt such a niggardly mechanism for treating verbs that the expression of tenses and moods has always been imperfect and awkward in its language'. Because Aryan languages were inflexive and given to decisive shades of expression and meaning, they formed a perfect vehicle for the advancement of subtle and refined thought, whereas the Arabic language's imperfect verb tenses and moods trapped the Semitic mind in a state of intellectual gridlock. Stuck with such an imperfect language, the Arabs, according to Renan, were 'still struggling against the linguistic error committed by their ancestors ten or fifteen thousand years ago'.[20] It stood to reason, therefore, that the rigid and seemingly timeless languages of the Semitic races would provide a window onto the state of their religious creeds.

As Tzetan Todorov has pointed out, the historical triumph of the Aryan race for Renan illustrated nothing less than the success of the reason of the Enlightenment (as the achievement of modern Europeans) over irrationality and superstition.[21] As for the Semitic races, their single meaningful contribution to Indo-European civilisation (and to human history on the whole) was the birth of Christianity, which was modified, tempered and vastly improved through its encounters with non-Semitic peoples: 'From the day when they [the Semitic races] committed the Bible to European science...they have had nothing more of consequence to do.'[22] Indeed, it was the Aryanisation of Christianity, after its contact with first the Greek and Latin civilisations and later the Germanic and Slavic races, which brought revelation into contact with reason and refined the former. Through this process, Christianity was able to balance its divine, mythic (Semitic) origins with a modern scientific temperament.

Islam, on the other hand, was an inferior cousin to its Semitic forebears and offered very little to humanity on account of its philosophical vacuity and implacable hostility to science and reason. In a lecture delivered at the Sorbonne in 1883, on the subject of Islam and science, Renan describes a puritanical, dogmatic faith deeply opposed to the spirit of scientific inquiry.[23] He achieves this by tying Islam to its origins in the Arabian Peninsula, whose tribes ('the least philosophical of men') had found in Islam a mere pretext for the activities of conquest, plunder and military adventure. Rational thought was extinguished at the hands of the first Arabian empire after the expansion of Islam but experienced a surprising revival under the succeeding Abbasid dynasty, whose Persian character purportedly sustained the Aryan/Iranian genius and inclination for philosophical thought. Renan thus acknowledges the considerable achievements in science and philosophy which occurred under Abbasid patronage by arguing that this owed nothing to the language of the Arabs or to Islamic culture, but was Greek in origin and Persian in inspiration.

According to Renan, the Aryan genius for philosophical thought and metaphysical speculation survived the Arab conquests, and was revived as a form of cultural resistance amongst Persians in the early history of Islam. Highlighting what Oswald Spengler would later call racial 'morphology' (denoting the spiritual survival of a race once conquered or overcome by another group), Renan argues that the real achievements of this period cannot be attributed to the Arab race, who were not capable of such intellectual development, but to the more sophisticated people they had overrun.[24] For this reason, he states, 'everything written in Arabic is not an Arab product', just as 'everything done in a Muslim country is not the fruit of Islam'.[25] The triumph of what is commonly referred to as Arab science therefore cannot be attributed to either the Arabs or to Islam but to the external, more 'energetic' races with which these came into contact.

Incidentally, Renan raised this very theme on the subject of his meeting with al-Afghani. Of their encounter in March 1883, which occurred shortly after al-Afghani's arrival in Paris, the philologist described his interlocutor as 'an Afghan; entirely divorced from the prejudices of Islam; he belongs to those energetic races of Iran, near India, where the Aryan spirit lives still so energetically despite the superficial layer of official Islam'. For Renan, al-Afghani was living proof that the Aryan genius could not be snuffed out by the dead hand of Islam and its brittle intolerance of spirit:

> The liberty of his thought, his noble and loyal character, made me believe while I was talking with him, that I had before me, restored to life, one of my old acquaintances – Avicenna, Averroes, or another of those great infidels who represented for five centuries the tradition of the human mind... Sheikh Jemmal-Eddin is the best case of ethnic protest against religious conquest that one could cite.[26]

For his part al-Afghani, to whom we now turn, resisted the idea that Islam is both antithetical to reason and instructed by its Arab origins, and substituted Renan's linguistic determinism with a more idealised, but no less homogeneous, conception of Islam. After their meeting, Renan noted that the matter of race arose as the one point on which the two disagreed and al-Afghani's doubts about the stultifying effects of the Arabic language are raised in his written response to Renan's Islam and science lecture. The Arabic language, al-Afghani opined, was not hostile to the Greek and Persian sciences in the immediate wake of Islam's expansion, nor did Islam curtail the reception of such knowledge. To support this point, al-Afghani exploited the flaw in Renan's argument by pointing out that all Arabic-speaking peoples must nevertheless be regarded within an Arab intellectual sphere, were their genius for science to be calculated:

> As for Ibn-Bajja, Ibn Rushd (Averroes), and Ibn Tuffail, one cannot say that they are not just as Arab as al-Kindi because they were not born in Arabia, especially if one is willing to consider that human races are only distinguished by their languages and that if this distinction should disappear, nations would not take long to forget their diverse origins.[27]

Here, al-Afghani gently recalled to Renan the philological premise of a language's capacity to condition and determine the national character of the people who use it.

On the subject of Islam's dichotomous relation to science and reason, al-Afghani tempered, so as to undermine, Renan's argument. At the outset, al-Afghani agreed with Renan that religion and science cannot be easily reconciled because the religious recourse to mythical symbols and emotions will always undermine science's reliance upon empirical knowledge. 'So long as humanity exists,' al-Afghani told Renan, 'the struggle will not cease between dogma and free investigation... a desperate struggle in which, I fear, the triumph will not be for free thought, because the masses dislike reason, and its teachings are only understood by... the elite.'[28] It is for this reason, al-Afghani affirmed, that wherever religion and philosophy have come into contact the former has sought to eradicate the latter, and it is precisely this which Renan had mistaken for the Arab's inability to accept science.

However, al-Afghani then placed the dichotomy between reason and revelation within a historicist framework that appears to resolve their differences as mere stages on the path to a truer civilisation. Because nations are born in ignorance, and were never guided by reason from the start, religions such as Islam provided leadership for humanity despite their imperfect systems of education. Whilst the effects of religious dogma would prove to be 'one of the heaviest and most humiliating yokes' a reason-deprived humanity was forced to bear, al-Afghani maintained that 'one cannot deny that it is by this religious education, whether it be Muslim, Christian or pagan, that all nations have emerged from barbarism and towards a more advanced civilization'.[29] Thus, al-Afghani established a teleological scheme in which religion, whilst fundamentally opposing reason, had nonetheless acted as a stepping-stone to its light. And because Christianity had a head start on Islam of many centuries, al-Afghani asserted that the latter's development, or catching up with the West, may simply be a matter of time. Eventually, Islam will succeed in 'breaking its bonds and marching resolutely in the path of civilization after the manner of Western society', for which Christianity's own intolerance was 'not...an invincible obstacle'.[30]

Such is the ambiguity besetting al-Afghani's notion of historical progress, in which religion opposes the use of reason at a given instant but has somewhat paradoxically played a part in its eventual triumph. And underlying this is the conviction that Islam, more than any other religion, is ideally compatible with modern science. Reason and rationality, for al-Afghani, reflect the spirit and essence of Islam in its original and truest form although centuries of religious misinterpretation have wrenched the two apart. When Renan asserted that Islam was hostile to reason, al-Afghani agreed with him precisely because Islam's historical institutions had, in his opinion, failed to live up to its innermost ideals, which are identical to those of a modern rational society. Thus, al-Afghani contributed to the perception – which was common amongst secular and religious Arab intellectuals of the *nahda* (renaissance) period – that the flourishing of Arab philosophy under Abbasid patronage had an essentially rational, and therefore Islamic, origin and emphasis.

The distinction that emerges in al-Afghani's thought between an ideal, philosophically rational notion of Islam and the irrationality of contemporary Muslim dogmatists is justified by the idea that there are essentially two levels of discourse where knowledge about divine truth is concerned. On one hand, there is the rhetoric of popular religious emotion, which employs mythological symbols, metaphorical tales and other such devices to capture the imagination of the masses, whilst on the other, there is the speculative philosophical discourse of a learned elite, whose abstract, rational and metaphysical arguments are accessible only to those who are trained in it. The notion of two parallel discourses, which was common to pre-modern philosophical thinking since the time of al-Farabi (870–950), enabled al-Afghani to distinguish Islam's innermost spirit (through the exercise of reason) from the superfluous commentaries and elaborations of contemporary Muslim dogmatists and theologians.[31]

Furthermore, a fixed and idealised conception of indigenous religions and cultures emerges in al-Afghani's anti-colonial arguments. For instance, in numerous writings and speeches, al-Afghani advocated a true and uncorrupted identity to which colonised peoples must return if they are to reclaim the strength and vitality which characterised their civilisation at its apogee. To an audience at Calcutta University in 1882, al-Afghani recommended India's pre-modern scientific heritage and common language as the source from which a collective Hindu-Muslim identity may be formed. Appealing to the cooperative unity of all Indians, he extolled India's ancient civilisation and common language as a basis from which to take up the struggle against British colonialism. Likewise, at a gathering in Egypt, al-Afghani made the same determination: that a pride in Egypt's ancient (and pre-Islamic) heritage is the basis of national strength and solidarity. In both cases, he repeated the assumption that a shared language and common culture of origin are the glue which bind the people of a modern nation together and underwrite their cooperative political effort. If al-Afghani refuted Renan's application of the theory of language to shape the racial and national character of the Arab Muslim mind, he strategically employed the same assumptions to encourage incipient national and anti-colonial sentiments.

This move towards the reclamation of a lost identity also imbued al-Afghani's conception of Islam. In several speeches and addresses, al-Afghani appealed to a global Islamic identity (the universal *ummah* or community of believers) as a source of social and political strength. On his travels through India, Afghanistan, Iran, the Hijaz and the Ottoman Empire, al-Afghani disseminated a pan-Islamist message amongst students and political elites that stressed the need for political and spiritual cooperation between the Ottoman Empire, India, Iran and Afghanistan.[32] Islam, he insisted, instils a selfless virtue in the individual which no other religion can match. Yet because of their disunity and sectarian political wranglings, Muslims had made themselves easy prey for predatory and exploitative European powers, and had fallen behind in the fields of science and industry. Al-Afghani's nationalist and anti-colonial sentiments fulfilled the wishful political vision of a pan-Islamic alliance, and the glue which held this together was his ideal conception of a non-sectarian and rationally empowered Islam.

To show that Islam was 'the closest of religions to science and knowledge'[33] and that it encouraged social justice and reform, al-Afghani turns to the life of the Prophet Muhammad and the ideal community which he formed. For al-Afghani, the Prophet and his companions upheld a rational ethic and morality whose standards contrasted radically with the benighted Arabian society that preceded them, and which they stunningly transformed. Of all the people in the world, al-Afghani proclaims, none were more 'established in barbarism' than the people of pre-Islamic Arabia. The nomadic Arabs were 'completely deprived of lofty intellectual stirrings, comprehensive rational concepts and great philosophical subjects' until the coming of Islam, which provided them with a moral education and hunger for knowledge, learning and reflection.[34]

Whilst this notion of the early Muslims as an ideal community (*as-salaf as-salih*, connoting the 'pious forebears') was already familiar to such pre-modern scholars as Ibn Taymiyyah and Muhammad ibn 'Abdul Wahhab, al-Afghani can be said to have interpreted it in a particularly modern way. In al-Afghani's prose, the Prophet appears as an advocate for rational thought whose influence on those around him did not depend on the validation of miracles and existing superstitions, but on the moral clarity and rational sense of the divine message. The old beliefs and customs of seventh-century Arabia were swept aside and in their place was nurtured a commitment to reason and a desire to understand the laws of nature and society. Striking a chord which has since become a cliché amongst Islamists and Muslim apologists, al-Afghani insists that because the community founded by the Prophet was rational, humane and perfect in every sense, it forms the ideological and moral base from which Muslim power must be regenerated.

Here, there is no clash between modern thought and Islamic revelation. In fact, it is the Qur'an which became 'the first teacher of philosophy to the Muslims'.[35] Whereas for Renan, the philological peculiarities of the Arabic language determine the ontological confusion of the Semitic mind, al-Afghani discovers an alternative, reason-centred ontology at the heart of Islam. And although al-Afghani refutes Renan's philological assumptions about the effect of a language on the intellectual culture of those who employ it, there is still, in al-Afghani's argument, a strong emphasis on the conceptual unity of an essentialised culture or people. In his attempt to prove that Islam is compatible with the best of modern thought, al-Afghani nonetheless contributes to the process of its objectification.

Muhammad 'Abduh's Theology of Reason

Whilst al-Afghani outlined an argument for Islam's compatibility with reason, the detailed systematisation of a modern rationalist theology in the Arab Middle East was to be undertaken by his pupil and collaborator, Muhammad 'Abduh.[36] Born in a village in the Egyptian delta in 1849, 'Abduh (d.1905) received a traditional religious education in the city of Tanta before moving to Cairo, where he enrolled at the al-Azhar university in 1866. Having graduated from al-Azhar as an *'alim*, 'Abduh gained a teaching position there and at the Dar ul-Ulum, a new educational institution designed to prepare teachers for government schools. During this period, 'Abduh came under the influence of al-Afghani, who exposed him to the study of Muslim classics in the fields of astronomy, logic, metaphysics, theology and mysticism, whilst sensitising him to the political problems of Egypt and the Muslim world under colonial rule.[37] 'Abduh soon became a leading advocate for modern educational methods and involved himself in the civilian wing of national opposition to the British- and French-supported regime of Khedive Tawfiq. For opposing the British invasion of Egypt in 1882, 'Abduh was imprisoned and sent into exile. After a short stay in Beirut, he met up with al-Afghani in Paris, where in 1884 the two established a journal, *Al-'Uwrah al-Wuthqa* (*The Strongest Bond*), to which he contributed significant articles on matters of social and religious reform. 'Abduh then returned to Beirut, where he taught in an Islamic school and composed a number of lectures summarising his theological ideas, which were later published as the *Risalah al-Tawhid* (*Theology of the Oneness of God*). He returned to Egypt in 1888, where he embarked on a civic career, becoming first a judge (*qadi*) in the national court system and, in 1899, Egypt's leading religious official (*mufti*). In this capacity, he actively reformed the religious courts and administration of charitable endowments (*waqf*) and issued religious opinions (*fatawa*, sing. *fatwa*) addressing issues relevant to the modern age, many of which were steadfastly opposed by the *'ulama* of the al-Azhar university.

For 'Abduh, as for al-Afghani, the effort to revive Islam's essential teachings finds him relating to it as a reified and fixed entity. In his writings, for instance, 'Abduh often refers to the example of the 'pious forebears' (*as-salaf as-salih*), whom he loosely associates with the Prophet's immediate companions and those generations of the first few centuries who stayed close to the spirit of Qur'anic revelation and the *Sunnah* of the Prophet. In a section of 'Abduh's fragmented autobiography, he states that the purpose of his life's work is:

> to liberate thought from the shackles of *taqlid* (the imitation of past tradition), and understand religion as it was understood by the elders of the community before dissension appeared; to return, in the acquisition of religious knowledge, to its first sources, and to weigh them in the scales of human reason, which God has created in order to prevent excess or adulteration in religion, so that God's wisdom may be fulfilled and the order of the human world preserved; and to prove that, seen in this light,

religion must be accounted a friend to science, pushing man to investigate the secrets of existence, summoning him to respect established truths, and to depend on them in his moral life and conduct.[38]

'Abduh develops a reason-based theology in his Beirut lectures, which were later collected and published as the *Risalah al-Tawhid* (*Theology of the Oneness of God*). Herein, the message of God's singular divinity is confirmed through the exercise of reason, from those proofs which are evident in the order of creation. Employing the Aristotelian categories which were familiar to medieval philosophers such as Ibn Rushd (and which were later used by Sufi intellectuals of the late medieval period), 'Abduh asserts that the world is moved by a chain of contingent secondary causes which prove the existence of a 'first cause', or God. Furthermore, God's mode of being is 'necessary' (*wajib al-wujud*), which is to say that God exists eternally and that nothing caused or sustains God's existence.[39] Reflecting an attitude which was commonplace amongst theologians associated with the rationalist Mu'tazilah tradition of theological thinking, 'Abduh argues that reason is self-sufficient for understanding God's signs as they appear in the secondary causes which move the physical universe.

A central concern of early Islamic theology to which 'Abduh returns is the need to ascertain the true extent of human freedom in relation to the divine will. For whilst the causes which move the universe are not independent of God's will (a will which has set all such causes in motion) this does not mean that God constrains or determines the lives of human beings. Rather, humans are considered free to choose from amongst a spectrum of decisions and actions already potentialised, or made possible, by God at any moment. This idea of 'potential actions', which humans then take as their own, refers us to the 'Asharite doctrine of *kasb* (acquisition). To say that humans are the independent 'creators' of their acts would be to situate them as co-creators with God. Thus, an emphasis on their freedom to 'acquire' actions (albeit a freedom limited to those actions which are potentialised at any given moment) protects the omnipotence of God whilst enjoining a sense of human responsibility and freedom.[40] To put it another way, 'Abduh argues that although there is a divine power behind each and every potential act, this power nonetheless includes the ability of human beings to *choose* their acts. Thus, the rationalist premise of 'Abduh's theology is combined with elements of 'Asharite doctrine. This does not mean that 'Abduh 'belonged' to either the Mu'tazilah or 'Asharite school, as some historians have supposed, for he clearly took up aspects of both.[41]

For 'Abduh, as for numerous Muslim theologians of the past, revelation serves the function of giving to reason what reason is otherwise incapable of attaining on its own: the metaphysical/transcendental truths that exist only in God's supreme wisdom.[42] And whilst reason cannot broach such issues as the divine essence or nature of the hereafter, its greatest use, as we have seen, is for discerning the message of divine unity (*tawhid*, or the 'oneness of God') in the phenomenal world. Yet, because 'Abduh establishes the existence of the divine being through rational proof, the denial of causality becomes in itself an act of false association with God. In other words, those who deny reason actually deny the sole faculty by which God's creation, or superior causation over the long train of secondary causes which move the created world, can be known. Such a person, 'Abduh concludes, commits the serious error of associating partners with God (*shirk*) on the basis that anything in this world which is not affected by God's causal agency must be attributed – negatively – to an agent or being other than God. Not coincidentally, 'Abduh elucidates this point with an appeal to reason's instrumental utility:

> It [denying God's causalities] is the belief of those who exalt other than God to Divine authority and presume to dispense with the means that He has given, such as military forces as the condition for victories in war, or the use of medicines (given by God) for the purpose of healing sicknesses, or the paths and precepts He has ordained whereby happiness might be ours in this world and the next.[43]

Here, reason's importance for monotheistic belief coincides with its usefulness for worldly power and success. Whilst this echoes the theological premise that good or bad social conditions stem from correct or incorrect religious belief and practice, 'Abduh does not reduce faith to a pragmatic social hypothesis. Rather, in 'Abduh, we witness the beginnings of a change in the conception of theology: from a branch of religious knowledge whose task was to discern and interpret God's attributes and signs, to a reason-based 'science', in the modern sense, whose role is bound up in the advancement and prosperity of a modern civilisation. Because science and reason represent the only valid means for social development, it is Islam's compatibility with reason which marks it as the wellspring, or source, of modern reforms. However, this emphasis upon Islam's rationality betrays a shift in the ontological foundations of faith, which I will pursue in the work of another influential modernist of the period.

Sayyid Ahmad Khan and the Authority of Nature

In the late nineteenth century, few modernists worked as hard to reconcile the claims of religion and science as the Indian reformer and educationalist, Sayyid Ahmad Khan (1817–1898).[44] Born and raised in the milieu of the Mughal aristocracy, Sayyid Ahmad found employment, as a young man, in the court system erected by the British East India Company, where he was soon elevated to the rank of *sadr amin* (sub-judge) in the province of Bijnaur. During this period, he composed a few pamphlets on the subject of religion and an impressive historical survey of the buildings and monuments of Delhi (*Athar al-Sanadid*, 1847). However, the events of the anti-British uprising of 1857, and subsequent reassertion of British authority, changed Sayyid Ahmad's life radically. Witnessing the immense destruction which the insurgency and its aftermath had wrought on the city of Delhi, Sayyid Ahmad sought to improve relations between the colonial government and India's Muslim community. Having demonstrated his loyalty to the colonial regime by personally intervening to save the European colony of Bijnaur during the rebellion, his enhanced status amongst colonial administrators and officials made it possible for him to gain support for various reformist initiatives.

Sayyid Ahmad's most significant reforms were in the area of education and scholarship. In 1864 he founded the Scientific Society, and

ISLAMIC MODERNISM AND THE REIFICATION 61

went on to promote the formation of educational committees across many districts of northern India. After an eighteen-month journey to England (1869–70), which saw him knighted for services to the British Empire, he launched the journal *Tahzib al-Akhlaq* for the purpose of spreading reformist ideas and practices amongst the Indian Muslim public. In 1875, he established the Mohammadan Anglo-Oriental College in Aligarh (which is now known as the Aligarh Muslim University) with the intention of giving Indian Muslims better access to, and representation amongst, the colonial government and administration. He also instituted the Muhammad Educational Conference, whose annual meetings sought to address the general educational needs of India's Muslim community.

In works targeting an English audience, Sayyid Ahmad sought to counteract the anti-Muslim sentiment of colonial officials in the aftermath of the 1857 uprising. Deploring the British perception of Indian Muslims as inherently fanatical and politically disloyal, he attempted, in three post-1857 works, to clarify the sociological, economic and political causes of the rebellion.[45] By way of a response to the new criticisms directed at Islam and the Prophet by the missionary polemicist and colonial official, William Muir (1819–1905), Sayyid Ahmad counselled the need to apply modern historiographical procedures to Islamic sources, though not in such a way as to undermine the veracity of the Prophet and reliability of the Qur'an. He advocated the historical re-evaluation and vetting of various *ahadith* (the reports, sayings and actions attributed to the Prophet) whilst asserting, contrary to Muir's criticisms, that the Qur'an was an authentic record of the words of Muhammad, regardless of the Muslim belief in its divine origins.

Addressing a domestic Muslim audience in numerous articles, letters and speeches composed in Urdu and Persian, Sayyid Ahmad declared his support for British rule and argued that the new security, science and industry brought by the empire were of benefit to all its subjects. Like his modernist contemporaries in Egypt, Sayyid Ahmad decried the intellectual stagnation and narrow-mindedness of the *'ulama*, whose attachment to superstition and reliance upon a pre-modern cosmological worldview barred them from reviewing traditional beliefs in light of modern scientific findings. Indeed, for Sayyid

Ahmad, this close-mindedness threatened to jeopardise the very survival of Islam as a modern culture. Thus he affirmed that 'if people do not break with *taqlid* (the imitation of past jurists)... and if they are going to prove unable to confront religion with present day scholarship and science, then Islam will disappear from India.'[46]

In his project for a new theology (*'ilm al-kalam*), Sayyid Ahmad argued that there can be no contradiction between the laws of the natural world and the sacred text of the Qur'an, no clash between the 'work of God' and the 'word of God'.[47] In the eyes of his opponents, this positivistic belief in the empirical sciences denied the possibility of religious miracles and undermined the conventional understanding of prophecy and divine guidance, for which they labelled him a 'naturalist' (*neichari*) and 'materialist' (*dahri*).[48] Yet, despite such criticisms, Sayyid Ahmad's rationalist theology did not so much seek to undermine the premises for religious belief as to found it upon those categories which, by his reckoning, made any such knowledge possible.

In the theoretical introduction to his commentary on the Qur'an, *Tahrir fi Usul al-Tafsir* (*The Principles of Exegesis*), Sayyid Ahmad responds to an opinion of the eighteenth-century theologian, Shah Wali Allah, concerning the manner in which revelation was transmitted from the angel Gabriel to the Prophet Muhammad. In his famous treatise, *Hujjat Allah al-Balighah* (*The Conclusive Argument from God*), Wali Allah had claimed that the words of the Qur'an became manifest 'only in the form of the Arabic language which was familiar to Muhammad and in which he could think, while the ideas flowed from the unseen to teach him as a means of God's nearness to men'.[49] Wali Allah thus intimated that for the sacred text to be comprehended by the Prophet's contemporaries, the words of the Qur'an must necessarily have been his own:

> They [the words of the Qur'an] became Divine Speech (*Kalam Allah*) ... only because the intention of the welfare of men became fixed in his (Muhammad's) thought: and this is what collected the words and composed them [so that the words of the Qur'an] unfolded in this composition and wore a dress... suitable for the mighty greatness of God.[50]

In Wali Allah's estimate, therefore, the Qur'an was revealed to the Prophet not in a certain phrasing of words but by the shape of ideas and feelings, impressed upon the heart, which the Prophet then poured out in his native Arabic tongue. By this account, the words of the Qur'an are as much the words of the Prophet, or the parlance of the society and culture in which the Prophet lived, as they are of God, whilst being no less divine for that reason.

Rejecting this notion that the Prophet received revelation in the shape of feelings which then became his (and God's) direct speech, Sayyid Ahmad marshals two arguments for why this could not be the case. The first of these defers to the Qur'an's own description of itself as 'an Arabic Qur'an' (12:2), or that which was revealed 'in the form of the Arabic language', to the Prophet by the 'faithful spirit' (*al-Ruh al-Amin*) (2:192–195). Because the Qur'an explicitly associates the event of its revelation with the Arabic language, it cannot as a matter of doctrine, be regarded as 'a pouring down of ideas' (*ma'na*) in which 'the medium, or words, in which these ideas were expressed were the Prophet's'.[51] This argument is familiar enough to various traditions of Qur'anic exegesis.

The other argument which Sayyid Ahmad makes in order to show that Wali Allah's conception of Prophecy is misplaced – and the more relevant one in this context – is that his very proposition is 'opposed to reason' (*'aql ke mukhalif*). According to Sayyid Ahmad, it is an established fact that:

> no idea divested of words can come to mind, nor can its pouring (into the heart) take place. The imagining and conceiving of any subject demand as a concomitant the imagination and conception of the words which are indicative of that subject. The occurrence of a content divested of words is a rational impossibility. Therefore, the glorious Koran was impressed upon the Prophet's heart in actual words as they are and the Prophet recited these same words in the same (original) order to the people.[52]

Sayyid Ahmad's insistence that there can be no separation between the word and its idea is not simply a defence of the notion that language is needed for ideas to be expressed or communicated. Rather, language in this instance is synonymous with a cognitive understanding which precedes feeling and emotion in the event of Prophetic revelation, which is to say that the Prophet did not *experience* insofar as he *thought* revelation, as I will attempt to show. This does not lessen the miraculous nature of Prophetic revelation but establishes a division of labour in which thought is placed above feeling, rationality over intuition, reason before miracles.

Let me highlight this with an argument Sayyid Ahmad makes about the very subject of miracles, in this instance, the 'miraculous' nature of the Qur'an. Sayyid Ahmad confirms the notion that the revealing of the Qur'an was miraculous, although he does this for reasons which are less than familiar to contemporary theological argument. Amongst classical exegetes since the time of 'Abd al-Qahir Al-Jurjani (d.1078), the doctrine of the 'miracle/immutability of the Qur'an' (*'ijaz al-Qur'an*) referred to the notion that the revelations received by the Prophet were an instance of divine speech whose miraculous nature is reflected in its aesthetic perfection and formal beauty.[53] According to this doctrine, the inimitable eloquence and literary brilliance of the Qur'an is sole proof of its miraculous stature. After all, didn't the Qur'an issue a challenge which no poet or belletrist of the Prophet's time or since has been able to meet, namely, to create anything of comparable beauty and eloquence?[54]

Whilst Sayyid Ahmad agrees that the Qur'an is characterised by the 'excellence' of its language and speech, he nonetheless considers this a 'superficial argument' in support of its miraculous status. The original miracle of the Qur'an, according to Sayyid Ahmad, is its appeal to the universality of reason. Because of its clarity and truth, of which 'not one word opposes nature or philosophy...an ignorant Bedouin and a holy maulvi would both receive from its literal meanings the same guidance as a philosopher from the intended meanings of the same words (*alfaz-i maqsud*)'.[55] It is this sense of reason and intelligence, before the aesthetic, onomatopoetic and emotional effects of the Qur'an, which underscores its true importance and enshrines the status of the empirical sciences in Sayyid Ahmad's theology.

The same approach to the evaluation of miracles accompanies Sayyid Ahmad's estimation of the phenomenon of prophetic revelation.

According to Sayyid Ahmad, prophecy is 'a natural thing (*ek fitri cheez hai*)' which can be said to exist 'in the prophets by exigency of their nature, as do the other human faculties'.[56] Thus, one may speak of a prophetic faculty, or habitus (*malakah-i nabawiyyah*), which is innate to human nature and which is not dissimilar to the senses of hearing, touch and sight. Prophets are not unlike other human beings except for being endowed with a greater sensitivity to the metaphysical, social and moral issues which the phenomenon of prophecy encompasses. In this context, the ability of prophets, their particular 'habitus', is denuded of every miraculous association save the 'miracle' of the message, which, as we have seen, confirms the divine appeal to reason. Because the faculty of prophethood already exists within human beings, there can be no interpolated angelic agency between God and prophet, attributed to a figure such as Gabriel:

> *Wahy* (revelation) is that which the source of God's overflowing bounty has engraved on the heart of the prophet, in accordance with the nature of prophethood. This stimulation of the heart sometimes makes itself heard by way of the outer ears like a speaking voice and sometimes this engraving on the heart (*naqsh-i qalbi*) appears in the form of somebody speaking. But in fact, there is no voice but the person's own voice, nor is there a person speaking.[57]

Nevertheless, prophecy's status as a human faculty does not abrogate the central Islamic tenet of Muhammad's finality as a messenger of God. Because the revelation (*wahy*) or inspiration (*ilham*) given to prophets and other social visionaries are of a lesser kind than that bestowed on the Prophet Muhammad, his experience of revelation was 'as nature would render perfect'. Only in this sense may one speak of the finality of prophethood (*khatm-i nabuwat*), which refers less to the severing of revelation between God and humanity after Muhammad's time than to prophecy's state of completion in him.[58]

A consequence of establishing prophecy as an internal human attribute is the reduction of a sense of God's immanence and closeness to humanity. Referring to the Qur'anic verse in which the angel of revelation descended to the Prophet 'to a distance of two bows length or nearer' (52:9), Sayyid Ahmad stated that even if such an event were visible to the Messenger (if it 'occurred by the outer eyes'), its visibility in fact represented 'the reflection of His divine epiphanies (*tajaliyyah rabani*), a reflection that appeared in accordance with the human and prophetic nature, and in reality was nothing but the habitus of prophethood which you might call Gabriel or something else'.[59] The consequence of confining what has been said to occur in the event of prophetic revelation to mental phenomenon, or the laws of the natural world, is that God cannot be known except through God's 'epiphanies' as they appear in nature and are apprehended by the empirical sciences.[60]

Moreover, the notion that God's epiphanies (*tajjali*) are present only in those secondary causes which govern the natural world cuts out the existence of that intermediary realm – the *'alam al-mithal* (imaginal world) – which once acted as a liminal zone between God and humanity.[61] As Fazlur Rahman explains, the *'alam al-mithal* in the pre-modern Islamic metaphysical systems of the Middle East and South Asia denoted a 'field of transition' in which the soul's power of imagination bridged the 'sensible and intellectual realms'.[62] Generally speaking, this cosmology reflected a productive fusion of the Aristotelian scheme of a world determined by secondary causes with the Neoplatonic theory of ideal forms emanating from God (who is the eternal maker or first cause of the Aristotelian model) to matter. Whilst I do not have the space to discuss this cosmology in detail, the *'alam al-mithal* was important for helping to explain those verses of the Qur'an which employ imaginary similitudes, parables and metaphors.

On some twenty-seven occasions, the Qur'an refers, in various ways, to instances in which God chose to communicate with humanity by the 'striking of similitudes/allegories' (*darb al-amthal*). Thus, for a theologian such as al-Ghazali (d.1111), God's use of similitudes points to two separate but complementary ontological realms: the spiritual and higher intellectual world of heavenly dominion (*malakut*) on the one hand, and the physical and sensory world of visible phenomena (*shahadah*) on the other.[63] Because everything in the physical world has its counterpart in the spiritual world, it follows that, on occasion, particular verses in the Qur'an appeal to two levels of meaning, pertaining to the literal and symbolic respectively. The interpretation of similitudes and metaphors thus serves an important function by pointing towards an imaginal realm (*'alam al-mithal*) which supersedes understanding based only on the observation of worldly bodies.

Yet, for Sayyid Ahmad, the *'alam al-mithal* has lost its epistemological validity insofar as he discounts the phenomenological or imaginative component of religious experience. In his theological writings, Sayyid Ahmad at no stage engages in the symbolic interpretation of Qur'anic similitudes, preferring instead to ignore or dismiss them as an inferior substitute for what science would otherwise better explain. Because reason forms an end in itself and is not a means to something outside of, or beyond, itself, it cannot address the role of the imagination within the sacred religious experience. Because Sayyid Ahmad entirely trusts science's claim to approximate a God's-eye view of the world, all that can be learned from the natural sciences encompasses all that anyone can know of humanity and religion. To put it another way, Sayyid Ahmad substitutes (in Hent De Vries' expression) 'a *science* of God for a science of *God*' in which religion and, with it, the theme of divine immanence are reduced to a category of objective study, like all other phenomena in the natural world.[64]

Indeed, Sayyid Ahmad's assertion of Islam's rationality, and compatibility with the laws of nature, echoes the 'natural religion' of the nineteenth-century Indologist and scholar of religion, Max Müller. Whilst Deism (the belief that reason plays an important role in determining religious knowledge) had dwindled in popularity by the nineteenth century, it continued to influence the modern study of religion, alongside the rationalistic atheism of thinkers such as Hume and Spinoza.[65] Nevertheless, one must not infer a clear line of influence between any specific Western thinker or school of thought, and the indigenous reformulation of such knowledge in the colonies during the nineteenth century. For the most part, there is no direct or obvious link between the production of knowledge amongst European scholars and colonial administrators, and the indigenous negotiation of such ideas. Whilst Muslim modernists were no doubt exposed to the sociological theories of Auguste Comte (1798–1857) and Herbert

Spencer (1820–1903), this came through various channels, including new educational institutions and intellectual societies, the translation of European works into indigenous languages, and the general acceptance of such ideas in social journals and the media as and when they impacted upon the political, cultural and theological issues of the day. My argument is not that modernist intellectuals were written over by European ideas but that they were compelled to negotiate the categories which made such knowledge possible in the first place.

And in this regard, the secular element of modernist thought poses a fundamental question for the contemporary conceptualisation of religion. Namely, if the symbols and metaphors employed by theologians and Sufis to describe the divine reality are now discounted as the stuff of imagination and fantasy, how can anything be known or said about God at all? Whilst the evidence of God's revelation and 'signs' (*ayat*) support a reason-based argument for the existence of a higher intelligence, the truth of God's similitudes, metaphors and mythical allegories (which include such descriptions as the day of judgment and afterlife) *cannot be known rationally or otherwise*. And if one cannot presume to know such matters through avenues of contemplative knowledge or mystical experience, as some pre-modern theologians and mystics had done, one can now only *believe* in God.

The notion of a belief emerging independent of, and supplementary to, reason contains an aporia which turns the project for a rational theology against itself. It is evident in Sayyid Ahmad's assertion that scriptural similitudes cannot be grasped by mere reason, whilst the content of faith nevertheless depends upon the rational proofs for God's existence encountered in the study of nature. If the transcendental content of religion cannot be known even obliquely, a belief now founded exclusively on God's causality in the natural world loses something in its quest for legitimacy.

Faith and the Limits of Reason

In Sayyid Ahmad's writings, 'faith' (*iman*) is often associated with the knowledge of scientific reason. And yet there is also a sense in which faith is anterior, or opposed, to reason. In a lecture delivered in 1884 to the *Anjuman-i Himayat-i Islam* ('Association for the Service of Islam') in Lahore, Sayyid Ahmad describes an uncritical type of faith which has existed amongst the masses and flourished for centuries. That this elementary faith has been so virile for so long, he concedes, must testify to its efficacy:

> millions of men have passed or are alive now or lived at the time of the Messenger of God whose heart accepted the instruction and who believed firmly in the truth of Islam, although they had no knowledge of the arguments for its truth. The only reason for their belief was that God had made their hearts in such a way that they would, even with a minimum of instruction, accept the Straight Path... These people in their heart believe Islam without knowing the proofs for its truth according to the principles of logic and philosophy.[66]

Having posited that this illogical type of faith reflects a predilection implanted by God in the human heart, Sayyid Ahmad goes on to categorise a second type of faith (his own) which nonetheless requires rational proof for acceding the truth of Islam. The problem with this second type of faith, however, is that it is inherently weaker than the sort which requires no proof at all:

> I am convinced that people who believe in Islam without the arguments and proofs of philosophy have a more solid faith than those who believe in Islam or hold it for certain on the basis of philosophical proofs and arguments. [Such people] do not need any logical proof or philosophical demonstration for knowing God and for believing in the Prophet. Whatever is stated to them as having been taught by God and the Messenger, be it irrational (*kharij az 'aql*) or unbelievable, be it true or false, they will believe in it. I consider such people the stars of true belief... and true Muslims.[67]

In this manner, Sayyid Ahmad praises the simple faith of the uncritical believer, which requires no a priori demonstration or rational validation of proof. Moreover, he later concedes that the more 'critical' variety of faith (his own) is weaker for the fact that it cannot subsist entirely in and of itself, but is vouchsafed by the labour of reason.[68] Thus the former, uncritical variant of faith can be counted as 'true belief' because it does not depend, as critical faith does, upon the 'doubt' and 'hesitation' which are necessary for a cognitive, reason-based negotiation of proof.

Herein lies the aporia at the heart of Sayyid Ahmad's theology, and of other rationalists like him in the nineteenth century: faith and rationality are now *paradoxically* dependent on one another. For instance, his concession to the strength of an 'uncritical faith' no longer refers us to the familiar notion that truth is available in two separate but mutually valuable registers (that of scriptural revelation and rational philosophy). It shows instead that because faith and reason are inseparable, neither is able to come into its own or properly coincide with itself. What arises, then, is an uneasy recognition of the inability of both faith and reason to satisfy the meaning of religion. Faith is at once both central to theology and is evacuated from it by a reason which does not, and cannot, take faith as its subject.

As I have tried to show, Muslim modernists reified the category of 'religion' and sought to concentrate their theology upon the practical, this-worldly requirements of their religious community. Yet their notion of faith was so firmly grounded in reason that, for Sayyid Ahmad, reason can admit to evacuating, or weakening, the very notion of an interiorised 'faith'. There was, therefore, no way for Sayyid Ahmad to combine a demystificatory scientific rationality and faith in the transcendental content of revelation *within* his project for a new theology. Whilst contemporary and later intellectuals sought to reconcile the divergence between reason and revelation,[69] this does not interest me as much as the way these opposing categories nurtured a dichotomy between Islamic and European sources of knowledge.

A Two-Worlds Theory and Its Ramifications

Amongst Muslim thinkers in the late nineteenth and early twentieth centuries, suspicions about the epistemological provenance and value of modern thought inform the distinction between domains of knowledge labelled 'Islamic', on one side, and (pejoratively) 'Western', 'materialist' (*dahriyyah, madiyyah*), 'non-religious' (*la dini*) or 'socialist' (*ishtirakiyyah*) on the other. An early example of this is al-Afghani's polemical tract 'The truth about the *neicheriyyah* [naturalist] sect and an explanation of the *neicheris*', which he composed in Hyderabad, in 1882, in opposition to Sayyid Ahmad's reformist theology.[70] In this pamphlet, al-Afghani set out to explain why the ideology of naturalism attacks all religious values and will lead, inevitably, to processes of historical corruption and decline. Here, as in most of al-Afghani's speeches and writings, there is a strong emphasis on the social unity, cohesion and strength which religion gives to society, and its compatibility with modern science. But beyond its polemical content, my interest in this work lies in the dichotomous ideological worldview it carves out.

When one compares their intellectual output, it becomes clear that al-Afghani and Sayyid Ahmad diverged more in their political attitudes towards colonial rule than in their thoughts about Islam and modernity per se. For, as Nikki Keddie points out, both reformers argued that Islam was wholly compatible with reason and made broadly similar claims on behalf of its importance to the resurgence of Muslim society.[71] However, al-Afghani, the staunch anti-imperialist, radically disapproved of Sayyid Ahmad's cooperative position on British rule and sought, for this reason, to identify and denigrate the 'materialist' bias in Sayyid Ahmad's theological system. This much can be inferred from the fact that al-Afghani never addressed Sayyid Ahmad's theological arguments in detail except to insinuate, in another pamphlet, that his reforms were part of a British-sponsored plot to divide, weaken and dispirit the Muslim community.[72] For my purposes, al-Afghani's anti-naturalist argument would not warrant analysis but for the fact that its positing of irreconcilable (Islamic and 'naturalist'/non-Islamic) worldviews has become an all too common feature of modern Muslim polemics.

In the ideology of naturalism, al-Afghani has found an age-old nemesis of religion which attacks the moral and ethical foundations of society. Naturalists, going back to the Epicureans and Cynics, held that all knowledge stems from matter, or nature, and cannot be attributed to the belief in God as the first cause or unmoved mover. This denial of revelation as a source of knowledge would later manifest itself in modern atheism and the Darwinian theory of natural selection. Because naturalists deny the existence of God, they would cut humanity off from the Islamic message of *tawhid* (connoting the oneness of God and God's creation) and the moral system taught by the prophets. For al-Afghani, Sayyid Ahmad fits into this movement by claiming that religion can only be understood through the study of nature, without recourse to revelation.

Here, al-Afghani portrays a rationally empowered Islam resisting the lure of this perfidious 'sect', whose acceptance would weaken the pillars of religion and morality. In this sense, naturalism provides an ideological foil for the assertion of a hermetically distinct and self-contained vision of Islam. And as I have pointed out, the homogenising effect of a singular definition of religion (very much present in the philological racism of the nineteenth century) is reproduced by al-Afghani in such a way that the determining element is no longer that of a particular language, or race, but the reified religious system to which historical generalisations – about language, race and culture – then referred. More broadly, this reflects the tendency of nineteenth-century thinkers to objectify, and then schematise, religious systems according to an estimation of their ideal and fixed content.[73]

Elements of modern thought pose a problem for al-Afghani, as for later reformers, precisely because they are thought to stem from an alien (Western) source whose fundamental value cannot be reconciled with the teachings of religion. The real challenge, as it occurs to modernist reformers, is that the separate value attached to Islamic and non-Islamic sources calls for the work of rejection or synthesis. This picture of two differentiated and opposing ideological spheres emerges after the negotiation of modern science's dual nature (which I mentioned at the beginning of this chapter), in which Western liberal claims to the neutrality of reason were undermined by its application to processes of colonial dominance. Because knowledge was not in fact value-free, it could not be accepted wholeheartedly or without consideration for its influence over religion.

This epistemic dualism certainly influences 'Abduh's attempts to identify the best aspects of modernity with Islam in its ideal, untrammelled form. Striking a chord to be repeated ad nauseam amongst later revivalists, 'Abduh discovers in Islam the origins of those European political and scientific concepts which are deemed to be of value for a modern society. The notion of democracy, for instance, is shown to have its origins in the Arab practice of tribal consultation (*shura*) and the provisions given amongst Muslim jurists for a notion of public welfare (*maslahah*) in decisions pertaining to the community at large. Likewise, the legitimacy given to consensus of opinion amongst Muslim jurists (*ijma'*) is cited as an early example of the modern democratic notion of public opinion.[74] Whilst such parallels may seem far-fetched, 'Abduh's efforts reveal the extent to which developments in modern knowledge had to be reconciled with, and relocated within, an Islamic discourse.[75] The negative value imputed to Western institutions, technologies and forms of governance – under the conditions of colonialism – required an Islamic veneer or precedent to make them more palatable.

Here, I have argued that the reification of religious systems in the modern period supports the idea that Islam exists in a pure form, above the exigencies of politics and history. Al-Afghani exemplified this in his desire to idealise an early, prototypical Islam, which he contrasted with a present state of moral and political decline.[76] This notion of history as a process of degeneration, in which the religious community is seen to drift further away from the spirit of its founding lights ('the pious forebears', *as-salaf as-salih*), was taken up by Muhammad Rashid Rida (1865–1935), who claimed that Western imperialism constituted a war of ideas as much as a political and material struggle.[77] Moreover, an a-historical, reified notion of Islam was employed in the Arab Middle East during the twentieth century by such intellectuals as the left-wing writer, Hasan Hanafi (b.1935), and the theoretical founders of Islamism, Sayyid Qutb (1906–1966) and Taqi al-Din al-Nabhani (1909–1977).

Conclusion

Despite its profound influence over later Muslim thought and culture, Islamic modernism is often presented as an intellectual capitulation to the certainties of Western scientism under the pressures of colonial rule. The seeds for this were no doubt planted by the European contemporaries of Jamal al-Din al-Afghani, Muhammad 'Abduh and Sayyid Ahmad Khan, who viewed Islamic modernism as an essentially Western-inspired (and therefore 'un-Islamic') intellectual movement. Those contemporaries include scholars such as Ernst Renan, whose estimation of al-Afghani as a 'free thinker' is cited above, and the colonial administrator Lord Cromer (1841–1917), who bluntly asserted that 'Islam cannot be reformed; that is to say, reformed Islam is Islam no longer'.[78] This pessimism finds an echo in the argument of later Orientalist historians that Islamic modernism 'failed' to provide a synthesis of Islamic and Western ideas, which led in turn to the anti-Western sentiments of revivalist thinkers from the 1930s onwards.[79] Yet modernist reforms can only be labelled a 'failure' if one has already charted the path of their historical destiny, which – for the proponents of this view – would have required such reformers to have abandoned Islamic 'tradition' for the successful adaptation of European intellectual models. The notion of failure is thus inappropriate, given that modernist thinkers were deeply engaged in negotiating the terms under which Islam and nineteenth-century thought might be reconciled.

To conclude, Jamal al-Din al-Afghani, Muhammad 'Abduh and Sayyid Ahmad Khan sought, in different ways, to bring Islam up to the conditions of religious faith and scientific rationality in the nineteenth century. For this purpose, the schematisation of Islam as a historical system – conforming to an unchanging scriptural/doctrinal essence – was particularly useful. By engaging with modern categories of thought, they were able to invert the Orientalist notion of Islam as an obstacle to the development of modernity, and laid the ground for later projects of theological and institutional reform. Their works do not, therefore, tell the story of a traditional (pre-modern) theology attempting to catch up with the demands of a modern civilisation. Instead modernist reformers were compelled to negotiate the value of a science whose role in the legitimation of European power could not be swept aside. Because reason is historically situated, its pretension to a God's-eye view of the world must be negotiated at a human level and is itself the product of a particular historical moment.

CHAPTER 2

LITERARY ROMANTICISM AND ISLAMIC MODERNITY: THE CASE OF URDU POETRY

The filthy archive of poetry and odes, more foul than a cesspool in its putridity,
By which the earth is convulsed as if by an earthquake, and which makes the angels blush in heaven,
Such is the place among other branches of learning of our literature, by which learning and faith are quite devastated.[1]

Introduction: Literature as Cultural Signifier

In the previous chapter I explained how Muslim modernists of the nineteenth century came to view Islam as a singular, reified civilisation, or culture, conditioned by a primary doctrinal or scriptural essence. This was seen, for instance, in the inclination amongst modernist reformers to ground an agenda for social and political rejuvenation in a return to the spirit of the early Muslim community. And yet, the influence on theological discourses of this quest for communal regeneration was, in some cases, less notable than its influence upon projects for cultural and social reform. One area of focus for Indian modernists of the nineteenth century was literature and the literary arts, including poetry, which were now deemed relevant to notions of cultural health, authenticity and decline. Under the dictum that a people's condition is reflected in their language, the themes of moral degeneration and reform came to have a strong bearing on the indigenous valuation of poetry and the literary arts, indeed challenging the criteria upon which such literature was judged.

Amongst Indian Muslims, the notion that literature should be used to inculcate 'correct' ideological and cultural attitudes was propagated by the founder of the Aligarh movement, Sayyid Ahmad Khan (1817–1898), and the poets in his intellectual orbit. After the 1857 rebellion, and the coerced reordering of political power beneath the British Crown, this movement interpreted the decline of Mughal authority as evidence of the corruption and moral ill-health of their society, which was reflected in, amongst other things, its literary and cultural productions.[2] To address this situation, Aligarh intellectuals, who included the belletrists Altaf Husain Hali (1837–1914) and Muhammad Husain Azad (1830–1910), attempted to ascertain where the poetry of the past had gone wrong and to show how it might contribute to the building of a modern 'civilisation'. Because poetry already held a pre-eminent place in the cultural life of the former service gentry of the Mughal courts, and the emerging middle classes of northern India's growing *qasbah* towns (which included urbanised Muslims, Hindus and Jains), it became the target for an agenda of reforms suited to the inculcation of a modern, bourgeois sensibility and ethic. For the traditional Urdu *ghazal* (a poem on the subject of love, usually comprised of a few double-line verses), this involved nothing less than the reconceptualisation of its central tropes and syllogisms.

The Aligarh movement for literary reform was influenced by the Anglicist vision for colonial education which, from the 1830s onwards, privileged the English canon over Indian high literature (in Sanskrit and Persian), and emphasised the study of the natural sciences, mathematics and history as the pathway to a career in the administrative system.[3] Sayyid Ahmad, for instance, revealed a utilitarian perception of Indian educational policy when he stated before the Education Committee (in an echo of Macaulay's famous *Minute on Education*) that the function of the Mohammadan Anglo-Oriental College (established in 1875) would be: 'to form a class of persons Muhammadan in religion, Indian in blood and colour, but English in tastes, in opinions and in intellect'.[4] The Aligarh Muslim University (as it became known) sought to improve the status and position of Indian Muslims amongst British policymakers and contributed to the formation of a new Western-educated bureaucratic class. Its students were taught scientific and secular subjects with the intention of preparing them for the *kacahri* milieu (denoting the administrative courts and offices of the colonial government) and reflected the utilitarian notion that a people's education is central to the elevation of their moral status.

Whilst Sayyid Ahmad often spoke out on behalf of vernacular instruction and contributed substantially to the development of a clear Urdu prose style, he nonetheless came to doubt the short-term efficacy of Urdu as a language of scholarship, morality and higher education. In 1882, he stated before the Education Committee that Urdu was too given to exaggeration, hyperbole and rhetorical convention to be of any use for the teaching of such subjects as history, logic, philosophy, political economy and jurisprudence, which required a clear and unambiguous mode of communication. 'As long as our community does not, by means of English education, become familiar with the exactness of thought and unlearn the looseness of expression,' Sayyid Ahmad affirmed, 'our language cannot be the means of high moral and mental training.'[5] However, this did not signal his unwillingness to work for the refashioning of those poetic and literary genres which were the wellspring of the Urdu spoken culture. That English became the new language of power, superseding Persian as a modern bureaucratic and instructional medium, was to have significant consequences for the way indigenous cultural traditions and systems of knowledge were evaluated.[6]

To learn English, for Sayyid Ahmad, was to be trained in the style, substance and culture of modernity. As David Lelyveld points out in his study of the Aligarh College's first generation of students, English became the sole medium by which a modern social temperament was picked up and internalised:

> What was primarily being taught was English: not only its vocabulary and grammar, but genres and styles of exposition and expression as they had developed in the historical tradition of

English literature. English was no neutral tool; it was to be an intentional instrument of acculturation to Victorian values and ideas.[7]

Precisely because language was presumed to temper and in part condition the ideological and cultural disposition of its speakers, English was conceived as the most suitable medium for understanding such subjects as science, history and law. One should not simply learn to speak English but adapt to, and internalise, its aesthetic standards and norms.

Furthermore, as Gauri Viswanathan points out, colonial administrators in British India saw the teaching of Western literary and aesthetic principles as a means to consolidate the ideological and political hegemony of empire.[8] Thus, for Britain's Indian subjects, the Indo-Persian literary heritage, with its strong influence over high Urdu poetry and prose, was to be replaced by Western aesthetic principles and tastes.[9] That such policies were interpreted by some Indians as an attack on their culture is reflected in a couplet by the nineteenth-century north Indian Urdu poet-satirist and critic of the Aligarh school, Akbar Allahabadi (1846–1921):

> We of the East break our enemies' heads, whereas they of the West change their opponents' nature.[10]

But to comment only on the disciplining role of colonial knowledge is not to tell the whole story. Indigenous reformers of the nineteenth century did not simply acquiesce in the grafting of European ideas onto their own societies, but were deeply involved in their reconfiguration. If, as Ranajit Guha points out, British techniques of persuasion were implicated in discourses surrounding the education and 'improvement' of Indian subjects – as a form of 'dominance without hegemony'[11] – this was in part a reflection upon the insecurities and fears of a colonial authority whose rule over a bewilderingly diverse and recalcitrant population could not be assured by force alone.

The appropriation of European thought by indigenous actors, then, is not a story of passive acceptance, mimicry and reproduction.

In fact, the reformist attempt to renew indigenous cultural and religious elements in the face of colonial criticisms represented a concerted effort to reshape the colonial discourse to indigenous needs.[12] In the context of the Aligarh movement for the reform (*islah*) and criticism (*tanqid*) of Urdu literature, this was seen in the transformation of that poetry's dominant tropes, spurred on by a new conception of what poetry's role in society should be. If, in the past, poetry was a self-referential art largely preoccupied with the formal conventions of language, metre and matters of taste, now it was to serve an educative and moral function.

In their appraisal of Urdu poetry, Aligarh reformers often evoke the notion that there is a special relationship between the life of a community and the literature and language that it produces. This attitude, which is reminiscent of Coleridge's '*lingua communis*', follows the Indian tracing of Victorian ideas through Urdu commentaries and translations of English works of literary and social theory, and is common amongst modernised, indigenous elites by the late nineteenth century. Concerning the 'afflicted state' of Urdu literature, Muhammad Azad opines that 'a people's literature corresponds to that people's condition, and its thoughts correspond to the state of the country and the country's education.'[13] That a people's literature bears a close historical relation to their own progress and improvement is also assumed by Altaf Husein Hali, whose *Introduction to Poetry and Poetics* highlights the effects of bad poetry on a society's moral condition.[14] Language is not simply the by-product of a civilisation, but may actively mould and shape that civilisation for better or worse.

This ideal connection between a society and its literature was demonstrated in Sayyid Ahmad's quest for a new literary realism which rejected, in turn, the symbols and habits of the old political order. To bring Urdu to the same level as the best modern English, it had to be wrested from the influence of the Mughal aristocracy, whose over-reliance on ornate and exaggerated forms of expression (familiar to the Orientalist depiction of Mughal rulers as decadent and effete) was felt to nullify the social utility of its speech and poetry.[15] In their efforts to promote a new language, Aligarh reformers rejected Urdu's social significance to the old political order and connected it, instead, to the aspirations of the rising middle classes in the many *qasbah* towns then proliferating across northern India. Rather than go down with the regime to which it once belonged, Urdu needed to become a truly universal language. To communicate and carry, with clarity and benefit, the best of the modern age, it had to transcend the conditions of the culture which developed it and adopt that rational sensibility – derived from the empirical sciences – which Aligarh reformers ascribed to modern systems of authority.

An exponent of this new didactic literature, Nazeer Ahmed (1836–1912), pioneered the modern Urdu novel in the latter half of the nineteenth century. Ahmed, who claimed to have penned his novels initially for the purpose of teaching his children by the use of exemplary moral stories, struck a balance between the polite language of the courtly aristocracy and near-colloquial idioms of everyday speech. Unencumbered by the high-flown rhetoric and artifice which marked the traditional *dastan* (long story) genre of the royal courts, Ahmed's most popular stories exemplified the struggle of urban Muslim families to preserve notions of cultural esteem in a changing social environment.

In *Taubat al-Nasuh* (*The Repentance of Nasuh*, a story inspired by the hortatory themes of Daniel Defoe's *The Family Instructor*), we meet Nasuh, a well meaning patriarch determined to set his family on the path of moral reform after suffering a bout of cholera in which he awoke to the seriousness of God's impending judgment. Attending to the religious re-education of his wife and children, Nasuh succeeds with the exception of his eldest son, Kalim, who is enamoured of the frivolous and dissipative lifestyle of the old aristocracy. The subject of particular disdain for Nasuh (as for the author) is Kalim's collection of classical Persian poetry, which is gathered up and thrown on a bonfire. 'Poetry is not bad in itself,' Nasuh later tells his daughter, 'but nowadays people use it for immoral purposes, or for satire, which is another name for slander, or for fulsome flattery, which is falsehood, or for lampooning religious men and precepts, which is contrary to the laws of Islam.'[16] In this instance, Urdu poetry's many genres, conventions and symbols are reconstituted as a type of civil discourse whose relationship to notions of modern citizenship and a proto-national Indian Muslim identity is of the utmost importance.

Before I describe this process of reform in greater detail, it is necessary to set out a brief summary of what the erotic Urdu *ghazal* most commonly represented for those who had developed and safeguarded its traditional conventions. An overview of the symbolic content of the normative *ghazal* and its mystically inspired conception of the theme of love (*'ishq*) underscores the radical nature of the changes which late nineteenth-century social and literary reformers set out to achieve.

Love (*'Ishq*) in the Pre-modern Urdu Ghazal

To understand the theme of love (*'ishq*) in the traditional Urdu *ghazal* of the pre-modern Indo-Persianate tradition is to contemplate its intriguing doubleness and reluctance to be subjected to any one type of interpretation. Much like the Persian and Central Asian courtly poetic canons which formed a prototype for the early Urdu *ghazal*, this doubleness was expressed through poetic conventions which were at once sensual and otherworldly. For instance, the theme of love was often described according to a set of romantic and erotic conventions which simultaneously carried an ideal notion of divine union informed by the Islamic mystical tradition. This gave an ambiguity to the poem which opened it up to different possibilities of interpretation and meaning. Thus, the subject of love may have evoked a metaphoric relationship (connoting the worshipper's relation to God) whilst its descriptive power, semantic affects and forums of appreciation (as a ritualised form of courtly, aristocratic entertainment) lent its erotic content a secular/worldly appreciation and context.[17]

In thematic terms, *ghazal* poetry frequently explored the alienation and loss experienced by a crazed or tortured lover (*'ashiq*), directed towards the absent, ambivalent and sometimes intentionally cruel figure of a human or semi-divine beloved (*ma'ashuq*). Whilst the lover/protagonist was suggested to be a man or woman, through its physical description or inflections of gender (it most often assumed a grammatically male voice), the beloved's gender was ambiguous, giving it the potential to be one of many things: an intensely beloved person, a theme such as 'fate' or a representation of God (who is the ultimate beloved). Sometimes the beloved was likened to a human or stone 'idol' (*but/sanam*), which was the poet's true object of adoration. At others, the beloved was compared to a tyrant whose glance was an arrow which could mortally wound or kill the anxious lover. The theme of separation, between lover and beloved, was expressed through transgression, in which the poet or protagonist was likened to a madman, a scoundrel, a mystical seeker, an apostate from Islam, a person speaking from beyond the grave, or a lover whose ideal match is socially or culturally off-limits.

That the conventional figures of lover and beloved in the Urdu *ghazal* did not represent the literal characters of a factual love affair is suggested by the theoretical distinction — made as early as the seventeenth century — between the *mazmun* of a poem, which was its chosen theme or content, and the *ma'ni*, which was its real significance or deeper meaning.[18] Far from representing an outpouring of the poet's subjective experiences, this distinction (between content and meaning) allowed poets to nuance the theme of love, depending on the apparent, or implied, meaning of the poem. Moreover, the ambiguity which surrounded the figure of the beloved enabled *ghazal* poets to manipulate a liminal space between the profane love of the phenomenal world (*'ishq-i mijazi*), on one hand, and the transcendental love of the mystical or divine-real (*'ishq-i haqiqi*), on the other. The tension established between the earthly-erotic and ideal-divine dimensions of the beloved, who was gendered and eroticised at one moment and ambiguous and absent at the next, opened the poem to the possibility, and delight, of variant and overlapping readings.

A common setting for the 'lover'/protagonist's search for mystical or worldly union was the wine tavern (*mekhanah*), in which the cupbearer companion (*saqi*) solicits the protagonist to deeper and yet deeper stages of drunkenness.[19] Referring to this theme, the following verse by the celebrated north Indian poet, Mirza Asadullah Khan Ghalib (1779–1869) may be interpreted as a direct statement about literary theory and poetics:

Harchand ho mushahadah-i haq ki guftugu,
Banti nahin hai badah aur saghir kahe baghair.

However much one may converse on the seeing of God/the truth,
Nothing is made without talk of wine and wineglass.[20]

Here, Ghalib admits to the play on metaphorical, intertextual understandings which comprise the poetic discourse and make it efficacious for the expression of higher truths. The stock of conventional poetic images associated with wine and drunkenness ('talk of wine and wineglass') are used to denote profound themes, such as the experience of divine union (the 'seeing of God' referred to in the first line).

Besides that of mystical intoxication, Urdu poetry incorporated cultural tropes and legends, such as the Arabic love story of Laila and Majnun, the Muslim-turned-infidel's love of his idol (be it in human form or otherwise) and the Persian romance between Khusrao and Shirin. Included, as well, were a number of non-anthropological poetic tropes, such as the nightingale's love for the rose, the moth's (self-destructive) love of the candle flame and so forth within a pleasure garden (*bagh*), the setting of which became a useful metaphor for the self-contained world of poetic discourse.[21] And to join this panoply of literary conventions describing themes of love and union, motifs of male-to-male erotic love (of the king for his slave or of a Sufi master for a young male initiate) were not uncommon.

One such scenario, which was familiar to the poetry of the Indian subcontinent, depicted the love of the eleventh-century Afghan king, Mahmud of Ghazna, for his young Turkish admiral, Ayaz.[22] What was important about this story is not so much the homoerotic nature of their love as its traversing of rank, wherein the renowned warrior king of Afghanistan is smitten by a love that dictates his complete surrender to the young officer, so becoming the contented servant of his warrior slave. Stories such as this performed a radical inversion of the social order which satisfied the notion of a love which transgresses all rational, social and worldly constraints. For all its allure, worldly power cannot usurp the divine splendor and beauty of the loving soul.

That love in the Urdu *ghazal* was sometimes the cause of radical social inversions – suggesting the theory of a 'reversible world' – has been the source of some scholarly misinterpretation.[23] It is claimed, for instance, that because the *ghazal* was not uniformly mystical, its erotic conventions might portray a more accurate picture of the social and historical environment in which such poetry was written. Thus, the transgressive, mystically intoned theme of an impossible and ideal love is supposed to have camouflaged the poet's own sexual predilections, frustrations and predicaments. A leading Western scholar to make this interpretation, Ralph Russell, argues that because love had nothing to do with the system of arranged marriages in pre-modern Indian society, the poet's experience of love was always for a woman 'already betrothed or married to someone else'. This, according to Russell, explains why love in the mystical *ghazal* was couched in themes of social transgression.[24] Likewise it is suggested, elsewhere, that transgressive themes formed the vehicle for a subversive type of social and political criticism.[25] Such enquiries are not without interest and Urdu poetry did quite often assume a form of social commentary of which the couplet by Akbar Allahabadi, given above, is an example. However, any attempt to procure sociological or cultural data must account for the problematic and often complex relationship between a text and its context, between the circumstances of a poem's making and the life that it takes on as social text thereafter, between its content and the already established formal conventions that it extends. In short, the *ghazal* may not always have formed a type of social commentary and did not attempt to represent – insofar as it was invested with – a psychological or social reality.

Thus the pre-modern Urdu *ghazal* was less concerned with depicting (or critiquing) contemporaneous social realities than with the virtuosic manipulation of language itself. As Francis Pritchett points out, Urdu poetry constituted a 'game of words' in which the formal principles of grammar, discourse, poetics and metre formed the criteria upon which its excellence and worth was commonly judged.[26] Shamsur Rahman Faruqi, in an interesting study of the development of early Urdu poetry, also argues that from the time such poetry established itself as a literary language in northern India – a development built in no small measure upon the mentoring system between an *ustad* (master poet) and *shagird* (novice) – it came to be recognised by formal literary techniques and notions of 'correct' and 'incorrect' language. The abovementioned theoretical distinction between the theme (*mazmun*) and meaning (*ma'ni*) of a poem (which are derived, in Faruqi's opinion, from Sanskrit theories of literature) enabled poets to generate variant and subtle possibilities of interpretation. To this end, the formalisation of such techniques as 'meaning creation' (*ma'ni afrini*), which involved a play, or punning, on words (*iham*) to suggest variant interpretations, came about.[27]

But all of this was to change, in the latter part of the nineteenth century, when Aligarh reformers sought to evaluate the Urdu *ghazal* according to new standards and attitudes. How they went about this and the consequences of their efforts is the subject of what follows.

'Natural Poetry' and the Creation of a Literary Teleology

The modern historical evaluation of Urdu poetry begins with Muhammad Azad's *Water of Life* (*Ab-e Hayat*, 1880) and Altaf Husain Hali's *Introduction to Poetry and Poetics* (*Muqaddimah Shi'r aur Sha'iri*, 1893).[28] Both works are unique for their time in their attempt to historicise Urdu poetry and aesthetics, to get under the surface of such poetry, to reveal its social and cultural influences. In both works, a teleological historical framework is established by pointing, at the outset, to a golden age in which poetry was presumed to be socially beneficial before identifying, in its later development, a process of degeneration and decline. Both works convey the notion that the poetry of the past was once 'honest' and 'natural' before it descended into a realm of stale mannerism, hyperbole and convention. Both assert, moreover, that contemporary poets must return to this naturalistic spirit if they are to speak to, and so improve, their people's moral and political condition.

Such attitudes reflect the influence of the nineteenth-century distinction between art and science, which informed contemporary notions of what were to be considered 'artificial' or 'natural' types of artistic expression. According to English literary critics of the period, poetry is no longer conceived as that which merely delights and moves the reader, and which finds its antithesis in the imperfect and randomly unpredictable stuff of history. Rather, poetry should be judged according to its presumed relation to the truth of particular feelings and experiences, the spontaneity and 'sincerity' of which is compared, by J. S. Mill and others, to the bland stuff of 'science' and the 'matter of fact'.[29] For the English utilitarian philosopher and colonial administrator, Jeremy Bentham, on the other hand, this distinction means that science, as the final arbiter of truth, will make poetry redundant.[30] Yet, on most counts, the distinction between poetry and science gives rise to the notion that the scientist passively receives and codifies data from the objective world whilst the poet interprets such information with the aid of feeling, intuition and emotion. If the poet's modification of such information is made in sincerity, the act of interpretation is no less 'truthful' than that of the natural scientist and may even be of a higher order.

It is to this notion of truth that Hali appeals in his *Introduction*. Poetry is true, posits Hali, insofar as it responds to concrete experience and emerges from the real excitement or passion (*josh*) which such experience elicits in the mind. In the middle section of his work, Hali states that poetry should essentially follow three principles, which he derives from Milton's theories of aesthetics. Namely, it should be simple (*sadagi*), it should spring from emotion (*josh se barha hua*) and be based on truth (*asliyyat*).[31] Central to these stipulations is the theme that poets should no longer seek to contrive artificial webs of hyperbolic language mired in stock metaphorical images and conceits. They should instead attempt to capture the truth of a subject embodied in genuine emotions, ordinary experience and the correct observation of nature. Hali reinforces the value of such 'truth' by his use of the term 'natural poetry' (for which he directly transposes the English word 'natural' into Urdu: *naicharal sha'iri*), the object of which is to address the themes, ideals and experiences of life as it is really lived. Thus, poetry is true or 'sincere' to the extent that it corresponds to the poet's individual or national (*qaumi*) state of mind.

In Hali's estimation, the lyrical *ghazal*'s sincerity is evident in its earliest (Arab, Persian and local) origins whilst the abuse of its conventional themes came about, in no small part, under the influence of the medieval Persian poetic and mystical traditions. The poetry of the ancient Arabs (whose formal poetic genres were carried over into Persian and Urdu) is upheld for its 'true emotion and exultation' before it degenerated into stale forms of flattery towards rulers and patrons (in the *qasidah* genre) or into conventional expressions of sexual eroticism and moral delinquency (in the *ghazal* and *masnavi* genres). The earliest Urdu poets once employed metaphors of wine, intoxication and the beloved to describe their philosophical insights and mystical states in an honest and morally sincere way. The same, however, cannot be said of contemporary poets who employ such themes to indulge their literal taste for alcohol and courtesans. That a once efficacious stock of symbols and metaphors were eventually transformed into a catalogue of real deeds and vices speaks to the historical and political degeneration of the Muslim community.[32]

The construction of a teleological scheme is also present in Muhammad Azad's *Water of Life*, which separates the 150-year history of Urdu poetry in northern India into five chronologically organised periods (sing. *daur*/pl. *adwar*).[33] Azad does not provide a theoretical justification for this periodisation, nor one for why the work and influence of particular poets lumped into different periods often overlap. Nonetheless, he uses the technique of periodisation to project the overarching theme of poetry's gradual artificialisation, corruption and decline. According to Azad, the poets of the first two periods expressed whatever entered their hearts in a simple and unaffected manner whilst later generations exhausted poetry's themes of relevance and meaning.[34] Commenting on the absence of new subjects in the poetry of the late nineteenth century, Azad compares the conventional themes and imagery of the Urdu *ghazal* (such as the beloved, garden, beauty and so forth) to 'morsels' of food which 'have already been eaten – or at least chewed – by other people'. His message to contemporary poets is clear: 'We chew on them and we're happy. Think about it – what relish do they still have left?'[35]

For Hali and Azad, the erotic *ghazal* could no longer fulfil its traditional role as an instrument of literary aesthetic pleasure but acted as an instructive marker for processes of social corruption. Both sought to historicise Urdu poetry within a teleological framework determining its downward movement from an idealised, uncorrupted period of purity to its present state of moral decay. As it stood, poetry's example would serve as a warning that no society can revert to a world of pure discourse, or retreat into the realms of fantasy, without losing its bearings. This assertion also spoke to poetry's (and the literary arts') transition from an abstract formal medium whose discursive properties were intertextual and preoccupied with matters of taste, culture and expertise, to its status as an expression of the inherent spirit of a nation (*qaum*) or civilisation. What Hali and Azad decried in the *ghazal* was its retreat into a realm of complete subjectivity in which the poet's rhetorical solipsism and exaggeration of emotion would defer the natural world for that of language games and artifice. What these intellectuals absorbed of Victorian literary ideals (albeit at second or third hand and through inaccurate translations) was not simply a vocation to express themselves sincerely, or to be true to nature, but to resist what amounted to a home-grown theory of 'literary decadence'.[36]

A Gendered Language: Verbal Effeminacy and the Heteronormative Ideal

Mrinalina Sinha argues for the need to historicise the ways imperial and indigenous discourses mobilised categories of gender in order to reinforce the hierarchical relations of power within colonial societies. As a general point, Sinha observes that an association of cultural decline with the self-perception of effeminacy was a common theme amongst the educated middle classes of Bengal, who compared their own supposed unmanliness to the sturdy masculine modernity embodied in their British rulers. Whilst one could easily point to this as the impact of 'Western' notions of masculinity upon traditional, indigenous conceptions of the same, Sinha usefully complicates an approach to both as discrete or mutually exclusive categories, thus showing their mutual implication in imperial politics.[37] This approach, I argue, is also useful for thinking about the self-image of Muslims in northern India, who were not as routinely effeminised by colonial administrators and indigenous elites as their Hindu counterparts in Bengal and other areas, but whose political decline was nonetheless attributed to the taint of wasteful unmanliness seen in the profligacy and decadence of their imperial courts.[38] This self-perception of effeminacy, which was associated with the aristocratic appreciation of erotic Urdu poetry, became a source of vexation for Aligarh reformers.

One area of concern was the genre of *ghazal* poetry referred to as *rekhti*, which originated during the late eighteenth century and had flourished in the imperial city of Lucknow from the 1830s to the 1850s. In *rekhti* poetry (the feminine noun of *rekhta*, a term denoting the 'mixed' Persian-Indic content of Urdu verse), the protagonist/poet adopted a feminine voice whose erotic and romantic fixation was concentrated upon the figure of a female beloved. This genre of poetry became famous in Lucknow's aristocratic courts, where one of its leading exponents, Yar Khan 'Rangin' ('colourful', 1756–1834), is remembered for having recited bawdy erotic verses in a high falsetto voice, dressed in female attire. Because such poetry was distinguished by the adoption of a female voice and all-female romantic themes, its male composers made a point of employing linguistic idioms and conventions commonly associated with women's domestic lives (*begumati zuban*), the courtesan's milieu and various regional dialects.[39]

Today, there is some scholarly discussion surrounding the truthfulness of *rekhti*'s depiction of lesbian romantic love, and female homoeroticism, in the context of north Indian culture. It has been argued, for instance, that *rekhti* poets were simply engaged in the popularisation of male fantasies about lesbian erotic desire, disclosing the structural patriarchy which was typical of Lucknow society in the early nineteenth century.[40] *Rekhti*'s most renowned poets, according to C. M. Naim, portrayed an early nineteenth-century man's-eye view of the women's *zenanah*, which at once belittled, eroticised and fantasised that domain for the mirth and titillation of a largely male audience.[41] Countering this interpretation, Ruth Vanita argues that *rekhti*'s play on 'low' forms of speech (which were then associated with the environments of the urban household, bazaar and courtesan's milieu) provided a space in which poets were able to 'depict, debate and playfully celebrate female lives and loves'.[42] Here, the partly sociological question as to why this genre simulated (or parodied) the conventions of women's speech and female homoeroticism does not concern me as much as the significance attached to it by Muslim reformers of the late nineteenth century. For it was only in this period that *rekhti* and other erotic poetic conventions were viewed with an eye to their possible sociological and historical significance, rather than according to internal formal or cultural criteria.

In his *Water of Life*, Azad lambasts *rekhti* for its superficial preoccupation with feminine and lesbian-erotic themes, which he describes as 'one cause of the effeminacy, lack of ambition and cowardice that has grown up among the common people'.[43] Here, the evocation of 'effeminacy' and 'cowardice' chimes with the colonial view that north Indian Muslims had cultivated a voluptuous, dissolute and dysfunctional courtly culture that had lost any claim to political legitimacy. This is especially significant for the city of Lucknow, whose time under the reign of Wajid Ali Shah (1847–1856) was associated in colonial discourses with immense profligacy and waste. Evoking this perception, Azad speculated that the 'volumes of Rangin and Insha' (two of Lucknow's most renowned *rekhti* poets) had 'sown the seeds of Lucknow's Qaiser Bagh and its affairs', so connecting *rekhti* to the catastrophic events of the 1857 'mutiny' and its aftermath.[44] The ease with which this discourse about literary decline was tied to a self-perception of cultural deterioration is also reflected in Abdul Halim Sharar's assertion, in the early twentieth century, that *rekhti* had done nothing to enhance notions of virtue and chastity in Lucknow, and must be placed outside the path of 'culture and moderation'.[45] Noting Rangin's admission to having learnt women's idioms in the city's brothels, Sharar accused the poet of composing his works with a view to excite and corrupt the female members of decent families.

Thus did the reformist critique of *ghazal* poetry seek to bolster the 'normal' (heteronormative) ideals of gender deemed appropriate for a modern Muslim society. Unsurprisingly, this discourse cast aspersions upon the presence of male-to-male homoerotic themes, and ventured against the homosexuality implicit in the beloved's taking on a male grammatical form (*ghazal-i muzakkar*) in the normative Urdu *ghazal*. In the conclusion to his biography of the Persian poet, Sa'adi, Hali blames the Persian tradition of poetry for introducing the theme of sexual pederasty into Urdu by laying the *ghazal*'s foundations 'in the love of youths and beardless boys'.[46] This was encouraged by the grammatical male gendering of the beloved, which, according to Hali, represents a 'vile and worthless custom which has scarred national morality'.[47] 'For a man to fall madly in love with a man and seek union and enjoyment with him,' he claims, 'is something that human nature entirely rejects.'[48]

Such sentiments echo that of the newly imposed colonial criminal code (1860), whose framing of homosexual sex as an 'unnatural' act and criminal offence reflected the modern state's desire to manage and police sexuality. In the context of modern Europe, as Michel Foucault points out in the first volume of his *History of Sexuality*, such laws contributed to an emerging bourgeois identity which was modelled upon heteronormative standards and ideas.[49] That such standards, imprinted in colonial legislation, also influenced indigenous constructions of bourgeois citizenship can be seen in Hali's reminder that the homoerotic themes encountered in the ancient poetry of Iran and India would be 'adjudged guilty according to the [British anti-obscenity] law'.[50] Commenting on the perceived influence of homoerotic roles, Hali and Azad sought to articulate a new type of masculinity, austerely heterosexual and rigidly aloof from feminine sentiment, to be the moral backbone for a reformed Muslim society.

De-sexing the Beloved, Redefining Love

Hali's reformist attitude towards the figure of the beloved no doubt held radical implications for its semiotic presence on the whole. Having collapsed sign and signifier into one another, Hali deemed conventional descriptions of a female beloved's beauty, etiquette, coquetry and so forth to be 'completely unacceptable' for a people who respect the position of women bound to the customs of segregation (*purdah*).[51] Moreover, the convention of referring to the beloved in masculine grammatical forms (*ghazal-i muzakkar*) only adds to the addressee's confusion over how the beloved's gender is to be understood. Thus, for Hali, a beloved so vaguely defined (as perhaps grammatically male or, unless specified, as female) may easily succumb to the attribution of both genders, whereby the beloved appears as: 'neither a man nor a woman, but a eunuch (*zenanah*) or transsexual (*hijra*)'.[52] If the symbol of the beloved is to serve its true function of advancing morally uplifting themes, and if it is not to fall into the hands of poets given to the literal description of their sexual predilections, its attribution of gender must be neutralised entirely.

On this matter, as Francis Pritchett observes, Hali's insistence on the genderlessness of the figure of the beloved marked a radical departure from conventional poetic practice by proceeding from the assumption that the gender of the beloved had *always* been established (overtly or covertly/grammatically) when in point of fact, the primary role of the beloved was to be sexually ambiguous, fantastical and generally absent from the poem.[53] Hali's assertions surrounding the theme of wine and the gendered nature of the beloved, for instance, abolished the conventional two-way interpretive dialogue and tension between the subject of an almost tangible worldly love (*'ishq-i mijazi*) and the mystical love of the divine real (*'ishq-i haqiqi*) that so characterised the traditional Urdu *ghazal*. Instead of the conventional, mystically inspired notion of an ambiguous (transcendental and/or worldly) love, which conflates the ideal and the erotic, Hali advocated a conception of love at the service of more realistic and morally uplifting themes. The eroticised beloved, and the half-crazed lover who transgresses all social boundaries in the vain hope of achieving union with him/her, were thus censored by a moral discourse containing provision only for the expression of a didactic and ideally 'natural' type of love.

Hali's support for a new type of 'natural poetry' (*naicharal sha'iri*), which posited a fundamental re-evaluation of the *ghazal*'s conventional themes, is argued thus:

> Love does not depend upon passion and lust and the worship of the beloved. Rather, the worshiper's love of God, the child's for its mother and father, brother's and sister's love for each other, a husband's love for his wife and a wife's for her husband, the servant's of his master, the subject's of the king, friend's for friends, man's love of the animal... and the peoples' love for their home, their country, their kingdom and their nation. In short, everything for which love arises or is able to cause affection. Within the *ghazal*, the themes of love may be established in such a way as to elucidate every type of spiritual and physical relationship and, as much as possible, no word should be included in which the object of love is male or female.[54]

Notably, this passage dismisses the traditional Sufi notion of love (*'ishq*) as Urdu poets had normally understood it. Love should now honour, as it supposedly did not in the past, such things as the emotional bond recommended to husbands and wives, social fraternity and the sentiments of national citizenship. To this end, the beloved's asexuality fulfils a didactic purpose for Indian Muslim society.

Yet in his attempt to establish a new conception of love, one which is true to the emotions and feelings elicited by the modern world, Hali achieves something else entirely. By desexualising the figure of the beloved, which is broadened to encompass new subjects and experiences, Hali invests the quotidian realm of the family, society and nation-state with a sacral, extramundane importance. For to maintain love as an ideal, albeit one derived from the real world, is to point to something beyond that world which exists still in the realm of the imagination. And regarding the tropes and similitudes which remained of the classical poetic tradition, Hali was able to derive a new social content from within them. They are transformed in their meaning and invested with a new, Romantic sensibility, to ferment the hopes and trepidations of India's Muslim community.

The 'Garden of Islam' and the Beginnings of Literary Romanticism

An early and fitting example of Hali's 'natural poetry' is his *nazm* (a thematic poem) on the subject of patriotism (*Hubb-i Watan*) delivered in 1874, at a series of assemblies hosted to encourage poetry after natural themes. In this work, Hali invokes the theme of separation which, rather than dwell upon the lover's ardent desire for an absent beloved, now denotes the stirred up emotions of a patriot towards the land of his birth:

Oh my country, my own heaven,
Where now are your earth and sky?

Distant from you, I'm an object of pain,
And released as well is my comfort and ease.

In your absence, the garden is ruined,
The sight of its flowers: an ugly scar.

Erased is the imprint of our life's work,
From you, comes the joy of living.[55]

Here, grief and the theme of separation are wholly transfigured from the psychological yearning of an unrequited metaphysical and/or worldly love to the homesickness of a patriot flung far from his land. This loss, which Hali likens to the separation of body and soul, confirms the ideological and emotional bond which modern citizens should feel for their country and not just the old ties of city, caste, or sect to which they once belonged. The poet's newfound feeling of repulsion about the garden, and the grossly scarred flowers within it, is especially important for referring us to the tradition Hali has left behind. In the garden of old, which stands for the political order of the Mughal courts and which was a central discursive and literary trope of the Persian and Urdu *ghazal*, the caged nightingale (*bulbul*) sang of its separation from the rose, whose scars were compared to marks on the beloved's lustrous face, or the craters of the moon. However, the garden (*bagh*) for Hali – as it appears in his most famous poem, *The Flow and Ebb of Islam* – is symbolic only of the desolation and ruin which has overtaken the Indian Muslim community. In a section of this poem, headed 'Simile of the community of Islam', Hali likens the civilisation of Islam to a garden which has been 'utterly devastated' (*ujra sarasar*):

Where rain acts as a poison, where the cloud of spring comes and weeps,

Which by anxious cultivation becomes still more desolate, which is suited neither by autumn nor spring.

There this cry is continuously raised: 'This is the ruined garden of Islam!'[56]

Whilst Hali conjoins the fantastical imagery of the garden often found in the poetry of Ghalib and Mir to the aesthetic referents of a modern style whose language should lean towards a greater naturalism of feeling and experience, *The Flow and Ebb of Islam* also announces the beginnings of a distinctly Romantic literary sensibility. The verse's simulated cry ('This is the ruined garden of Islam') evokes the impassioned though formalised expressions of mourning familiar to the elegiac genre (*marsiyyah*) of Shi'a ritual, whilst auguring a turn to the mythopoetic, counterfactual and sublime.[57]

Lamenting the degradation into which Muslims have fallen, Hali recounts the stunning moral, political and intellectual achievements of the earliest Islamic civilisation. Drawing an obvious comparison between the Muslim world's decline and that of the pre-Islamic *jahiliyyah* (period of ignorance), he lauds the Prophet as an exemplary moral reformer who taught his followers the 'value and worth of time' through the desire to work hard and perform good deeds.[58] Whilst the influence of Victorian social values on Hali's modernism is on display here, his admonitions were no doubt intended to prick the conscience of contemporary Muslim society and highlight the sorts of values (honesty, diligence, hard work and so forth) to which it must aspire. Thus, the teleological historical sensibility of Hali's poem, which emphasises the Muslim world's contemporary decline, points back to an ideal, universal Islamic civilisation that transcends the realm of historical time.

Here, the dialectical relationship between an abject present and better future – which is based, in turn, on the premise of returning to the spirit of an ideal past – brings Hali's counterfactual and imaginary Romantic vision to the fore. It emerges in the juxtaposition of ages and times, in which a causal theory of historical decline is tied to a promise of salvation and renewal.[59] This vision certainly bears the influence of a reified Muslim identity (as mentioned in the previous chapter), in which the golden age of Islam, coterminous with the life of the Prophet and his immediate companions, is established as an exemplary paradigm for a modern religious life.

Furthermore, Hali transfers a notion of the sublime from its former place in traditional religious theology and mysticism to the factual and everyday content of the modern world. Thus for the numerous Muslim (and non-Muslim) communities across northern India who embraced Hali's poem, its teleological vision of a process of historical degeneration auguring a renewal of faith catalysed a distinctly modern understanding of religion's place in society.[60] Here, the emotional sentiment of a unitary community of faith (which was always, in actuality, a historical fiction imposed over a diverse array of linguistic communities and castes) laid the ground for a shared conception of Islam, most notably in its cultural and social dimensions.

National Honour and the 'Loss' of a Literary Culture

In drawing this chapter to a close, I would like to say something about the consequence and current perception of this movement for literary reform. Since the second half of the nineteenth century, supporters of Sayyid Ahmad's reformist project have presented him as the saviour of India's Muslim community, whose dignity he restored after the trauma and degradation which accompanied British reprisals in the wake of the 1857 uprising. This no doubt began with Hali, who in 1910 published the first proper biography of his mentor, and extends down to the present day.[61] Nevertheless, there is also a view that along with the improvements Sayyid Ahmad and his circle brought to the status of Indian Muslims, there was an irretrievable cultural loss.

According to Shamsur Rahman Faruqi (b.1935), Sayyid Ahmad's social reforms salvaged the esteem of India's Urdu-speaking communities at the expense of their literary culture. Precisely because Sayyid Ahmad insisted on maintaining the honour of the Indian Muslim nobility and landed gentry, the community of Urdu-speaking Muslims trusted his social reforms and not his new theology:

> Never mind the blasphemous views that Syed Ahmad Khan was alleged to profess, or did profess. That was between him and his God. What was here and now was a new hope for regaining some of the moral ground lost since 1857.

Faruqi continues:

> This seems to me to be the reason why a community even more broad-based than that of the Indian Muslims, I mean the literate and literary community of Urdu speakers throughout the subcontinent, let Syed Ahmad Khan demolish the old-established

notions about the nature of their literature. Furthermore, they accepted without demur Syed Ahmad Khan's agenda to refashion Urdu literature after the English model. If our old literature was effete and decadent and if it would help us regain our self-respect were we to reject that decadent literature and embrace a new regime, so be it.[62]

For Faruqi, a respectable, bourgeois modernity came at the price of one of the world's richest literary poetic traditions. Unnecessarily, in Faruqi's estimation, Sayyid Ahmad and the literary reformers in his company cast this culture in a derisory light, thus handing it an 'inferiority complex' which the literary community 'cheerfully accepted' on the premise that it bestowed 'the gift of self-respect, and a sense of purpose and self-worth'.[63]

The impact of Sayyid Ahmad's movement for literary reform or why, for literary critics such as Faruqi, it had such a harmful effect on the poetic tradition does not merely stem from the idea of 'sincerity' and its condemnation of poetic artifice. Rather, the damage is done by the way this notion of truth, or fidelity to experience, overrode the cultural criteria and practices of connoisseurship which once guided the *ghazal* tradition. Specifically, it is the theoretical distinction between the subject of a poem and the vast array of meanings and associations which the poet wrought from that subject which established the pleasure effect, or surprise, of so much pre-modern *ghazal* poetry. On a conceptual level what was lost was not the notion of love per se, but a liminal ambiguity or tension (between the phenomenal and mystical worlds), relating to the figure of an absent beloved. In its place, Hali sought to create a new beloved, whose ideal qualities were to be safeguarded precisely for being denuded of any erotic or gendered associations. As a consequence (and I am here extrapolating from Faruqi's thought), older sensibilities towards sexuality, which alluded to the complex role of gender and language in north Indian society, were supplanted by the 'modern' (heteronormative) attitudes recommended by British ideology.

But however much Urdu poetry's normative conventions were downgraded, the power of its tropes could not be erased. For instance, the romantic sensibility which Hali initiated was to be echoed by arguably the most renowned Urdu poet of the twentieth century, Muhammad Iqbal (1877–1938). In particular the trope of the ruined garden, as developed in Hali's *The Flow and Ebb of Islam*, recurred in Iqbal's *Complaint* (*Shikwah*), in which the poet laments the historical misfortune of India's Muslim community and promises hope for its renewal:

> The time of the rose has gone, the instrument (*saz*) of the garden is broken.
> Those who adorned the garden with melodies have flown away from the branches.
> But one nightingale is still absorbed in song.
> With a storm of melodies still contained in its breast...
>
> May hearts be rent by this lone nightingale's song.
> May hearts be roused by this caravan-bell.
> I mean, may hearts come alive with this new pact of faith.
> May hearts drink again from this ancient wine.
> If the pitcher is Persian so what? The wine that I drink is *hijazi*.
> If the song is Indian so what? The tune that I sing is *hijazi*.[64]

The nightingale of Iqbal's poem sings on behalf of the poet, whose new vision of social and philosophical reform would transmute the abandoned garden of Islam, so heralding 'a new pact of faith'. In this sense, Iqbal puts a new twist on the wine metaphor, by supplanting the poet's state of worldly/mystical intoxication with the essential spirit of Islam.[65] 'What does it matter if I adopt Persian idioms in an Indian language?' the poet asks his audience. 'What really matters is that my message is true to the spirit of Islam as it first arose in the *hijaz* region of Arabia.' Whilst I will detail the romantic nature of Iqbal's reforms in the fourth chapter of this book, the trope of the ruined garden in Urdu poetry augurs a new aestheticisation of the modern political and social realms.

The birth of literary Romanticism in Urdu poetry therefore represented an unanticipated, though not unwelcome, consequence of the hortatory naturalism recommended for Urdu literature by Aligarh reformers. Hali's revisions on the theme of love, for instance, did not conform to the ideological agenda of colonial Anglicists and Aligarh reformers, which was to wean Indian Muslims away from the traditional folk tales, erotic verses, and romantic literature of the past and guide them towards a more 'natural' and morally upright understanding of the world around them. Instead the 'decadent' literature of the aristocratic and Mughal courts gave way to a new kind of romance, in which the community of believers (*ummah*) or nation-state (*watan*) came to stand in for the once absent, mystical/erotic beloved. By attempting to supplant the traditional aesthetic of intoxicated beauty and mystical union with a didactic form of 'natural poetry', Hali created a vision of historical decline promising hopes for spiritual and moral redemption.

CHAPTER 3

EDUCATION AND THE STATUS OF WOMEN

Introduction

During the nineteenth century, issues of women's reform were closely bound up with emerging notions of civil society, national belonging, and various claims to religious and cultural authenticity. This was as true for European populations as it was for the indigenous elites under colonial rule, who felt a strong concern to educate women as to their proper (private and semi-public) roles within the newly emergent institutions of the colonial state. Modern schools, the postal system and expansion of print capitalism (through the widespread dissemination of vernacular books, pamphlets and journals) led to an increase in literacy and letter writing, which held implications for the symbolic status and roles of women. Whilst early Muslim societies were no doubt characterised by the gendering of various public-versus-private spaces, the late nineteenth century is unique for witnessing the symbolic identification of women with the family home, as well as the formation of nascent national and religious identities. In this chapter, I will examine the issue of women's education amongst indigenous reformers in the colonial societies of Egypt and northern India.

At the outset, it is important to register the significant social and economic changes which informed the construction of the modern

Muslim wife, mother and homemaker during the nineteenth century. Colonial Egypt, beginning with Muhammad 'Ali's ambitious project for economic industrialisation in the 1830s, is commonly seen as the starting point for discussions about women and modernisation in the Middle East (although the main patterns of social and economic change which occurred there would be reproduced, at varying speeds, in other colonised territories). Although there was a limited increase in women's participation in educational institutions during the late nineteenth century, structural changes which accompanied the rise of the modern state had negative consequences for the majority of lower-class and peasant women.[1] Egypt's incorporation into the colonial economy as an exporter of raw cotton (amongst other materials), the emergence of private property within its state institutions, and the onset of global capitalism reduced its market for textile production and other industries involving women.[2] Thus, the majority of peasant and lower middle-class women experienced little, if any, access to the language, culture and apparatus of government.

Regarding the symbolic status of Muslim women in the modern Middle East, attitudes amongst indigenous reformers were influenced by the negotiation of their political and economic domination by colonial Western powers.[3] In particular, as Leila Ahmed points out, practices of women's segregation and veiling acquired a new symbolic importance amongst Muslims, which was partly precipitated by the colonial regime's critique of the 'backward' nature of Islamic culture. Concluding that the unequal treatment of women in Islam was one of the reasons that Muslims had fallen behind European standards of progress, administrators such as Lord Cromer (1841–1917) adopted a feminist line to bolster the argument that Egyptians ought to be 'persuaded or forced into imbibing the true spirit of Western civilisation'.[4] Moreover, Orientalist discourses amongst colonial administrators, scholars, policy makers and European travellers frequently depicted Muslim women as the hapless victims of ingrained customs whose denigrated status was indicative of Islam as a whole.[5] To support his argument that the practice of women's segregation had contributed to the stagnation of Muslim societies, Cromer cited a prominent British Orientalist of the time, Stanley Lane-Pool (1854–1931), who asserted that 'the degradation of women in the

East is a canker that begins its destructive work in childhood, and has eaten the whole system of Islam'.[6]

Yet unlike their colonial counterparts, indigenous reformers did not hold religion accountable for all of society's ills. They instead argued that Islam in its truest form nurtured a vision of respect and equality for women that even Europe would struggle to emulate. This is encapsulated in an article in Egypt's *al-Manar* journal by the leading Egyptian modernist of the time, Muhammad 'Abduh (1849–1905). According to 'Abduh, Islam shows that men and women are equal before God both spiritually and with regard to the quality of their works. Therefore 'the claim of Europeans to have been the first to honour woman and grant her equality', 'Abduh proclaimed, 'is false'. Although 'Abduh conceded that the status of women in Muslim societies lagged behind that of contemporary Europe, he and his reformist contemporaries blamed this on a lack of women's education, and the continuation of outdated social regulations (such as slavery, polygamy, the employment of wet nurses and so forth). 'Muslims have been at fault in the education and training of women, and acquainting them with their rights,' asserted 'Abduh, 'and we acknowledge that we have failed to follow the guidance of our religion, so that we have become an argument against it.'[7] In their responses to Western criticisms, and as they formulated new solutions to redeem the position of women in their societies, indigenous male reformers nonetheless accepted the premise (implicit in colonial critiques of their culture) that women were the signifiers of a society's strength and weakness, its progress and decline.

A reformist poem, titled 'Homage to Silence' (*Chupp ki Dad*, 1905), by the north Indian poet Altaf Husain Hali (1837–1914), confirms this perception of women in tones of sympathy and endearment verging on the clichéd:

> You are the picture of piety,
> The councillor of chastity,
> Of religion the guarantee.
> Protection of the faith,
> Comes from you...

There lived virtuous men,
Who knew not when their virtue was lost,
Oh virtuous ones of the world!
Whatever virtue now costs,
It comes from you.[8]

In what follows, I will argue that calls for women's education and the re-evaluation of their place in society furnished a discourse which was at once emancipatory in tone but also ambivalent about the potential consequences of such reforms. This ambivalence was not a symptom of the failure to educate women, but was indicative of the idealised role into which modern conceptions of 'progress' and 'improvement' now placed them.

My analyses of texts will focus primarily on the work of two indigenous reformers: the Egyptian lawyer and social critic, Qasim Amin (1863–1908), and the reformist *'alim* in northern India, Ashraf 'Ali Thanawi (1863–1943). These reformers were of the same generation, but lived in different parts of the Muslim world and were brought up in starkly different educational settings. The son of a Turkish Ottoman lieutenant-general, Qasim Amin received a secular education in Alexandria and Cairo, before entering the Khedival school of law, from which he graduated in 1881. Thereafter, he went to further his studies in Paris, where he collaborated on the reformist journal, *al-'Uwrah al-Wuthqa*, which was produced by the leading modernists Jamal al-Din al-Afghani and Muhammad 'Abduh. Whilst in Paris, he became convinced of the need to reform Arab women's living conditions, which he compared unfavourably to that of women in Europe. After returning to Egypt in 1885, Amin engaged himself in the movement for modern educational and social reforms for women, and wrote two important books on the subject. Ashraf 'Ali Thanawi was born in the same year as Qasim Amin (1863) in the city of Thana Bhawan, in north-eastern India. In the early years of his life, he received a traditional religious education at the Dar al-'Ulum *madrasah* in Deoband, from where he graduated in 1884. Thanawi then settled in the nearby city of Cawnpore, where, for the next fourteen years, he taught the *Dars-i Nizami* syllabus of traditional religious scholarship, and acquired some of the prestige and authority that surrounded spiritual figures of the *silsilah* tradition of the Chisti-Sabiri school of Indian Sufism.[9] Mixing traditional and reformist attitudes in his writings, Thanawi spoke up on the need for a modern home-based educational curriculum for women, and advocated on behalf of changes to unfair divorce laws in the Indian Hanafi interpretation of Islamic law.

Despite their differences in culture and education, I have selected Qasim Amin and Ashraf 'Ali Thanawi because they each advocated for women's education whilst differing on how best to enact an agenda of social reform. In their respective works, for instance, the issue of women's reform is crucial to a vision of social resurgence and selectively invokes categories of national citizenship, Islamic identity and the homogeneity of an emerging middle class. Yet what is interesting in both cases is the peculiar ambiguity which marks their reformist projects. In my analysis of this, I will focus, first, upon Amin's appropriation of the Western, bourgeois notion of conjugal romantic love, which underpinned his vision of marriage and was spurred by sentiments of national citizenship. Then I will look at how Thanawi advocated on behalf of women's education to support the spiritual reform of Indian Muslim women.

Qasim Amin and Conjugal Love

From the first half of the nineteenth century, local elites in the Middle East sought to devise a programme for social and political reform grounded in a teleological vision of national 'progress'. A significant voice in this movement, the Egyptian lawyer and magistrate Qasim Amin wrote two books towards the end of the nineteenth century which have generated heated discussion and controversy until the present day. Amin argued in his first book, *The Liberation of Women* (*Tahrir al-Mara'ah*, published in 1899) and then again in *The New Woman* (*al-Mara'ah al-Jadidah*, published in 1900) that Egyptian society will not gain the strength to throw off its colonial subservience and achieve true social prosperity until its women have been properly educated and their social bonds loosened. Women must be tutored in the subjects that will enable them to carry out their tasks as wives, mothers and homemakers in a modern, urban environment. Only then will they be able to fulfil their role as national citizens and contribute to the building of a strong and rational society.

At the outset, it must be pointed out that Amin's reformism draws more on arguments for Egypt's social and economic expediency than on the priority of religious reform for its own sake. Whilst he argues that medieval Muslim jurists and rulers had distorted religious tradition by denying women their true rights under Islam, religious principles are not his main focus of concern.[10] He instead argues that Western-style educational and social reforms are in themselves morally evident and self-justificatory. The impetus to human development and progress is, according to Amin, a 'strange power that compels a human being to every scientific or literary idea once it crystallizes in the mind, and once it is accompanied by the belief that it will benefit the process of future generations'.[11] To this end, Amin embraces a vision of society, and model of national citizenship, which is grounded in the political and social sciences of the day.

In his agenda for reform, Amin emphasises the need for women's education in literacy, mathematics and a general understanding of science, history and political affairs. Primarily, this will benefit Egyptian mothers by enabling them to raise healthy, well-educated children. Because good mothering is essential to the formation of rational adult men and women, and thus to the stability of the family unit, Amin advocates that women be trained in the correct techniques of housekeeping, hygiene, family economics, motherhood and childrearing. If the mother is the locus of the family, and the family is the locus of the modern state, then the competence of the nation's mothers will no doubt determine the intellectual abilities of the nation as a whole.

This conception of *tarbiyyah* (upbringing/education), which explicitly links the issue of women's education to the idea of national progress, was a common feature of nationalist metropolitan and anti-colonial discourses during the latter part of the nineteenth century.[12] For instance, Anne McClintock identifies a parallel discourse amongst the bourgeois classes in British cities towards the 'domestic degeneracy' of the indigent poor and lower classes.[13] In a metropolitan centre such as London, as in the colonies, concerns about the negligent habits of lower-class mothers sustained the construction of a national identity whereby progress in the areas of scientific childrearing, hygiene, rational science and political organisation was paramount to a sense of the nation's ascendancy. Such attitudes deferred to generally accepted pseudo-Darwinian theories about national 'survival' and were particularly useful, for anti-colonial nationalists, to articulate a vision of future independence in which the best parts of indigenous cultures are somehow preserved through modernisation.

In *The Liberation of Women*, Amin decries the inability of educated middle-class Egyptian men to relate meaningfully to their often illiterate and uncouth spouses. Underscoring the sociological origins of this, he replays the desire of the urbanised middle classes to distinguish themselves from the 'ignorant' customs and habits of the rural peasantry.[14] The abilities of rural women, whose simple, rustic and repetitive chores nonetheless kept them on a par with rural men, are wholly inadequate, Amin argues, for the complex demands of an expanding urban middle-class environment:

> ... in spite of her ignorance, an Egyptian peasant woman is a partner to her husband, attending to her household and helping him in his work in the fields. This is facilitated by the fact that rural life is simple, almost elementary, with very few needs for the family. On the other hand, running a household in an urban area can be compared to administering a large business organization. The urban environment with its advanced way of life, its proliferating needs, and its numerous economic opportunities has contributed to this change of family roles. Thus an urban woman, given authority over the private domain of the family, cannot administer it without the necessary education and training.[15]

Women should be educated in order to improve on household-oriented roles and tasks. As rational partners in the 'business' of running a household, their potential benefit to national growth is encoded in the language of economic efficiency.

Furthermore, Amin assumes that the sum of his reforms will promote a greater level of harmony between husbands and wives, to culminate in feelings of matrimonial love and trust. Such love, he insists, can only occur between two people of like mind and does not flourish in a society which upholds inequality as the norm. Only such women as are educated and of a sound temperament may overcome the deficiencies of their socialisation and connect with their husbands on an intellectual and emotional level. This emphasis on the ideal of marital love, which Amin declares to be 'the secret of happiness', and compares to 'the bliss of paradise',[16] marks a shift in the popular conception of marriage during the nineteenth century: from marriage as an economic, sexual and procreative contract to that of an emotional, romantic pact.

Here, the lack of connection between husbands and wives is attributed to contemporary practices of gender segregation, veiling and seclusion, which were wasting the physical and intellectual potential of Egypt's women.[17] By cloistering its women within the family home, Egyptian society is poisoning the relations between them and other women, their husbands' families. Instead of encouraging emotions of love and friendship between husbands and wives, the censure of tradition reinforces feelings of possessiveness and jealousy which defines the boundaries of a woman's supposed virtue and honour. In imploring tones Amin advocates for practical legal and social reforms in the spheres of education and family law. A 'refined and sensitive man', he argues, knows that 'his heart will not be at ease living with an ignorant woman, regardless of the barriers he erects between her and other men'.[18] Such barriers were not only spoiling the relations between men and women, but were adversely affecting other aspects of Egyptian society, including religious laws, the stability of families, and design of domestic homes.

However, such reforms were not as emancipatory as Amin's rhetoric would suggest, for the call to ease women's social restrictions in the name of promoting their overall wellbeing accompanied his intention to discipline and regulate areas of women's lives that men had previously exercised little control over. This is especially evident when Amin rails against the character and habits of common, uneducated women. According to Amin, Egyptian women were inferior to men only insofar as contemporary Egyptian customs had repressed and inferiorised them. As a consequence of this, they exacted power over their husbands through tactics of surveillance and subordination. This evidently irked Amin who comments on the techniques of manipulation, secrecy and gossip that women would employ with their spouses and other relations:

> At times she compares him with the husbands of her neighbours...Sometimes she sets herself to finding a way to change his feelings towards his relatives ... Nor does she fail to supervise his conduct with the servant girls and observe how he looks when women visitors call...she will not tolerate any maid unless the maid is hideous...You see her with neighbours and friends...raising her voice and relating all that occurs between herself and her husband and her husband's relatives and friends, and her sorrows and joys, and all her secrets, bearing what is in her heart until no secret remains – even matters of the bed.[19]

This hostility towards women's wiles, manners and habits not only betrays Amin's class prejudice and patriarchy, but also reveals a profound unease with the autonomous, feminine-gendered spaces which women carved out in the otherwise male-ordered world of pre-modern Egyptian society. The overbearing dislike towards middle-class Egyptian wives disclosed in some of the more scathing passages of Amin's text are not simply derived from the currency of 'European and Egyptian men's self-representations' and stereotyping of women,[20] but stems from an anxiety over the distinct domains of power occupied by the sexes in the nineteenth century.

Thus, as Lila Abu-Lughod points out, Amin's reforms represent both an effort to support the modern bourgeois ideals of conjugal love and scientific childrearing for the improvement of Egyptian society, on one hand, and an attack on the customary roles and social networks which urban women traditionally participated in, on the other.[21] Because such women's networks fell outside the domain of state organisation, and so of male control, Amin's interventions worked towards, and were enabled by, the power of the colonial state to regulate, control and govern the lives of its subjects in new and more effective ways. A common feature of the late nineteenth century, this large-scale modernising project required the state, to the best of its ability, to survey, organise and discipline the family household as a means to facilitate the creation of 'modern' subjects.[22]

Moreover, as Talal Asad observes in the context of Muhammad 'Abduh's re-evaluation and codification of *shari'ah* law, the new legal definition of the 'family' (*'ailah*), as belonging to a private space which is nonetheless the object of legal jurisdiction, reflects a distinctly modern understanding of laws pertaining to the formation of the 'private' individual.[23] This is certainly reflected in 'Abduh and Amin's conceptualisation of the family household as a micro-political unit whose moral wellbeing was crucial to the health of civil society at large. Indeed, the attitudes of both reformers, whilst they differ over important details, nonetheless relate to modern categories. For instance, both posit a framework of separate (public-from-private) domains contiguous to an emerging template of civil society, and accept the right of the state to oversee changes in the family's organisation and legal status. This is mirrored in Amin's appeal for legal and institutional reform in the areas of women's health and education, for which he emphasised the role of modern urban households in the development of Egypt's economic and political prosperity.

Yet what interests me here is the way indigenous reformers linked the secular modern understanding of the 'family', and the discourse of national health on which it rested, to the status of women and the tensions this entailed. Thus, I argue that the subject of women's reform cannot be approached only according to that liberal/modernist narrative which, for Amin, posited the gradual emancipation of women. Instead, Amin's call for the aristocratic and upper-middle classes of Egyptian society to embrace the ideal of matrimonial love and to release their daughters from the bonds of repressive tradition performed a double movement. On one hand, it promised to liberate women from the patriarchal mores of Egyptian life, whilst, on the other, it clamped down vigorously on what spaces for gender autonomy and communal self-understanding women then shared.

Constituted as a field of intense ideological dispute, the issue of women's reform was also advocated by religious intellectuals whose concepts exacted their own claims over the modern civil subject. The encounter could not have occurred otherwise if one considers that the colonial state provided the institutional and legal framework within which various types of political and social action were legitimated. In what follows, it will become clear that the new parameters and assumptions established by modern notions of bourgeois civility were upset by the very conditions that the idealised status of women placed upon them.

Ashraf 'Ali Thanawi and the Ideal Muslim Woman

That modernity was a double-edged phenomenon which brought new promises but also new trepidations and anxieties is evident in reformist concerns that the avenues opened to educated women might simultaneously work to undermine society's moral foundations. In northern India, calls for women's education ushered in the fear of how such an education, and the empowering tools of literacy and writing, would adversely affect the roles prescribed for women by venerated social and religious customs. From the viewpoint of some sections of the religious *'ulama*, women's education was to be embraced insofar as it contributed to the religious and spiritual reform of the Muslim community. And thanks to the rapid expansion of print media during the latter half of the nineteenth century, individual religious and lay reformers were able to shape women's lives as never before.[24] For instance, the widespread production of religious pamphlets and didactic manuals allowed male reformers to disseminate their judgments on contemporary social trends to a broad audience. In their efforts to adapt religious tenets to the conditions of modern life, they addressed such topics as the legitimacy of superstitious rituals, practices associated with saint worship and various, indigenous women-led practices and customs.

In the first decade of the twentieth century, an influential leader of the Deoband *'ulama* in northern India, Ashraf 'Ali Thanawi (1864–1943), wrote a guide for the correct spiritual and moral conduct of Muslim women in matters covering almost every aspect of their social lives.[25] Titled *Bihishti Zewar* (*Ornaments of Paradise*), the book was first published in 1905 and has been reprinted many times in northern India, in the original Urdu, and translated into an array of other Indian and European languages. In it, Thanawi set out to imbue a new religious self-consciousness amongst Indian Muslim women, which required the re-evaluation of their place in society and their relation to the new opportunities and threats presented by the modern world.

Like Qasim Amin, Thanawi saw education as a means to both instruct women in their domestic functions and to reform the customary traits and habits of illiterate and 'ignorant' women. Unlike Amin, however, he did this by evaluating women's customs according to their conformity to, or variance from, the template of sacred laws and practices set out in God's *shari'ah* as he understood it. Bolstered with citations from the Qur'an and various *ahadith* (containing the deeds and sayings of the Prophet), Thanawi ran through a long list of the social customs and manners practised amongst Muslim women that fell outside the boundaries of Islamic law, and exhorted both men and women to be more conscious of their religious and social responsibilities.

In matters of social comportment, he paid great attention to the abolition of that distinctly feminine language which women employed within the family home and at all-female gatherings and festivities. As historians such as Gail Minault have observed, the largely segregated and distinct world inhabited by urban Muslim women in northern India during the eighteenth and nineteenth centuries produced a uniquely idiomatic and colloquially feminine style of language. Termed *begumati zuban* (women's language), this type of speech developed in the all-female spaces of patriarchal, urban households and catered exclusively to women's lifestyles and concerns.[26] Amongst themselves, women would discuss their personal affairs, relationships and matters of sexual intimacy in a dialect seldom heard in the public, male domain. In its ambivalence towards the blend of cultivated Persian and high Urdu used by courtly male society of the time, *begumati zuban* constituted an independent and autonomous linguistic realm which reflected the circumscribed but no less significant self-sufficiency that women possessed.[27]

The language and habits in which women indulged during festivals and all-female gatherings are, for Thanawi, a particular source of moral approbation. Such congregations provided a forum in which, against all prohibitions, 'everyone settles down to gossip, complaining of this one, engaging in backbiting about that one, slandering the other, reproaching someone else'. Thanawi is critical, also, of the prayers and invocations which women customarily use at the commencement of such gatherings. Expressions such as 'Remain a beloved wife', 'May you bathe in milk and enjoy grandsons' and 'May your husband live long' have supplanted the use of conventional Islamic formulae, and represent a contravention of normative religious practice.[28] Furthermore, women become so engrossed in such events that they forget to retreat to a closed room or veil themselves in the presence of male servants and palanquin-bearers, thus violating the strictures of *purdah*.[29] To rectify this, Thanawi reminds women of the salutations, rituals and deference needed to accord due respect to one another, their elders, other family members, as well as non-familial acquaintances.[30] In this sense, Thanawi contributes to the construction of an urbane, *ashraf* (noble) identity in which the regulation and refinement of contemporary women's habits, language and customs is central.[31] Yet as dangerous to the social order as the culture and habits of unreformed women are, one must also account for the new and equally serious threat posed by the freedoms an education affords.

Of particular interest, in this regard, is Thanawi's advice concerning the subject of women's letter writing and access to India's newly introduced postal service. According to Thanawi, the emerging, semi-public realm of women's letter writing posed a challenge to the prohibitions and customs of sexual segregation (*purdah*) practised in the urban centres of northern India. Whilst women must spend most of their lives within the family home, the ability to read and write letters opened new avenues of communication, perhaps with total strangers who may include undesirable suitors. Thus, Thanawi counselled women who do not transgress in their social relationships with people outside their family to observe the same restrictions in the 'virtual' relationships that letter writing enabled. To this end, women are advised not to write letters to men with whom Islamic law forbids social intercourse, except in matters of the direst necessity. Women are instead advised to correspond only with their familial relations, always observing the same compunctions of etiquette as those which are practised in the family home. And just as women should not roam freely in the public domain, unsupervised by a husband or close male relative, so too should their letters be vetted by either of these male figures. Akin to those traditional laws which stipulate the regulation of women's activities in the public sphere, this is justified on the familiar theological premise that men's social responsibility over women derives from their superior intellect (*'aql*) and common sense in worldly matters.[32]

In the following example of a 'correctly written letter', hypothetically sent by an uncle to his young niece, Thanawi finds occasion to remind girls that an education does not license them to forego established customs of respect and civility:

> I have heard that you are somewhat saucy and do not have regard for the respect due anyone. I felt grieved at hearing this, because a person's honour does not only derive from being able to read and write. Until you learn to have regard for *adab* (civility), people will not love and cherish you. Along with reading and writing, it is necessary for boys and girls to learn civility, for with civility a person is dear to the heart of everyone and everyone seeks to please that person.[33]

This excerpt provides a reminder to young people to observe established social and moral standards. Here, the regulating power of hearsay (conveyed by uncle's use of 'I have heard...') supplies the premise for a lecture on the importance of retaining the ideal, socially defined qualities of courtesy and *adab* (connoting respectfulness and civility) amongst boys and girls. Whilst Thanawi includes both sexes in this moral lesson, the effect of hearsay, gossip and private conversation no doubt served to reinforce the social, cultural and religious standards which regulated women's domestic lives.

As the ability to read and write came increasingly to be identified with one's social status around the turn of the century, new literature proffering advice in the areas of women's education, etiquette and social customs increased exponentially. This is seen, for instance, in the proliferation of didactic reformist novels, home magazines, journals, poems, plays, manuals and literary tracts that offered moral self-improvement for both women and men. Amongst the new forums that addressed issues of women's reform (including the earliest Urdu novels, women's home magazines and periodicals), educational and religious reformers set out their vision for the ideal Muslim woman. And although many such periodicals were founded by enlightened men, they nonetheless provided an opportunity for educated and upper-class women to contribute towards discourses on personal piety, education and moral reform.[34]

Around the turn of the century, debates over the extent of women's education, and what constituted suitable reading for women, reveal the uneasy standing of women vis-à-vis the construction of the modern colonial citizen subject. Rather than allow *ashraf* women to read the same texts as their male relations, the common refrain was that women should only read such elementary religious and household-oriented works as were relevant to their daily tasks and functions. For this reason, women should not be exposed to the belles-lettres poetry and *dastans* (epic tales) which made up the Indo-Persian literary heritage on the grounds that such works would distract them from their allotted tasks as mothers, wives and housekeepers. After all, girls had little need for secular learning and high literature when most of their time is taken up with learning to cook, sew, and care for younger children and older relations.

Moreover, a basic level of education for girls could be obtained privately, within the family home and without the aid of state-funded schools. Testifying before the Indian Education Committee in 1882, Sayyid Ahmad Khan pronounced that there was no need to establish a school for girls at the Aligarh college on the presumption that existing regimes of home learning, and what knowledge girls might glean from their more educated male relations, were sufficient for the time being:

> The question of female education much resembles the oriental philosopher who asked whether the egg or the hen was first

Education and the Status of Women

created. Those who hold that women should be educated and civilized prior to men are greatly mistaken... The present state of education among Muhammadan females is, in my opinion, enough for domestic happiness, considering the present social and economic conditions of the Muhammadans of India.[35]

The apparently dismissive tone of Sayyid Ahmad's speech may be attributed to his conviction that men are better placed than women to achieve necessary short-term social reforms and should therefore be educated first. For this reason, he might have wished to see whatever funds and resources were available pooled directly towards his college for Muslim boys. It has been observed, also, that a number of Sayyid Ahmad's modernist contemporaries did not share his cultural conservatism on the issue of women's education. At any rate, he was merely delaying the inevitable, and modern schools for Muslim girls, such as the Aligarh Girls School, were established by the second decade of the twentieth century. However, the statement that women should not be 'educated and civilized *prior to...* men' is revaling, for it is the promise of *becoming civilised*, and the threats this entailed, which weighed on the minds of male reformers.

That the reformist vision of bourgeois civility did not allocate the same citizenship status to both men and women comes as no surprise to anyone familiar with Carole Pateman's interpretation of the role of classical 'contract theory' in liberal notions of civil society. According to Pateman, the antinomous (public-versus-private) domains which came to define the organisation of modern civil society institutionalised a division of power in which men are allocated control over the civic, 'rational' public sphere, and women are associated with the 'natural' private domain. Because, as Pateman argues, the 'private, womanly sphere (natural) and the public, male sphere (civil) are opposed but gain their meaning from each other... the civil freedom of public life is thrown into relief when counterposed to the natural subjection that characterises the private realm.'[36] Civil society's identification of maleness with the rational public sphere simultaneously relies upon the subjection of femininity to the less rational and circumscribed abode of the private domain. But if the private sphere is the natural foundation of civil life, it may nonetheless come to influence the public sphere in covert and non-confronting ways.

Here, I am not interested so much in the fact that indigenous reformers sought to identify women with the domestic space of the urban family household, or that the citizenship allocated to women was deficient when compared to that offered to men. Rather, I am interested in how the necessary steps to women's reform so disturbed the idealised position of women as civil subjects that this status was put under pressure. To bring women up to the correct social, moral and religious standards, male reformers sought to reorder and control the all-female networks and environments to which urban women were socially accustomed. But the effort to educate and so extract women from pre-modern social circles had its own consequences, which reveal a profound unease with the separate public/masculine and private/feminine spheres on which notions of modern citizenship were constructed.

Taking his place among those recommending a minimal, household-based education for women, Thanawi's reformist tract is exemplary for incorporating the aforementioned vision of civil society into a religio-spiritual framework for reform. This is achieved by identifying women's symbolically protected and domesticated status with a universal Islamic template of personal piety. In the eighth section of Thanawi's manual, for instance, he presents an account of the virtuous life and deeds of the Prophet Muhammad. Like many didactic religious works of the nineteenth century, the Prophet's life story is upheld as the exemplary model upon which Thanawi's female readers may live as close to the divine laws prescribed in the *shari'ah*, and the prophetic *Sunnah*, as possible. In this instance, examples from the Prophet's life are given not so much for the purposes of intellectual reflection as to allow the believer to emulate, aspire to, and obtain something of the Prophet's immense spiritual charisma (*barakah*). As Thanawi explains to his female readers, one reads the Prophet's biography in order to:

> ... gain the blessed power that is in his story, so that those who read it may learn about the Apostle and about his habits and may

thus love and follow him. It goes without saying that all people gain the treasure of goodness in no other way but through the blessed power of the Prophet. The women of the early community gained it through the presence of his light; the women of today's community gain it through the *Shari'ah*.[37]

Whereas Amin sees the educated woman as a productive and potentially useful private citizen, Thanawi is more preoccupied with ensuring that she retain the Islamic virtues upon which a moral society is maintained. Although Thanawi, like Amin, appeals for women's education and literacy so that they may better manage their domestic affairs, his central concern was to purify the substance of their spiritual lives. In Thanawi's reformist tract, then, the educated mother and housewife is conjoined to the ideal of the pious Muslim female in terms which bear little relevance to the end goals of the modern civil subject. In this sense, Thanawi's project worked against the aim of contemporary advocates for women's education, which was to engender a liberal secular order in the contemporary imperial world. This is seen in his appropriation of certain British imperial and Indian nationalist themes into a practical model for the God-conscious, feminine soul. Women should be organised, efficient and self-restrained in their daily tasks and rituals, he argues, not just for the social and material benefit of their community, but for the otherworldly, spiritual gains which such actions accrue. Thanawi, after some criticism of extra-Islamic practices and superstitions, is thus able to re-invoke the workable elements of a mythic Islamic consciousness for his female readers.

An Ambivalent Rhetoric

In the late nineteenth and early twentieth centuries, reformist discourses concerning women's education were unable to conceal an ambivalence which accompanied the goal of 'improving' women's lives. Indeed, Thanawi's reformist tract points to a vision of modernity in which the idea of 'progress' through women's education simultaneously raises the threat of women's moral disobedience. This sense of ambivalence is encapsulated by the contemporary north Indian poet-satirist, Akbar

Allahabadi (1846–1921), who explicitly links the question of national improvement to the idealised status of women and the fears which accompany their introduction to the Western system of education:

> It is not a women's obligation (*fard*), to be trapped within four walls,
> Unless it is the bond of modesty and self-restraint.
>
> Ah! But such restraint and modesty do not come easily,
> To speak of them is easy, to perform them is less so.
>
> Of the restraint that we profess, where is its discipline?
> Does our nation's pride, conqueror-like, spread over the land?
>
> Of today's education, to whom is it not freely prescribed?
> But for our noble women, the Western mould is ill-advised.[38]

Throughout the poem, Allahabadi links the rhetoric of women's emancipation to the preservation of that 'modesty' and 'self-restraint' which must accompany their newfound status as modern civil subjects. In the fifth line, he queries the absence of such virtues in the community as a whole, reminding men of their meekness in the face of colonial power. That 'today's education' (a euphemism for the colonial system of education) or the 'Western mould' of the final verse, is 'ill-advised' for Indian women alludes to the dangers that such an education was thought to present to the aforementioned notion of women's virtues. Allahabadi thus ironises that anxiety which accompanied the issue of women's reform whilst reflecting upon the fact that such efforts took place within, and were shaped by, the discursive parameters of the European coloniser. His satire is effective for showing us that reformist constructions of feminine virtue were in part a gesture of self-compensation for the loss of authority and cultural prestige felt amongst colonised communities.

Conclusion

Whilst the faith of Muslim reformers in women's education during the second half of the nineteenth century would appear to hold great promise for society at large, this was undercut by the new demands which the idealisation of women's status exacted. For instance, Amin and Thanawi in their different ways saw women's education as a means to limit the autonomy women once exercised in the all-female quarters of traditional patriarchal urban households. Whilst the spread of literacy promised to liberate women from the constraints of 'backward' or 'un-Islamic' customs, male reformers nonetheless feared that it would allow them to slip from the roles in which they were traditionally valued – as wives, mothers and housekeepers. Such concerns contributed to Amin and Thanawi embracing the common strategy of modern imperial, national and religious discourses to idealise the status of women as a reflection upon the internal character of a homogeneous national or religious community. Their attitudes towards women's education reflected an ambivalence which was indicative of the new status of women as private civil subjects.

This ambivalence did not represent the failure of such societies to become modern, but points to the complex ways in which modernity was interpreted. After the significant social, cultural and economic changes augured by colonial rule (which included the attribution of cultural inferiority to indigenous practices of gender segregation), self-criticism became the only path to maintaining the virtues that reformers still wished to preserve of their culture. The negotiation of modern themes is therefore central to conceptions of women's duties in this period, just as it provides an ideological launching pad for later constructions of Islamic femininity.

CHAPTER 4

MUHAMMAD IQBAL, ISLAM AND MODERN NATIONALISM

There is a world still lost in our hearts,
A world that still waits for the call of 'Rise!'
A world without distinctions of blood and colour,
Where evening shines brighter than morning in the West.[1]

Introduction

In the first half of the twentieth century, new types of religious and cultural exclusivity were bound up in the formation of national identities amongst peoples of the colonised and decolonising world. This was certainly evident in British India, where the political push towards national independence culminated in the partition and independence, in 1947, of the newly formed states of India and Pakistan (and then later Bangladesh). This event was accompanied by the enormous trauma of sectarian killings, mass rape, arson, and the displacement and exchange of up to 16 million people, as Muslims, Hindus and Sikhs fled from India to Pakistan and vice versa. Such violence – and the political conditions that enabled it – did not make it easier for ruling elites to nationalise the populations of their fledgling states in the years after 1947.[2] To a large extent, this nationalisation was achieved through the imagining of discrete 'Hindu' and 'Muslim' polities, languages and cultures, which compartmentalised the past in new ways.

In its populist guise, 'history' on both sides of the India–Pakistan border has consolidated the nation-state as a home and refuge for supposedly timeless identities of a religious or secular nature. As a bulwark for the 'two-nation' theory, nationalist histories have often asserted the existence of homogeneously separate and self-defining Hindu and Muslim national communities. This was mobilised in the defence of an intrinsic religious/cultural identity, in Pakistan and amongst Hindu nationalists, or was counterposed with a tradition of indigenous pluralism, amongst Indian secularists. Such national traditions are then projected backwards onto the various calamities and sacrifices, social and economic traumas, partitions, wars and so forth, which paved the road to modern statehood.

That this understanding of history has direct implications for the present can be seen in the rise to power of the Hindu nationalist BJP party in India from the early 1990s to 2004, which stimulated considerable debate about the apparent 'crisis' of Indian secularism, and called for a rethinking of the dichotomy between 'secular nationalist' and 'communal' notions of identity.[3] It has been observed, for instance, that right-wing Hindu nationalists of the 1990s and early 2000s claimed to represent 'secular' interests when pandering to the populist fears of a politicised Hindu majority, by typecasting India's Muslim minority as a sign of 'communalism', 'fanaticism' and 'backwardness'. In this sense, 'secularism' accommodates the imposition of a majority–minority structure onto the national culture through the exclusion of a vulnerable religious community.[4] In Pakistan, from which religious minorities have long since fled while those who remain are so small in number as to be negligible, similar charges were levelled against the country's heterodox communities, as seen in the 'Qadiyyani controversy' of 1952.

Recent studies, since Benedict Anderson's influential *Imagined Communities*, have shown how modern technologies and social formations enabled the imagining of national citizenship and a teleological narrative which was then to be written as the national past.[5] Under colonial rule in the nineteenth century, religious, regional and/or ethnic notions of identity accompanied the expansion of print capitalism, the modern postal system, the creation of communally based legal codes, census operations and electoral systems. As Gyanendra Pandey points out, British policy makers no doubt contributed to this process by assuming that Indian society was defined by primordial, religiously based communal identities.[6] Drawing upon popular nineteenth-century Orientalist conceptions of religion, race and class, colonial sociology sought to understand and so govern Indian society by establishing a theory of social origins which placed Hindus and Muslims apart from one another, thus minimising the many folkways and customs which the urbanised, peasant and rural classes had in common. This gave to Hindu nationalism the revisionist narrative of a primordial Hindu nation ground down by 'foreign' Muslim invaders, which such historians of ancient and medieval India as Romila Thapar and Richard Eaton have contested. Contrary to the Hindutva narrative, these historians claim that it was only in the colonial and post-independence periods that such identities *were constituted as persuasive political categories*.[7] This is not to posit a seamless continuity between the discourses of colonialism and modern religious nationalism. Rather, it is to say that the modern (colonial European) theory of origins laid the ground for those notions of belonging and difference which contributed to the identity of postcolonial nation-states and their communal subsets. Whilst the historical study of caste, ethnicity and nationalism in India and Pakistan can be traced to attitudes and social categories of the pre-modern era, such identities were only isolated, theorised and produced as legal and political categories under modern colonialism.[8]

Thus, nationalist claims to represent the sentiments of primordial religious communities cannot be taken for granted, nor should we accept their differential construction against the putative threat posed by a real or imagined 'other'. The role of the 'other' is fulfilled by India and Pakistan to one another, or is found internally, amongst those religious, ethnic, sexual or political identities which fall outside the nation's ideological parameters. Nevertheless, to show that Hindu and Muslim communalism in its present form belongs to the policies of the colonial period, and that India and Pakistan make few obvious historical claims upon pre-modern polities and social formations, is less interesting than to explore how the idea of nationhood (and its use of racial and cultural categories) constituted new pathways for ideological thought and the formation of identity. The emergence of a national politics in India and Pakistan, far from representing the belated survival/liberation of fixed pre-modern communities, was a joint product of colonial sociology and the indigenous elites who worked within and sometimes against it.[9]

Although he died some nine years before its creation, Muhammad Iqbal (1877–1938) is officially regarded in Pakistan as the ideological founder of that nation. Of the decades preceding Pakistan's creation, nationalist histories depict Iqbal struggling alongside Muhammad Ali Jinnah (1876–1948) for the creation of the new state against the self-interest of British administrators and Congress Party nationalists. In this narrative, Iqbal plays the poet/philosopher/ideologue who conceived of Pakistan along theoretical lines, and whose vision was consolidated by Jinnah at a political level.[10] In this national storytelling, historians, even those who acknowledge, as Iqbal did, the 'artificial' nature of national identities, too frequently succumb to the claim that Indian Muslims possess a 'unique', proto-national character which sets them apart from other religious communities.[11] Yet such histories raise a problematic which is larger than the question of which national identity (Pakistan's or India's) most gravely distorts a complex and heterogeneous past. It is one which relates to Iqbal's own writings. Namely, can India's Muslims, or Muslims generally, be defined as a 'nation' or *qaum* in the modern sense, and if the answer is yes (which Iqbal concluded it was), then what sort of *qaum* are they?

Iqbal's thought was informed by the perception that India's Muslim community had fallen into a state of historical servitude and weakness. Witnessing an escalation of Hindu–Muslim violence in the Punjab during the 1920s, Iqbal was wary of the Congress Party's appeals to a united Indian nationalism and warned that the democracy planned for India could not guarantee the adequate representation of provinces with a Muslim majority. Were they to become a religious sub-class subject wholly to the whims of a Hindu-dominated, centralised Indian state, the very things which defined Islam in the Indian subcontinent would be diluted and lost. To consolidate the political sway of Indian Muslims in the Punjab, Iqbal called for separate, communal electorates, which set him against Congress Party nationalists during the late 1920s.

From 1930 to 1934, Iqbal provided ideological leadership for the Muslim League and in his presidential address to it in 1930, announced:

> I would like to see the Punjab, North-west Frontier Province, Sindh and Baluchistan amalgamated into a single state. Self-government within the British Empire with or without the British Empire, the formation of a consolidated North-west Indian Muslim state appears to me to be the final destiny of the Muslims, at least of North-west India.[12]

In this oft-quoted speech, Iqbal called for the creation of an autonomous Muslim province on the grounds that India's Muslims 'are the only Indian people who can be fitly described as a nation in the modern sense of the word'.[13] Although Iqbal died before the creation of Pakistan, such language was taken up by Muhammad Ali Jinnah, who requested that the League officially adopt the so-called Pakistan Resolution.

Much has been made, both then and now, of Iqbal's attributing a separate nationality to the Muslims of India. According to Iqbal's political opponents, his presidential address of 1930 seemed nothing less than a call for the entrenchment of communalism, signalling his betrayal of the national movement and rejection of Indian unity. Taking up this line, Edward Thompson, a keen observer of Indian politics, warned that Iqbal's 'Pan-Islamic plotting' threatened to derail the vision of the Indian Federation.[14] Responding to Thompson's charge, Iqbal stated that he made no demand for an independent Muslim state outside the British Empire but was simply anticipating the 'redistribution of India into provinces with effective majorities of one community or another', in keeping with the suggestions of the Nehru report.[15]

Yet such disclaimers have done nothing to counter the retrospective glorification of Iqbal as a Muslim 'separatist' in the national imagination of Pakistan. Moreover, various historians and Islamic revivalists have since established Iqbal as a proponent for the idea that Muslims must live under an Islamic state.[16] In 1986, the then President of Iran, Sayyid Ali Khamenei, delivered a lecture on the importance of Iqbal's philosophy in which he concluded that the Islamic Republic's 'policy of self-reliance is identical with Iqbal's views'.[17] Yet the linking of modern nationalist aims to Iqbal's philosophy is tenuous at best. It not only fails to account for the volatile political environment in which Iqbal formulated his ideas but smothers the peculiar ambivalence which marked his notion of Muslim nationalism.

Defining Nationalism

The Arabic word, *qaum* (denoting a kin group, tribe, race or people), from which is derived the modern term, *qaumiyyah* (nationalism), has been revised often in the thoughts of national and religious reformers of the nineteenth and twentieth centuries. In the Arabic of the Qur'an, a *qaum* denotes any group of people regardless of whether they are defined by a common genealogy or mythical origin. With the weakening of the Ottoman Empire and assumption of British and French control over the Middle East in the modern period, however, Arab nationalists invoked a common Arab identity (*al-qaumiyyah al-'arabiyyah*) with which to counteract forces of political fragmentation and distinguish them from their European colonisers.[18] Mirroring the development of nationalism in other parts of the world, the *qaum* became a powerful conceptual and imaginative trope with which to validate the myth of a primordially unified or homogeneous people.

In northern India during the second half of the nineteenth century, Sayyid Ahmad Khan extolled British India as the land to which both Hindus and Muslims owed their common allegiance. India's Hindus, Muslims and Christians are one *qaum*, Sayyid Ahmad attested, and must therefore cultivate a shared sense of patriotism (*hubb al-watan*).[19] Such patriotism, he argued, was owed to one's countrymen as well as to the British, who had brought order, stability and a well-managed system of government to the land. Yet, whilst he lived before the time of the two-nation theory, Sayyid Ahmad underscored the religious and cultural unity of India's Muslim community in order to enhance its political representation amongst colonial authorities. To this end, he propounded the view that Indian Muslims also understand the term '*qaum*' not in relation to land or ethnicity, but 'purely with reference to religion'. It is in this context, he stated, that 'a man may belong to any country or race – but as long as he is a Muslim, he is of the same *qaum*'.[20] Thus, he tied the identity of Indian Muslims to the notion of a universal *ummah* (community) which transcends the limitations of occupation, class, ethnicity and geography.

During the 1920s and 1930s, intermittent communal violence and hostility between Hindus and Muslims contributed to the notion of distinctly separate *qaum*s and raised the intensity of arguments surrounding the two-nation theory. Yet those who opposed the creation of Pakistan, such as the leader of the Jami'at-i 'Ulama-i Hind, Husain Ahmad Madani (1879–1957), argued for a vision of national unity reminiscent of Sayyid Ahmad Khan's late nineteenth-century patriotism. The Muslims of India, Madani opined, are particular only insofar as they constitute a separate *millat* (religious community) who abide by religiously prescribed laws (*shari'ah*), folkways and customs. The notion of a national *qaum*, on the other hand, is defined according to broader criteria: 'India will have geographical and political boundaries of an individual whole and as such is the common homeland of all its citizens irrespective of race and religion', said Madani. 'From the national point of view every Muslim is an Indian.'[21]

Iqbal contested Madani's definition of nationality and invoked, in its place, an identity exceeding Sayyid Ahmad Khan's other, more religious use of the term. According to Iqbal, nationality (*qaumiyyah*) amongst Muslims is expansive in its universality and cannot be tied to worldly constraints. It is 'a pure idea' which has 'no material basis' comparable, for example, to a nationality defined by geographical borders.[22] Because, for Iqbal, Islam's sole rallying point is a 'mental agreement for a certain view of the world' with its own moral and political philosophy, it differs from other nationalisms whose defining elements are mundane in a worldly sense. And as we shall see, Islam does not focus solely on the spiritual consolidation of the individual, but seeks to transform the 'national and racial viewpoint' into a 'purely human consciousness'.[23]

Thereafter, Iqbal's philosophical notion of a distinct Muslim *qaum* was revised by Muhammad Ali Jinnah to fit his secular vision for the new state of Pakistan. Immediately after Pakistan's creation and during his first presidential speech to its Constituent Assembly on 11 August 1947, Jinnah announced that 'in course of time Hindus would cease to be Hindus and Muslims would cease to be Muslims, not in the religious sense, because that is the personal faith of each individual, but in the political sense as citizens of the state'.[24] Such statements reveal Jinnah's concern to stretch the fragile skin of the nation over Pakistan's many religious, sectarian, ethnic, social and linguistic differences.[25] Nonetheless, the paradoxes inherent in Jinnah's stance have been commented on elsewhere and do not need reiterating now.[26]

What interests me is not the concept of a national *qaum* promoted by Pakistan's ideological defenders, but the ambiguities which beset this theme for he who did the most to explain it in philosophical terms: Muhammad Iqbal. Whilst I do not provide a systematic chronology of Iqbal's intellectual development, my focus upon his philosophy draws upon the dominant themes of his major lectures, *The Reconstruction of Religious Thought in Islam*, and some other writings. Because Iqbal used poetry as a means to express the religious and philosophical themes of his work, I have also selected examples from his poetic oeuvre. In particular, I will analyse how Iqbal's conception of Muslim identity is entangled in, and complicated by, race-based nationalism and how he sought to overcome it. But first, I must lay the ground by explaining something of the highly individualistic philosophy which animated his dynamic and original conception of Muslim history.

Khudi

Iqbal's notion of Islam, its morality, metaphysical precepts and historical institutions, promote a vision of the individual ego defined by dynamism, movement and constant action. For Iqbal, the self in Islam is 'a force, an energy, a will, a germ of infinite power, the gradual unfoldment of which must be the object of all human activity'[27]. Indeed, the true Muslim, or 'man of faith' (*mard-i momin*), is one who has realised the potential inherent in the Islamic doctrine of personality, for which

Iqbal employs the term '*khudi*', or 'selfhood'. He explains that, in an ethical sense, *khudi* means 'self-reliance, self-respect, self-confidence, self-preservation, self-assertion' and the power to stick to such concepts as truth, justice and duty.[28] As I will show, Iqbal's philosophy is a rich and complex amalgamation of the mystical and theological heritage of Islam, on one hand, and the dominant philosophical and intellectual currents in England and Germany during the first half of the twentieth century, on the other.

Having established himself as an Urdu poet of considerable repute in his early twenties, Iqbal graduated with degrees in law and philosophy from the Government College in Lahore, where he came under the influence of Thomas Arnold, the Orientalist scholar and reader in Arabic and Persian.[29] Encouraged by Arnold to travel to Europe, he spent the years from 1905 to 1908 studying in England and Germany. In England, Iqbal qualified as a barrister from Lincoln's Inn and studied philosophy at Trinity College, Cambridge, where he sat under two of the leading lights of English neo-Hegelian philosophy, John McTaggart and James Ward. In Germany, he attended a course at Heidelberg and enrolled at the University of Munich, to which he submitted his doctoral dissertation, titled 'The Development of Metaphysics in Persia', in 1907. This was to be a formative period in Iqbal's intellectual development, during which he absorbed the writings of various European poets and philosophers.[30]

Iqbal was particularly responsive to European Romantic and idealist trends in philosophical thinking, absorbing the works of Hegel, Kant, Schopenhauer, J. G. Fichte, Henri Bergson and Nietzsche. Some of the preoccupations of these philosophers – in particular, their mystically intoned emphasis on life not as a question of being but as a process of becoming – supported Iqbal's theory of selfhood, which he derived from the Qur'an and traditions of intellectual Sufism. In particular, Iqbal's philosophy gains from a comparison to that of the German idealist, J. G. Fichte (1762–1814).

From the Kantian premise that human freedom is a transcendental ideal enabling individuals to act outside the rigid, causal laws which determine the natural world, Fichte constructed a system of philosophy with the absolute autonomy and freedom of the individual as its starting point.[31] Unlike those philosophical systems in which knowledge is gained from the world outside the mind, idealism posited that experience and knowledge are generated by those tensions and encounters which attend the ego's own process of thinking. According to Fichte, self-realisation can only occur when the ego confronts the objective world (the 'other'), which naturally opposes and limits its activity. Thus, the ego is not a pre-existing thing or substance, but is produced by its activity of thought. For this reason, self-consciousness is not a given but derives from the *acting* ego's encounter with, and relation to, a non-ego.[32] Because reality is subjectively known, such encounters can also be said to bring the objective world, or non-ego, into being.[33]

To Iqbal as well, the life of the ego is 'a kind of tension caused by the ego invading the environment and the environment invading the ego'. For this reason: 'The ego does not stand outside this arena of mutual invasion. It is present in it as a directive energy and is formed and disciplined by its own experience.'[34] Thus Iqbal describes thought 'not as a principle which organises and integrates its material from the outside, but as a potency which is formative of the very being of its material'.[35] This notion of the self making the world, and realising itself, through its encounter with an 'other' is vividly expressed in Iqbal's most famous mystical poem, *Asrar-i Khudi* (*Secrets of the Self*):

> The form of existence is an effect of the Self,
> Whatsoever thou seest is a secret of the Self,
> When the Self woke to consciousness,
> It revealed the universe of thought.
> A hundred worlds are hidden in its essence;
> Self affirmation brings no-Self to light.[36]

And whilst the objects of the external world are an 'effect' of the self, this does not discount their reality. Instead Iqbal stresses their existence as the stuff through which the self achieves its fullest consciousness and state of individuation:

> Light transformed itself into an eye,
> And moved to and fro in search of beauty;

> The grass found a means of growth in itself,
> Its aspiration clove the breast of the garden.[37]

The soul is tasked, then, to overcome the multiplicities inherent in God's creation and enter into the unity of God's being (pure being) which underlies and precedes all diversity. Self-individuation becomes a proviso for personal immortality when, at its highest point of ascension, the ego confronts the ultimate ego, or God.[38] It is in this sense that Iqbal says: 'Personal immortality... is not ours as of right; it is to be achieved by personal effort. Man is only a candidate for it.'[39]

Although the refinement of one's self is a process of constant struggle, for Iqbal, its mysterious impulse towards movement honours the divine trust bestowed on humans at the moment of their creation:

> If you are among the living, fashion your own world.
> Life is the secret of Adam, the essence of the words 'Be and it was'![40]

Drawing upon the mystical tradition of Islamic thought, Iqbal sets out to reaffirm the relationship between God and humanity. According to the doctrines of classical Sufism, the essences which inhere in the phenomenal world are but an outward manifestation of God's own attributes. Put another way, the external world can be likened to a mirror which serves the purpose of reflecting God's attributes back to God's self. In this sense, God's relationship to the material universe entails a process of self-revealing, or as Iqbal put it: a 'rationally directed creative life' which 'unfailingly realises the infinite possibilities of His being'.[41] Conceiving God not only as pure being, but as pure ego, Iqbal posits an organising principle of unity, behind the created world, to which the human ego aspires. Because the ego strives for individual freedom, and God is the free individual par excellence, the ego must approach the divine on terms which fulfil the promise of its own freedom and immortality.

For Iqbal, then, the divine encounter represents a coming together of independent and mutually empowered selves, which is expressed through the theme of love. In mystical parlance, the soul's love for God (*'ishq*) is that which brings the seeker into closest proximity with the essence of the divine reality, and which the Indo-Persian poetic tradition often metaphorised as a beloved person or thing.[42] In his philosophical writings and much of his poetry, Iqbal underscored the importance of a love which bridges the gulf between the human soul and its divine maker. But, as Iqbal made clear, the experience of an intoxicating love does not simply facilitate the *'ashiq's* (lover's) dissolution into the figure of a metaphysical-divine *m'ashuq* (beloved), as so much conventional Urdu and Persian poetry would suggest. Love is that which instead reinforces the distinct personalities and potentialities of both:

> The Ego is fortified by love (*'ishq*). This word is used in a very wide sense and means the desire to assimilate, to absorb. Its highest form is the creation of values and ideals and the endeavour to realize them. Love individualizes the lover as well as the beloved. The effort to realize the most unique individuality individualizes the seeker and implies the individuality of the sought, for nothing else would satisfy the nature of the seeker.[43]

For Iqbal, Islamic mysticism's true ideal was to realise the 'I' as a metaphysical force not at the moment of its dissolution in the divine reality (*fana*) but at the point of its worldly return (*baqa*), which is 'the highest stage of self-affirmation'.[44] The mystical seeker's temporal but immediate experience of God, encountered (in Fichteian terms) as an 'independent other self' fulfils this process of self-individuation.[45]

Moreover this encounter cannot be entered passively. In a long poem on the subject of Islam's historical decline, the ego abrogates for itself the right to challenge God, to complain (as the poet does) about the perceived lack of favour shown to his community.[46] And, at its most refined, the ego's aspiration to power enlists God as a partner in the fashioning of its destiny:

> Raise the self to such lofty heights (*Khudi ko kar buland itna*) that before the realisation of each destiny (*taqdir*),
> God should ask the human being: 'tell me, what is your desire?'[47]

That this cannot be done in a tensionless state underscores the importance of oppositional energies in Iqbal's philosophy. Such opposition gives necessary shape and meaning to life's quest, in regard to which I cannot resist citing Iqbal's appreciative evaluation of the role of Satan (*Iblis*), from his Persian poem *Tashkir-i Fitrah* (*Nature's Purpose/Design*). After the penalty of his disobedience, Satan plans the fall of humanity by showing Adam that his life in the Garden of Eden is an insipid one, devoid of fervour and energy. The real meaning of life, Satan tells Adam, is in the creation of passion:

> A life of ceaseless strife is better than perpetual peace,
> The dove becomes a falcon when struggling under a snare...
> Know ye not that union [with God] only means the end of desire,
> The secret of eternal life is in incomplete burning![48]

Adam later admits before God that the state of his life would have lacked something integral were it not for Satan's temptation. In this instance, Satan's role is to provide the negative forces – of struggle and conflict – against which the ego stakes its aspiration to eternal life.[49]

Islam and History

In his writings and speeches, Iqbal points to history as a discipline in which the 'spirit of Islam', its underlying principles and ethics, may be known as a kind of 'world-fact'.[50] In this regard, history bears witness to the unfurling of the human spirit, upon which truly dynamic moral figures, including the Abrahamic Prophets and various political actors, have left their mark and influence. This universal history does not begin with Islam, although the latter's contribution was crucial in combining the strictest monotheistic principles with the formalisation of an all-inclusive social creed. The same could not be said, Iqbal avers, of Islam's Semitic forebears, whose doctrines were hollowed out by sentiments of racial community (in the context of Judaism) and an anthropomorphised divinity (in the figure of Christ). Moreover, Islam's own historical record, with its flourishing intellectual culture and expansive imperial dynasties, gave practical expression to the ontological reality of the ego as an expression of will committed to principles of movement and dynamic change.

Regarding the situation of Muslims in British India, Iqbal made it clear that Islam cannot flourish whilst its adherents have no control over their political destiny. In a statement which reflects the rise of incipient nationalist sentiments across northern India in 1910, and some years before the idea of Pakistan was first mooted, he wrote:

> To my mind government, whatever its form, is one of the determining forces of a people's character. Loss of political power is equally ruinous to a nation's character. Ever since their political fall, the Musalmans of India have undergone a rapid ethical deterioration. Of all the Muslim communities in the world, they are probably the meanest in point of character.[51]

To posit a loss of political authority as both the symptom and cause of ethical deterioration is to suppose that Islam's moral philosophy cannot thrive outside such channels. Indeed, Iqbal's interest in history reflects a preoccupation with figures and motifs of political rejuvenation, power and authority. Whilst he rebukes the European misconception of Islam as a warmongering religion, Iqbal nonetheless commemorates the vitality of such diverse political/religious leaders as Muhammad ibn 'Abdul Wahhab, Aurengzeb and Kamal Atatürk (despite the latter's commitment to secular statism), who are each felt to have re-invigorated and transformed – through sheer force of will – the tenor of the age in which they lived.[52] In these personalities, Iqbal valorises a world-conquering dynamism which confirms his faith in Islam's energetic spirit. If Iqbal romanticises Muslim history, he does so in order to emphasise the dynamic potential inherent in his vision of *khudi*, upon which are pegged his hopes for communal regeneration.

An important aspect of this romanticised history is Islam's own contribution to the founding of history as a secular discipline. In a lecture delivered under the title 'The Spirit of Muslim Culture', Iqbal identifies 'ruling concepts' intrinsic to Islam, which belie a 'process of ideation' coterminous with the true spirit of the religion.[53] Prominent amongst such ruling concepts is the finality of Muhammad's prophecy – denoting the end of *all* prophecy – which accompanied the Qur'anic call to human understanding through logical induction.

In this sense: 'the constant appeal to reason and experience in the Qur'an, and the emphasis that it lays on Nature and History as sources of human knowledge, are all different aspects of the same idea of [prophetic] finality.'[54]

The Qur'an's appeals to human reason, and insistence on the finality of prophecy, thus laid the basis for an empirical scientific understanding of such subjects as time, causality and history. For Iqbal, this is wholly congruent with the Islamic principle of the unity of existence and concept of life as a continuous, creative movement which cannot be predicted or determined. Qur'anic rationality was not an end in itself but provided a framework for the self's intuitive search for a higher moral and spiritual life. Thus to objectively study the sources of nature and history is to apprehend the 'signs' of God, which are an essential part of the mystical quest for the ultimate reality.[55] Moreover, this orientation was distinctly 'anti-classical' in its spirit. It opposed the speculative and otherworldly assertions of Greek metaphysicians and gave Muslim intellectuals a 'greater maturity of practical reason' about 'the nature of life and time' upon which a scientific approach to history was founded.[56] This introduces Iqbal's objection to the influence of Hellenistic thought in Islam, which he saw as reducing the living God of prophetic revelation to an abstract and immovable 'first cause'.

Reviewing the Islamic civilisation's contribution to universal history, Iqbal commemorates a long-running intellectual revolt against Greek philosophy, which made significant contributions to the inductive/empirical scientific culture of the modern world. After the initial reception of Greek thought in Arab Muslim circles, thinkers such as Abu Bakr al-Razi, Ibn Taymiyyah, and those within the 'Ashari school of theology rejected the theory of Aristotelian causes (and its notion of a world comprised of essentially static and unchanging forms), developing instead new techniques of experimentation and verification. This is seen, for instance, in the works of the mathematician al-Biruni, who argued for a non-static view of the universe, foreshadowing Whitehead's theory of relativity. Likewise, al-Jahiz's observations concerning the development of plant and animal life are seen to anticipate the modern science of evolution. In Iqbal's estimation, the efforts of these thinkers stemmed from the essential, Qur'anic emphasis on the observation of nature and history without regard to the unscientific, metaphysical assertions of Greek philosophers.[57] Whilst Iqbal acknowledges that his claims surrounding the Islamic philosophical contribution to modern scientific ideas and methodologies are not conclusive, he nonetheless associates a disparate array of scientists, philosophers, theologians, Sufis and poets with a historical vision – the Qur'anic conception of life – forged by a dynamic view of the universe.

Furthermore, Iqbal's notion of Muslim culture as a 'world fact' mirrors various assumptions familiar to the German historicist tradition after the time of Hegel.[58] This is seen in Iqbal's notion of history, which in its reference to elements of human nature conforming to the Qur'anic vision of life recalls William von Humbolt's summary of the transcendent purpose of historicism: 'Like philosophy after the first cause of things, art after the ideal of beauty, so history strives after the picture of the human destiny in perfect truth, living fullness and pure clarity.'[59] Just as Iqbal embraced the idealist, post-Kantian vision of a soul unencumbered by the predetermined laws of the natural world, so did he share the aversion of Romantic thinkers and historicists to a conception of history compelled only by whimsy, chance, random causes and their unintended consequences. Human history instead contains a logical vitality which participates in the revealing of Islam's essential truths.

Like many European Romantics, Iqbal's philosophy of history regards various cultures, or nations, as individual entities bearing their own nature, internal logic and processes of development. Thus he asserts, in tones reminiscent of thinkers such as Johann Gottfried Herder (1744–1803) and Oswald Spengler (1880–1936), that the particular genius and character of a national culture corresponds with, and is shaped by, the unique ideas, customs, folkways, rituals and language which inhere in that nation's deepest fabric. To such thinkers, the 'idea' of a national group expressed what was felt to be its timeless and essential character. To Iqbal, Islam as a 'political ideal', or 'corporate individuality', develops a new form of nationality (a new 'idea') in which the real and concrete exigencies of human life are wedded to an ideal, abstract and universal moral system.[60]

Yet for this system to be realised it must first negotiate other, less principled systems on the terrain of ideological and political conflict. History (to be thought about henceforth in its purposive upper case form) is moved by a process of competition and struggle amongst divergent ideas that reflect the ethical spirit of the various races or nations which harbour them. This does not mean, as it did for some amongst the early German historicists, that all nations are incomparably unique or that there is no universal standard against which to measure their relative values. Rather, an environment of rivalrous and sometimes conflicting national cultures is necessary for the 'spirit' or 'idea' of Islam to come into its own.

The other parallel between Iqbal and German historicists after the time of Humbolt (1767–1835) that I wish to touch upon is their emphasis on the formation of state power to assert the internal character of a national culture. For Iqbal, the developed institutions of a self-governing Muslim polity will no doubt protect the rights of its Muslim and non-Muslim citizens according to Islamic principles of justice. However, this alone is not the state's *raison d'être*. Instead, the state is conceived as something akin to a free individual in which the collective (and in Islam's case, individualising) aspiration of its people may be realised.[61] Thus, the construction of an Islamic state, or federation of states, seems legitimate to Iqbal only insofar as its striving for power accomplishes an innate movement towards Islam's higher ethical and moral goals. This emphasis contravenes that of Islamist activists in the twentieth century, for whom the establishment of a religious state is often seen as the precondition for an eventual, yet-to-be-realised moral utopia.

East and West in Iqbal's World History

Accompanying the historicist notions which underpin Iqbal's world history is the view that there is an essential and long-standing division between a Europe which is civilised, rational and materialistic, on one hand, and an East made recognisable by a preponderance of contemplative, 'spiritual' philosophies, on the other. The distinction between a rational West and spiritual East (outlined by Max Müller in the second half of the nineteenth century) was once a staple of

Orientalist discourses and provided a basis for Romantic and anti-colonial/nationalist critiques of modern European thought.[62] Amongst German intellectuals, the Romantic interest in India's contribution to the history of ideas is a case in point, for it accompanied a comparative and often critical evaluation of the Enlightenment faith in reason and science.[63] Likewise, Friedrich Nietzsche often invoked Islam in a demonstrative fashion, for the purpose of highlighting those aspects of Judeo-Christian modernity and Germanic culture which he found deserving of criticism.[64] Yet even when they asserted the superior philosophical or political calibre of Eastern religions, such thinkers remained within a theoretical discussion (about religion, society and political thought), the focus of which derived from, and returned to, the example of Europe.

Nevertheless, the imaginary construction of a 'mystical East' must also take account of those South Asian intellectuals who recommended it for the furtherance of their own anti-colonial, nativist and nationalist ideas. In India, prophets for a spiritual East, aside from Iqbal, include such important and diverse social reformers as Rammohun Roy, Dayananda Saraswati, Swami Vivekananda, Rabindranath Tagore and Mohandas Karmchand Ghandi.[65] For Iqbal, the East/West division did not merely explain why the Muslim world trailed Europe in the areas of rational thought and industry. It contributed instead to a pure vision of Islam, which might act as a type of panacea for the West's own spiritual desolation.

In his negative evaluation of Western power, Iqbal harnesses the anti-Eurocentrism of German Romantic thinkers, which he tweaked for his own purposes. Reflecting the nineteenth-century obsession with the Greek origins of Western history, his characterisation of the West begins with the Muslim world's encounter with, and reaction to, Hellenic philosophy in the ninth century, which I have already touched upon. Though he underscores the West's status as an inheritor of the modern scientific spirit once pioneered by Muslim thinkers, the causes for which modern science and technology have since been put to use reveal the West's inability to connect the outward phenomenon of the natural world with the deeper spiritual reality that underlies it. That European knowledge had led to the formation of the contemporary capitalist system and order of nation-states, which its imperial arms have hoisted across the earth, speaks less of its technological supremacy than of its unbound materialism and thirst for power. In the 1930s, Iqbal contends that modern nationalism served no other purpose than to facilitate the designs of European imperialists to fragment and thereby weaken the Muslim *ummah* (global community).[66] The idea of belonging to a country (*watan*), Iqbal posits, is useful only insofar as it denotes one's natural fondness for a geographical region. It is purely in this sense that one can speak about Chinese, Arab or Japanese people.[67] But when nationalism takes the form of a political concept or ideology, it counteracts the egalitarian content of Islam which is 'neither national and racial, nor private and individual, but purely human'. Because Islam's purpose is to 'unite and organise mankind', regardless of its 'natural distinctions', it cannot be relegated to the private sphere, as modern nationalists would want it to be.[68] Thus, for Iqbal, the secular regime's separation of religion from public life empties the political arena of that moral orientation which is humanity's only check against the forces of oppression and exploitation. Indian nationalists were wrong to assume that land was simply the basis of national belonging and that devotion to one's country, in this sense, could be reconciled with the duties of religious faith.

Yet if Iqbal is wary of secular nationalism, the democratic presumption of equality amongst individuals nonetheless strikes him as 'the most important aspect of Islam regarded as a political ideal'.[69] So long as it does not reduce individuals to the sum of their votes, which necessarily limits self-authenticity and subjects minority communities to the brute politics of majoritarian power, Iqbal argues that Islam and democracy are wholly compatible. To show this, he favourably compares the democratic idea in Islam, which respects the potential of individuals, with Nietzsche's 'aristocracy of supermen', which conveys a distinctly bourgeois elitist point of view. True democracy, according to Iqbal, should galvanise the aspirations of all its citizens, regardless of their social rank:

> Nietzsche... abhors the 'rule of the herd' and, hopeless of the plebeian... bases all higher culture on the cultivation and growth

of an Aristocracy of Supermen. But is the plebeian so absolutely hopeless? The democracy of Islam did not grow out of the extension of economic opportunity, it is a spiritual principle based on the assumption that every human being is a centre of latent power, the possibilities of which can be developed by cultivating a certain type of character. Out of the plebeian material Islam has formed... men of the noblest type of life and power. Is not, then, the Democracy of early Islam an experimental refutation of the ideas of Nietzsche?[70]

So why hasn't this ideal, democratic notion of Islam flourished in the East yet? Invoking Orientalist notions of Eastern mysticism and spirituality, Iqbal attributes the lack of intellectual, scientific and economic progress in a country such as India to a paucity of rational thought brought on by its attachment to philosophies of worldly renunciation. Whilst such tendencies are endogenous to India's native Hindu and Buddhist religions, they entered the Muslim world through the external civilisations of Persia and Greece, in the philosophies of 'Magianism' and Neoplatonism. In both of these trends, Iqbal decries a tendency towards self-renunciation whose origins in the ancient world did not diminish its contemporary relevance.

Magianism, as Iqbal describes it, was believed to have started in parts of the Middle East and Central Asia, amongst Zoroastrians, Jews, Nestorians, and the Chaldean and Sabean religions. After the early Arab conquests and as Islam took root in areas of Iran and the Middle East, Magian beliefs and practices came to influence its theological and mystical traditions. Employing a common theme of the German thinker Oswald Spengler, Iqbal described Magianism as a type of culture in which the concept of prophecy is characterised by a continuous and ongoing process of revelation.[71] Because Magian thought denied the end of revelation expressed in the doctrine of the Prophet's finality, it prevented the self from taking its place as an active and engaged force in the world. By directing humanity to an unending state of divine intervention and miraculous atonement, it slighted the affairs of this world and usurped the presumption of a transcendent moral authority. Whilst Islamic teachings represented a significant rebuttal of this trend, Magianism, according to Iqbal, had a contemporary resonance in the Persian Bahai and Indian Qadiani movements, both of which promised the return of a messianic saviour who would supersede and abrogate Muhammad's prophecy.[72]

A similar and equally pervasive trend towards self-dissipation arose in those strands of Islamic mysticism which came to view the ego not as a premise for, but as an obstacle to, self's union with the divine. From about the ninth to the twelfth centuries, the Islamic mystical tradition came firmly under the influence of Greek Neoplatonism which established an ideal world, parallel to this one, in which disembodied forms descend (and later ascend) from God, through humanity, to the inert substance of matter. This metaphysical system found its expression in Ibn al-'Arabi's theory of *wahdat al-wujud* ('oneness of being'), which seemed to relativise and in doing so, erase, the distinction between God and God's creation. On Indian soil, it found a counterpart in Vedantic monism, which similarly blurred the distinction between God and reality, Brahman and Atman. Such a theory, for Iqbal, was only one step away from a pantheistic belief in the divinity of everything, whose enervating effect on the mind was not dissimilar to that of Magianism.

Whilst Iqbal embraced philosophical Sufism in its life-affirming aspects, he distanced himself from those facets of the Indo-Persian Sufi tradition to which he attributed the Muslim community's historical decline. In a section of *Asrar-i Khudi* (*Secrets of Self*), which he later omitted because of the unhappy response it provoked amongst his audience, Iqbal attacked the poet Hafiz, 'the wine dealer, whose cup contains deadly poison', and the Hafizian/Persianate theme of mystical intoxication for its soporific effect over the Muslim mind.[73] For the Hafiz-inspired mystic, 'weakness becomes something beautiful...and renunciation brings satisfaction'. And although nations 'try to hide their indolence and inactivity...behind the façade of renunciation', they cannot prosper once they have denied the reality of a self committed to processes of struggle and upward striving.[74]

For Iqbal, then, the bifurcated cultural and geographical entities of East and West facilitate a world history based on the creative realisation of ego. And into this dichotomy are inserted the essentialising categories of 'race' and 'nationhood', which constitute a significant point of tension for his philosophical and political thought.

Islam and Race

The rise of nationalism in the late nineteenth and early twentieth centuries was tied up with the acceptability of the idea of race, even though no coherent or unified theoretical conception of the latter existed. Instead, the anthropological and scientific approximation of racial categories sat alongside 'folk' conceptions of racial difference which resided in the common language of popular discourse and which included a range of characteristics not always connected, even tangentially, to processes of scientific analysis.[75] A satisfactory definition of race, therefore, is pertinent not only to notions of scientific superiority and inferiority, but to the flexible economic, social and cultural conditions in which modern notions of racial difference arise. Racism is an ideology or assumption which interprets any form of collective physical, ethnic, cultural or religious difference as somehow innate, determining and unchangeable. Because understandings of racial difference preceded – and have outlasted – their heyday in the scientific (eugenic) and anthropological professions, we must employ a definition that is broad enough to encompass such seemingly innocuous words as 'culture', 'religion', 'demography', and so forth.

Because it contravenes the Islamic conception of an egalitarian community, Iqbal points to the idea of race as Islam's 'greatest enemy'. If existence is realised through unceasing movement and energy, then a nationality based on notions of racial or geographic exclusivity can only be a 'temporary phase in the enfoldment and the upbringing of life', and not its final destination.[76] Adopting the imperative tone of Keith Arthur's *The Problem of Race* (1931), Iqbal argues that Islam's historical mission is to 'deracialise' a humanity driven towards a future of 'internecine warfare' amongst belligerent and irreconcilable nation-states.[77] But, as I will show, this notion of 'deracialisation' is undermined by Iqbal's simultaneous reliance upon the categories of race. On one hand, Islam alone supplies the moral basis for a politics of inclusion, set against the divisive categories of race and nation which are carving up the world's peoples. Yet, on the other hand, Iqbal does not conceive of the relations between Islam and race-based nationalism in solely oppositional terms, and often employs racial categories as a basis for social belonging.

An example of this has already been given. Iqbal's interpretation of Islamic history posits the enervating influence of Magian culture over an otherwise vital Muslim core. Whilst this relationship provides an obvious justification for Iqbal's idealised notion of Islam, it is also instructive with regard to his views about race. Of Magianism, Iqbal says: 'It had its ruling concepts, its philosophical discussions, its truths and its errors. But when a culture begins to show signs of decay, its philosophical discussions, its concepts and its forms of religious experience become fixed and immobile.' In the same passage, he contrasts the stasis of the Magian inheritance to the essentially dynamic and fluid nature of Islam: 'There is definite evidence in the Qur'an itself to show that Islam aimed at opening up new channels not only of thought but of religious experience as well.'[78] Iqbal thus exploits the presumption of stasis inherent to methods of racial typology (that a culture can only be defined when its general characteristics become 'fixed and immobile') which, it is implied, is itself the product of cultural 'decay'. Because Islam is characterised by dynamism and change, it cannot succumb to the above-mentioned process of stagnation and presumably contains no qualities commensurable to that of static races.

This raises the question: how did Iqbal's notion of race cohere with his concept of Islam as a national 'idea' (amongst other nations) in the early twentieth century? I submit that his strategic use of the terms 'nation' and *'qaum'* to describe India's Muslim community reveals a reliance upon, and not just a subversion of, racial ideas for his own definition of Islam. This ambiguity is inherent in Iqbal's appropriation of the theme of nationality, and explains how a moral system so opposed to any recognition of class or race could itself be constituted as a *'qaum/* nation', in order to rival and outflank other nations.

Because, according to Iqbal, the divine ego is all-inclusive, and the human ego participates in the self-revealing of the former, it follows that all human beings are equal. When the Qur'an speaks about different human groups, then, it does so 'for purposes of identification only' and not to prescribe an eternal truth.[79] More pointedly, the Qur'an explicitly advocates the overcoming of petty racial and linguistic divisions as a step towards human peace and equality. An example of this is the Islamic form of association in prayer, in which all believers stand shoulder to shoulder, regardless of their individual status or class, suggesting what Islam can achieve for humanity at large.[80] However, Iqbal concedes that whilst Islam resists the ideology of race-based nationalism, 'it cannot be said that Islam is totally opposed to race'. Moreover:

> Its history shows that in reform it [Islam] relies mainly on its scheme for gradual deracialization and proceeds along the lines of least resistance... Considering the mightiness of the problem of race and the amount of time which the gradual deracialization of mankind must necessarily take, the attitude of Islam towards the position of race, i.e. stooping to conquer without itself becoming a race-making factor, is the only rational and workable attitude.[81]

Because Islam's moral message is universal and all-inclusive it must logically supersede the ideology of nationalism. But this will only occur when it has changed the national characteristics of the various races or groups it encounters into Islamic ones. The logic of race and nation is denied by the universalising claims of Islam only insofar as it will replace them with its own 'nationality' (*qaumiyyah*) in the long term.

Despite the teleological end point inferred by Iqbal's putting Islam to the task of 'deracialisation', his concept of Islam nonetheless reproduces that dualism which lies at the heart of European racial discourses. Modern racism was dualist insofar as it attempted to differentiate and categorise people who otherwise belonged to the one human family. Indeed, as George M. Fredrickson has pointed out, the force with which European racism disavows the 'other' and marks him/her/them as inferior is often developed in a 'context which presumes equality of some kind'.[82] In the nineteenth century, the anthropological endeavour to typologically categorise various human groups both particularised and differentiated the essential qualities which those groups were thought to possess. By the same token, Iqbal's argument for a universal, non-racial Islamic identity is somewhat paradoxically predicated upon the essentialisation of various religious and national groups. The influence of static races is read into Muslim history and comes, in turn, to represent the negative constraint from which Islam is liberated and made universally relevant to the contemporary age. On one hand, Islam dissolves difference and stands opposed to race-based theories of nationhood whilst on the other its 'stooping to conquer' involves a dialectical concession to the power and logic of race. In this regard, Magianism was not the only force that Islam had to contend with.

It is no small irony that Iqbal conceives of Islam as a force for 'deracialisation', to unite people of different ethnic and religious persuasions, whilst embracing a notion of history informed by the presumption of static racial and cultural types. In his famous presidential address to the All-India Muslim League at Allahabad in December 1930, Iqbal voices his uncertainty about the future of nationalism, which reflects a rare, though significant, ambivalence in his conception of Islam as a historical force:

> I do not know what will be the final fate of the national idea in the world of Islam. Whether Islam will assimilate and transform it, as it has assimilated and transformed... ideas expressive of different spirits, or allow a radical transformation of its own structure by the force of this idea, is hard to predict.[83]

Here, Iqbal concedes that the presumption of stasis inherent to generalisations about race and culture may indeed threaten to contain, or reshape, that dynamism which defines Islam. However, we should not assume that Iqbal places Islam and the 'national idea' at such opposite extremes that one will abolish the other. My argument, rather, is that he defers to the same Romantic notions (about the homogeneous unity of a 'culture', 'race' and 'people' animated by a particular 'idea') upon which modern racial and national identities are built. To put it another way, his attitude towards modern nationalism mirrors that ambivalence which attended the concept of race in the first half of the twentieth century.

The Fruition of Ambivalence

One cannot explain Iqbal's attitude towards race-based nationalism without considering the productive oppositions and tensions which animate, and underlie, his philosophical conception of Islam. Amongst such tensions, a site of conflict has already been identified in the self/other binary that underpins Iqbal's theory of *khudi*. Tension is seen, also, in the frisson that arises between his philosophical exhortation to free will, on the one hand, and notion of metaphysical predestination on the other, as commented upon by Alam Khundmiri.[84] That Iqbal places a high priority on the ego's creative freedom whilst simultaneously affirming its absorption into the divine being inevitably leads him to such oxymoronic statements as 'the searching ego affirms itself at the very moment of its self-negation'.[85] This, as Javed Majeed observed, shows a tension between the metaphysical assertion of ego's creative energy and striving, on one hand, and the theistic concept of union with an omnipotent God, on the other.[86] Such tension also underlines the extent to which ambivalence and contradiction constitute the forces by which Iqbal's theory is sustained.

Faiz Ahmed Faiz (another of Pakistan's most renowned and interesting postcolonial poets) observed as much, when he pointed out that Iqbal's commitment to a philosophy of constant struggle and 'man's fight against the hostile forces of nature' made the destination of an eternally languid hereafter seem 'entirely irrelevant' to his thought and poetry.[87] Faiz may have had the following verse from *Payam-i Mashriq* (*Message from the East*) in mind, in which the poet's striving for God becomes a destination of its own:

> I do not seek the beginning or the end;
> I am full of mystery and seek the realm of mysteries.
> Even if the face of truth were unveiled,
> I would still seek the same 'perhaps' and 'maybe'.[88]

So it is that a non-resolving path, which is likened to the encounter of the self with the other (God) in Iqbal's philosophy, supplies a normative ontological description of the human condition. In this sense, there is no 'end of history' because that would presuppose the end of human activity. Life's 'realm of mysteries' is its essence, and points to something crucial that lies both within and beyond the self–other dichotomy.

Such ambivalence no doubt problematises attempts to conflate Iqbal's thought with a national, or Islamist, political agenda. For instance, Iqbal's conflicted attitude towards modern nationalism cannot explain his posthumously acquired status as the 'architect' of Pakistan, a nation formally bound to imposed geographical borders and strained by regional and ethnic divisions. Indeed, I would go so far as to say that to cast Iqbal in the mould of a nationalist figure is to smother the complex and productive tensions which animated his work. Whilst modern Islamists and contemporary historiographers are quick to demonstrate Iqbal's 'fundamentalist' leanings, he certainly gave more credence to Islam's liberal-minded reformulation in light of modern knowledge than to theories about why Muslims should live under the sway of an authoritarian religious state.[89]

How, then, is Iqbal so easily put within a nationalist framework? I propose that Iqbal's ambivalence contains an aporia which is integral to the construction of modern national identities and which may just as easily work to undermine them. According to Homi Bhabha, the modern social imaginary which defines a homogeneous nation, culture or community presupposes an archaic form, or point of origin, the articulation of which 'emerges in the narrative ambivalence of disjunctive times and meanings'.[90] This 'narrative ambivalence' (as I understand it) provides for the essentialisation of a community whose myth of origin must always be recouped, organised and performed in the disjunctive, or incomplete, context of the present. What pushes this narrative forward, for Bhabha, is a 'supplementary space' which allows for the combination of the pedagogical and performative elements which go into the construction of a modern national identity. And just as this 'supplementary space' acts to bridge the archaising and contemporary aspects of modern nationalism, so too may it reveal their illegitimacy. That the contradictory force in Iqbal's thought cannot be reduced to one or another polarity is suggestive of this extra element, which Bhabha calls the 'third space'. It is there, in 'the realm of mysteries', about which Iqbal affirms: 'Even if the face of truth were unveiled, I would still seek the same "perhaps" and "maybe"'.

Because opposition, contradiction and interminable conflict are integral to Iqbal's thought, I do not see as much need to decry Iqbal's theoretical inconsistencies (what Iqbal Singh labelled his ideological 'self deception')[91] as to defend their germinative value for his intellectual project. Precisely because, in Iqbal's philosophy, the self engages in a dynamic movement committed to the absorption of obstacles, oppositions, tensions and conflicts, it must necessarily retain something of their ambiguities and erasures. To construe Iqbal's legacy is to remain as open to what his ambivalence enables as to what it cancels out. We have seen that the appropriation of national and Orientalist themes are decisive to Iqbal's notion of Islam as a force for the remaking of these categories. But this was just as important as a creative, liberatory impulse which refuses such categories for a higher calling.

CHAPTER 5

THE THEORY OF DIVINE SOVEREIGNTY

Introduction

Since the 1970s, few ideological movements have evoked as much consternation amongst scholars, policy analysts, political scientists and public intellectuals as those which come under the heading of 'Islamism'. This is no doubt due to circumstances in which Islamist parties have sought to influence state power in countries such as Iran, Egypt, Sudan, Algeria, Afghanistan and Pakistan, and is exacerbated by the threat of modern terrorism. By their insistence that Islam is both a religion and a system of government (*din wa dawlah*), Islamists challenge the theoretical 'separation of church and state' upon which the doctrine of political secularism is based. In particular, the Islamist theory of divine sovereignty (*hakimiyyah*), which asserts God's authority over the private lives of individuals and the public powers of the state, is seen to oppose the liberal, democratic presumption that autonomous, free-willed individuals are best placed to decide upon matters pertaining to the common good. Theocentrism, it appears, has no place in a modern liberal society.

Amongst intellectuals on the political right and left, including neo-conservative and liberal-Marxist thinkers, the Islamist view of political authority is often interpreted within behaviourist/social science models

THE THEORY OF DIVINE SOVEREIGNTY 149

as an expression of political totalitarianism. For instance, Francis Fukuyama opines that the characteristics of what he calls 'Islamofascism' bear comparison with those of European fascist movements in the early part of the twentieth century. In psychological terms, this includes a disillusionment felt by those who have undergone a rapid process of urbanisation and modernisation, which leads, in turn, to the construction of an unreal, mythical identity. At a broader political level, Fukuyama cites the failure of Muslim countries to embrace 'the global economy and lay the foundations for sustained development', which he regards to be symptomatic of Islam's 'problem with modernity'.[1] Extending this theme, the Syrian-German sociologist Bassam Tibi warns that because Islamism's proponents would wish to replace secularism with a divine order: 'the notion of *hakimiyya*/Allah's rule...is nothing less than a vision of totalitarian rule – exercised, shamefully enough, in the name of God'.[2] Such sentiments inform the dominant discourse towards Islamism of many governments in the West and across parts of Asia, Africa and the Middle East. (Although the flagrant human rights abuses perpetrated against Islamists and other dissidents by authoritarian regimes in these parts of the world seem to warrant less concern. Significant examples include the massacre at Hama of an estimated five to ten thousand members of the Muslim Brothers by the Syrian government of Hafiz al-Assad in February 1982, and frequent imprisonment and torture of Islamists by the governments of Egypt, Saudi Arabia and Israel, amongst others.)

As such, the depiction of Islamists as totalitarian and fascist appears to stem less from the results of their actions than from the secular conviction that religious faith is inherently irrational and should bear no moral authority over public life. Thus, for Bassam Tibi, Islamism is to be distinguished by its animus towards the West's 'cultural modernity', connoting a secular political disposition of rational individualism, which is the wellspring of modern liberal systems of governance.[3] Amongst some political philosophers, moreover, one encounters the assumption that 'religion' freights an obscurantist, monistic impulse which has resurfaced, since the Enlightenment, in such anti-rational movements as fascism and Nazism. To substantiate the claim that 'Modern politics is a chapter in the history of religion', John Gray describes the twentieth century's utopian projects (of Communism, Nazism, 'scientific racism' and so forth) as nothing less than a 'vehicle for religious myths' whose notions of apocalyptic redemption and the end of history were dressed up 'in secular terms'.[4] It would seem normal, from this perspective, to identify the worst totalitarian movements of the twentieth century with that ideological 'fundamentalism' which now seems to threaten secular states on the very basis of religious doctrine.

Yet just as this simplistic characterisation of the opposition between religious and secular forces in the modern world premises an all-too-generalised conception of the West, it also fails to account for the internal contradictions and ambivalences which mark Islamist ideas of modernity. After the rise of religious nationalisms amongst Hindus and Sikhs in India; Christians in Eastern Europe, the United States and Latin America; Buddhists in Sri Lanka; Jewish settlers in Israel; and Muslims across part of Asia, the Middle East and North Africa, it is widely accepted that a politicised religious ideology can make the same claims as secular nationalist theories over the powers of the modern state. This is hardly surprising given that modern institutions throughout the twentieth century have been the vehicle for numerous agendas of political and social reform. I am informed, on this point, by Talal Asad's observation that 'Islamism's preoccupation with state power is the result not of its commitment to nationalist ideas but of the modern nation state's enforced claim to constitute legitimate social identities and arenas'.[5] Nonetheless, what is often missing from the historical analysis of Islamist ideology is an attention to the internal complexities and divisions that nuance its relationship to the secular modern imagination. I will address this here, by showing how the Islamist theory of divine sovereignty negotiates modern categories on the political, aesthetic, and philosophical terrains.

Abul A'la Maududi and the Abstract Moral State

The theory of an Islamic state, with God as its sovereign, was first developed by the Indian revivalist Sayyid Abul A'la Maududi (1903–1979), to address the political insecurities faced by Indian Muslims in the first half of the twentieth century.[6] Born in Aurangabad in the

THE THEORY OF DIVINE SOVEREIGNTY   151

Deccan, Maududi was schooled to the age of fifteen, before deciding to pursue a career in journalism. Having moved to Delhi in 1918, he immersed himself in the Indian nationalist struggle against British rule and found work at the Congress-affiliated *Taj* newspaper in Judalpur. Thereafter, he wrote and edited for the newspapers *Muslim* (until 1923) and *al-Jami'ah* (from 1925 to 1928), which were both linked to the pro-nationalist Jami'at-i 'Ulama-i Hind. In this period, Maududi associated with members of the Deoband and Ahl-i Hadith movements, under whose inspiration he pursued a formal religious education following the *dars-i nizami* syllabus of Indian religious scholarship.

Like many anti-colonial Muslim thinkers in India during the 1920s, Maududi supported the Indian Caliphate movement, which opposed the break-up and division of the Ottoman Empire amongst Europe's colonial powers and raised hopes for a pan-Islamic confederacy of states to resist European imperialism across the Middle East and Central Asia. Though by the time of 'Abdul Mejid (who reigned from 1922 to 1924) the status of Caliph was a redundant and ceremonial office of no political importance, the call to reinstitute it as a figurehead for the Sunni Muslim world temporarily united India's regionally, linguistically and ethnically diverse Muslim communities. Whilst a Caliphate never existed in India, as it did for instance in Abbasid Iraq or Fatimid Egypt, its important symbolic function served to catalyse the political engagement of Indian Muslims. In its opposition to British imperial hegemony over the Middle East and South Asia, moreover, this movement fostered a sense of cooperation between Muslim organisations and other nationalist groups, such as India's National Congress Party.[7]

After Atatürk's dissolution of the Caliphate in 1924 and the movement's subsequent collapse, Maududi experienced a change of heart concerning the desirability of Indian nationalist aims. In the face of an increasingly assertive Hindu nationalist movement, and against the backdrop of rising communal tensions between Hindus and Muslims in northern India, Maududi became convinced that the secular democratic thrust of Congress party ideology would only guarantee the welfare of India's dominant religious community. For this reason, in 1928 he left journalism, severed his association with the pro-Congress Jami'at-i 'Ulama-i Hind, and turned his thoughts to the task of

Islamic revival. In the period leading up to the withdrawal of British authority, Maududi affirmed that the very survival of India's Muslims depended on them living by the practices and institutions of Islam, as he interpreted them. The theory of an Islamic state, with God as its sovereign, sought to realise this.

Maududi's notion of a religious state represents a concerted attempt to de-secularise the political domain and ground it in the language of morality. According to Maududi, God is lord and sovereign (*hakim*/حاكم) over every aspect of creation, which applies as much to the social and moral dimensions of human life as it does to the natural world. This is encompassed by his interpretation of the doctrine of *tawhid*, denoting divine unity and the unity which binds God and God's creation to humanity. As Maududi put it: 'The belief in the unity [*tawhid*] and the sovereignty of Allah is the foundation of the social and moral system propounded by the Prophets. It is the very starting point of the Islamic political philosophy.'[8] Because God's sovereignty is universal (*kainat-i hakimiyyah*), Maududi conceived of Islam as a political system (*nizam*) with the divine being as its architect and legislator.[9]

Human beings, as God's representatives or 'viceregents' (*khulafa*) on earth, are therefore obligated to fulfil the moral telos imputed by this notion of divine authority. Because a Muslim is someone who submits wholly to God and no other, one's practice of worship (*'ibadah*) must eschew that which comes between self and God's authority in either a spiritual or a material sense. In a letter to Chaudhari 'Ali Ahmad Khan, Maududi claimed that certain verses of the Qur'an clearly associate a definition of God as *rabb* (lord/nurturer) with the role of a *hakim*, or worldly ruler. 'If anyone acknowledges the sovereignty of a human being', explained Maududi, 'he lays claim to being Rabb and Allah', which is no different to the practice of 'association in *'ibadah*' (worship), or 'polytheism' (*shirk*).[10] God's status as *hakim* thus involves a dispensation to legislate over human affairs, ordering both the public laws of the state and the private life of the individual. For this reason, an Islamic state 'will be entitled to obedience in its capacity as a political agency set up to enforce the Divine law and only if it acts in that capacity. If the state disregards God's prerogative to authority, its jurisdiction will not be binding on its believer-citizens.'[11]

This totalising conception of God's authority is encompassed by Maududi's notion of Islam as *din*, denoting not only a 'religion' in the privatised, secular sense of the term, but a complete and all-encompassing 'way of life'.[12] Whilst the term *din* connotes different things within the nuanced revelational and semantic contexts of the Qur'an, it is interpreted by most commentators to denote the concept of 'religion': not as that which binds humanity to God (given by the term *religio*) but as an obligation of individual submission to God's will and favour (keeping in mind that the etymological sense of 'Islam' means 'surrender').[13] For Maududi, the term – whilst encompassing both meanings – owes less to this notion of surrender than to the political structures and cultural forms which are presupposed to guarantee a religious life. This was made explicit in a Friday sermon of 1938–39, in which Maududi explained that:

> Acknowledging that someone is your ruler to whom you must submit means that you have accepted his *Din*...*Din*, therefore, actually means the same thing as state and government; *Shari'ah* is the law of that state and government; and *'Ibadah* amounts to following and complying with that law.[14]

Yet, despite this linking of divine authority with worldly power, Islamists of the early part of the twentieth century felt an ambivalence towards modern nationalism which was reflected in Maududi's antipathy, during the early 1940s, for the idea of Pakistan. In fact, Maududi founded his political party, the Jama'at-i Islami, partly in opposition to the Muslim League's decision (in the Lahore Resolution of August 1941) to make the creation of Pakistan its political objective. Unlike the Indian *'ulama*, who endorsed secular political rule so long as it guaranteed freedom of religion and worship, Maududi rejected the idea of Pakistan on the grounds that the global Muslim community (*ummah*) is universal and cannot be reconciled with a singular, worldly construction of identity. Because Islam addresses the human condition in its entirety, it cannot be expressed as a national movement without submitting to the limiting ideological conditions (of demography, geography, ethnicity and language) which nationalism enforces.

However, after the events of 1947, the Jama'at-i Islami formed into two separate (Indian and Pakistani) wings, with Maududi and a number of its leading members relocating from India to Pakistan, where they sought to prepare the ground for an Islamic state. Pakistan, they reasoned, was now a country with a clear Muslim majority and would create an ideal base from which to engage in *da'wah* (proselytising activities) amongst the lay Muslim population. In his writings, Maududi addressed the secularised national elite and Westernised middle classes (rather than the rural peasantry) of India and Pakistan, amongst whom he wished to inspire an 'Islamic revolution' (*Islami inqilab*) similar to that undertaken by the Prophet and the early Muslim community.[15] Whilst this emphasis upon social revolution reflected Maududi's adoption of an insurgent Marxist-Leninist rhetoric, his was a pragmatic approach to political change which eschewed the formation of secret societies committed to acts of political violence.[16] Instead, Maududi expressed the need to raise the people's consciousness of Islam as a living social reality which, in time, would necessarily shape its institutions and processes of governance.

Whilst the Jama'at-i Islami would participate in Pakistan's often fragile democratic process through which they have until now garnered little electoral success, Maududi could not reconcile his vision for an Islamic state with the founding ideals of a secular democracy.[17] 'Islam', he declared, is the 'antithesis of secular Western-democracy' for the latter would usurp God's authority and reduce the very concept of sovereignty to a materialistic, ends-driven process of parliamentary decision-making and majoritarian politics.[18] Since secular democracies do not work within a moral framework, they cannot sustain the spiritual and ethical dimensions of human life. Moreover, democracy is conceived as an unlimited and unrestrainable process of governance. The very freedom it guarantees is, for Maududi, a freedom from, rather than for, morality.

As if to highlight this, Maududi likened what he saw as the West's amoral and atheistic culture to the 'period of ignorance' or *jahiliyyah* of pre-Islamic history, whose attractions he first decried amongst the urbanised middle classes of Delhi in the 1930s.[19] Amongst the early commentators on the Qur'an, the indigenous customs and practices of

Arabian society before the time of the Prophet were associated with a state of paganism anterior to the knowledge of God and the divine laws of Islam.[20] By linking the depredations of this historical period with the contemporary age, Maududi reconceptualised the *jahiliyyah* as an ontological condition transposable to any time or place, framing lives in which Islamic morals are ignored and untended. That the *jahiliyyah*, or 'age of ignorance', characterised the period called for a reform movement no less radical than that undertaken by the Prophet and the early Muslim community. Maududi thus counterposed a revived Islamic morality, with its accompanying social and political system, against the processes of cultural degeneration which were a product of both the moral weakness of Muslims and their attraction to Western ways.

Whilst Maududi claimed to reject Western cultural influences, Islamist designs for a moral state offer a strong comparison with liberal-universalist theories of political governance precisely because they reproduce the form, sentiment and rhetoric of modern draft constitutions and declarations. Maududi's *Human Rights in Islam*, for instance, establishes Islam as the original and best vehicle for a system of universal human rights. In doing so, it relegates Western human rights schemes to the non-universal values and cultural prejudices of the modern West. Yet, the fact that Maududi mimics a notion of universal rights – rather than arguing for the presence of opposed, non-universal standards – speaks to the comparable nature of his endeavour.[21]

By the same token, Maududi's proposal for an Islamic state contains the sort of ambiguity which is familiar to modern draft charters and declarations. For whilst he is clear on some features of a future Islamic society (such as the unequal political standing of non-Muslims and a domesticated role for women), Maududi's overall vision proffers little beyond an outline of the sorts of abstract principles to which the state must aspire.[22] This is seen, also, in Maududi's assertion that an Islamic constitution shall remain 'unwritten' until such time as the historical conditions required for an Islamic state to live up to its ideals have been properly realised.[23] This vague quality seemed to underlie his proposals (delivered to the Law College in Lahore on 18 February 1948) regarding the future constitution of Pakistan, in which he suggested:

> That sovereignty in Pakistan belongs to God Almighty alone and that the government of Pakistan shall administer the country as His agent.
>
> That the basic law of the land is the Islamic *Shari'ah* which has come to us through our Prophet (peace be upon him).
>
> That all those existing laws which may be in conflict with the *Shari'ah* shall in due course be repealed or brought into conformity with the basic law and no law which may in any way be repugnant to *Shari'ah* shall be enacted in the future.[24]

What is striking about these proposals is their lack of legislative detail, the absence of political content, beyond stating the symbolic necessity of establishing a moral/religious framework for government. This recalls the observation of a respected historian of Islam in South Asia, Wilfred Cantwell Smith (1916–2000), who noted that:

> ... the essential significance of the Islamic state does not lie in the content of the concept. For various Pakistanis it has diverse content, and for some it would seem to have no content at all. Being religious, it transcends precise apprehension as well as transcending objective actuality.[25]

Whilst Smith was not referring to Maududi's theory (of which he was critical) but to the very idea of Pakistan as a Muslim homeland, his observation that the Islamic state's significance 'does not lie in the content of the concept' captures something of the ambiguity attending Islamist designs for a religious state. This ambiguity does not merely describe the tension between the ideals of a religious society and how those ideals are to be borne out in practice. It underscores a deeper division: between the Islamic state as a legitimate authority (vested in the sovereignty of God), and the terrestrial acts by which such authority is brought into being.

This division has been commented upon by Jacques Derrida who, in the context of modern Western political theory, draws a distinction between the ideal of justice and the means by which it is actualised in law.[26] Justice, according to Derrida, can only exist through a process of enforcement, through the law, and despite the fact that justice precedes the law as its legitimising condition. Thus, there is a fundamental aporia at the heart of modern legal structures, between a notion of justice which legitimates the enforcement of laws whilst existing simultaneously in a position that is prior to them. This aporia, which inhabits the space between justice and its imperfect (therefore unjust) enforcement within the law, is useful to my analysis of Islamist theory.[27] The difference between justice and law can be likened to the distinction between a system which claims to uphold the principle of God's divine authority, on one hand, and the terms under which that authority is realised, on the other. In particular, this distinction underscores the silence of theorists such as Maududi concerning how the ideal and the real dimensions of an Islamic system are to be reconciled. I will now address this aporia, and the effort to overcome it, in the work of an important Egyptian Islamist of the twentieth century.

Sayyid Qutb and the Islamic Conception

Born in the village of Musa in the district of Asyut in 1906, Sayyid Qutb was sent to a traditional religious school (*kuttab*) where, by the age of ten, he had memorised the Qur'an.[28] At 13, he moved to Cairo, where he received a secular secondary school education which prepared him to enter in 1929 the Dar al-'Ulum Teachers' College. There, he studied modern methods of education, graduating as a Bachelor of Education in 1933. Qutb then found employment as an educational instructor at both the Dar al-'Ulum, and with the Egyptian Ministry of Education (from 1933 to 1939). During this period, he established himself as a leading social activist and forward-thinking poet, critic and man of letters in the intellectual circles of Cairo.

In his literary orientation, Qutb fell under the influence of the modernist Diwan school and one of its leading poets and theoreticians, 'Abbas Mahmud al-'Aqqad (1889–1964). In the intellectual quarrel between the traditionalists and modernists of contemporary Arabic poetry, the Diwan school advanced the argument that language cannot be contained in old forms and conventions. Rather, poetry must respond to the scientific, political, economic and social developments of the age. Influenced by such English writers as Wordsworth, Shelley, Byron, Burns, Hazlitt and Carlyle, the theorists of this movement argued that poetry must contain an organic formal and thematic unity as a subjective reflection of the human heart and sincere expression of the individual's place in the world. Poetry thus acts to bridge the real and the ideal, embodying the hopes and aspirations of a people or nation.[29] During the 1930s and 1940s, Qutb's approach to poetry was grounded in the supra-rational experiences of empathy, intuition and feeling. Thus he developed a highly subjective poetic style, whose themes of restlessness, mortality, unhappiness, the idealised beloved and so forth were intended as a reflection upon the turbulent and uncertain spiritual condition of the Egyptian nation.[30]

In the 1940s Qutb's interest in political affairs, and contributions to the Egyptian press, established him as an outspoken critic of official corruption and the royal government's collaboration with British imperial interests. It is believed, for instance, that his work as a political activist led to his being sent to America, in 1948, by the Ministry of Education, for the purpose of studying modern systems of education and training. Once in America, the Egyptian government hoped he would gain a positive impression of Western culture, education and society.[31] Yet Qutb's 21-month trip through New York, Washington DC, Greely in Colorado, San Francisco, Palo Alto and San Diego only enforced his impression of the country's materialism, racism and sexual permissiveness.[32] Registering his disdain towards such American phenomena as rampant industrial production, mass consumerism, the romantic mingling of men and women, and support for the Zionist occupation of Palestine, Qutb sharpened a dichotomous image of the relationship between Islam and the West.

This anti-Western sentiment had first emerged in his early writings on literature and nationalism, and was explicitly rendered in his first major work of social theory, *al-'Adalah al-Ijtima'iyyah fi al-Islam* (*Social Justice in Islam*). Published in 1949, and written before Qutb left for the United States, *Social Justice* sought to establish Islam as a rival social and political doctrine (*'aqidah*) to that of Western capitalism,

THE THEORY OF DIVINE SOVEREIGNTY 159

whilst commenting critically upon the political, social and economic policies of the Egyptian government during the interwar period.[33] After returning from the United States in 1950, Qutb's idea of Islam as an alternative social model to that of Western capitalism, socialism and Arab nationalism attracted him to the organisation of the Muslim Brothers (*al-Ikhwan al-Muslimun*), whom he officially joined in 1953, and for whom he became an important ideological advocate.

In any analysis of Qutb's late works, a connection between the trajectory of his intellectual development and the adverse political circumstances under which he spent his final years must be taken into account. After the Free Officers' Revolution in Egypt of 1952, the polemical tone of Qutb's writings on issues of social justice and reform saw him targeted by the regime of Gamal Abdul Nasser during its crackdown on the Muslim Brothers in 1954. By this stage, significant political differences had emerged between the Muslim Brothers and the ruling regime, accompanied by armed clashes, an attempt upon Nasser's life and accusations of a plot to attack civilian infrastructure.[34] Furthermore, Nasser had no time for Qutb's pointing to Islam as a higher form of 'nationality' (*qaumiyyah*), whose '*aqidah*' (belief) or 'programme of life' would claim to supersede Nasser's Arab nationalist agenda.[35] Qutb was accused of plotting against the state and sent to prison, where he remained for ten years. It was during this period of incarceration that he penned his most influential and radical works, notably his commentary on the Qur'an, *Fi-Zilal Al-Qur'an* (*In the Shade of the Qur'an*), sections of which were put into his final book, *Ma'alim Fi al-Tariq* (*Signposts on the Way*). *Signposts* was published in November 1964 and was used as evidence against Qutb for a conspiracy charge against the government which saw him re-arrested (after a brief release from prison), condemned to death and executed in 1966. An environment of suspicion, state censorship and torture seemed to intensify Qutb's dedication to a theocentric vision of political sovereignty which, from his prison cell, was marshalled against the Egyptian government and its cooperative citizenry.[36]

Whereas Maududi used the opposition between *hakimiyyah* and *jahiliyyah* to gauge the moral temper of an Islamic society, this distinction acquires a particular force in Qutb's late writings, which were no doubt influenced by Maududi's themes.[37] Although he never refers to Maududi directly, Qutb acknowledges the notion of *jahiliyyah* in the work of another Indian reformer and associate of Maududi, Abul Hasan 'Ali Nadwi's *Madha Khasira al-'Alam bi-Inhitat al-Muslimin* (*What has the World Lost with the Decline of the Muslims?*, published in Cairo in 1950). In this work, Nadwi argues that in contrast to the period of the rightly guided Caliphs, the Muslim world has since fallen into the grip of ignorance, which – like Maududi – he associates with Western history and culture.[38] In an appreciative introduction to Nadwi's work, Qutb explains that his concept of *jahiliyyah* demonstrates 'the difference between the spirit of Islam and the spirit of Materialism which prevailed before the advent of Islam and which has prevailed in the world ever since Islam lost its [position of] world leadership'.[39] Thus, for each of these thinkers, the gap between the theory and realisation of an Islamic society takes the form of eradicating the presence of *jahiliyyah* from contemporary Islam. Yet whilst Maududi identifies *jahiliyyah* with the culture of the modern West and, by association, with Westernised Muslims, for Qutb it has completely overtaken Muslim society and must therefore be fought from a position within society.[40] In Qutb's last and most radical work, *Signposts on the Way*, the struggle between Islam and *jahiliyyah* (which is also the struggle between a system that acknowledges God's natural sovereignty over the universe, on one hand, and an ideology which mistakenly allocates the right of sovereignty to human agents, on the other) acquires an urgent tone:

> If we look at the sources and foundations of modern living it becomes clear that the whole world is steeped in *jahiliyyah* and all the marvellous material comforts and high-level inventions do not diminish this ignorance. This *jahiliyyah* is based on rebellion against the authority [*sultan*] of God on earth, which is the most special aspect of divinity, namely: His sovereignty [*hakimiyyah*]. It [*jahiliyyah*] supports the sovereignty of men, and makes some lords over others.[41]

It is with *Signposts* in mind that various political commentators have drawn an association between Islamism and the desire for a totalitarian state founded upon acts of political violence.[42] In a radical idiom, Qutb called for the formation of a 'vanguard' (*al-tali'ah*) which would withdraw from society and seek moral purification as a prelude to acts of social change. A spur to such change lay in the conviction that God's sovereignty (*hakimiyyah*) cannot be reconciled with a system in which the power to distribute justice is relegated to a non-divine source. 'The nature of this religion, and its function,' posited Qutb, 'is to declare God's lordship (*rabbaniyyah*) over the world, and the freedom of humanity from all forms of servitude ('*ubudiyyah*), to anything other than God.'[43] The acknowledgment of God's sovereignty therefore entails the rejection of all human systems. Conceptually, the presence of *jahiliyyah* in Qutb's thought is co-extensive with the force of a political tyranny (*taghut*) whose depredations impinge on the individual at all times. Yet there is no clear evidence which substantiates the portrait of Qutb as a radical totalitarian and advocate for violence. Whilst he no doubt stipulated the need for a total social and political transformation, Qutb never condoned acts of violence. The phenomenon of Islamist violence in Egypt must instead be attributed to conflicts between some elements of the Muslim Brothers (and various splinter organisations) and the ruling regime, which played out irrespective of Qutb's ideology.

Regarding the above-mentioned aporia between the ideal and real dimensions of an Islamist system, Qutb's work is important for combining an Islamist ideology with aspects of the anti-rationalist, literary aesthetic theories he developed in the 1930s and 1940s as a poet and literary critic.[44] For just as Qutb asserted that the best poetry possessed an organic coherence and unity, by joining humanity's inner feelings to the external world, so did he come to identify the same qualities (of unity, harmony, coherence with the real, and so forth) with the literary, aesthetic and ideological aspects of the Qur'an. In his work on the Qur'an's formal expressive and artistic devices, *al-Taswir al-Fanni fi al-Qur'an* (*Aesthetic Portrayal in the Qur'an*), of 1945, Qutb writes the following:

> *Taswir* [the portrayal of a mental image or conception] is the preferred tool/element in the style of the Qur'an. By palpable

fancied images, it designates intellectual meanings, psychological states, perceptible events, visual scenes, human types and human nature. It then elevates these images it draws, and grants them living presence or regenerative movement; whereupon intellectual meanings become forms of motions, psychological states become tableaux or spectacles, human types become vivid and at hand, and human nature becomes visible and embodied. As for events, scenes, stories and sights, it renders them actual and immediate, pulsating with life and with movement.[45]

Here, the concept of unity and integration (of meaning and environment) which Qutb applied to secular poetry in the 1930s and 1940s is extended to the literary qualities of the sacred text. For, according to Qutb, the Qur'an creates an image (*taswir*) in the consciousness of the listener, which is also an experiential *representing* (in the active participle) of its spiritual message. And whilst this image is carried upon the formal devices of literary effect, atmosphere, expression, rhythm, word sounds and so forth, its true power resides in the extraordinary unity and coherence of feeling, experience, intuition, and imaginative representation which the text conveys. To add to this, one must note Qutb's childhood appreciation for the Qur'an, which he recalls with a sense of awe at the semantic power that the sacred text held over his young imagination.[46] With the Islamic *taswir* at the front of his mind, Qutb seeks to develop a palpable, hermeneutical experience in which the reader is drawn into the Qur'an's inner reality, above the level of its rational discursive understanding.

In *Khasais al-Tasawwur al-Islami wa Muqawwimatuhu* (*The Special Characteristics and Constituents of the Islamic Conception*, first published in 1962), this supra-rational, aesthetic appreciation for the Qur'an is tailored to the vision of an Islamic ideology. Here, Qutb describes an 'Islamic conception/perception/worldview' (*al-tasawwur al-Islami*) which is derived from the Qur'an, and which is the basis for a proper Islamic ideology.[47] In particular, Qutb's idea of an Islamic *tasawwur* connotes a mental representation, conceptualisation or depiction. It is the active participle of the verbal root ص-و-ر, denoting the Qur'an's way of representing/conceptualising/depicting a particular image or imaginative tableau. Thus, the Qur'an's immanence, which is distinguished by 'vigour, harmony, immediacy and inspiration', is experienced by the reader in both an aesthetic and moral sense.[48] The features of the Islamic *tasawwur*, for Qutb, are intended not simply to improve one's understanding of the Qur'an, but to 'equip the soul with emotions, perceptions and experiences similar to those that accompanied' its revelation. For such were the perceptions 'that prevailed in the life of Muslims as they received it [revelation] in the course of battles... as they experienced effort and sacrifice, fear and hope, weakness and strength, error and awakening.'[49]

This experiential approach to the sacred text (and to Islam on the whole) is evident in Qutb's critique of the over-reliance upon reason present in the modernist reforms of Muhammad 'Abduh (1849–1905). According to Qutb, 'Abduh's mistake was to submit his reforms to the intellectual premises of nineteenth-century Western thought, with its emphasis upon the efficacy of reason. To judge Islam according to a foreign system of ideas, he warned, is not to reform Islam but to create a new 'deviation' in place of the old.[50] To the degree that 'Abduh was confronted by the supremacy of European science, and a chorus of Orientalist scholars flouting a distorted picture of Islam, it is understandable that he succumbed to the dialogical parameters marked out by his interlocutors. Yet, whilst the reasoning mind (of 'Abduh's reforms) is a useful tool for knowing the world, Qutb is adamant that 'revelation is greater and more comprehensive than the other [reason], and... was destined to be the source to which the other refers, the balance on which it weighs its concepts and ideas'.[51] Because the content of revelation is divine, and therefore perfect, a reason necessarily subjected to the elisions of the human mind cannot be given equal status to revelation in its quest for truth. Thus, Qutb advocates the need to replace reason-based interpretations of the Qur'an with an 'emotive logic' (*al-mantiq al-wijdani*), which may appeal more directly to the reader's sense of intuition, feeling, sentiment and emotion.[52] Above all, the Qur'an's literary qualities substantiate a worldview based upon the realisation of human feeling and activity, in a practical, this-worldly context.

For Qutb, then, the tension between the ideal and real aspects of an Islamic system is resolved by a notion of praxis based upon an ontological experiencing of the sacred text. A case in point would be Islam's 'realism', which Qutb identifies as one of the main components of the Islamic conception. Because 'the divine reality is a positive and effective reality in our actual existence, and its characteristics and attributes are reflected in its real impact on our actual existence', Islam cannot be defined according to abstract mental and theoretical concepts.[53] This builds upon Qutb's assertion, in *Social Justice in Islam*, that the reality (*waqi'i*) of Islam conforms to truth (*haqiqah*), and cannot be associated with that of a particular people or nation.[54] For this reason, experience is both a criterion for ascertaining the ontological truth of the Qur'an, and a basis for practical action in establishing an Islamic society. Whilst Qutb's prison writings (his commentary on the Qur'an) approach the text with a view to uncover its ideological foundations – in order to fashion a message applicable to solving the social dilemmas of Arab society – they also evoke the theme of a Qur'anic *tasawwur*, or 'conception', by which Islam becomes a force for the moral transformation of human life. Thus for Qutb, the intellectual rationalisation of the Qur'an's spiritual and moral authority is of secondary importance to the practical experience of its lived reality.[55]

Moreover, the notion of an Islamic *tasawwur* substantiates Qutb's rejection of the epistemology of reason in Islamic philosophical and theological discourses. According to Qutb, the advent of Muslim philosophising represented an attempt to mix Islamic ideas with the incompatible thought systems of Greek (Aristotelian and Neoplatonic) philosophy. This is identified in the works of al-Farabi (d.950), Ibn Sina (d.1037) and Ibn Rushd (d.1198), who are accused of distorting Islam's conception of the divine nature (and its meaning for life) with theories borrowed from Greek materialism and atheism.[56] To complement his critique of modern rationalism, then, Qutb repudiates reason's influence over the intellectual heritage of Islam and, in particular, its historical role in the development of Muslim philosophy and theology.[57] Reason's sole value is thus to understand and implement an Islamic social system, without downgrading it as an emotive force in the interior lives of individuals.

More interestingly, Qutb's attack on reason extends to the fallible biases by which it conceives religion as an artificial, man-made 'culture' or 'philosophy'. Because reason is socially and historically constructed, Qutb seems to say, we must not accept its claim to the status of a universally self-evident, or transparent, category. 'Divinity', which is the first characteristic and the source of the Islamic conception, must therefore be distinguished from 'the philosophical concepts established by the human mind concerning the nature of God, the universe, and mankind, and the relations between them'.[58] This is because Islam is not a 'theory' (*nazariyyah*) that works on assumptions, but a 'system' (*minhaj*) that operates on actuality, which is to say that it cannot be contained by the rules from which man-made ideas and institutions are built.[59] Because the ideal aspects of an Islamic system correspond with its lived reality, Qutb argues that Islam is not simply a body of knowledge to be contained or attested to in verbal formulae, but is also, and more importantly, a practical and realistic system of life whose true purpose can only be understood through feeling and activity.

However, Qutb's effort to overcome the dichotomy between the theoretical and real dimensions of an Islamic system cannot be separated from the same Western ideological influences he otherwise criticised. For, as I have pointed out, his description of the Qur'anic art (*fann*) or portrayal (*taswir*) no doubt defers to the secular aesthetic attitudes and theories which he acquired as a literary critic in the 1930s. Moreover, the notion of an Islamic worldview (*tasawwur*), denoting an idea, concept or something formed by the human mind, jangles discordantly against the claim that divinity (*uluhiyyah*) and the divine nature (*rabbaniyyah*) are the main features of Islam. Because, as Hamid Algar argues, the divine nature cannot correspond with a fallible mental construct, Qutb seems less concerned with the nature of religious truth, or experience per se, than with 'the making of an Islamic ideology'.[60] This conceptual paradox (of an ideology which denies its own status) suggests that the epistemic conditions of modern thought cast a wider net than Qutb himself may have acknowledged.

A reliance upon modern ideas is also reflected in Qutb's admiration for the contemporary French physician and pro-Fascist political theorist, Alexis Carrel (1873–1944), whom he described as 'one of the greatest scholars of the twentieth century'.[61] In particular, Qutb was influenced by Carrel's critique of Western civilisation in *L'homme, cet inconnu* (*Man, The Unknown*, 1935) which he read, in its Arabic translation, in 1959 or 1960.

A Nobel Prize-winning physicist, eugenicist and supporter of the Nazi-dominated Vichy government in France, Carrel argued that modern scientific and industrial societies have undermined the spiritual and religious dimensions of human life. Particularly, the tendency of modern scientific thought to grasp for abstract concepts and ideas has ignored the fundamental aspiration of human beings to the immediate and non-utilitarian experiences of beauty, pleasure, sorrow and so forth. By the same token, Western democratic theories have violated the natural biological distinctions which gave rise to the inequalities between men and women, the white and non-white races, and upper and lower classes. For this reason, the 'white races' of Europe and the United States must strengthen their best elements through the new science of eugenics, whilst using 'euthenasic institutions' for the criminal classes and criminally insane. To bring this about, Carrel called for the institution of a new 'science of man', to be spearheaded by a small forward-looking intellectual aristocracy who are sworn to a monastic regimen of social segregation, self-discipline, education and contemplation.[62] Such men, Carrel believed, would be able to diagnose and thus remedy the social, economic, physiological and psychological ills of the modern world.

Whilst Qutb ignores Carrel's argument for the inherent inequality of human classes and races, he is certainly influenced by the latter's vision of an industrialised society which cannot fulfil the biological and spiritual needs of human beings, and whose decline into 'barbarism' (as Carrel put it) must be rectified by a trained vanguard, acting from within society.[63] Moreover, a notable element of Carrel's ideology from which Qutb draws obvious inspiration is his hypothesis concerning the as yet unrealised or 'unknown' qualities of human nature, which hold great potential for human improvement. In *The Special Characteristics and Constituents of the Islamic Conception*, Qutb cites a passage from Carrel's book which alludes to the unexplored dimensions of human life. As Carrel put it:

> mankind has made a gigantic effort to know itself. Although we possess the treasure of the observations accumulated by the

scientists, the philosophers, the poets, and the great mystics of all times, we have grasped only certain aspects of ourselves. We do not apprehend man as a whole. We know him as composed of distinct parts. And even these parts are created by our methods. Each one of us is made up of a procession of phantoms, in the midst of which strides an unknowable reality.[64]

For Carrel, these 'phantoms' include a present state of ignorance about the complex physiological, cellular and biological workings of the body, the relationship of these to consciousness, and the entire spiritual makeup of the human soul. Moreover, this poorly developed state of self-awareness is attributed, by Carrel, to three factors: firstly, the legacy of our human ancestors (their practices and methods of survival); secondly, the complexity of human nature; and thirdly, the determining structure of the human mind.[65] In Qutb's estimation, the most important of these explanations is the third, wherein, as Carrel argues, our mind's 'delight in contemplating simple facts' has reduced the complex phenomena of human life to flat mental abstractions.[66] According to this argument, the dominant tendencies of the rational mind, with its penchant for simple formula and systematisation, have distorted our conception of human life. Clearly, this 'unknown' element is crucial for validating Qutb's attack on rational formalisation, and his alternative of an Islamic conception.

Nonetheless, Qutb's anti-theoretical orientation only exacerbates the aporia of an Islamic state based on God's sovereignty. For just as Maududi lacked the details of an Islamic constitution, so Qutb's vision of an Islamic society failed to describe that vision/society in any detail.[67] In this sense, the idea of an Islamic state, or theme of divine sovereignty, compares to Derrida's appraisal of the idea of justice. It cannot be present in and of itself but is always *'avenir'* (to use Derrida's term), or still 'to come'.[68] Of course there were differences in emphasis and imperative between Maududi's and Qutb's theories. Maududi, no doubt, accepted ideological compromises and adaptations in the hope of realising an Islamic state one day, as when he relocated to Pakistan, and became embroiled in the wider political issues of that country.[69] The circumstances of Qutb's imprisonment, torture and death sentence, on the other hand, made him less amenable to compromise, and brought the distinction between theory and praxis to a head. For Qutb, as for the numerous Islamists to follow his inspiration, there is a sense in which the desire to describe and so quantify the Islamic state would undermine it, by reducing it to the status of a man-made system or idea.

This underlines what I consider to be the primary theoretical dilemma of Islamism. That is, how can one seek to implement a transcendental religious and moral order when the means of its construction cannot claim a transcendent origin or value? This refers us to the above-mentioned distinction between the real and the ideal dimensions of an Islamic state, and the efforts of Maududi and Qutb to overcome it. Furthermore, the Islamist theory of divine sovereignty addresses a quandary which is now the challenge of much modern (and postmodern) theology, and which follows from the question raised above. That is, how does one not exchange one's religion for the *logos* (or idol) of modernity (bound up in the theory of an Islamic state, or a human conception of the sovereignty of God) when they have become interchangeable? What occurs when conceptions of religious truth, of a transcendental order, are transferred to the mundane realities of worldly power?

The Etatisation of Shariʿah Law

In modern times, the notion that Islamic law represents a simple yet comprehensive system of rules for the ordering of a modern state has served to replace its diverse legal traditions and jurisprudential models with a reified conception of the sacred law. As Maududi put it, *shariʿah* law represents 'a complete scheme of life and an all-embracing social order in which nothing is superfluous and nothing is lacking'. Comparing its many parts to the organisms of the human body, Maududi upheld *shariʿah* law as a perfect social and cultural expression of Islam, to be implemented in its entirety.[70] Yet this notion of a complete (organically whole) religious and political system has little precedent in traditional theories of Islamic law or statecraft. Whilst the divine law was often categorised by pre-modern thinkers in immutable terms, and formed a moral reservoir from which religious scholars could advise secular authorities, it was never a complete blueprint for the ordering of government. It is telling that when he advocated *shari'ah* as a complete system of law, Maududi ignored the interpretive prerogative of India's Hanafi *'ulama*, choosing, instead, to engage in the ad hoc application of divine tenets to contemporary social and political issues.[71]

However, Maududi's systematic conception of the divine law was not without precedent, for it built upon earlier attempts to incorporate *shari'ah* law into the juridical structures of the colonial and postcolonial nation-state. This began with the European-inspired *majallah* code (from 1869) of the Ottoman Empire in the second half of the nineteenth century, in which some aspects of *shari'ah* law pertaining to the Hanafi school of jurisprudence were codified, alongside other secular decrees and principles, as the laws of the state.[72] Reforms in the administration of Islamic law were then pushed forward by the modernist theologian, Muhammad 'Abduh (d.1905), who sought to extend Islamic jurisprudence (*fiqh*) in the application of law through a revival of the use of *ijtihad* (independent scholarly reasoning) and by allocating greater weight to the consideration of public interest (*maslahah*).[73] During the same period, European colonial regimes furthered the etatisation of religious/sectarian doctrines and laws by incorporating them into their systems of justice, which limited the *shari'ah*'s jurisdiction to matters of 'private' religious, personal and family law. By codifying certain aspects of Islamic law within the legal paradigms available to the colonial states of the nineteenth and twentieth centuries, modernist reformers replaced the flexible and evolving features of the Islamic legal tradition with the kind of determinacy that one encounters in a civil law code.[74]

In British India, for instance, a system of 'Anglo-Muhammadan law' was established in the colonial courts (initially, by the British East India Company) whose service to the centralisation and bureaucratisation of the colonial state distanced it from established practices of jurisprudence (*fiqh*) amongst Indian Muslims.[75] Whilst the new system claimed to protect venerated traditions of indigenous law, it nonetheless had the effect of reifying the *shari'ah* within the canonical certainties of a modern juridical system.[76] An example of this is seen in the new status given to *fatawa* (sing. *fatwa*) in government courts. In the past a *fatwa*, or legal opinion, was a non-binding judgment or sanctioned course of action, issued by a jurist in response to a specific query or problem. *Shari'ah* law, in its broad conception, was built upon the evolution of varying juristic opinions, all of which were extrapolated from religious precepts contained in Islam's foundational texts (of the Qur'an and prophetic *Sunnah*). Under the new system, however, such legal opinions were applied to situations in which a verdict of guilt or innocence was shackled to a structure of case law and legislated as a binding legal sentence. The concretisation of such laws into a 'personal code' (covering such 'private' issues as marriage, divorce, inheritance and so forth), after the events of the 1857 Indian uprising, secured a place for British sovereignty on the one hand whilst contributing to the formation of a modern Muslim legal identity on the other.[77]

After the gradual formation of a fixed conception of Islamic law during the latter part of the nineteenth and first half of the twentieth centuries, it was easy for certain postcolonial states to manipulate this theme in their quest for political legitimacy. This is evident in the programme of political Islamisation initiated by the regimes of Muhammad Zia ul-Haq in Pakistan (1977–1988) and of Ja'afar Muhammad al-Numeiri in the Sudan (1980–1985), in which Islamic laws were crudely extended to the public sphere through the implementation of *hudud* (a juristic term denoting the penalty for acts that are proscribed by the Qur'an) punishments for such crimes as theft, adultery and so forth. In such cases, appeals to *shari'ah* law did not augur a meaningful programme of social and structural reforms, but were used as a political slogan in the manipulation of populist hopes for such things as social justice and equality.[78]

Moreover, appeals to the implementation of *shari'ah* law have recently found a foothold in non-political social arenas through their penetration of such forums as the internet and satellite television. Yet the fact that *shari'ah* law lacks any detail with regard to social and political policy – beyond personal strictures, designated family laws and public punishments – guarantees its survival as an abstract model which pertains to the moral and symbolic, rather than the institutional, outline of an Islamic state. For this reason, the claim amongst Islamists to enact an Islamic system is always cast as an ethical endeavour, enjoining true Muslims to return to the moral imperatives located in Islam's sacred sources and the example of the Prophet. However, the return to Islam's founding principles becomes a difficult task when the means to achieve this (in the example of a religious state) makes its own demands on the way such principles are approached.

Contesting the Islamic State

A significant and interesting critique of Maududi's ideology was raised by a prominent member of the Indian *'ulama*, Wahiduddin Khan (b.1925). Born in a village near the town of Azamgarh in northern India, Khan received a traditional religious education at the Madrassat al-Islam in Sarai Mir, where he graduated as an *'alim* in 1944.[79] Thereafter, he became disillusioned with the traditional religious education of his upbringing, which did not seem to meet the challenges of modern life. After experimenting briefly with agnosticism, Khan rediscovered Islam through the comprehensive worldview and vision of social change espoused by Maududi. In 1949, he joined the Indian wing of the Jama'at-i Islami, the Jama'at-i Islami Hind, of which he became an important spokesperson. Yet, after a decade, Khan became convinced of the impractical nature of the Jama'at's agenda to establish an Islamic state, which in his opinion did not suit the needs of Indian Muslims. Having studied Maududi's writings in depth, Khan concluded that his ideology purveyed a fundamental misunderstanding of the nature of Islam and its role in the world. In 1962, he resigned from the Jama'at-i Islami Hind, and for a time joined the Tablighi Jama'at, with which he eventually developed ideological differences. Khan has since been an independent voice of intellectual reform both for Indian Muslims and for other Muslim communities throughout the world.

Taking issue with Maududi's definition of such terms as *din* and *tawhid*, Khan identifies an 'interpretive error' in Maududi's conception of Islam, which distorted the human–divine relationship and social vision derived from it.[80] Maududi is not wrong, Khan argues, to conceive of Islam as a system (*nizam*) which of itself encompasses and informs different areas of life; but this element is only an external manifestation of the true *din* and is not its essential spirit. Rather, Maududi's conceptualisation of the Islamic *din* foregrounds the political and social aspects of human life without giving proper attention to its moral and spiritual dimensions.[81] In his explanation of this, Khan accuses Maududi of misunderstanding the nature of God's divinity as connoted by the terms *ilah* (God) and *rabb* (lord, nurturer), which, in turn, warps his entire conception of worship (*'ibadah*) in Islam. Because God is conceived in terms of divine power (*iqtidar*), the concept of worship in Maududi's thought denotes a state of submission coded by this relationship of political authority. But *'ibadah* (worship), cautioned Khan, does not merely refer to an individual's entering a social system of command and obedience that humans only have to submit to in order to guarantee their salvation. Rather, the true reality of *'ibadah* is to enter a 'loving and humble relationship' with God, which the Qur'an characterised as one of 'intense love' (*hubb shadid*).[82] By insisting that Islam is first and foremost a 'system of life' (*nizam-i hayat*) or social system, Maududi instrumentalises notions of submission, faith and so forth. By moulding Islam into a socio-political ideology or movement, he relegates the spiritual values of worship and love to the peripheries.[83]

To understand the salience of Maududi and Qutb's thought, Khan points to a 'defeatist mentality' which accompanied the decline of Islam's traditional institutions in the pre-modern period, and which reached its nadir during the colonial period. When Muslims lost their cultural self-confidence, argues Khan, they developed a siege mentality which has resulted in the differential construction of the European other as an oppressor or foe. Hostility and suspicion towards non-Muslims then became the premise for the way Muslims engaged with the outside world, warping their moral sensibilities and alienating them from the peaceful content of Islam. It is this alienation, according to Khan, which has led to the 'political interpretation' of Maududi's Islamism, in which religion is transformed into a system of state, and the status of worship is equated with fulfilling a vision of political power.[84]

Here, Khan mobilises the selfsame theory of historical decline commonly employed by Islamists (that modern Muslims have been progressively alienated from the content of their religion), but he does so in order to delegitimise the theory of an Islamic state. Were Muslims to find themselves in a position of power in which their sacred laws could be implemented into political forms through peaceful means, then Khan is adamant that *shari'ah* law 'would require them to do exactly that'. But because the Muslims of India are not in any such position, it is not their duty to establish an Islamic political system, 'nor are they required to set in motion political initiatives calculated to create opportunities to do so'. Because political power is a 'gift' from God (and 'politics is only a relative and not a real part of Islam'), it cannot be counted as a divine prerogative when the real struggle before Muslims is to inculcate an 'Islamic character' (of piety and moral action) in their innermost selves.[85] For this reason, Khan makes a clear separation between the activity of *da'wah* (an 'invitation' or 'calling' to faith) whose goal is the Islamisation of the individual, and that political activism which seeks to influence or co-opt the powers of the state. The moral content of Islam is not an expedient element in the creation of an Islamic state and is endangered by any theory which establishes such a state as its ultimate goal.

What interests me about Khan's argument is that it works within the parameters of an Islamist discourse, as when he develops a comparable notion of activism (*da'wah*) by which the Muslim community may be brought closer to the essential spirit and teachings of Islam. And yet, Khan implicitly links Maududi's conception of Islam to the secular political themes he otherwise intended to reject. This occurs when Maududi makes of Islam a state 'system' (*nizam*) without any regard to its force for spiritual and moral reform, and the internal experiences of love, mercy, and so forth, which conventionally animate the human–divine relationship. Khan's critique of the idea of an Islamic state thus demonstrates that the conjoining of politics and religion in Islamist discourses is neither guaranteed nor above contestation. Moreover, secular categories are reworked, by Islamists and their opponents, within competing claims over Islamic tradition.

This does not indicate a failure to detach Islam from the premises of political secularism, but points to a complex negotiation of these categories. For instance, Khan's critique touches upon the above-mentioned aporia, which Derrida attributes to modern systems of legal authority. Because God's divinity is recognised through the experiences of faith (*iman*) and worship (*'ibadah*), these are the natural preconditions for an Islamic society. However, the veracities of faith and worship partake of a transcendent relationship, which is to say that the external authority of an Islamic state can neither confirm nor guarantee their presence. Like justice in its relation to the institutionalisation and enforcement of law, the sovereignty of God cannot be guaranteed through a man-made system, which Maududi's theory of an Islamic state and Qutb's idea of an Islamic conception (*tasawwur*) in fact must be. Like the ideal of justice as discussed by Derrida, the notion of divine sovereignty cannot be present in itself but is always deferred to the non-temporal horizon of human prayers, ideals and expectations. It is always yet to come.

Conclusion

The Islamist attempt to ground political theory in the domain of morality – under the arch of God's sovereignty (*hakimiyyah*) – represents an appeal to a different or alternate type of modernity. Sayyid Qutb's notion of divine sovereignty, for instance, was presented as an alternative to the materialism, corruption and abuse of power which he associated with the secular dictatorship of Nasser's Egypt. However, Qutb's attempt to overcome the perennial distinction between the real and ideal dimensions of an Islamic system drew on his own reservoir of poetic and literary aesthetic theory. It is therefore less accurate to say that Qutb failed to protect Islam from the premises of Western aesthetic, social and political theories, than it is to say that his conception of Islam is reconstituted within these categories.

Furthermore, the theory of an Islamic state may not always determine doctrines of political dictatorship and violence. Whilst Islamist theories have certainly been interpreted in repressive ways and cited to justify acts of violent insurgency (and may continue to be so), one must avoid the tendency to conflate a particular idea with a pattern of historical interpretations, doctrines and practices as though the connection were somehow natural. Whilst some Islamist thinkers attempt to foreclose questions of interpretation and intellectual pluralism (as when Qutb denies the 'theoretical' nature of his reforms), I submit that – albeit unintentionally – they are expanding the parameters for an appraisal of contemporary Islam.[86] To put it another way, the tension between the ideal and the real dimensions of an Islamic state has, in the case of Wahiduddin Khan, encouraged the re-evaluation of what constitutes an Islamic system and the role of human beings within it. Contrary to the notion that Islamists reject modernity, secular categories and understandings form the epistemological ground from which they seek to reclaim Islam as a moral reality.

CHAPTER 6

MAUDUDI AND THE GENDERING OF MUSLIM IDENTITY

The social role which the Western woman is being made to play, is not in reality 'emancipation' but perversion and enslavement and as a result of false and misleading propaganda, women are trying to 'de-womanize' themselves. They think it is degrading to fill their natural place in life and to perform the tasks assigned to them by nature. Instead they seek honour in manly pursuits. Western civilization has proved to be very cruel to its womanhood. On one hand, it wants women to bear the burden of nature single-handed and on the other hand, this civilization calls her out to perform the multifarious duties of a man. Thus she has been squarely placed between two grindstones. Moreover this same propaganda has enticed women in such a way that they feel they must make themselves more and more attractive to the opposite sex and thus outrage their decency... They have been turned into play-things in male hands.

Abul A'la Maududi, in a letter to Margaret Marcus, aka Maryam Jamila, 1 April 1961[1]

Introduction: The Subject of Experience

This chapter will analyse the place of women in the thought of the influential twentieth-century Islamist, Sayyid Abul A'la Maududi

(1903–1979). Maududi's theory of an Islamic social system, I argue, relies upon a notion of female shame, which is encompassed by the term *haya*. Yet, Maududi's thought, like that of other Islamists during the first half of the twentieth century, was so dependent upon the example of women in the West that his reforms cannot be separated from the contemporary history of Western sexual politics and morality. By drawing upon the recent feminist analysis of gender, this chapter will critically examine Maududi's conceptualisation of female shame and his essentialisation of the role of women in general.

The excerpt given above is from a letter sent by Maududi to Margaret Marcus (b. 1934), a young woman living in the United States who had recently converted to Islam. Styling herself as an advocate for Muslim causes, Marcus addressed a range of concerns focusing on the need to separate so-called Islamic values and ethics from those which exist in Western societies. As one born and raised in the United States, she conveyed her dislike of the materialism of contemporary Western society and defended the clear moral and ideological alternative she had found in Islam. Her letters contain all the verve and excitement of one whose mind had been opened to a new spiritual and intellectual orientation and her observations dovetailed with Maududi's in ways which surprised the latter and encouraged both correspondents. Their letters cover a period of almost one and a half years (from December 1960 to May 1962) until Marcus (or Maryam Jamila, as she became known after her formal conversion and as I will henceforth refer to her) left the United States to live in Pakistan. There, she hoped to live a life closer to Islamic values.

In her letters to Maududi, Jamila declares that contemporary European fashions and styles 'do all they can to make the modern Western woman look like a street walker', and are 'designed exclusively for commercialized sex'.[2] Such fashions, she asserts, are a morally corrosive feature of the ideology of capitalism by which many Westernised Muslims are also enthralled. In particular, Jamila's fondness for Islam as a way of life justifies her rejection of the supposed 'freedoms' which monopolise the lives of Western women:

> One of the very first things I did after accepting Islam and saying my prayers was to lengthen all my skirts. My relatives were

most surprised to see me wearing skirts almost to the ankles when all the women are wearing their dresses above the knee. There is loud propaganda in American popular magazines about the increasing 'emancipation' of women in Muslim lands due to the impact, of course, of Western education and the mass-media. Although I believe that every woman should be educated for the fullest use of her intellectual capacities, I certainly question the advantages of taking women out of the home (particularly those with young children) to compete in business offices and factories with men and substituting nurseries and kindergartens for a home upbringing. This is exactly what has happened in Soviet Russia and Communist China where the so-called 'emancipation' of women is being deliberately used by the rulers to destroy the family. To a lesser degree, a similar situation exists in my country.[3]

And from a later work which purports to evaluate Western feminism from an Islamic viewpoint:

Feminism is an unnatural, artificial and abnormal product of contemporary social disintegration which in turn is the inevitable result of the rejection of all transcendental, absolute moral and spiritual values.[4]

These passages touch upon many of the themes which were to dominate Jamila's career as a spokesperson for Islamic revivalism. They include her personal stake in rejecting Western society's secular, 'materialistic' worldview, and her dissatisfaction with its detrimental influence on the Muslim world. Notably, Jamila's narrative links her conversion to her rejection of a stereotyped Western femininity evoked by demeaning women's fashions and broken (working women's) families. Yet her rejection of what she assumes to be Western norms and values problematises attempts to locate, and so theorise, the autonomy of Muslim women. In particular, her hostility towards the changing status of American women confounds assumptions that the theoretically autonomous, self-creating woman should be attracted to, and not repelled by, the then emerging liberal feminist tenets of women's emancipation, sexual liberation and so forth.

To cite another example, secular liberal intellectuals often presume that Islam is inherently hostile to women's natural rights and freedoms. Commenting on the status of Arab women in modern interpretations of Islamic law in the Middle East, the entry on 'woman' (*al-Mar'a*), by N. Tomiche, in the *Encyclopaedia of Islam* offers the following:

> [The] sacralising of her inferiority is perhaps the main reason for the problems of the Arab woman. She is regarded from an ontological point of view as a second-rate human being, coming after man in the order of God's creatures. She submits to her duties, is limited in her powers and is mistress neither of her own development nor of her own body. Everything about her is considered taboo.[5]

Pointing to the injustices perpetrated against women by modern Muslim legal systems in the Arab world, Tomiche rightly criticises those laws which have prevented women from assuming rational control over their intellectual and physical development. Yet the attribution of an 'ontological point of view' concerning Arab women is deeply problematic. For whilst aspects of Islamic law may discriminate against women, questions nonetheless arise about the agency of those women who not only submit to, but consciously endorse its interpretations and practices. It is not my intention to contest the generalisation that women hold a lowly position under Arab Islamic legal systems but to suggest that even in cases where this seems self-evident, one cannot always assume the denigration of such women's autonomy, particularly in cases where they stake their self-development on the tradition in question.

Furthermore, the conventional sociological analysis of women's participation in contemporary religious movements tends to ignore the autonomy of such women except when it takes the form of 'resistance' to patriarchal power and other assumedly repressive social forces. This is observed by Saba Mahmoud, who calls for a critical rethinking of the search for women's agency and 'resistance' to patriarchy on the grounds that such notions are inappropriate to many real women's lives. According to Mahmoud, the sociological attribution of 'autonomy' carries teleological assumptions – contiguous to Western feminist ideas about individual liberty and freedom – which cannot account for the social conditions and bodily rituals which give meaning to the lives of religiously conservative women.[6] Following Mahmoud's argument, one might ask: what are we to make of those contemporary Islamist women who endorse a model of piety which all but forbids them access to the public sphere while insisting that Islam is a quintessentially non-discriminatory and non-sexist religion? Is it feasible to label such women the victims of a type of 'false consciousness' on the assumption that if they knew better, they would resist that ideology which seems, ostensibly, to enforce their passivity?

Maryam Jamila's personal adoption of an Islamic view of womanhood fundamentally opposed to, and corrective of, the 'unnatural' lifestyle of the West does not match the conception of Muslim women as passive and oppressed. Whilst the decision to lengthen her skirts spoke to her ideological conservatism, Jamila's conversion to Islam (and to a Maududian view of Islamic femininity) was, by her own account, an act of cultural subversion. In it, she rejected the capitalist market's commodification and exploitation of women's bodies and the material philosophy upon which this is based. Far from the vision of sexual equality that 1960s feminists espoused, Jamila adopted a religious ideology assigning wholly separate (and some would say discriminatory) functions to women and men. Amongst the responsibilities allocated to women by Islam, as Jamila understood it, was the duty to serve one's husband, maintain the family household and devote one's life to the upbringing of children. Her rejection of contemporaneous Western liberal notions of equality would therefore confound the expectations of those who might otherwise champion her will to autonomous and rational self-definition.

A significant problem for the way we theorise the agency of women in the modern Muslim world is the notion of an easily defined, homogeneous and recognisable women's 'experience'. For instance, Western liberal societies have by now accommodated (albeit not without resistance) some aspects of that second-wave feminist worldview which conceives of 'woman' as an essentially stable subject category defined prescriptively in her relation to persistent and essentially universal types of male power. Yet as the contemporary feminist historian, Joan Scott, points out, the search for a female 'experience' in the analyses of gender may just as easily be incorporated into a vision of unequal and oppressive social and political relations.[7] Where women are assumed to be universally on a par regarding their internal nature or the causes of their oppression (patriarchy), other contingent and no less decisive categories, including that of race, social class and ethnicity, may go unacknowledged. In such cases, the notion of a natural, timeless and reified female experience may actually reduce, rather than enhance, the particular agency of the female subject. The idealised category of 'woman' is not always a space for liberation, but may just as easily act to reinforce the discursive formations which have ensured her subjugation to, and differentiation from, men in the first place.

Clearly the gendered female subject cannot be conceived outside those social relations through which she acts and is defined. Moreover, any attempt to recognise women's agency according to a universal notion of femininity will run up against lives which are too complex, heterogeneous and ambiguous to be reduced and explained so simply. Informed by Scott's criticisms, I argue that one must historicise the categories of experience and identity which have contributed to our notions of gender and the subjects which they produce. The idea that women are shaped solely by their experience of an unchanging femininity (notwithstanding their experiences of ethnicity, class and religion), if it ever held true for women in Western societies, is doubly confounded by the example of women in the 'global South', whose identity is as inextricably caught up with religious, cultural and nationalist constructions of the self as it is with resistance to patriarchal domination.

In short, one must be wary of idealising women without regard for the external, discursive, social and political forces which work upon and through them. This is not to suggest that women in Muslim countries do not face problems and difficulties stemming directly from their status as women (they certainly do), but that even where obvious examples of gender discrimination exist, contemporary global feminist discourses nonetheless tend to romanticise the notion of women's autonomy as a cipher for acts of resistance. The clear problem with such a strategy is that it actively conceals other relationships and ways of being. Furthermore, the desire to recognise Muslim women according to a universal notion of women's 'experience' mirrors the Islamist tendency to essentialise women according to supposedly 'natural' dispositions and roles. One must not simply rebuff the Islamist model with a simplified liberal feminism which then recasts women according to similarly timeless notions and expectations.

To critique the essentialised constitution of female and male identities, however, is not to suppose that there is no such thing as autonomy, or that individuals are simply written over by dominant forms of social power. We must instead seek to contextualise, rather than romanticise, the agency of individuals, and of the female voice. As such, the modern Muslim woman may well carve out her own strategy within the outwardly patriarchal programme of contemporary Islamist thinking. Attention to subjectivity should therefore recognise that whilst individuals are co-opted by the external social and political discourses which sustain overarching configurations of power, there are still real experiences in the consciousness of subjects that exist independently of these discourses. As David Lamberth points out, it is the work of conscious, free-willed people to 'respond to and produce the more subjective experiences of community (love, justice, and liberation) that mark faith communities oriented around some sense of divinity'.[8] Despite its susceptibility to the corrupting influence of worldly power, the religious community *in toto* is not a parasite on the natural liberty and rights of the individual. In fact, it often supplies the moral framework within which individuals seek to affirm notions of self-worth and value.

I have included these cautionary thoughts on women's agency and the subject of experience as a necessary caveat and prelude to the proper subject of this chapter, which is the reductive view of gender encountered in the writings of the South Asian ideologue, Sayyid Abul A'la Maududi. Writing from his home in Lahore, Maududi responded thus to Jamila's anxieties over the nature of Western women's fashions:

> I am very much pleased to know how much you despise this [Western] form of dress. If you manage to learn Arabic or Urdu

and study direct the detailed instructions which the Holy Prophet Muhammad (peace and blessings of God be upon him) has given pertaining to women, I hope you will find them exactly corresponding and appropriate to the real womanly nature.[9]

The last four words of this last sentence and the discursively construed West-versus-Islam nexus on which Maududi and Jamila concurred will be the focus of my discussion in the remainder of this chapter. Unquestioning assumptions about 'the real womanly nature' were not peripheral to Maududi's vision for social stability, nor were they an offshoot of more structuring moral values. Rather, the idealisation of women was central to Maududi's conception of Islam as a way of life and social 'system' (*nizam*).

Human Nature for an Islamic System

The notion that women have a special role to fulfil in society is based, for Maududi, upon a theory of human nature (*fitrah*) which facilitates a radical conception of men's and women's social and sexual difference.[10] Whilst this theory sometimes defers to pre-modern authorities, its essential content derives from modern, early twentieth-century conceptions of gender. Medieval Muslim conceptions of the human soul recognised 'natural' differences between men and women which derived from their ostensibly different functions and capacities. When the Muslim scholar al-Zamakshari (1075–1144) wrote that God had 'favoured' (*faddala*) men over women with regard to their 'intelligence, physical constitution, determination and physical strength', for instance, he undoubtedly posited a fundamental distinction between the sexes.[11] Yet this was justified according to the contextual, historically contingent social, political and economic roles which distinguished men from women. The idea of difference did not gain its meaning, as it did in the earlier twentieth century, from such 'rational' disciplines as medicine and science, which presumed to dispense the final word on the physical and mental constitution of human beings. For Maududi, references to sexual difference in traditional Islamic thought are confirmed by modern medicine's positing of separate biological and psychological functions to women and men.

For instance, the notion that women should not copy the social roles of men but are best suited to a life of childrearing and domesticity would seem justified by traditional religious sources, but is nonetheless reliant upon Western medical data available to Maududi during the 1930s. When a woman experiences menstruation, she loses body warmth, her pulse and blood pressure fall below 'normal' levels, her endocrines, tonsils and lymphatic glands undergo change and her ability to metabolise proteins and gases deteriorates, rendering her digestion slow and ungainly. Respiration decreases, her muscles become tired, she feels lethargic and loses the ability to concentrate. Maududi thus concludes that the serious nature of these biological and physiological changes render her manifestly 'unwell' and incapable of fulfilling important social responsibilities.[12] Maududi's selective use of contemporary medical data is intended to confirm, as traditional sources perhaps cannot, that the differences between men and women are intrinsic to their essential nature.

This notion of gender difference intersects with a profoundly dualistic conception of the human soul. According to Maududi, human beings are part 'animal' (*hevaani*) and part 'human' (*insaani*). In the struggle between these forces, our 'humanity', which characterises and maintains the features of a civilised life, is tasked to commandeer the 'animality', cast as sexual lust and desire, which seeks to unravel it. Sexual lust, for Maududi, is an anti-social urge which produces selfishness, egoism and anarchy. For this reason, it must be integrated into, and controlled by, the social order.[13] Whilst the institution of marriage would fulfil the licit sexual needs of men and women, only a regime of gender segregation can protect society from the overpowering aura of women's sexuality. Maududi's vision for an ideal Islamic society is therefore based on the need to monitor, discipline and control the intense sexual and physical attraction which women create in men.

Gender Segregation

In *Beyond the Veil*, the Moroccan anthropologist and feminist historian Fatima Mernissi argues that the social mechanisms developed to subordinate women throughout the history of Western and Islamic societies are different according to their respective evaluation of women's sexuality. In the history of the Christian West, women were cast in an inferior light to that of men and were seen as the essentially passive and inactive partner in the sexual and procreative act. In stark contrast to this passive and inferior characterisation, the Muslim conception of female sexuality portrays it as an active, powerful and even threatening force, which is of equal strength to that of men. Initially, Islamic tenets accepted the reality of sexual libido without projecting good or bad moral connotations onto it, which Mernissi considers to be in keeping with the fundamentally egalitarian nature of Islamic teachings. However, once the first religious community was established under the Prophet Muhammad's guidance, the need arose to regulate and control women's and men's sexual instincts. In this context, female sexuality became associated with the destructive, anti-social forces of temptation and sedition (*fitnah*) to which the society of men was susceptible.[14]

Whilst Mernissi claims that both systems possess an inherently negative view of women's sexuality, the regulations which they imposed upon women differed according to their established conceptions. If Western Christianity attempted to check women's sexuality internally, by associating it with negative, sinful experiences of guilt and shame, Muslim cultures sought to control it through a system of external, spatial and territorial regulation, as the custom of women's segregation would indicate. Upon this premise, Mernissi sees no need for Arab Muslim women to emulate the arguably incomplete path to liberation that women in the West have taken on the grounds that theirs is a profoundly different set of circumstances requiring different solutions. Mernissi's most optimistic and interesting speculation is that women's liberation in the Arab Muslim world (when it occurs) may achieve more than the liberation of women in the West, considering that the former are not subordinated by a theory of their inherent inferiority. Muslim women are instead dominated by the tacit recognition and consequent fear of their equal potential.

Mernissi's thesis is interesting and provocative. However, its validity, and that of other theories like it, depends upon whether modern

Muslim women are indeed dominated by a system of segregation and not by an ideology of difference. As a point of discussion, it provides a useful entrée to Maududi's theory, which refutes the notion that external forms and practices of segregation constitute the operative means for curtailing Muslim women in the social sphere. Whilst Maududi certainly endorses practices of gender segregation, his theory places a stronger emphasis upon the experience and consciousness of female shame. To establish a truly Islamic sense of piety, women must retreat before men not just physically but in their innermost thoughts.

According to Maududi, Islam holds up a social blueprint which is perfectly attuned to the requirements of human nature. For instance, Islamic law not only enforces punitive laws to uphold social order (which include the punishments prescribed for sins such as adultery, false accusations of the same and theft) but contains moral and ethical mechanisms to dissuade the very intentions which precede acts of social or sexual anarchy. Prominent amongst such mechanisms is the presence of *haya* (an Arabic word), which Maududi defines as the emotion of 'shame/shyness' (*sharm*, in Urdu) so needed to protect an individual's 'modesty' and 'sense of decency'.[15] As Maududi explains, *haya* is 'the force which prevents humans from indulging in indecency and obscenity'. Without it, humans would be left to commit sins under the impulse of their 'animality', the result of which would destroy their 'sense of modesty'.[16]

Bolstering Maududi's theory of sexual *haya* are a number of selectively marshalled prophetic traditions which he links to those verses in the Qur'an which enjoined seclusion to the Prophet's wives in the city of Medina.[17] Amongst the early Muslim community, the Prophet's adversaries had attempted to make his wives the objects of slander and sexual intrigue in order to undermine the Prophet's moral authority and the integrity of the political alliances that some of his marriages represented. It is after these incidents that the Qur'an instructed the Prophet's wives to seclude themselves from the rest of society and to refrain from any activities which may expose them to such intrigues:

> Wives of the Prophet, you are not like any other woman. If you are truly mindful of God, do not speak too softly in case the sick

at heart should lust after (or expect favours of) you, but speak in an appropriate manner.[18]

Following the patriarchal interpretive norms observed amongst various medieval legalists, Maududi claims that this verse relates a timeless warning against the capacity of the female voice to act as a medium for morally wicked thought and behaviour. Whilst an unrelated man and woman may engage in seemingly 'innocent talk', Maududi argues that beneath the veil of their speech 'hidden motives of the heart are at work', the effects of which would 'render the voice increasingly sweet, the accent more affectionate'.[19] Thus it is that the very inflexions and intonations of such otherwise mundane chatter lead to the realisation of erotic desires and acts. Other elements which reduce *haya* and jeopardise the social order are the sounds emitted by a woman's jewellery, the effect her perfumed body or clothing may have on men even when she is not in their company, and a woman's ever-present 'urge to display' her beauty and ornaments to men directly (*jazbah-i namaish-i husn*).[20]

Reinforcing the notion of *haya* as an internal emotion recommended to the individual's deepest experiences of modesty and shame is Maududi's reminder that the supposedly 'natural' urge of a woman to display her beauty must apply not only to those situations in which she is exposed to non-related (*ghair maharim*) males, but also to her husband in circumstances where the exposure of her 'shameful parts' is of a disrespectful or vulgar nature.[21] Such prudishness, even towards the nudity of lawfully married partners, underscores the comprehensive nature of Maududi's conception of *haya*. It covers 'every aspect of human life' including, as we have seen, 'even the slightest lapse of the self in sexual affairs'.[22] A deeply felt consciousness and experience of shame is thereby necessary on the part of the morally upright Muslim woman as 'only she can search her heart' to detect its 'hidden desires'.[23] Spatial segregation as a check on socially inappropriate interactions between men and women is insufficient unless an experience and awareness of *haya* is already nurtured in one's deepest conscience. Maududi thus calls us to examine the value of shame and the manner in which it might support or undermine an individual's moral integrity.

Shame and Feminine Subjectivity

Because all notions of femininity and masculinity are imbricated in historical (social, cultural and political) settings, there can be no experience of shame which is not a product of these settings. Indeed, notions of pride, honour, shame and guilt are as closely related to our idea of human nature as the subjectivities and experiences they produce. In recent decades, theorists such as Michel Foucault and Nikolas Rose have explored those modern forms of discursive and objectifying power which provide the ground upon which individuals forge their experiences of subjectivity, and define themselves as meaning-giving subjects.[24] Such work reminds us that the notion of an interior and autonomous self does not exist outside human history and may not always have existed in its current form. Because the self is necessarily bound up in, and formed through, the structures, matrices and contingencies of social power, emotions such as shame cannot be properly understood outside their historical setting. This is not to deny the influence of modern notions of subjectivity but to problematise their conceptualisation as 'natural' or taken-for-granted categories.

It is a curious feature of recent anthropological, psychological and philosophical studies that the phenomenon of shame is so often likened to a state of visibility or exposure before a judge or audience. According to the philosopher, Gabriele Taylor, shame is a matter of being 'seen through', which Gerhart Piers likened to the consciousness of God as an all-knowing arbiter of human actions.[25] Yet, for Taylor, the emotion of shame is defined according to two identifiable and overlapping experiences. On one hand, an individual experiences internal feelings of self-criticism and moral self-judgment, which is the premise for shame, and which accompanies the experience of being observed and judged before an external audience, on the other. The role of the audience, according to Taylor, constitutes an essential point of reference, in which the moral importance and weight of the individual's misdeed, or misgiving, becomes clear to her. An individual thus experiences shame when she is able to assess herself from the viewpoint of a real or metaphorical observer, before whom she realises the extent of her own moral degradation or wrongdoing. An interior self-consciousness thus forms itself through the 'concept of another', which fulfils the emotion of shame.[26] It is the experience of being seen or observed, alongside the quality or nature of one's fault, which defines this emotion.

Concerning that which catalyses shame in the first place, an individual must feel herself contravening, and wishing to re-align herself to, an important moral standard or value. Thus, for Taylor, shame is bound up in those notions of right and wrong which the individual takes from society and makes her own. To deviate from such values is to know that one has strayed from what is socially acceptable and it is this conception of stepping beyond an established moral norm which charges the experience of shame. However, such values do not derive – in modernised Western societies – from a collective identity. Rather, the values one would be ashamed to deviate from are those which most intimately nourish a person's self-respect and sense of integrity: 'A person can have self-respect, or a sense of her own value, only if she believes some form of life is worth living, and that by and large she is capable of leading such a life.'[27] To experience shame is thus to register how one has betrayed one's own values (which are nonetheless derived from one's environment) and, as a consequence, injured one's own integrity. The analogy of sight and exposure, in this case, reinforces the broad, social base or grounding from which an individual's integrity is constructed.

Here, I will compare Maududi's analysis of shame with that of Taylor's, and then with Taylor's feminist critics, who have raised useful questions surrounding the role of shame in the discourses and structures of social power. For Maududi, the tenets provided for humanity by Islam are the universal, God-given moral and ethical foundations upon which personal integrity and the ties of communal harmony are built. In this regard, both Maududi and Taylor reinforce the individual's commitment to principles which endow the self with a sense of meaning and value. And just as Taylor's individual is able to assess herself from an exterior point of view, so Maududi's believer experiences *haya* before an audience: 'The meaning of *haya* is *sharm* (shame/shyness/modesty)... which a wrongdoer experiences *before his own inherent nature (khud apni fitrah ke samne) and before his God*.'[28]

Thus, the theme of visibility before God and self plays a large part in Maududi's system of gender segregation (*purdah*). For instance, it is women who are endowed with a supposedly 'natural' urge to display themselves to members of the opposite sex, at which time male participation is associated with the lustful, or sexually 'seditious look' (*fitnah-i nazar/chor nigah*) that passes between them. This seditious look is gendered as an act which men perform on women, and for which the latter are responsible if they have not resisted the desire to expose themselves to men. This is because men are 'by nature outgoing/ aggressive' in their desires towards women, whereas women assume the passive role of making themselves more attractive to men.[29] The practice of women's self-display, which the Qur'an forbade in the context of pre-Islamic social customs and fashions, is therefore assumed by Maududi to represent a universal trait of the female sex.[30] In his estimation: 'no law can be made to check and control this tendency, as it springs from a woman's own heart'.[31]

Women, then, are to be made aware of their causal relationship to that seditious male gaze which can only be diverted through methods of segregation and self-monitoring. This highlights a process of internal, self-objectification which John Berger eloquently described in another context:

> *Men act* and *women appear.* Men look at women. Women watch themselves being looked at. This determines not only most relations between men and women but also the relation of women to themselves. The surveyor of woman in herself is male: the surveyed female. Thus she turns herself into an object – and most particularly an object of vision: a sight... She has to survey everything she is and everything she does because how she appears to others, and ultimately how she appears to men, is of crucial importance.[32]

Maududi invokes a comparable notion of female self-observation in his moral invocation against a woman's 'natural' inclinations towards self-display and the response that this elicits in men. *Haya* is that internal emotion of shyness and shame which enables women to control their innermost thoughts and tendencies by seeing themselves precisely as men (according to their nature) see them. And added to this are the external practices of veiling and gender segregation, which are presumed to reinforce the presence of *haya*.

Whilst assigning a positive moral value to the function of shame, Maududi's conception of its effect upon the self highlights the difference between his and Taylor's views concerning the extent and limits of human freedom. If, for Maududi, the system of values to which an individual relates is permanently laid out in universal Islamic doctrines then integrity, per se, is a fixed entity. Taylor, on the other hand, does not presume to know what the common good is, or should be, and accepts that social and individual values will be as diverse and changing as the multifarious historical contexts and conditions in which they arise. Thus Taylor's notion of integrity is not moored to any particular doctrine and will change according to the shifting standards and expectations of a liberal society.

Because Taylor does not underscore the efficacy of all types of shame in reinforcing individual integrity, her theory allows for the possibility that one may experience detrimental or 'false' types of shame. False shame, according to Taylor, cannot aid one's moral sense but undermines the foundations upon which integrity is built. If shame is to serve a positive function, the individual has to know that the values, behaviours and standards to which one aspires are in fact true values which are worth defending. To suffer from 'false shame', on the other hand, is to experience a shame derived from values which are tenuous and unfounded, leading to a misdirected kind of integrity.[33] Taylor therefore assumes that where the rightness of an individual's views is assured, shame has a positive value to productively confirm those beliefs in which the self holds equilibrium. Where shame arises over values which are false or incorrect, it can only harm and further disorient the individual.

The distinction between 'true' and 'false' shame nonetheless gives rise to a host of problems which cannot be satisfactorily answered. Feminist scholars have pointed out, for instance, that Taylor's positive appraisal of the function of shame does not account for its imbrication in the categories of race, class, religious faith, political ideology and gender. Nor, they claim, are individuals always able to judge and discriminate amongst the various and diverse kinds of shame which one may experience.[34] Whilst Taylor assumes that an individual should ideally be able to distinguish right from wrong values and experiences, the notion that people of different social circumstances will experience shame differently and according to the conditions prescribed by their belonging to a particular race, gender or class goes unacknowledged. So what does one make of the fact that the self is conditioned to affirm the integrity of men and women in diverse ways, and with a very different value attached to the importance of shame?

Jennifer Manion argues that Taylor's analysis of shame is incomplete to the extent that it does not account for the negative social constructions and experiences of gender which society allocates to women.[35] Precisely because conceptions of femininity are socially and historically constructed, women are not always free to know – let alone reject – the validity or 'truth' behind their experiences of shame. One might suppose, for instance, that a girl berated by vicious peers for some aspect of her appearance may experience a profound shame without knowing – as Taylor supposes she should – that this is 'false' or misplaced. Taylor's feminist critics therefore rightly hold that the distinction between 'genuine' and 'false' shame places the spurious and impossible onus on individuals to know, or distinguish, right from wrong values and practices. Whilst Taylor recognises that all such values are historically situated, she is nonetheless blind to their entanglement in the matrices of social, cultural and political power. As such, Taylor's conception of shame reflects common liberal assumptions about the formation of the modern self. Her conception of the individual as a morally free agent, whose choice it is to distinguish 'true' from 'false' types of shame, replays the Kantian presumption of an autonomous self whose access to notions of morality may somehow be separated from environmental circumstances and conditions.

For Maududi, however, the true metaphysical will of the individual is determined and known not by him or herself but according to an essentialised conception of human nature (*fitrah*) which does not accept the idea of changeable or historically evolving values. Yet in spite of this, Maududi's conception of shame places as much force as Taylor's on the notion of self-authority and individual responsibility. Women are tasked by Maududi with the responsibility of monitoring their emotions and feelings. They are assumed to know the differences between right and wrong not through a process of autonomous moral choice but through their own natural instincts.

Whilst Taylor attempts to distinguish 'true' from 'false' types of shame, Maududi asserts that shame, in whichever manner it arises, is 'true' for conforming to a women's innermost nature. Recall, for instance, his concern to present the experience of *haya* as something inherently 'natural' and appropriate to the feminine sex. Moreover, such shame intensifies an instinctual propensity towards 'modesty' and 'resistance' in all women:

> Shame [*sharm*], modesty [*haya*], inhibition/resistance [*taman'a*], flight [*farar*] and the means to desist are found, more or less, in every woman. But whilst the qualities of flight and resistance are found in the females of other species, their power and quantity are greater in the human female, and are intensified further by the emotions of shame and modesty.[36]

Whilst Maududi seems unaware of the Darwinian nature of this evolutionary-type argument (in which human activities are meaningfully compared with that of other animal species), his use of it to gender the emotion of shame nonetheless works against the aforementioned notion that humans are given an equal share of human (*insaani*) and animal (*hevaani*) instincts.

This is most obvious in Maududi's view of male sexuality. Whilst women are the objects of male attraction, they are nonetheless endowed with those civilising (*insaani*) instincts (of shame, shyness, modesty, and so forth) which provide for the maintenance of social harmony.[37] Men, on the contrary, are the bearers of a powerful sex drive from which women must be protected lest the institution of the family, and the entire social order, descend into sexual anarchy. Whilst the heightening of male lust is nature's mechanism for committing them to the activities of marital union and the construction of a civilised communal life,[38] men come across in Maududi's writings as the weaker sex insofar as they are not deemed capable of regulating their instinctual urges. The burden of self-mastery falls upon women if they are to remain safe from the potentially destructive and animalistic (*hevaani*) compulsions of lust and sexual desire to which men are susceptible. For this reason, Maududi's notion of masculinity becomes a site of potential conflict. Men bear the responsibility to uphold and regulate the public sphere but are not deemed morally capable of regulating their own sexual desires. They are given authority over women and are infantilised at the same moment by a discourse which seeks only to humour their lack of restraint and modesty.

This aspect of Maududi's theory reproduces contemporaneous notions of the male libido as a rapacious and irrepressible force next to which female sexuality is cast in a passive and inferior role. Amongst Indian Muslims of Maududi's generation, the assumption is taken from popular psychoanalytic theories of the early twentieth century and is linked, retrospectively, to Islam's sacred and classical legal sources. A contemporary of Maududi and member of the Deoband *'ulama* in northern India, 'Abdul Majid Daryabadi (1892–1977) uses such theories (in his commentary upon the Qur'an) whilst arguing for the right of husbands to beat their wives. Taking a view associated with the influential psychoanalyst and feminist, Helene Deutsch (1884–1982), Daryabadi posits that masochism is deeply embedded in a woman's psychological, sexual and reproductive experience. To this end, he quotes a Western source confirming that: 'what [a] woman ultimately wants in marriage is to be raped and violated, what she wants in mental life is to be humiliated; menstruation is significant...because it feeds masochistic fantasies, childbirth represents the climax of masochistic satisfaction'. Daryabadi then notes the English taste for the sadomasochistic practice of sexual 'flagellomania' amongst women, and cites studies to demonstrate that the practice of wife-beating is so widespread across Europe as to constitute a normal and even desired aspect of marital life.[39] That modern psychoanalysis and science have associated weakness and a pathological desire for pain with the female sex leaves little room for doubt regarding the interpretation of those sacred sources which seem to confirm practices of social patriarchy.

Muslim Wives/Western Whores

Over the last century numerous Muslim revivalists, Maududi and his followers amongst them, have linked the role of women in the West to the cultural differences which are attributed to European/

Western societies, on one hand, and the colonised, or formerly colonised, Muslim world, on the other. The presumption is that European and American cultures have destabilised the natural system (or 'way of life') advocated for humanity by Islam. Most often, such thinking refers to a series of perceived economic, social and biological contexts which have alienated Western women from their instinctive nature. And because the unbalanced culture of the West is felt to impinge on Muslim societies, a truly Islamic society cannot be established without rolling back the influence of Western values. Islamism thus establishes a universal template with which to challenge the putative universality of the Western 'way of life'. Moreover, Maududi's conception of Muslim femininity cannot be separated from the negative presence of an oppressive and lascivious Western culture.

In an example of what the Algerian theorist, Malik Bennabi, termed 'colonisability', Maududi and the revivalists under his influence contend that Western imperialism would not have succeeded but for the simultaneous weakening of Muslim society through a process of internal moral decline.[40] Employing this argument, Maryam Jamila attributes the influence of Western ideas amongst middle-class Muslim women to the prior dissolution of patriarchal power in the family home. According to Jamila, the rebellion of Muslim women only came about 'when men...ceased to fulfil their religious function and lost their virile...character'. Because the father, husband and patriarch is like the *imam* (spiritual guide) of the family, and his authority 'symbolizes that of God in the world', his collapse into effeminacy augured nothing less than the dissolution of the social order. Women, who were once the beneficiaries of male guidance, 'no longer felt the authority of religion' and were thus exposed to non-Islamic influences from the West.[41] For Jamila, the spread of Western cultural influences follows the endogenous weakening of men's and women's natural roles.

If Jamila employs a modern (psycho-historical) understanding of decline and regeneration in her analysis of Muslim society, this is no less present in Maududi's view of Western women, which defers to a number of contemporary European and American thinkers who railed against the perceived loosening of social and moral standards during the first three decades of the twentieth century. Armed with such sources (which include sociologists, physicians and social critics such as

Paul Bureau, Hugo Van de Veld, Richard von Krafft-Ebing and George Riley Scott), Maududi warns his readers of the new sexual attitudes which are corrupting the family system and eroding the norms which once defined the West as a moral society.[42] Of particular interest, for my purposes, is how Maududi contrasts the good Muslim woman, who is a mother, wife and homemaker, to her failed Western counterpart, the self-centred abortionist, career woman and prostitute.

In Maududi's analysis, the decline of the modern Western woman began with the ascendance of the eighteenth-century Enlightenment ethic of individualism which set the course for a self-seeking and atomised conception of human life. Historical events, such as the French Revolution, augured significant changes in women's social conditions and laid the ground for pleasure-seeking sexual attitudes which were supported by Neo-Malthusian ideas towards sexual contraception in the nineteenth century. For Maududi, the introduction of contraceptive methods did more than allow a country to regulate its population for the health of its economy. It instead signalled a decline in moral standards by permitting sexual indulgence under the banner of individual freedom and recreation. That a woman was now able 'to surrender herself to a man, without fear of having children and its responsibilities' held dire social consequences which included the destruction of her fundamental roles as a wife and mother.[43]

Echoing nineteenth- and early twentieth-century nationalist discourses which linked the health of a nation to the moral protection and stability of the family unit (and the central place of mothers and wives within it) Maududi warned that the self-indulgence and moral laxity accompanying women's access to state contraception eroded those 'natural motherly feelings' (*fitri jazbah-i madari*) which are 'the basis not only of civilisation but of the human species itself'. In dire tones, he warned that the West's preoccupation with attributing God-like reproductive rights and liberties to women initiated nothing less than a form of 'national suicide' (*qaumi khudkashi*).[44]

Sustaining this line of analysis, Maududi finds support in the apparent connection, drawn by George Riley Scott, between the entry of women into the workforce under the pressures of industrialisation and rising levels of prostitution.[45] An influential sociologist of the early twentieth century, Scott had argued that a woman's access to notions of sexual freedom and her newfound status as an object of erotic interest were the levers that enabled her to reject the institution of marriage and supplement a meagre workplace income through prostitution as a type of amateur vocation. For Maududi, the results of this were ruinous to society. Because a sexually free culture is one in which the male libido is stimulated beyond 'normal' levels, women will inevitably be co-opted into the commodification of their sexuality. In Maududi's prose, the dark and marginal figure of the prostitute, who threatens all familial and social values, is brought shockingly close to home. His readers are asked to imagine a world in which their daughters and female relations are transformed (as Western women have already been) into the objects of male lust:

> But where will these women come from? They must come from the very society in which they were raised, as someone's daughters or sisters. Thousands of such women, who could have been the queen of a home, the founder of a family, a nurturer to numerous children – will have to be taken and installed in the markets. Like the municipal urinals, they will make a place where the needs of promiscuous men are given relief. All of the special qualities of feminine nobility will be removed from them. For this cause, they will be taught to flirt and conditioned to sell their love, hearts, bodies, beauty and charms to a new buyer, every hour.[46]

Thus the values of materialism and personal gain, for which Maududi coined the ironic term the 'new moral philosophy', are condemned in popular Indian culture, romantic films and Urdu literature. Moreover, those women who embrace the Western idea of sexual freedom are worse off than prostitutes because a conventional prostitute (according to Maududi) has no access to that relativistic moral philosophy which transforms 'sin into virtue and virtue into sin'. Unlike the women who wilfully give themselves up to men in the romantic literature which Maududi deplores, prostitutes perform their activities (or so Maududi supposes) 'with an awareness of their dishonour and sin'.[47]

That Maududi saw the transformation occurring in Western Europe as a symptom of moral degeneration rather than of ineluctable economic conditions underlines his perception of those changes as a cultural/ideological challenge to Islam. Indeed, the impending threat of Western values ranked amongst the issues which vexed him the most. When queried as to whether any single event spurred his determination to bring about an Islamic revival, Maududi remarked:

> I am not the kind of person whose life can be drastically changed by any one incident. It is only after a great deal of thought and consideration that I establish my goals and then I work gradually to achieve them. But there was one incident that had a considerable impact on me. In 1937, after staying in Hyderabad for nine years, I went back to Delhi where I witnessed a great change among the Muslims; they were rapidly moving away from Islam. In Delhi, the situation was completely different from Hyderabad. I saw Muslim 'shurafa' ['noble'] women walking in the streets without 'purdah', an unthinkable proposition only a few years ago. This change shocked me so greatly that I could not sleep at night, wondering what had brought about this sudden change among the Muslims?[48]

Whilst Indian Muslims did not undergo the same shifts in sexual and moral attitudes that occurred in parts of America and Europe during the 1930s, Western cultural influences nonetheless made enough headway for Maududi to feel as though central Islamic values were under threat. Exposed to the allure of an ostensibly more permissive and materially advanced culture, he feared that Indian Muslims would lose their moral bearings to the Western way of life.

Explanations for the rise of Western feminism, amongst many Islamist thinkers, provide a justification for what are presumed to be 'natural' (God-given) human tendencies and essences. When women lose their maternal role, their nurturing instincts disappear altogether, as Maududi sought to establish. The maternal drive is then usurped, displaced and redirected to the male arena where women cannot possibly hope to compete as equals. Historically, this led to the demand amongst Western women for the chimera of 'equality' which must be distinguished from the ideal of 'justice' provided for women by Islam. To really treat women equally, for Maududi, is to respect their spiritual equality with men, whilst observing their different natural roles and functions. Because the psychological and physical make-up of women differs fundamentally to that of men, Islam's recognition of this gives to women more respect than Western society is able to give them. As a bulwark against the threat of change, feminist calls for the enhancement of women's rights and freedoms are dismissed as one front in a Western 'attack' on true Islamic values and principles.

Conclusion

In Maududi's writings, the example of Western culture acts to shadow his conception of what is true to the spirit and teachings of Islam. Indeed, the prior repudiation of negative Western influences goes a long way towards making the construction of an ideal Islamic system and the place of women within it possible. Within the supposed dichotomy between Western and Islamic values, Maududi develops a specific understanding of human gender, in which a woman's sense of shame and physical 'retreat' act to preserve her from male animalism. Yet this essentialist notion of human nature (*fitrah*) and understanding of modern sexual relations is so intimately corrupted by an exaggerated Western stereotype as to be inseparable from it.

Moreover, the Maududian understanding of Islamic universality repeats the tendency to approach women according to essentialised feminine faculties and characteristics. As I have pointed out, this approach cannot account for those aspects of women's lives which do not conform to the supposedly natural swelling of *haya*/shame, restraint and sexual modesty. Just as recent feminist critics have deconstructed the concept of a universal feminine 'experience', so is it necessary for Muslim thinkers to question and re-conceive the ethical implications of historical gendering. We must at least work from the premise that there is no 'natural' female subject, one which exists independent of the diverse ways femininity is conceived in historical, social, cultural and political terms, if we are to critically understand the tenuous generalisations which are so often attributed to women's (and men's) sexual and social identities.

CHAPTER 7

PROGRESSIVE ISLAM: THE HERMENEUTICAL TURN

The pressure exerted by modern ideas and forces of social change, together with the colonial interregnum in Muslim lands, has brought about a situation in which the adoption of certain key Western ideas and institutions is resolutely defended by some Muslims and often justified through the Qur'an, the wholesale rejection of modernity is vehemently advocated by others, and the production of 'apologetic' literature that substitutes self-glorification for reform is virtually endless. Against this background the evolving of some adequate hermeneutical method seems imperative.

Fazlur Rahman (1919–1988)[1]

The distinction...between the eternal and temporal aspects of the word of God seems to be absent in modern Islamic theology.

Nasr Abu-Zayd (1943–2010)[2]

Introduction

The efforts of some progressive Muslim intellectuals to devise a new method of Qur'anic interpretation will mark the central theme of this chapter. Here, the term 'progressive' Islam (like that of 'liberal Islam', as others describe it) will denote a recent trend amongst like-minded intellectuals who are not bound to any specific political ideology, school or context.[3] What does unite these thinkers beneath a single appellation, in my view, is the concern to establish new principles of reform upon a thorough, and non-essentialist, contextualisation of Islam's sacred sources.[4] Over the last few decades, progressive Muslim intellectuals have sought to address an impasse in hermeneutical thinking brought about by a lack of contextualisation vis-à-vis the Qur'an and selective disaggregation, and recombination, of Islam's legal and theological traditions. This process was initiated by modernist reformers in the second half of the nineteenth century and has become a conspicuous feature of the way Islam is imagined in the present day. In order to address this, progressive Muslims have advocated a hermeneutical approach which is sensitive to the presumptions and contexts that underpin the task of religious interpretation. This strategy no doubt mirrors, and is influenced by, global developments within the social sciences and humanities since the 1950s and 1960s, including the rise of structuralist, poststructuralist, feminist and postcolonial theories. For the thinkers analysed in what follows, one cannot claim to 'know' Islam without accounting for the circumstances and historical conditions which have brought such knowledge into being.

The modernist approach to Islamic thought was typified, at the outset, by the replacement of existing traditions of exegesis with an individualised hermeneutical stance so that Islam's sacred sources could be reinterpreted to meet the demands of a new age. Sayyid Ahmad Khan (1817–1898) indicated aspects of this approach in his *Tahrir fi Usul al-Tafsir* (*Treatise on the Principles of Exegesis*) when he criticised traditional Muslim scholars for failing to address modern conditions, and argued that if the discoveries of science were to be superseded by new forms of knowledge then the Qur'an would have to be interpreted anew.[5] Although Sayyid Ahmad stressed that this did not make the Qur'an a 'plaything' (*khilona*) in people's hands, his approach nonetheless underscored the need to base one's interpretation of the Qur'an upon the knowledge contingencies of one's time.[6]

This change in attitude was significantly influenced by the historical shifts that occurred, in places such as India and Egypt, under the administration of the colonial empires of the nineteenth century. The emergence of incipient anti-colonial nationalist movements; the rise of a new urbanised middle class with greater access to education and literacy; and the etatisation of religious laws by the colonial and modern nation-state all contributed to a transition of religious leadership, from traditional religious scholars to lay activists, local leaders and political elites. During the twentieth century, the rejection of pre-modern traditions was reflected in the theory of an Islamic state, as formulated by Sayyid Abul A'la Maududi (1903–1979) and Sayyid Qutb (1906–1966), which did not meaningfully relate to any traditional school of Muslim law or statecraft.[7] Moreover, in the last few decades, the forces of global capitalism and spread of electronic media and communications have decoupled religious ideologies (including Islamism) from the classical sociological locus of the nation-state and its subsidiary formations. As Olivier Roy observes regarding Muslim communities within Europe (though it seems to be as true of Muslims at large), globalisation has broadened religion's sphere of influence and opened new avenues for its participation in the evolving configurations of civil society.[8]

With this context in mind, I will argue that the intellectual disaggregation of Islamic traditions in the modern period has laid the ground for a serious rethinking of the way religion is to be interpreted and understood. For instance, the presumption of epistemological finality assumed by Sayyid Qutb (for denying Islam's status as a manmade 'theory' or 'philosophy') raises concerns not merely about the correct or incorrect interpretation of Islam, but of how such knowledge is constituted in the first place.[9] As one scholar put it, Islamists assume a position of 'epistemological privilege' for supposing that their interpretations are not, in fact, a human endeavour but an expression of Islam's true reality.[10] The observation is pertinent to a number of modern-day revivalists, who conceive of Islam as something which is ahistorically fixed, perfect, and beyond further investigation. It is this foreclosing of spaces for interpretation, I argue, which has contributed to the above-mentioned impasse in hermeneutical thinking.

Whilst Muslims have always interacted with the Qur'an according to the perspective and needs of their age (as any survey of the differences in medieval *tafsir* literature would indicate), the thinkers described in what follows address the area of hermeneutical theory in a particular way. For just as they are concerned with the need to reform Islam, so are they aware that any such attempt premises an awareness of the epistemological conditions for such reform. By this I do not mean to suggest that pre-modern thinkers never considered hermeneutical issues. Questions of methodology and interpretation were important to the formation of Islam's legal schools in the pre-classical period, and medieval jurists thereafter took great pains to demonstrate that the principles of interpretation are derived from a serious evaluation of the sacred text's rhetorical meaning and contextual significance. In this sense, it was not the literal meaning of the Qur'an's injunctions, but the spirit behind them, which guided the effort of jurists to determine the meaning of the law. As Ebrahim Moosa points out, this contributed to a reservoir of considerable intellectual creativity from which new and more properly modern hermeneutical methodologies were developed.[11] Within Islamic history, moreover, there is a long tradition of self-reform (*islah*) and renewal (*tajdid*) which has normatively drawn upon such principles of adaptation for the revival of the religious community.[12]

Whilst the reformers of the past strove to question and critique the veracity of other interpretive procedures, they did not busy themselves with theoretical questions about the conditions under which interpretation becomes possible. The medieval juristic tradition, for instance, was more concerned with establishing normative juristic precedents as a basis for the further imitation and extrapolation of legal rulings, than with the need to renew those laws within the evolving/changing conditions of knowledge as a whole. By the same token, the *islahi* tradition conventionally focused upon the need to bring contemporaneous beliefs, practices and institutions within the spirit of Islam's sacred sources, and was less concerned with what Paul Ricoeur calls the 'epistemology of interpretation' that exists behind such judgments and decisions.[13] What distinguishes contemporary progressive reformers from those of previous times is their working from the premise that interpretation itself has been brought to a point of instability and crisis. This chapter will explore the diverse implications of this in the work of such Muslim thinkers as Fazlur Rahman, Amina Wadud, 'Abdolkarim Soroush, and Mohammad Arkoun, amongst others. Whilst I will not attempt to analyse the complete oeuvre of these scholars in every detail, salient elements of their work will be highlighted insofar as they contribute to my analysis of a new hermeneutical approach.

The Universality and Contingency of Islamic Thought

Fazlur Rahman's (1911–1988) call for an 'adequate hermeneutical method' with which to interpret the Qur'an represents an important starting point for the themes of this chapter. Born in an area of the Punjab in what is now Pakistan, Rahman was educated in Lahore and went on to study modern methods of historical criticism at Oxford, where he wrote a PhD in 1949 on the thought of Ibn Sina.[14] There, he came under the influence of the renowned Orientalist Hamilton Gibb (1895–1971), and formulated the need to develop a historical understanding of Islamic thought and practice. In 1962 he returned to Pakistan, where he was appointed head of the Institute of Islamic Studies in Karachi, under the patronage of General Ayub Khan. This position gave him the opportunity to disseminate a progressive intellectual agenda on matters of Islamic scholarship, economic policy, family planning, and the social implementation of religious principles, which was opposed by Pakistan's conservative religious parties. In 1968, Rahman resigned his post and left the country under intense criticism from sections of the religious right and the political opponents of Ayub Khan's regime.[15] Thereafter, he worked as an advisor to the Indonesian government on matters of Islamic education and, from 1968 to 1988, as a scholar at the University of Chicago.

The problem with traditional and modern Muslim exegetical readings of the Qur'an, according to Rahman, was that they approached it in a piecemeal fashion and so failed to grasp its universal worldview. If the traditional verse-by-verse method of Qur'anic *tafsir* (commentary) was valuable for elucidating the Qur'an's literal and lexicographical meanings, and for uncovering the contexts in which particular verses were revealed, it nonetheless contributed little to an understanding of its complex doctrinal unity.[16] Moreover, this inability to view the Qur'an as a whole resulted in the compartmentalisation and divergence of Islam's mystical, theological, philosophical and legal traditions. The example of early Islamic philosophy's failure to absorb Hellenic thought on its own terms, according to Rahman, was a case in point. Because the adoption of Greek philosophy was not satisfactorily derived from the principles of the Qur'an, it created a two-tiered system in which philosophical truths were tenuously equated to religious truths. This created a state of disharmony between the theological and philosophical traditions which culminated in the 'Asharite reaction against independent philosophical inquiry, to which Rahman attributes a decline in theoretical thinking.[17] In the modern period, Orientalist scholars fared no better in their analysis of the Qur'an by focusing on the text's chronology of revelation, collation and so forth, without regard for its integral wholeness.[18]

For the Qur'an to be understood as a whole, Rahman argues, the difference between its 'normative' and 'historical' content must be taken into account.[19] Here, normative Islam connotes the universal moral teachings and principles which are encapsulated in the Qur'an and the life of the Prophet, whilst historical Islam refers to the manner in which such principles and teachings were formulated in a given historical context. Normative Islam denotes principles which may be interpreted for any time and place, whilst historical Islam refers to the teachings and doctrines which grew out of a specific political and cultural milieu, and which should not be reproduced as though they were literal, or universal, injunctions. Whilst this distinction stipulates a return to the spirit of Islam's sacred sources, and thus echoes the sentiments of various *salafi* and other revivalist movements, Rahman's reformist ideas are distinguished by a will to properly historicise the context in which Islam's moral injunctions were revealed. Whilst he concedes that his approach is 'new in form', and represents a novel form of *ijtihad* (connoting the independent reason-based analysis of sacred texts), Rahman nonetheless connects it to the efforts of early Muslim scholars and compilers of *hadith* who sought to understand specific Qur'anic verses within the contextual settings of their revelation (referred to as *sha'n al-nuzul*, or the 'causes/occasions of revelation').[20]

Then there is the matter of the nature of Qur'anic revelation with regard to the role of the Prophet. According to Rahman, the true content of the Qur'an, which is the 'moral law' of Islam, was not revealed exclusively through words, but through an organic combination of words, feelings and ideas.[21] Whilst the Qur'an was not an expression of the Prophet's subjective personality, nor was it completely external to the Prophet, which is to say that he did not simply receive and reproduce it in a mechanical way. Instead the Qur'anic message was both external to, and intimately bound up in, Muhammad's prophecy, for the creation of a new social and moral order. Whilst God is wholly transcendent, and assumes a position of otherness with respect to humanity, the message of the Qur'an was explicitly concerned with the religious mission of the Prophet, and its social and political consequences. In this sense, Rahman asserts that: 'the Qur'an is entirely the word of God and, in an ordinary sense, also entirely the word of Muhammad'.[22]

Yet, according to Rahman, this sense of the Qur'an's duality was ignored by early Muslim exegetes, who privileged the otherness, objectivity, and verbal character of prophetic revelation over its concern for the inner reality of the Prophet's life.[23] Effective though it was in settling inter-doctrinal controversies during the early development of Islamic thought, this emphasis upon the objective, literal and external features of the sacred text nonetheless obscured its universal moral content.[24] Rahman therefore argues that the Qur'an cannot be approached as a legal manual made up only of literal injunctions and specific rules. It should instead be viewed as a moral document whose aim is to create a 'good and just society... with a keen and vivid awareness of a God who enjoins good and forbids evil'.[25] Islam is a religion which calls its adherents to realise such principles in the context of today's world, over and above the imitation of its endogenous forms in the classical period.

Here, my analysis of Rahman's distinction between the normative and historical content of Islamic doctrine becomes relevant to a broader formulation of what exegesis means for an agenda of progressive reform. Because the interpreter does not exist in a void, the universal message of the Qur'an cannot simply exist for itself, but must meaningfully refer to the interpreter's own experience, knowledge and environment. For Rahman, this highlights a circularity of meaning: between the reader's prior understandings and the text's own normative content, which returns meaning to, and for, the reader. This movement, 'from the present situation to Qur'anic times, then back to the present', is the basis of any living intellectual tradition.[26] The same principle is explained by the Egyptian-born thinker, Nasr Abu-Zayd (1943–2010):

> The understanding of the first Muslim generation and the generations to follow are by no means final or absolute. The specific linguistic encoding dynamics of the Qur'anic text always allows an endless process of decoding. In this process the contextual socio-cultural meaning should not be ignored or simplified, because this level of meaning is so vital to indicate the direction of the particular significance of the text. Knowing the direction of meaning facilitates moving from 'meaning' to 'significance' in the present socio-cultural context.[27]

Only when the Qur'an's 'linguistic encoding' within a specific social and historical context is understood will the interpreter be able to outline its universal principles, for the purposes of present understanding.[28]

This emphasis on contextualisation, with its promise of meaning for the present, rebuts the Islamist presumption that the message of the Qur'an is somehow fixed, or that knowledge moves in a straight and uncomplicated line from the text to the knowing subject. For the Egyptian-American legal scholar, Khaled Abou El Fadl (b. 1963), this is seen in the Islamist formulation of *shari'ah* law as a ready-made legal code for the creation of an ideal religious society, which seems to deny the fallible and contestable nature of human knowledge. Because the understanding of God's law presupposes the 'subjective interpretive determinations' of Muslim jurists (*fuqaha*), Abou El Fadl asserts that the essential content of the sacred law is naturally separate from the temporal and contingent understanding of that law. This distinction (between a law which is divine and therefore perfect, on one hand, and our understanding of it, on the other) means that *shari'ah* law cannot be likened to a pre-formulated legal code:

> Either the law belongs to the state or it belongs to God, and as long as the law relies on the subjective agency of the state for its

articulation and enforcement, any law enforced by the state is necessarily not God's law. Otherwise, we must be willing to admit that the failure of the law of the state is in fact the failure of God's law and ultimately of God Himself. In Islamic theology, this possibility cannot be entertained.[29]

Thus, for Abou El Fadl, Islamists depart from normative practice when they hold *shari'ah* law to be the final statement of God's will, rather than a contingent, potentially fallible interpretation of that will.

This raises questions about the proper status of intellectual inquiry and hermeneutical considerations in Islamic thought. How, for instance, can the status of knowledge in Islam be returned to its rightful place as a human endeavour which nonetheless respects the proper omniscience of God? The solution, as Abou El Fadl sees it, lies in a return to the normative complexity, heterogeneity and intellectual sophistication of Islam's pre-modern legal and theological traditions. Because normative juristic tradition upheld God's law to be separate from the contingent, human understanding of it, it necessarily embraced a plurality of opinions concerning the sacred law.[30] This latitude of judgment, on the part of Muslim scholars, reflected the view that the human understanding of the divine truth is limited, which is to say that one cannot presume to speak on behalf of the divine will. This separation of knowledge does not point to a deficiency in the content of faith but is grounded in an acceptance of the natural imperfection of human knowledge before the omniscience of God. For Abou El Fadl, Muslim thinkers should acknowledge the contingency of human understanding already posited by traditional epistemologies of Islamic law.

The point highlights a tendency amongst progressive reformers to regard Islam's interpretive diversity as the precondition for its proper historical realisation. 'Since the message of Islam is believed to be valid to all human beings, regardless of time and space', Abu-Zayd asserts, the Qur'an requires 'an endless process of interpretation and reinterpretation which cannot but differ in time'.[31] This does not mean that the essential meaning of the text is open to change inasmuch as its application to different circumstances implies the contextual re-signification of that meaning. To separate the normative from the merely historical content of the sacred text, then, is to establish the terms under which interpretation is made. A recent example of this is found in the contemporary 'feminist' critique of the patriarchal norms maintained amongst various Muslim traditions of exegesis.[32]

Islamic Feminism and the Challenge to Patriarchal Hermeneutics

Amongst some recent feminist reformers and historians of gender, the patriarchal interpretations of historically conservative religious scholars and modern revivalist movements calls for a critical re-evaluation of the ways gender is understood in Islam's sacred sources and traditions of jurisprudence. For scholars as diverse as Fatima Mernissi, Leila Ahmed, Asma Barlas, Barbara Stowasser and Amina Wadud, to name a few, exegetical approaches which rely either on the authority of the text, tradition or reason to bolster a patriarchal understanding of Islam are not above contestation.[33] Rather, as Rahman points out, the process of interpretation is understood to be circular, which is to say that one must acknowledge a transferral of meaning: from the reader, to the text, for the reader. With this in mind, a new and potentially 'liberatory' hermeneutic of the Qur'an premises a methodological awareness of the way male exegetes have transferred hermeneutical authority: from the divine text, to the interpretation of that text, and subsequently, to the interpreter himself.[34] In this respect, the feminist and postcolonial academic focus upon gender as a category of historical analysis has proved useful in attempting to distinguish the universal moral kernel of Islamic doctrine from subsequent (mis)interpretations.

The African-American scholar Amina Wudud was born in 1950, in Bethesda, Maryland, USA. The daughter of a Methodist minister, and the descendent of Muslim Berber and African slaves on her mother's side, she converted to Islam at the age of 22, and went on to obtain a PhD in Arabic and Islamic Studies at the University of Michigan, in 1988. Thereafter she worked as a scholar at the International Islamic University in Malaysia, where she remained until 1992, and in the Department of Philosophy and Religious Studies, at the Virginia Commonwealth University.[35] Influenced by both the second-wave feminist movement and the American civil rights campaign under the leadership of Dr Martin Luther King Jr., Wadud has developed a hermeneutical approach to the Qur'an which addresses the issues of gender justice and social reform. This is reflected not only in her scholarship, but in her close involvement with Malaysia's Sisters in Islam movement and other activist groups, including LBGTQ Muslim organisations, and African-American women's collectives.[36]

Wadud's scholarship is pertinent to a criticism of the way male interpreters have projected patriarchal mores and assumptions onto the sacred text which arguably do not belong to it. Traditional Qur'anic commentaries (*tafasir*), she asserts, were written exclusively by men and tended to approach women's issues from a singularly male perspective.[37] It is the absence, or 'voicelessness', of women during the formative period of the Qur'an's interpretation in Islamic history, then, which accounts for a view of women as socially weak and handicapped. To redress this, Wadud develops a hermeneutical model which is based upon a consideration of the context in which Qur'anic verses were revealed, the grammatical structure of the text, and the general worldview which the text conveys. A 'female inclusive' reading of the Qur'an intends to show that whilst the work of past exegetes reveals no positive concern for women, this cannot be said of the text itself.[38]

An interesting element of Wadud's effort to contextualise the way males and females are treated in the Qur'an is her analysis of the text's grammatical inflexions and uses of gender. Because the Arabic language contains no gender neuter, there are no nouns, verbal nouns and other correlatives in the Qur'an which do not defer to the conventions of linguistic gendering as encountered in the *parole* of seventh-century Arabian society. This gendering of language constitutes the 'prior text' (in other words, the historical usages, assumptions and conventions associated with the application of gender) which is a vehicle for meaning, and from which various male exegetes have drawn male-centric interpretive conclusions. Wadud's attention to the Qur'an's uses of gender seeks to demonstrate how male interpreters, past and present, have departed from the text's original meaning and intent.

Within the Qur'an, Wadud distinguishes three ways in which women are referenced, and which are not adequately accounted for by traditional male exegetes. These types of references to women are: a) those which address matters specific to their social and historical situation within the early Muslim community, b) those which apply to women's universally accepted biological and social functions (of childbirth, caretaking and so forth), and c) those which address both women and men with regard to their shared humanity, in a universal, non-gender specific context.[39] The figure of Mary, as she appears in the Qur'an, is a case in point. Normatively, Mary is upheld by conventional exegetes as the ideal Muslim woman and mother who, alongside the Prophet's wives, represents an exemplary role model for the behaviours and practices of women in general. Yet, as Wadud points out, the Qur'an's classification of Mary as 'one of the *qanitin*' (66:12, which is often translated to mean 'obedient' and, by extension, obedient to one's husband) makes no special reference to the biological or social attributes of her gender.[40] Rather, the word *qanitin* (which Wadud interprets to refer to one who is obedient: not as a women might be to her husband but as a 'characteristic or personality trait of believers towards Allah')[41] is given in the masculine plural form, connoting a relevance to both women *and men*. The significance of Mary in the context of this particular verse thus cannot be used to justify a doctrine of marital obedience for women, when the Qur'an upholds her as an exemplary figure for *all* believers.

From this textual example, and others like it, Wadud concludes that the Qur'an's own language and uses of gender belie a message of equality which presents hitherto misunderstood implications for the relations between men and women. That the sacred text is able to overcome the limitations of its own (the Arabic language's) reliance upon linguistic gendering stands as evidence for the themes of gender inclusion which male interpreters have hitherto overlooked.[42] After the reformist ideas articulated by Fazlur Rahman, Wadud attempts to contextualise the Qur'an's references to men and women for the purpose of constructing a more ethical approach to gender relations in the contemporary Muslim community.

'Abdolkarim Soroush: The Religious Defence of Democratic Pluralism

In the Islamic Republic of Iran, where a modern interpretation of Shi'a doctrine has acquired the authority of state ideology since 1979, the issue of Islam's relationship to the political sphere is raised by the reformist philosopher, 'Abdolkarim Soroush. Born in Tehran in 1945, Soroush (whose real name is Hossein Dabagh) became intellectually engaged in Iran's numerous Islamic student associations and intellectual societies which preceded the political ferment of the 1979 revolution.[43] Studying pharmacology at the University of Tehran, he developed an interest in Islamic philosophy, which he learned from a student of Morteza Mottahari (1920–1979), and attended lectures of the sociologist and influential pre-revolutionary thinker 'Ali Shari'ati (1933–1977) at the Husainiyyah-i Irshad. After travelling to Great Britain to study analytical chemistry, he enrolled as a PhD student at the Chelsea College of Science and Technology. There he researched a thesis on the history and philosophy of science, which encompassed such fields as epistemology and modern European philosophy.

After the Islamic revolution of 1979, Soroush returned to Iran and became a high-ranking ideologue of the Islamic Republic. In this role, he publicly defended the state's religious ideology against that of secular Marxist and other leftist movements, such as the Mujahidin-i Khalq. In the post-revolutionary ideological confrontation between the supporters of Karl Popper's scientific positivism and those critics of Western thought who were influenced by the German historicist tradition, Soroush sided with the Popperians, arguing that Iranians had nothing to fear from Western knowledge.[44] As a member of the Advisory Council of the Cultural Revolution, he played a key role in the re-opening of Iran's universities and defended the utility of the social sciences and humanities from those who would frame these as part of a pro-Western 'cultural invasion' of Islam. From the early 1980s, Soroush began to apply his knowledge of epistemology and the history of science to the study of religion, as a result of which he has been at odds with conservative segments of the ruling regime. As a historian of science, he posited that developments in scientific understanding must have a bearing on the development of epistemology, so that changes in knowledge will necessarily influence new social, religious and cultural worldviews. In recent years, he has advocated the institutional reform of Iran's clerical authority and called for a radical rethinking of the political project of Islamism in general.

Despite the particular significance of a modern version of Shi'a theology to the Iranian revolution, Soroush's thoughts concerning the construction of religious knowledge are pertinent to discussions about the way religion is politicised in the broader Muslim world. At the outset, Soroush establishes the above-mentioned distinction between religion (*din*) and religious knowledge (*ma'rifat-i din*) otherwise explained by Rahman and Abu-Zayd. Because, for Soroush, religion is 'sacred and heavenly' but the understanding of religion is 'human and earthly', the former remains unchangeable (in consonance with its divine origins) whilst the latter is a fallible product of human understanding which must be the subject of constant criticism and reconstruction.[45] The usefulness of this premise is that it historicises the oppositional categories (of continuity and change, reason and revelation, tradition and modernity) which are the perennial intellectual stumbling blocks for projects of religious criticism and reform.

An important aspect of this theoretical division for Soroush's theory of politics is his unwillingness to engage in the arbitration of a final understanding, or version, of historical truth. Because the content of religion is human and non-divine (despite its divine origins), it cannot accommodate the sense of finality that accompanies the theology of Islamism.[46] Instead, Soroush advocates the need for a theory, and subsequent political model, which is responsive to 'the process through which religion is understood and the manner in which this understanding undergoes change'.[47] Such a context/practice/understanding of religion can only come about in a society which respects the values of intellectual pluralism, which Soroush associates with democratic secularism. Because the knowledge of religion is entirely human, any political body which claims to speak or legislate on behalf of the divine will – as Iran's highest religious and political offices, the *Velayet-i Faqih* ('Rule of the Jurist') and Council of Guardians, have done – will inevitably distort it. For religion to play an organic part in Iran's social development, Soroush advocates 'a religious civil society' (*jama'a-ye madani-ye dini*) in which religious knowledge cannot be monopolised by any political institution.

Here, it is necessary to clarify what democratic secularism means with regard to Soroush's idea of a 'religious society'. In an early essay, entitled 'The sense and essence of secularism', Soroush argues that true secularism has an affinity with the founding principles of philosophical nominalism in that it valorises the independence of reason in non-universalising terms.[48] Because secular democracies refuse to take the metaphysical finality of theological doctrine as the basis for their legitimacy, they guarantee that intellectual freedom which is the standard bearer of a healthy pluralistic society. Moreover, secular democratic theory is a natural inheritor of that epistemological transition which Soroush identifies with the advent of modernity: from a fixed, static, pre-Platonic view of nature and society, on one hand, to a rationalist theory which confers a dynamic, this-worldly agency to our understanding of the world, on the other. Secularism is therefore concordant with modern reason and represents the best model for a society committed to principles of intellectual pluralism.

In his valorisation of this reason-based secular model of governance, Soroush draws upon a theory of justice derived from Mu'tazilah theology.[49] Because justice can be attained through the exercise of reason, and does not rely on the interpretation of religious divines to make it just, its value cannot be conflated with any particular religious order or institution. Rather, it is the task of human beings to make religion just, which is a prerequisite for the implementation of religious values.[50] The essential ethical/moral content of religion is therefore not guaranteed by the institutions of a religious state, but through the capacity of rational individuals to promote justice as the basis for a pluralistic religious society. When reason becomes the fulcrum for evaluating what is just and unjust, religion may be detached from the artificial sanctifications of the state, and in fact becomes the guarantor of a secular-civic sphere which does not allow the dominance of any particular ideological doctrine.

Soroush thus calls for a secular space for religion in order to protect the natural plurality of Islam's human understanding and interpretation. By submitting religious knowledge to the same reasoning which governs other areas of intellectual activity, including the physical and social sciences, he forwards a strong philosophical argument for why religion must participate – democratically – in the civic sphere, and cannot be reified into a static political doctrine. Needless to say, this does not match the process of democratisation advocated for Iran amongst those in Europe, the United States, and Australia, who have typically characterised secularism as the liberation of reason from the irrational bonds of religious dogma. By claiming political secularism for the purpose, ostensibly, of defending universal religious principles, Soroush rejects Western secularism's peremptory claim to the rationalisation of human life. Rather, religion must retreat *into* the secular sphere (and take its place in civil society) to protect it from the co-opting effects of political power. By sanctifying a notion of civil society which is non-coercive and intellectually pluralistic, religion nurtures a type of secularism within itself.

In this sense, Soroush argues against the notion that religion must be relegated solely to the private domain or that secular criticism represents the most enlightened repository of social knowledge. He instead points to a type of secularism which is aligned with the protection of religious values within a defence of political, religious and social pluralism. Because secularism is a human project, and does not exist outside time and space, history and geography, it cannot be abstracted from those historical conditions which answer to the preservation of human values. It is the very absence of coercive doctrine within secular democracies which allows for the free growth and development of religious knowledge. Secular democracy is appropriate, for Soroush, to the extent that it ensures the protection of a genuinely religious society. And this can come about only when religion is freed from the ideological grip of a clerical elite who claim to speak on behalf of the divine law.

Mohammed Arkoun: Deconstructing Islamic Logocentrism

Born in 1928, in Taourit Mimoun in the Kabylia region of Algeria, Mohammed Arkoun studied at the Faculty of Literature of the University of Algiers, before taking up a post at the Sorbonne in Paris. There, he established himself as an authority on the Muslim Arab historian and humanist philosopher, Miskawayh, whose treatise on ethics, *Tahdhib al-Akhlaq wa Tathir al-Araq*, he translated into French in 1969. Lecturing and writing at the Sorbonne until 1992, and as an editor of the journal *Arabica*, Arkoun has exercised a considerable influence over Western-language scholarship on Islam. In his methodology, Arkoun draws upon the modern social sciences and humanities disciplines, employing the techniques of structuralism, semiotics, structural anthropology, discourse analysis and poststructuralism, to mount a considered reappraisal of the Orientalist study of Islam. Influenced by the 'hermeneutical turn' in philosophical thinking (formulated by such thinkers as Schleiermacher, Dilthey, Heidegger, Gadamer and others) he calls for a reconstruction of historicist thought vis-à-vis Islam's traditions of knowledge, and the imaginary entities of 'Islam' and the 'West' which pervade modern-day Orientalist and Islamist discourses.

At the outset, Arkoun is critical of modern Muslim revivalists 'who reject...questions of an epistemological nature' and are 'only sensitive to discussing the "facts" according to the meaning and in the cognitive framework which they themselves have chosen'.[51] This highlights the problem of logocentrism in Islamic thought, which Arkoun locates in Islam's formative theological, philosophical and heresiological debates. Islamic logocentrism, as Arkoun defines it, is the tendency to confine all knowledge to a narrow selection of religious texts, and the discursive assumptions, commentaries and social/cultural/political worldviews attributed to these.[52] Because the revealed word of God is a basis for absolute certainty (*'ilm al-yaqin*), it became the fundamental premise of every other branch of knowledge, including traditions of religious reason and logic. Logocentrism thus connotes the discursive parameters which have guided the historical understanding of particular religious texts beyond an analysis of their formal content and style.

Yet, when Arkoun refers to the 'logocentrism of Islam' he is not pointing to an explicitly 'Islamic' phenomenon. Rather, the concept of 'logos' (as derived from Aristotle) is a fundamental component of the historical development of Jewish, Christian and Muslim thought. Over time, the intellectual legacy of Greek (Aristotelian and Neoplatonic) rationalism came to influence these three scriptural, monotheistic religions within the common gestalt of the 'Mediterranean space'.[53] For Arkoun, the paradigm of the Mediterranean space is 'more cultural than geographic and strategic'. It encompasses those cultures which were originally influenced by 'Iranian religions and the great ancient cultures of the Near East... all before the invention of Greece, Rome, Byzantium, and "Islam".'[54] In the early medieval period, moreover, the dominance of Hellenistic philosophy in this shared cultural-epistemic location gave rise to those common semantic tensions (between such categories as faith–unbelief, soul–body, essence–existence and reason–revelation) which have instructed the rational theological, philosophical and heresiological discourses of these religions.

This represents a clear riposte to the modern academic notion (which is shared by modern religious revivalists) of Islam as a religion bound to the force of its sacred sources, without regard for broader influences and contexts. For too long, Arkoun argues, modern historians have conflated the western Mediterranean cultures of Spain, Portugal, Greece and Italy with the imaginary entity of 'Europe', or 'the West', whilst the eastern Mediterranean lands inhabited by the Turkic- and Arabic-speaking peoples were relegated to the rarefied domain of 'Oriental' or 'Islamic studies' departments. Consequently, Islam is the exclusive subject of area specialists and historians who are unable to link its traditions of knowledge with the broader preoccupations of humanist scholarship and philosophical reflection, let alone the intellectual history of those societies which make up the modern West.[55] To correct this, Arkoun argues that Islamic history must be linked to those broader environments which have determined the discursive and logical methods to which it, and Europe, owe their formation.

Thus, Arkoun establishes a comparative epistemological framework for subjects which might otherwise be relegated to the separate fields of 'Oriental' and 'European' history. When he speaks of an Islamic *'imaginaire'* (or imaginary), for instance, he refers to the long historical processes – common to Europe and Islam – by which modern collective social, religious, linguistic, ethnic and national identities are formed.[56] For the modern Muslim world this took a particular form, when the intellectual struggles of colonialism and decolonisation nurtured a mythical Muslim identity with which to rebut certain aspects of the modern world. Whilst this imaginary notion of Islam is a source of legitimation for those who believe that it and the West are engaged in a 'clash of civilisations', it is, nonetheless, a transparently ideological construction, which cannot advance the objectives of historical and philosophical inquiry. Crucial to Arkoun's argument is the notion that the human construction of Islam is not primordially unified and cannot exist outside time and history. The theme of the *imaginaire* serves a deconstructive purpose, in enabling historians to resist the imposition of an essentialised Muslim identity.[57]

Declaring that *'there is no access to the absolute* outside of the phenomenal world of our territorial, historical existence', Arkoun intends to remove Muslim history's transcendental reference points, and sharpen its historical focus.[58] He points out, for instance, that contemporary Muslim thinkers rarely entertain questions about the historical status of the Qur'an, or consider that its content and language might have been influenced by the conditions and circumstances of the society to which it was revealed. Yet, by doing this, they ignore a vigorous and rich theological debate of the classical period over the 'created' (historical and non-divine) or 'uncreated' (in the sense of being divine and co-eternal with God) stature of the Qur'an. During the early centuries of Islam, this debate addressed the tensions that arose between the Qur'an's universal and contingent nature, as between its eternal and merely temporal elements. By denying the historical properties of the sacred text (in order to maintain its transcendent qualities), Muslims have lost touch with the rich genealogy of this issue in their own religious history.[59] Thus, for Arkoun, one must not detach the category of revelation (*wahy*) from its historical conceptualisation within premodern and modern Muslim theological discourses.[60]

Here, Arkoun's theoretical distinction (between the transcendental content of religion and its human explication) becomes less a concern of theology than of epistemology. Just as Derrida once argued that 'there is nothing outside textuality' (meaning that both the world and the language used to refer to it participate in the 'marks' and 'signs' which constitute signifying systems), so Arkoun may be taken to mean that there is no knowledge (secular or religious) which is not constituted by the language which that knowledge constructs.[61] The terms of Arkoun's critique are thus grounded not in a search for the hidden structure, or programme, of Islamic thought (as it is for Fazlur Rahman) but in the promise of contemporary critical theory and cross-disciplinary analysis to forge new areas of historical inquiry. In this sense, Arkoun does not see himself working within the reformist tradition of religious (*islahi*) thinking.[62] He instead opts for a deconstructive approach which, as we have seen, is alive to the epistemological limitations that such traditions impose.

Arkoun's most useful theme, for my purposes, is his dialectical notion of the history of reason in the conceptual imaginaries of Islam and the West. For Arkoun, the use of reason in Muslim history has oscillated between the polarities of (in his words) the 'thought and unthought' (or the 'thinkable and unthinkable') within Islam's various intellectual traditions. Again, this was not a unique occurrence, for Islam's encounter with Hellenistic/Mediterranean rationalism certainly can be compared to (and indeed influenced) the flowering of theological reason which occurred in medieval Christian thinking after the time of Thomas Aquinas (1225–1274). In both cases, the encounter with Greek philosophy altered the parameters of the thinkable and unthinkable in terms of philosophical and religious reason although the historical consequences of this for Islamic history were different to that of Europe, given the different historical, political and cultural conditions under which such intellectual activities were waged.[63]

In the modern period, moreover, Islam is as much a victim as its Judeo-Christian forebears of that 'tele-techno-scientific reason' (the term is borrowed from Derrida) which expanded with the rise of global capitalism and its concomitant technological forms.[64] Whilst some of the newly independent regimes of North Africa and the Arab Middle East embraced the emancipatory but unrealisable promises of 'progress' and 'rationalisation' in their interpretation of socialist ideology, this gave way, after the Cold War, to the disintegrative influences of the neo-liberal capitalist market. For Arkoun, the influence of global capitalism upon Islam's intellectual traditions has been as disastrous as its influence on other Third World cultures, and is exemplified by the philosophically impoverished forms of religiosity embraced amongst contemporary Muslim revivalists. The same global, tele-techno-scientific process which augured the secularisation of Western societies has thus had the effect of denuding Islam's essential religious values of their intellectual and cultural support. Instead of addressing these issues, contemporary Muslims have worked to expand the realm of the 'unthought', beneath a defensive and exclusionary form of religious reasoning.

In his diagnosis of this, and to make the unthought potentially thinkable, Arkoun calls for a new paradigm, which he finds in the concept of 'emerging reason'. For Arkoun, this is:

> concerned with the philosophical subversion of the use of reason itself and all forms of rationality produced so far and those which will be produced in the future so as not to repeat the ideological compromises and derivations of the precedent postures and performances of reason.[65]

This notion, as I interpret it, intends to subvert reason by balancing it against that which reason opposes. In the context of the modern academy, it intends to expand reason beyond the limits of that 'Western historical logosphere' which authorises the superior self-conception of reason in modern secular societies.[66] In the study of Islamic history, moreover, it seeks to account not only for the logocentrism of Islam's traditions of knowledge, and reason-based exegesis, but for the silences (the unthought) which are a counterpart to these. Emerging reason, or 'reason in crisis' is capable of addressing the human condition to the extent that it lends an ear to the 'heterodox' and marginalised voices of Muslim history.[67]

There is an aspect of Arkoun's notion of an 'emerging' and necessarily incomplete process of reason (of a reason which is prohibited from fulfilling its claims to finality) which is useful for my analysis of the aims of a progressive Muslim hermeneutical theory. Primarily, it is the above-mentioned sense that the task of interpretation is open-ended (or as changeable as the historical structures of human thinking in which reason inheres), which in turn caters to the need for a deontological (or foundationless) theory of religion.[68] Here my use of the term 'deontological religion' does not refer to a theology with no sound basis in knowledge, nor is it a religion without God. Instead it denotes a theology in which the contingencies of knowledge (as it relates to the interpretation of sacred sources) are necessarily incomplete and fallible. This sense of openness, of a religion whose actualisation in human life is always unfinished, is touched upon by Amina Wadud in a passage of her book, *Inside the Gender Jihad*:

> Those who opposed my analysis boisterously hurled their opposition directly in my face, claimed certain of my comments were blasphemous, according to their interpretations of Islam, and eventually labelled me a 'devil in *hijab*' (head-covering). At the time I was utterly stunned by the presence of such insolence from other Muslims. Since that experience, however, I have moved towards a new, albeit uncomfortable, reflection: neither their 'Islam' nor my 'Islam' has ultimate privilege. We are all part of a complex whole, in constant motion and manifestation throughout the history of multifaceted but totally human constructions of 'Islam'... Curiously enough, relinquishing the idea that there exists a perfect thing called Islam devoid of the consequences of human interactions allowed me to relinquish my own self-agonizing expectations that I could one day become a perfect Muslim.[69]

The moment in which religion becomes conscious of its own constructed/human status is the moment in which Arkoun's theme of 'emerging reason', of a reason which is critical of the search for immutable foundations, comes into its own. Furthermore, this insistence on contingency in the production of religious knowledge leads to a deontological theory of religious truth very much resembling the postmodern deconstruction of knowledge systems. This deontological standpoint, I argue, is essential for a morally responsible reformist agenda. For only when one has studied the epistemological basis (and sociological provenance) of religious thought can one reconstruct Islamic themes within the fields of social criticism, political theory and ethics. This is also achieved dialectically, against other interpretations and against the background of contemporary understandings. It is therefore necessary to place religion in the emergent, and continually unfurling, position of that reason, and knowledge, to which it defers. As Wadud puts it, 'Islam is no longer the goal, but a process'.[70]

Conclusion: Islam and the Future of Religion

For the progressive thinkers analysed above, one cannot conflate Islam with an all-encompassing theme, ideology, or social programme, without simultaneously denying the very conditions under which the human understanding and interpretation of religious knowledge becomes possible. For this reason, one must return to questions not only of correct methodology, but to the epistemological ground from which subjective interpretations of religion are based. For Fazlur Rahman, the separation of Islam's 'normative' content from its 'historical' practice and understanding achieves this, by allowing the Qur'an's moral-universal worldview to come into focus. Likewise, amongst feminist thinkers, this distinction is used to show how male interpreters have exploited the sacred text, how the text resists such types of interpretation, and how the reader may yet form a better understanding of it in light of present concerns. This takes an interesting turn for 'Abdolkarim Soroush, whose attempt to separate, and so protect, Islam's normative content from the distortions of political power, leads to the valorisation of a secular scheme that preserves religion within the sphere of civil society.

In the reconstruction of Islam's intellectual traditions, one cannot underestimate the value of those recent philosophical, poststructuralist and semiotic theories which attend not simply to the rules of language but to the conditions of its various and changing contexts and uses. For as we have seen, with respect to the thought of Mohammed Arkoun, the hermeneutical advantage of the linguistic turn is not to determine where the interpretations of the past went wrong and how they can be put right in a once-and-for-all manner. It is instead to arrive at an understanding of the historical contingency of all interpretations, so precluding the implementation of an eternally determined or hegemonic notion of religious truth (which is the perceived flaw of Islamist doctrine, as of any constraining 'ontotheology'). Thus, for the thinkers analysed above, the value of a deontological hermeneutical theory is its refusal to conflate the human understanding of divinity with the thing itself. Such can only be the future of religion when one acknowledges the man-made (rather than divine) aspects of contemporary religious thought.

Moreover, to place this current of thought within the ideological opposites of 'religion' and 'secularism' (whose distinctions contribute to the condition of our global modernity) is an interesting proposition. Because progressive Islam is marked by the search for an interpretive position which is responsive and adaptable to the complex development of religious forms in modern life, it does not uniformly support the will of some secularists to banish religion from the public sphere. It instead seeks to preserve religious principles within contemporary discussions about political democracy, gender equality and intellectual pluralism. To this end, progressive Muslim reforms provide us with one further example (amongst those already described in the earlier chapters of this thesis) of how religion draws upon contemporary resources to mark its place in the modern world.

CONCLUSION

From the liberal imperialism of the nineteenth century to Francis Fukuyama's thesis concerning the 'end of history and the last man', history has often played witness to the passions of a triumphalist, lopsided notion of modernity that frames the world in singular, self-defining terms. This is no doubt true of the contemporary study of Islam, in which analysts have often opposed Islam to a distinctly Eurocentric notion of the modern world, as my introduction sought to show. Notable cases include the ideological representatives of nineteenth-century European imperialism (including administrators such as Lord Cromer and the Orientalist scholars, Stanley Lane-Pool and Ernst Renan) as they do the present-day historians and intellectuals aligned to commensurable ideological and nationalist agendas. For many such intellectuals, modernity is felt to have developed exclusively within Europe, to be exported elsewhere at a later stage. This relies upon a false dichotomy: between the 'original' intellectual developments of the European metropole, and what are perceived to be a series of derivative, compensatory gestures occurring at the periphery of empire. Yet the world in the nineteenth century was shaped as much by the new contexts and environments which colonialism created, as by the intellectual productions of its manufacturing centres.

As the nineteenth-century indigenous critique of imperialism reveals, the liberal tenets of 'reason', 'improvement' and 'progress' were clearly undermined by the unequal relations of colonial power which such tenets helped to validate. This contradictory gesture is repeated in the twentieth century, when the 'uneven development' attributed to Third World countries by theorists of modernisation led to policies which in fact impeded modernisation's universalist notions of political and economic 'convergence'. Because history does not move in a straight line, it makes little sense to continue with a teleological model that posits the supposed 'failure' of Islamic reforms, or of Islam on the whole, to achieve modernity. To ask 'what went wrong?' of Muslim history (as Bernard Lewis does) is not to observe the failure of Muslim societies to become modern, but to disclose one's own failure in conceptualising the conditions under which modernity is constituted. Thus throughout this book I have raised the need to conceive of modernity as a complex process that arose globally, and often at cross-purposes to itself, under the conditions of modern colonialism and international capitalism. It is less accurate to speak of modernity as a singular ideology or doctrine than as an epistemological condition which gave rise to the dichotomies (of science–religion, reason–superstition, public–private and so forth) through which the modern world emerged. In this sense, modernity cannot be conflated with any singular culture, tradition, people, nation or essence.

My analysis of this began in chapter 1, where I focused upon three modernist thinkers of the nineteenth century (Jamal al-Din al-Afghani, Muhammad 'Abduh and Sayyid Ahmad Khan) who sought to reform Islam in relation to the epistemological categories of European thought. Each of these thinkers were impressed by Western science and argued – contrary to colonial criticisms – that Islam was wholly compatible with modern reason. Yet because reason played a central role in the instrumentalisation of colonial rule, modernist reformers felt compelled to distinguish its beneficial from its harmful elements. To this end, they developed a theory of separate ('Islamic' and 'materialist') epistemologies, whose essentialisation of Islam (as a reified system, civilisation, or culture) mirrored changes in the concept of 'religion', or of religious systems, occurring within Europe. In this sense, modernist reforms were influenced by the categories of nineteenth-century thought. My second and third chapters focused upon the consequences of this for particular projects of literary revival and female education around the turn of the century.

To properly contextualise Islamic reformism in the twentieth century is to understand its complex engagement with the theories of modern nationalism. Thus, my fourth chapter highlighted the ambiguous appropriation of Romantic nationalist themes by the celebrated Indian philosopher and poet, Muhammad Iqbal. Iqbal's conception of Islam is interesting precisely for appropriating the concepts of modern nationalism (especially, its theory of separate national peoples or races) in a theoretically self-conscious way. Because he harnessed the contradictory forces that are built into the modern ideologies of race and nationhood, Iqbal cannot be associated with projects of religious nationalism, Islamism, or any such totalising ideological construction.

Around the middle of the twentieth century, the transformation of Islam into a political 'system' (*nizam*) or ideological 'conception/ worldview' (*tasawwur*) amongst such Islamist thinkers as Sayyid Abul A'la Maududi and Sayyid Qutb represents a decisive moment in the reification of religious themes. Yet, as my fifth chapter showed, this conceptualisation of Islam creates a theoretical rift between the real and the ideal dimensions of a religious system, or state, which neither Maududi nor Qutb were able to satisfactorily resolve. Moreover, as the internal criticism of Islamist doctrine in the work of India's Wahiduddin Khan reveals, the theory of an Islamic state is too deeply embedded in secular categories to realise its own claims to ideological purity. This was further explored in chapter 6, where I discussed Maududi's idealisation of the role of Muslim women and his evident reliance upon the (quasi-)scientific, sociological and psychoanalytic essentialisation of gender.

If the notion of Islam as an ideological system is a distinguishing feature of the modern period, so too is the hermeneutical impasse brought about by this idea, which I analysed in chapter 7. Because various reformers in the modern period have selectively disaggregated and recombined elements of Islam's sacred sources and intellectual traditions, progressive Muslim intellectuals call for a proper hermeneutical theory with which to reconstruct religious knowledge. For the most part, this is done by re-evaluating the historical conditions and contexts under which the Qur'an can be interpreted, for the purpose of retaining its universal moral principles. Employing critical theoretical discoveries in the fields of philosophy and the social sciences, this interpretive methodology is important for contextualising the manner in which Islam is to be understood, and provides a firm reminder of its responsiveness to critical trends in contemporary thinking.

To speak of Islam and modernity at all, in light of the above, is to account for the interaction of disjunctive ideas and responses, beyond the scope of a singular religious tradition, culture, or essence. As such, the complicated and sometimes hazy distinctions which modernity validates (between notions of progress–decline, reason–irrationality and so forth) must be historicised against one another, if we are to understand the true meaning of such terms as 'reason', 'civilisation' and 'progress'. This historicising gesture resists the dichotomous thinking that would pit Islam and modernity against one another, and clears a space beyond this dichotomy. From this point, one can better understand how Muslim reformers encountered, and worked within, those categories of knowledge, experience and feeling, through which the contemporary world emerged.

This task becomes all the more necessary when notions such as 'civilisation' and 'Enlightenment' are used to justify the superiority of one people over another, or to scapegoat a national, ethnic or religious minority for political purposes. One notices with alarm, for instance, a rise in conspiracy theories about Muslim minorities amongst right-wing and far-right political parties in Europe and America. This is promoted by various media pundits, policy analysts, and self-appointed 'experts', such as Daniel Pipes in the USA and Melanie Phillips in the UK, who warn against the Islamisation of Western society, or the 'shariah-isation' of democratic legal systems, as though Western Muslim minorities are uniformly working against Western societies. By conflating the threat of global terrorism with the presence of Muslim faith, the proponents of such theories indeed undermine the civil ethics and values of human dignity which they claim to be defending. An example of this is the legislation passed in many American states in 2010 which sought to ban the observation of shari'ah law (however that is conceived) in local courts – even though it is customary for American courts to account for religious codes in matters of civil arbitration. A similar paranoia surrounded the national referendum in Switzerland, in 2009, which succeeded in banning the construction of minarets throughout the country on the assumption that minarets are a political symbol of Islamic radicalism. Thereby it is possible to espouse the promotion of liberal values whilst traducing the rights of those who are not deemed worthy of them.

However, I do not suggest that because universalist paradigms are self-undermining or because the modernist themes of progress and rationality have not always lived up to their promises, we should somehow renounce them or seek an alternative elsewhere. On the contrary, we cannot simply discard our universalisms, let alone our cultural, national, religious and sexual identities, when these are valuable to sustaining the categories (of belonging, subjectivity, faith, gender and so forth) by which we make sense of the world and our place in it. Moreover, universalising theories of the human good are a valid means by which we project our hopes, aspirations and impetus for social change into the future. We should be aware of the conditions of our historical moment, and remain critical of those who manipulate history to foster prejudice and exclusion.

NOTES

Introduction: Islam, Postcolonialism and Modernity

1. Francis Fukuyama, 'Has history started again?', *Policy*, 18, 2002, pp. 3–7.
2. Recent examples, amongst many, of this type of analysis are: Michael J. Mazarr, *Unmodern Men in the Modern World: Radical Islam, Terrorism, and the War on Modernity*, Cambridge University Press, New York, 2007; Lee Harris, *The Suicide of Reason: Radical Islam's Threat to the Enlightenment*, Basic Books, New York, 2007; and Thomas L. Friedman, *The Lexus and the Olive Tree*, HarperCollins, London, 1999.
3. Alain Badiou, *Infinite Thought*, London, Continuum, 2003, p. 115.
4. See Uday Singh Mehta, *Liberalism and Empire: A Study in Nineteenth-Century British Liberal Thought*, University of Chicago Press, Chicago, 1999; and Thomas R. Metcalf, *Ideologies of the Raj*, Cambridge University Press, Berkeley, 1995.
5. Because 'liberty, as a principle, has no application to anything anterior to the time when mankind have become capable of being improved by free and independent discussion', John Stuart Mill asserted that 'despotism is a legitimate mode of government in dealing with barbarians, provided the end be their improvement'. John Stuart Mill, *On Liberty and Other Essays*, John Gray (ed.), Oxford University Press, Oxford, 1998, pp. 14–15. See also, James Mill, *The History of British India (to 1834)* (5th edn), Horace H. Wilson (ed.), James Madden, London, 1858.
6. See *Subaltern Studies*, vols 1–12, Oxford University Press, New Delhi; Partha Chatterjee, *The Nation and its Fragments: Colonial and Post Colonial Histories*, Oxford University Press, Delhi, 1995; Dipesh Chakrabarty, *Provincializing Europe: Postcolonial Thought and Historical Difference*, Princeton University Press, Princeton, 2000; and Ranajit Guha, *History at the Limits of World-History*, Columbia University Press, New York, 2002.

7. Homi Bhabha, *The Location of Culture*, Routledge, London, 1994, chapter 4.
8. Sayyid Amir 'Ali, *Memoirs and Other Writings of Syed Ameer Ali*, People's Publishing House, Lahore, 1978, pp. 285–286.
9. Ibid.
10. Frantz Fanon, *The Wretched of the Earth*, Constance Farrington (trans.), Penguin Books, London, 2001, p. 251.
11. Bhabha, *The Location of Culture*, pp. 157–158. Alongside the works mentioned in footnote 5 of this introduction, see Gyan Prakash, 'Introduction', *After Colonialism: Imperial Histories and Postcolonial Displacements*, Gyan Prakash (ed.), Princeton University Press, Princeton, 1995, pp. 3–19. The ambiguity and contradictions besetting the application of Western liberal ideas in the colonies during the nineteenth century is discussed in Mehta, *Liberalism and Empire*.
12. Chakrabarty, *Provincializing Europe*, pp. 28–46.
13. Abdallah Laroui, *The Crisis of the Arab Intellectual: Traditionalism or Historicism?*, Diarmid Cammell (trans.), University of California Press, Berkeley, 1976.
14. Ibid., pp. 1–10.
15. Arthur Strum, 'What Enlightenment is', *New German Critique*, 70, 2000, pp. 106–136. For the thinkers of the Romantic Enlightenment, see Isaiah Berlin, *The Crooked Timber: Chapters in the History of Ideas*, Henry Hardy (ed.), John Murray, London, 1990.
16. David Kolb, *The Critique of Pure Modernity: Hegel, Heidegger, and After*, University of Chicago Press, Chicago, 1986.
17. Robert J. C. Young, *White Mythologies: Writing History and the West*, Routledge, New York, 2004.
18. Edward Said, *Culture and Imperialism*, Vintage, New York, 1994.
19. Three studies which analyse the role of colonialism in the formation of British imperial mythology are: Jenny Sharpe, *Allegories of Empire: The Figure of Woman in the Colonial Text*, University of Minnesota Press, Minneapolis, 1993; Saree Makdisi, *Romantic Imperialism: Universal Empire and the Culture of Modernity*, Cambridge University Press, Cambridge, 1998; and Gauri Viswanathan, *Masks of Conquest: Literary Study and British Rule in India*, Columbia University Press, New York, 1989.
20. Peter van der Veer, *Imperial Encounters: Religion and Modernity in India and Britain*, Princeton University Press, Princeton, 2001.
21. See Arjun Appadurai, *Modernity at Large: Cultural Dimensions of Globalization*, University of Minnesota Press, Minneapolis, 1996; and Oliver Roy, *Globalised Islam: The Search for a New Ummah*, Hurst, London, 2004.
22. For a good study of the relationship between Islam and modern Islamic revivalism on one hand, and modern Western political and Orientalist

discourses on the other, see Armando Salvatore, *Islam and the Political Discourses of Modernity*, Ithaca, Beirut, 1997.

23. Whilst the themes of 'rationalisation' and 'disenchantment' are commonly drawn from the work of Max Weber, Walter L. Wallace points out that the simplified definitions since put to use by theorists of modernisation do not exhaust the complex meanings which Weber invested in these themes. See Walter L. Wallace, 'Rationality, human nature, and society in Weber's theory', *Theory and Society*, 19 (2), 1990, pp. 199–223.

24. Max Weber, *The Protestant Ethic and the Spirit of Capitalism*, T. Parsons (trans.), Allen & Unwin, London, 1930.

25. Nils Gilman, *Mandarins of the Future: Modernization Theory in Cold War America*, Johns Hopkins University Press, Baltimore, 2003.

26. Daniel Lerner, *The Passing of a Traditional Society: Modernizing the Middle East*, Free Press, New York, 1964.

27. Ibid., pp. 49–50.

28. Ibid., p. 405. Brian S. Turner critiques the universalist pretensions of modernisation theory in his *Weber and Islam: A Critical Study*, Routledge, London, 1974, pp. 151, 158 and 170.

29. Samir Amin, *The Arab Nation: Nationalism and Class Struggle*, Zed Press, London, 1978, p. 24. Other examples of dependency theory include: Roger Owen, *The Middle East in the World Economy: 1800–1914*, Methuen, London, 1981; and Haim Gerber, *The Social Origins of the Modern Middle East*, Mansell, London, 1987.

30. See S. N. Eisenstadt, 'Multiple modernities in an age of globalization', *Canadian Journal of Sociology*, 24 (2), 1999, pp. 283–295; and Nulifer Gole, 'Snapshots of Islamic modernities', *Deadalus*, 129 (1), pp. 91–117.

31. Lisa Anderson, 'Policy making and theory building: American political science and the Arab Middle East', *Theory, Politics and the Arab World: Critical Responses*, Hisham Sharabi (ed.), Routledge, 1990, p. 65.

32. See G. E. von Grunebaum, *Modern Islam: The Search for Cultural Identity*, University of California Press, Berkeley, 1962, p. 209.

33. See Anderson, 'Policy making and theory building', p. 66. For an interesting thesis which addresses the idea of an incomplete or 'distorted' process of modernisation without reductively essentialising Arab culture, see Hisham Sharabi, *Neopatriarchy: A Theory of Distorted Change in Arab Society*, Oxford University Press, New York, 1988.

34. See *Association for the Study of the Middle East and Africa* website, <http://www.asmeascholars.org/index.php?option=com_content&view=article&id=4&Itemid=6> (accessed 8 July 2011).

35. Bernard Lewis, *What Went Wrong? Western Impact and Middle Eastern Response*, Oxford University Press, Oxford, 2002.

36. Ibid. See Lewis' preface and references to Osama bin Laden and the Taliban on p. 159.
37. Ibid., pp. 96–99.
38. Bernard Lewis, 'Islam and liberal democracy', *Atlantic Monthly*, 271 (2), 1993, pp. 96–97.
39. Ibid.
40. Bernard Lewis, *Islam and the West*, Oxford University Press, New York, 1993, pp. 46–56.
41. The argument that the Ottoman Empire did not adapt to the modern global economic system sufficiently to facilitate the creation of a capitalist bourgeois middle class derives in part from the work of Weber. See Brian S. Turner, 'Islam, capitalism and the Weber thesis', *The British Journal of Sociology*, 25 (2), 1974, pp. 230–243; and by the same author, *Marx and the End of Orientalism*, George Allen & Unwin, London, 1978, p. 46.
42. Lewis, *What Went Wrong?*, p.158. Because pre-modern Muslim polities are characterised by 'intensely personal' structures of authority, Lewis asserts that: 'In principle, at least, there is no state, but only a ruler; no court, but only a judge. There is not even a city with defined powers, limits and functions, but only an assemblage of neighbourhoods, mostly defined by family, tribal, ethnic, or religious criteria, and governed by officials, usually military, appointed by the sovereign' (Lewis, 'Islam and liberal democracy', p. 94). As Andre Raymond points out, this habit of defining a non-city, or a city by what it lacks, had a long pedigree amongst Orientalist scholars who looked to the Middle East and lamented the disappearance of the Graeco-Roman city-structures of antiquity. Andre Raymond, 'Islamic city, Arab city: Orientalist myths and recent views', *British Journal of Middle Eastern Studies*, 21 (1), 1994, pp. 3–18.
43. Lewis, *What Went Wrong?*, p. 100.
44. N. J. Coulson, *A History of Islamic Law*, Edinburgh University Press, Edinburgh, 1964, chapter 9.
45. See Ira M. Lapidus, 'The separation of state and religion in the development of early Islamic societies', *International Journal of Middle Eastern Studies*, 6 (4), 1975, pp. 363–385. For the complex and mutually dependent relations between the caliph and religious authorities in Muslim history, see Wael B. Hallaq, *The Origins and Evolution of Islamic Law*, Cambridge University Press, Cambridge, 2005, chapter 8.
46. Halil Inalcik, *The Ottoman Empire: The Classical Age 1300–1600*, Phoenix, London, 1994.
47. Lewis, *What Went Wrong?*, pp. 128–132.
48. Ibid., p. 129.

49. Benedict Anderson, *Imagined Communities: Reflections on the Origins and Spread of Nationalism*, Verso, London, 1991. See also Francis Robinson, 'Technology and religious change: Islam and the impact of print', *Modern Asian Studies*, 27 (1), 1993, pp. 229–251.
50. Lewis, *What Went Wrong?*, p. 159.
51. Bernard Lewis, 'The roots of Muslim rage', *Atlantic Monthly*, 266 (3), 1990, p. 60.
52. Ibid., p. 49.
53. For instance, Faisal Devji asserts that al-Qaida's contemporary importance lies not in its use of violence but in its ability to fragment traditional structures of clerical and mystical authority which are then recombined in unprecedented and novel ways. See Faisal Devji, *Landscapes of the Jihad: Militancy, Morality, Modernity*, Hurst, London, 2005.
54. The notion of the *salaf* in relation to the thought of al-Afghani and Muhammad 'Abduh is explored in more detail in chapter 1 of this book.
55. Seyyed Vali Reza Nasr demonstrates that the twentieth-century Indian revivalist, Sayyid Abul A'la Maududi's vision of an Islamic state 'left no room for the *'ulama* as leaders, judges and guardians of the community. By encouraging the independent study of Arabic, the Qur'an, Hadith and other religious sources, Maududi rendered them superfluous.' Seyyed Vali Reza Nasr, *Maududi and the Making of Islamic Revivalism*, Oxford University Press, Oxford, 1996, p. 115. For the Muslim Brothers' attitude towards the *'ulama* of al-Azhar, see Richard P. Mitchell, *The Society of the Muslim Brothers*, Oxford University Press, London, 1969, pp. 211–212.
56. Sami Zubaida, *Law and Power in the Islamic World*, I.B.Tauris, London, 2005.
57. Bernard Lewis, *Semites and Anti-Semites: An Inquiry into Conflict and Prejudice*, W.W. Norton, New York, 1999, pp. 145–146.
58. Joel Beinin contends that Lewis' Zionist sympathies, and corresponding eagerness to establish an essentialist and monolithic theory of Arab culture, leads to some curious omissions. Political leaders such as Pierre Gemayal, the founder of Lebanon's Phalange (an organisation modelled after the Hitler Youth), and his son Bashir, who was an ally of Israel in Lebanon, are not included in his study. Nor does he mention the pro-Fascist sentiments of the revisionist Zionists who cooperated with Mussolini and expressed admiration for the Nazis. Moreover, the much larger phenomenon of anti-Arab racism in Israel is dismissed by Lewis as a belated historical reaction (arising only in the 1980s) to Arab anti-Semitism. Joel Beinin, 'Bernard Lewis' Anti-Semites', *Middle Eastern Report*, 147, 1987, pp. 43–45.
59. Fouad Ajami, *The Arab Predicament: Arab Political Thought and Practice Since 1967*, Cambridge University Press, Cambridge, 1992, p. 23.

60. Samuel Huntington took the 'clash of civilisations' theme from Bernard Lewis' aforementioned article 'The roots of Muslim rage', p. 60. Samuel Huntington, *The Clash of Civilizations and the Remaking of World Order*, Touchstone Books, London, 1997. Huntington's thesis was first published in the journal *Foreign Affairs* in 1993.
61. Reflecting the stance of an ex-Cold War warrior who is blind to instances of influence and adaptation between cultures and civilisations, Huntington enshrines processes of opposition and conflict with such useful aphorisms as: 'we know who we are only when we know who we are not and often only when we know whom we are against.' (ibid., p. 21). For a good analysis of the powerful influence of Carl Schmitt's friend/enemy distinction on American conservative thinkers, see Brian S. Turner, 'Sovereignty and emergency: Political theology, Islam and American conservatism', *Theory, Culture and Society*, 19 (4), 2002, pp. 103–119.
62. Huntington, *The Clash of Civilizations*, pp. 217–218.
63. See George W. Bush, 'Address to a Joint Session of Congress and the American People' (20 September 2001), http://www.washingtonpost.com/wp-srv/nation/specials/attacked/transcripts/bushaddress_092001.html (accessed 8 July 2011).
64. Resisting this paradigm, Mahmood Mamdani demotes 'culture talk' for a more useful analysis of the rise of radical Islam in the political context of the late Cold War. See Mahmood Mamdani, *Good Muslim, Bad Muslim: America, the Cold War, and the Roots of Terror*, Doubleday, New York, 2005.
65. Bernard Lewis, 'A time for toppling', *From Babel to Dragomans: Interpreting the Middle East*, Phoenix, London, 2004, p. 470. This article was first published in the *Wall Street Journal*, 28 September 2002. In a later article, Lewis stressed that those considerations of self-preservation and self-interest which attended the doctrine of 'mutually assured destruction' (MAD) and so prevented nuclear war between the United States and Soviet Union, cannot be applied in the instance of Iran. Because the clerical regime under the leadership of Mahmoud Ahmedinijad harbours a religiously inspired 'apocalyptic vision' of world history which is eschatological, destructive and cataclysmic, 'the deterrent that worked so well during the Cold War would have no meaning [in the case of Iran]'. See Bernard Lewis, 'Does Iran have something in store?', http://www.metransparent.com/old/texts/bernard_lewis_does_iran_have_something_in_store.htm (accessed 8 July 2011).
66. For a good analysis of the reality underpinning America's invasion of Iraq and rhetorical stance concerning democracy and 'freedom' in the Middle East, see Rashid Khalidi, *Resurrecting Empire: Western Footprints and America's Perilous Path in the Middle East*, I.B.Tauris, London, 2004.

67. See Anouar Abdel-Malek, 'Orientalism in crisis', *Diogenes*, 11, 1963, pp. 103–140; Sayyid Hussain Alatas, 'The captive mind in development studies', *International Social Science Journal*, 24 (1), 1972, pp. 9–25; Laroui, *The Crisis of the Arab Intellectual: Traditionalism or Historicism?*; and Fanon, *The Wretched of the Earth*.
68. For the early contributions of scholars associated with the insights of the anthropologist historian, Talal Asad, see *Anthropology and the Colonial Encounter*, Talal Asad (ed.), Ithaca, London, 1973.
69. Edward Said, *Orientalism: Western Conceptions of the Orient*, Penguin, London, 1995.
70. Ibid., pp. 22–23.
71. This insight is explored in greater detail in Said, *Culture and Imperialism*.
72. This does not mean that all Orientalist scholars were corrupted by power or had no sympathy for their subject of research, as various critics of Said's thesis have claimed. Nor does it imply that only non-European, so-called Third World scholars are somehow qualified to write the history of their societies. It simply means that despite the sincere and often salutary work of scholars who sought a profound and real interaction with the history, peoples and cultures of the Orient, the dominant conceptions and themes of historical scholarship were never entirely free from broader political concerns and stances. The same no doubt remains true today.
73. Michel Foucault, *The Order of Things: An Archaeology of the Human Sciences*, Vintage, New York, 1994.
74. See also Michel Foucault, *The Foucault Reader*, Paul Rabinow (ed.), Pantheon, New York, 1984, pp. 77–100.
75. For a review of the influence of Said's theory over the anthropological study of the Middle East, see Lila Abu-Lughod, 'Anthropology's Orient: The boundaries of theory on the Arab world', *Theory, Politics and the Arab World: Critical Responses*, Hisham Sharabi (ed.), Routledge, 1990, pp. 81–131.
76. Regarding the situation in Holland, see Peter van der Veer, 'Pym Fortuyn, Theo Van Gogh, and the politics of tolerance in the Netherlands', *Political Theologies: Public Religions in a Post-Secular World*, Hent De Vries and Lawrence Sullivan (eds), Fordham University Press, New York, 2006, pp. 527–538.
77. Quoted in 'Fraser was warned on Lebanese migrants', *The Australian*, 1 January 2007.
78. Lewis, 'The roots of Muslim rage', pp. 53–54.
79. Bassam Tibi's description of Islam as a civilisation accords with the anthropological historian Clifford Geertz's notion of a cultural system. Although Islam encompasses a diverse range of the world's population, its principle

doctrines unite its adherents within a common civilisation. 'Culture', according to Tibi, represents a 'locally constrained production of meaning, while a civilization combines a set of similar and related local cultures in a civilizing process. There exists a variety of Islamic cultures, however, only one Islamic civilization.' Bassam Tibi, 'Islamic law/shari'ah, human rights, universal morality and international relations', *Human Rights Quarterly*, 16 (2), 1994, p. 287, f.n. 41.

80. It must be observed that Habermas places modernity within the field of philosophical and not of aesthetic discourse. See Jurgen Habermas, *The Philosophical Discourses of Modernity*, Frederick Lawrence (trans.), MIT, Cambridge Mass., 1990.

81. Bassam Tibi, *The Challenge of Fundamentalism: Political Islam and the New World Disorder*, University of California Press, Berkeley, 1998, pp. 64–70.

82. Bassam Tibi, 'Culture and knowledge: The politics of Islamization of knowledge as a postmodern project? The fundamentalist claim to de-Westernization', *Theory, Culture and Society*, 12, 1995, p. 7. The term 'fundamentalism' is one that I will quote but avoid using, given that it bears connotations that are unfamiliar to the intellectual history of Islamic reform. Although some Muslims have adopted the notion of *usulliyah* (denoting a return to elemental religious sources), this bears only a superficial resemblance to the description of a 'fundamentalist' and unhelpfully connotes a very dissimilar set of political and social attitudes.

83. Tibi, *The Challenge of Fundamentalism*, p. 13.

84. According to Tibi: 'An international morality that promotes human rights and is accepted by all civilizations must be founded on secularity...in the meaning of a separation of religion and politics.' Ibid., p. 203.

85. Ibid., p. 210.

86. Tibi, 'Islamic law/shari'ah, human rights', p. 282.

87. Ibid., p. 289.

88. Ibid., p. 297.

89. Ibid., p. 292.

90. Tibi, 'Culture and knowledge', p. 9.

91. See Leszek Kolakowski, *Modernity on Endless Trial*, University of Chicago, Chicago, 1990; and Paul Berman, *Terror and Liberalism*, W.W. Norton, New York, 2004.

92. Roger Scruton, *The West and the Rest: Globalization and the Terrorist Threat*, Continuum, London, 2002, p. 108.

93. Ibid., pp. 68–83.

94. Gayanendra Pandey, 'The secular state and the limits of dialogue', *The Crisis of Secularism in India*, Anuradha Dingwaney Needham and Rajeswari Sunder Rajan (eds), Duke University Press, London, 2007, p. 157.

95. Joan Wallach Scott, *The Politics of the Veil*, Princeton University Press, Princeton, 2007.
96. Hent De Vries, 'Before, around and beyond the theologico-political', *Political Theologies: Public Religions in a Post-Secular World*, Hent De Vries and Lawrence E. Sullivan (eds), Fordham University Press, New York, 2006, pp. 1–89.
97. Thomas Nagel, *The View From Nowhere*, Oxford University Press, New York, 1986.
98. Benhabib's counsel to shift 'from a substantialistic to a discursive, communicative concept of rationality' leads to a post-metaphysical universalist position which, with great benefit to the historian, recognises the finitude of reason and sheer contingency of substantive truths. Seyla Benhabib, *Situating the Self: Gender, Community and Postmodernism in Contemporary Ethics*, Polity Press, Oxford, 1992, p. 6.
99. For a discussion of the interplay between nationalist and nativist discourses in postcolonial Iran, see Mehrzad Boroujerdi, *Iranian Intellectuals and the West: The Tormented Triumph of Nativism*, Syracuse University Press, New York, 1996.
100. Talal Asad, *Formations of the Secular: Christianity, Islam, Modernity*, Stanford University Press, Stanford, 2003, p. 25.
101. Ibid.
102. William E. Connolly, *Why I Am Not a Secularist*, University of Minnesota Press, Minneapolis, 1999, p. 4.
103. Alasdair MacIntyre, *After Virtue: A Study in Moral Theory* (3rd edn), Duckworth, London, 2007, p. 222.

Chapter 1. Islamic Modernism and the Reification of Religion

1. See Colin A. Russell, 'The conflict of science and religion', *Science and Religion: A Historical Introduction*, Gary B. Ferngren (ed.), Johns Hopkins University Press, Baltimore, 2002, pp. 3–12; and David B. Wilson, 'The historiography of science and religion', in the same volume, pp. 13–29.
2. John Hedley Brook, *Religion and Science: Some Historical Perspectives*, Cambridge University Press, Cambridge, 1991.
3. Ignaz Goldziher, 'The attitude of orthodox Islam towards the "ancient sciences"', reprinted in *Studies in Islam*, M. Schwartz (ed.), Oxford University Press, Oxford, 1975, pp. 185–215. For a criticism of Goldziher's thesis, see Dimitri Gutas, *Greek Thought, Arabic Culture: The Graeco-Arabic Translation Movement in Baghdad and Early 'Abbasid Society (2nd – 4th/8th –10th centuries)*, Routledge, New York, 1999, pp. 166–175.

4. See A. J. Arberry, *Reason and Revelation in Islam*, Allen & Unwin, London, 1957, chapter 3.
5. See Michael E. Marmura, 'Ghazali and demonstrative science', *Journal of the History of Philosophy*, 3 (2), 1965, pp. 83–209; and by the same author, 'Ghazali and Asharism revisited', *Arabic Sciences and Philosophy*, 12 (1), 2002, pp. 91–110.
6. For references to the continuation of philosophy after the time of al-Ghazali, see Dimitri Gutas, 'The study of Arabic philosophy in the twentieth century: An essay on the historiography of Arabic philosophy', *British Journal of Middle Eastern Studies*, 29 (1), 2002, p. 13; and Khaled el-Rouayheb, 'Sunni Muslim scholars on the status of logic, 1500–1800', *Islamic Law and Society*, 11 (2), 2004, pp. 214–232.
7. The social and historical roots and motives behind the Arabic translation movement (in which numerous works of mathematics, philosophy, medicine, astronomy, natural history and theories of music were rendered from Greek into Arabic, mostly via Syriac, as well as works of history and statecraft from Pahlavi into Arabic) are examined in Gutas, *Greek Thought, Arabic Culture*.
8. Ahmad Dallal, 'Science, medicine and technology: The making of a scientific culture', *The Oxford History of Islam*, John Esposito (ed.), Oxford University Press, Oxford, 1999, pp. 155–213.
9. Shibli Nu'mani, *'Ilm al-Kalam aur al-Kalam*, Nafis Academy, Karachi, 1979, pp. 209–210.
10. The term 'modernist' is here used as a heuristic category. It loosely designates those intellectuals of the late nineteenth and early twentieth centuries who sought to prove the compatibility of Islam with modern knowledge, and does not designate a uniform movement or ideology.
11. As Wilfred Cantwell Smith points out in the context of European thought, the notion of a 'religion' as something that can be reduced to a definite or fixed form was influenced by the new intellectualism of the Enlightenment; the nature of contemporary polemics between conflicting religious parties within Europe; and a deeper knowledge of other religions which existed beyond Europe's shores. Wilfred Cantwell Smith, *The Meaning and End of Religion*, Harper & Row, New York, 1978, chapter 2.
12. Jonathan Z. Smith, 'Religion, religions, religious', *Critical Terms for Religious Studies*, Mark C. Taylor (ed.), University of Chicago Press, Chicago, 1998, pp. 269–284.
13. Jonathan Z. Smith, *Relating Religion: Essays in the Study of Religion*, University of Chicago, Chicago, 2004, pp. 362–374.
14. See Johann Gottfried Herder, *On the Origin of Language: Two Essays*, Alexander Gode (trans.), University of Chicago Press, Chicago, 1966, pp. 85–176;

NOTES TO PAGES 46–51

Maurice Olender, *The Languages of Paradise: Race, Religion and Philology in the Nineteenth Century*, Harvard University Press, London, 1992; and George G. Iggers, *The German Conception of History: The National Tradition of German Thought from Herder to the Present*, Wesleyan University Press, Middletown, 1988.

15. Quoted in Olender, *The Languages of Paradise*, p. 5.
16. Herder, in his *Essay on the Origin of Language*, argued that because the earliest words were used as signs to represent ideas or things, speech became wholly coincident with human thought. Upon this basis, he made the argument that different languages faithfully reflect the national characteristics of the *Volk* or people who have developed them. See Herder, *On the Origin of Language*.
17. Edward Said, *Orientalism: Western Conceptions of the Orient*, Penguin, London, 1995.
18. Gyan Prakash, *Another Reason: Science and the Imagination of Modern India*, Oxford University Press, New Delhi, 1999.
19. For the following details of al-Afghani's life, I have referred to Nikki R. Keddie, *An Islamic Response to Imperialism: Political and Religious Writings of Sayyid Jamal ad-Din 'al-Afghani'*, University of California Press, Berkeley, 1968; and Albert Hourani, *Arabic Thought in the Liberal Age, 1798–1939* (2nd edn), Cambridge University Press, Cambridge, 1983.
20. Quoted in Tzvetan Todorov, *On Human Diversity: Nationalism, Racism and Exoticism in French Thought*, Catherine Porter (trans.), Harvard University Press, Cambridge Mass., 1993, p. 147. See also, Edward Said, *The World, The Text, and The Critic*, Harvard University Press, Cambridge Mass., 1983, chapter 12.
21. Thus, according to Todorov, Renan's 'assertion of the superiority of Aryans over Semites is only an anthropomorphic transposition of the superiority of science over religion'. Todorov, *On Human Diversity*, p. 149.
22. Ibid., p. 148.
23. Ernst Renan, 'Islamism and science', *The Poetry of the Celtic Races and Other Studies by Ernst Renan*, William G. Hutchinson (trans.), Kennikat Press, New York, 1978, pp. 84–108.
24. See Ernst Renan, *Studies of Religious History and Criticism*, O. B. Frothingham (trans.), Carleton, New York, pp. 237–238; and Oswald Spengler, *The Decline of the West* (first published 1926), Charles Francis Atkinson (trans.), Allen & Unwin, London, 1980.
25. Quoted in Keddie, *An Islamic Response to Imperialism*, p. 92.
26. Ibid. Renan's interpretation of Averroes (Ibn Rushd) as an atheist and free thinker, and the Latin Averroists of the Renaissance as secular precursors to the Enlightenment, was to have a significant influence on nineteenth- and

twentieth-century historiography. See Craig Martin, 'Rethinking Renaissance Averroism', *Intellectual History Review*, 17 (1), 2007, pp. 3–19.
27. Keddie, *An Islamic Response to Imperialism*, pp. 185–186.
28. Ibid., p. 187.
29. Ibid., p. 183.
30. Ibid.
31. See R. Walzer, 'Al-Farabi's theory of prophecy and divination', *Journal of Hellenic Studies*, 77 (1), 1957, pp. 142–148. Nikki Keddie discusses al-Afghani's use of the pre-modern philosophical distinction between rational philosophy and religious symbolism in Keddie, *An Islamic Response to Imperialism*.
32. Jacob M. Landau, *The Politics of Pan-Islam: Ideology and Organization*, Clarendon Press, Oxford, 1990, pp. 13–21.
33. Keddie, *An Islamic Response to Imperialism*, p. 107.
34. Ibid.
35. Ibid., pp. 113–114.
36. For the following details of 'Abduh's life, I have referred to Hourani, *Arabic Thought in the Liberal Age*; Malcolm H. Kerr, *Islamic Reform: The Political and Legal Theories of Muhammad 'Abduh and Rashid Rida*, University of California Press, Berkeley, 1966; and Anke von Kugelgen, 'Muhammad 'Abduh', *Encyclopaedia of Islam* (3rd edn).
37. For al-Afghani's influence on the Sufism of the young Muhammad 'Abduh, and the *pir-murid* relationship they established, see Oliver Scharbrodt, 'The salafiyya and Sufism: Muhammad 'Abduh and his *Risalat al-Waridat* (Treatise on Mystical Inspirations)', *Bulletin of SOAS*, 70 (1), 2007, pp. 88–115. Scharbrodt also discusses the efforts of 'Abduh's disciple and biographer, Rashid Rida, to present 'Abduh as a defender of orthodox Sunni Islam. To this end, Rida distanced the latter from any perceived unorthodoxies, including Sufism.
38. Quoted in Hourani, *Arabic Thought in the Liberal Age*, pp. 140–141.
39. Muhammad 'Abduh, *Risalah at-Tawhid: The Theology of Unity*, Ishaq Musa'ad and Kenneth Cragg (trans.), Islamic Book Trust, Kuala Lumpur, 2004, pp. 45–52. Muhammad 'Abduh, *Risalah al-Tawhid*, Majlis Idarah al-Azhar, 1345 h.
40. For the use of this concept in early theological discussions about divine pre-destination and human responsibility, see W. Montgomery Watt, *The Formative Period of Islamic Thought*, Edinburgh University Press, Edinburgh, 1973, pp. 192–193.
41. For 'Abduh's appropriation of certain aspects of Mu'tazilah and 'Asharite theology, see Kerr, *Islamic Reform*, pp. 111–112.
42. 'Abduh, *Risalah at-Tawhid*, Ishaq Musa'ad and Kenneth Cragg (trans.), chapter 6.

NOTES TO PAGES 59–65

43. Ibid., p. 64.
44. The following details of Sayyid Ahmad's life are derived from Aziz Ahmad, *Muslim Modernism in India and Pakistan: 1857–1964*, Oxford University Press, London, 1967; and Christian W. Troll, *Sayyid Ahmed Khan: A Reinterpretation of Muslim Theology*, Vikas Publishing House, Delhi, 1978.
45. These are: *The History of the Bijnor Rebellion* (1858), *The Causes of the Revolt* (1858) and *The Loyal Muhammadans* (1860–61).
46. Quoted in Troll, *Sayyid Ahmed Khan*, p. 128.
47. Sayyid Ahmad Khan, *Tafsir al-Qur'an*, Dost Association, Lahore, 2004, p. 30.
48. The intense opposition generated amongst various religious scholars and traditionalists to Sayyid Ahmad's theology is pointed out in Sheikh Muhammad Ikram, *Mauj-i Kausar*, Idarah-i Thaqafat-i Islamiyyah, Lahore, 2000; and Altaf Husain Hali, *Hayat-i Javid*, Saleem Akhtar (ed.), Sang-i Meel, Lahore, 1993. Al-Afghani's opposition to Sayyid Ahmad Khan's theological reforms will be discussed later in this chapter.
49. Khan, *Tafsir al-Qur'an*, p. 44. See also, 'Sir Sayyid Ahmad Khan's principles of exegesis translated from his *tahrir fi usul al-tafsir*', Muhammad Daud Rahbar (trans.), *Muslim World*, 46, 1956, p. 106. Whilst I have referred in much of what follows to the able translations of Muhammad Daud Rahbar and Christian W. Troll, some changes have been made to these translations for greater accuracy and clarity of meaning.
50. This is quoted in Khan, 'Sir Sayyid Ahmad Khan's principles of exegesis', p. 106. See also, *The Conclusive Argument from God: Shah Wali Allah of Delhi's Hujjat Allah al-Balighah*, Marcia K. Hermansen (trans.), Islamic Research Institute, Islamabad, 2003.
51. Khan, 'Sir Sayyid Ahmad Khan's principles of exegesis', p. 106.
52. Ibid.
53. For an overview of the formation of the doctrine of the Qur'an's inimitability within the systematic body of *kalam*, see Richard C. Martin, 'The role of the Basrah Mu'tazilah in formulating the doctrine of the apologetic miracle', *Journal of Near Eastern Studies*, 39 (3), 1980, pp. 175–189. Al-Jurjani was the first theologian to assert that the miraculous status of the Qur'an could be ascertained from the study of its language and eloquence. See Nasr Abu-Zayd, 'The dilemma of the literary approach to the Qur'an', *Alif: Journal of Comparative Poetics*, 23, 2003, pp. 15–18.
54. Qur'an 2:23 reads: 'If you are in doubt as to what we have revealed to Our Servant, then produce a Sura similar to it and call upon your witnesses other than God, if you are truthful.' See also 10:38 and 11:13.
55. Quoted in Troll, *Sayyid Ahmed Khan*, pp. 326–327.
56. Ibid., p. 281.

57. Ibid., p. 283.
58. Ibid., pp. 294–295.
59. Ibid., p. 284.
60. Just as, for Sayyid Ahmad, revelation (*wahy*) and natural law are not able to contradict one another, so too are Qur'anic references to the role of angels, devils, *jinn*, the day of judgment and paradise interpreted in scientific terms. Thus, he rationalised scriptural stories involving miraculous events as misunderstood natural occurrences or metaphorical devices made congruous with the superstitions and beliefs of the people to whom they were revealed.
61. Sayyid Ahmad Khan, *Maqalat-i Sir Sayyid*, vol. 3, Ismail Panipati (ed.), Majlis-i Taraqi-e Adab, Lahore, 1984, pp. 184–185.
62. Fazlur Rahman, *Revival and Reform in Islam: A Study of Islamic Fundamentalism*, Ebrahim Moosa (ed.), Oneworld, Oxford, 2000, p. 175.
63. The work in question is Abu Hamid al-Ghazali's *Mishkat al-Anwar*. See Abu Hamid Muhammad al-Ghazali, *The Niche of Lights*, David Buchman (trans.), Brigham Young University Press, Utah, 1998; and Kristin Zahra Sands, *Sufi Commentaries on the Qur'an in Classical Islam*, Routledge, New York, 2005, p. 37.
64. Hent De Vries, *Minimal Theologies: Critiques of Secular Reason in Adorno and Levinas*, Geoffrey Hale (trans.), Johns Hopkins University Press, Baltimore, 2005, p. 51. I have maintained De Vries' use of emphasis, only substituting his quotation marks with my own italics.
65. For the influence of Deist ideas on the historical study of religion, see Peter Byrne, *Natural Religion and the Religion of Nature: The Legacy of Deism*, Routledge, London, 1989.
66. Quoted in Troll, *Sayyid Ahmed Khan*, pp. 308–309.
67. Ibid., p. 310.
68. 'There was nothing on the basis of which they could call themselves Muslims, except the faith in God and His Messenger. But I assure you, I consider their [non-rational] faith to be much more solid than my own faith.' Ibid.
69. A contemporary of Sayyid Ahmad, Shibli Nu'mani (1857–1914) sought to retain something of Islam's spiritual, other worldly and non-rational content by affirming that science cannot claim to understand everything of the natural world. Whilst Shibli endorsed the modernist agenda to reinterpret Islam in the light of modern thought, he nonetheless doubted reason enough to accept that some very important truths fell beyond its jurisdiction. See Shibli Nu'mani, '*Ilm al-Kalam aur al-Kalam*; and Mehr Afroz Murad, *Intellectual Modernism of Shibli Nu'mani: An Exposition of His Religious and Political Ideas*, Kitab Bhavan, New Delhi, 1996.
70. For a translation of this, see Keddie, *An Islamic Response to Imperialism*, pp. 130–174.

71. Ibid., pp. 67–68.
72. The accusation of collusion with the British is made in an Arabic article, titled 'The materialists in India', which was published in 1884, in *al-'Urwah al-Wuthqa*. See Keddie, *An Islamic Response to Imperialism*, pp. 175–180.
73. Smith, *The Meaning and End of Religion*.
74. Despite the apologist tone of these examples, one should not infer that Muhammad 'Abduh supported the idea of representative government by popular vote. Rather, 'Abduh, like many amongst his generation of reformers, counselled for the presence of a strong autocratic government which could ensure the implementation of modern systems of education, regular taxation, public security, and some political consultation. In the years preceding the 'Urabi revolt of 1882, 'Abduh concluded that the Egyptian people were not yet ready for a full-fledged constitutional system and spoke up for the Khedive of Egypt, Tawfiq, to act as just such an enlightened authority. See Youssef M. Choueri, *Islamic Fundamentalism*, Twayne, Boston, 1990, pp. 38–42; and Kerr, *Islamic Reform*, pp. 135–136.
75. 'Abduh's reconciliation of Islam with the tenets of modern government is recapitulated, only with greater intensity, by those twentieth-century apologists who claimed that the Qur'an predicted or alluded to all that would later be discovered by modern science. See Ahmad Dallal, 'Science and the Qur'an', *Encyclopaedia of the Qur'an*, Jane Dammen McAuliffe (ed.), Brill, Leiden, 2005.
76. This is underscored in Aziz Al-Azmeh, *Islams and Modernities*, Verso, London, 1996. Whilst I concur with Al-Azmeh that Afghani's insistence on a unitary notion of Islam bears parallels with European Romanticism in the nineteenth century, I have also tried to show that this tendency amongst Muslim modernists is as deeply imbricated in the Western Orientalist study of religion during this period as it is in the work of 'anti-rationalist' figures such as Herder.
77. Drawing upon the more doctrinally rigid figures of Sunni Islam, notably Ibn Hanbal and Ibn Taymiyyah, Rida stated that Islam must learn from Western civilisation only as much as will enable it to recover its material self-sufficiency whilst retaining its moral integrity. For a sensitive analysis of Rida's interpretation of the eighteenth-century scholar al-Shawkani, within the context of his debt to al-Afghani and 'Abduh's reforms, see Ahmad Dallal, 'Appropriating the past: Twentieth century reconstructions of pre-modern Islamic thought', *Islamic Law and Society*, 7 (3), 2000, pp. 325–358.
78. Earl of Cromer, *Modern Egypt*, vol. 2, Macmillan, London, 1908, p. 228. For a modern historiographical work that emphasises the religiously insincere or illegitimate nature of al-Afghani and 'Abduh's reforms, see Elie Kedouri, *Afghani and 'Abduh: An Essay on Religious Belief and Political Activism in*

Modern Islam, Frank Cass, London, 1966. The charge of insincerity is echoed by twentieth-century Muslim revivalists who have sought to invoke a purer version of Islam, uncorrupted by modernist thought. See, for instance, my reference to Sayyid Qutb's interpretation of the reforms of Muhammad 'Abduh in chapter 6 of this book.

79. For the 'failure' of Islamic modernists to adapt pre-modern theological paradigms to nineteenth-century ideas and institutions, see Kerr, *Islamic Reform*. A work which has adopted this premise in the context of Indian Islam is Martin Forward, *The Failure of Islamic Modernism? Syed Ameer Ali's Interpretation of Islam*, Peter Lang, Bern, 1999. For a critique of the theme of 'failure', see Charles Smith, '"The crisis of orientation": The shift of Egyptian intellectuals to Islamic subjects in the 1930s', *International Journal of Middle Eastern Studies*, 4, 1973, pp. 382–410; and Dallal, 'Appropriating the past'.

Chapter 2. Literary Romanticism and Islamic Modernity: The Case of Urdu Poetry

1. Altaf Husain Hali, *Hali's Musaddas: The Flow and Ebb of Islam*, Christopher Shackle and Javed Majeed (trans.), Oxford University Press, Delhi, 1997, pp. 192–193.
2. The post-1857 context and its impact on Urdu literary culture is discussed in Francis W. Pritchett, *Nets of Awareness: Urdu Poetry and its Critics*, University of California Press, Berkeley, 1994.
3. Peter van der Veer, *Imperial Encounters: Religion and Modernity in India and Britain*, Princeton University Press, Princeton, 2001, p. 41.
4. Quoted in David Lelyveld, *Aligarh's First Generation: Muslim Solidarity in British India*, Princeton University Press, Princeton, 1978, p. 207. In his *Minute on Education*, Thomas Babington Macaulay articulated the need to produce a 'class of persons, Indian in blood and colour, but English in taste and intellect', who would serve under the British as dependable officials and bureaucrats. See Thomas Babington Macaulay, *Selected Writings*, John Clive and Thomas Pinney (eds), University of Chicago Press, Chicago, 1972, p. 249.
5. Ibid., pp. 206–207.
6. Bernard Cohn, *Colonialism and its Forms of Knowledge*, Princeton University Press, Princeton, 1996, chapter 2. For the role of Persian as an administrative and high cultural language in north Indian society, see Mazaffar Alam, *The Languages of Political Islam: India 1200–1800*, University of Chicago Press, Chicago, 2004.
7. Lelyveld, *Aligarh's First Generation*, p. 207.

8. Gauri Viswanathan, *Masks of Conquest: Literary Study and British Rule in India*, Columbia University Press, New York, 1989.
9. As Viswanathan points out, educationalists in India sought to offset the cultural and ideological appeal of 'Oriental literature' amongst Indians in a manner profoundly at odds to the kind of syllabus recommended for those in the home country. If 'Englishmen of all ages could enjoy and appreciate exotic tales, romantic narrative, adventure stories and mythological literature for their charm and even derive instruction from them, their colonial subjects were believed incapable of doing so because they lacked the prior mental and moral cultivation required for literature – especially their own – to have any instructive value for them.' Ibid., p. 5.
10. Quoted in Ralph Russell, *The Pursuit of Urdu Literature*, Zed Books, London, 1992, p. 133.
11. Ranajit Guha, 'Dominance without hegemony and its historiography', *Subaltern Studies: Writings on South Asian History and Society*, vol. 4, Ranajit Guha (ed.), Oxford University Press, Delhi, 1985, pp. 210–309.
12 An important study of this in the context of colonial Bengal is Partha Chatterjee, *The Nation and its Fragments: Colonial and Post Colonial Histories*, Oxford University Press, Delhi, 1993.
13. Muhammad Husain Azad, *Ab-e Hayat: Shaping the Canon of Urdu Poetry, Muhammad Husain Azad*, Francis Pritchett (trans. and ed.) in association with Shamsur Rahman Faruqi, Oxford University Press, New Delhi, 2001, p. 91.
14. Altaf Husain Hali, *Muqaddimah Sh'ir aur Sha'iri*, Khazinah 'ilm o adab, Lahore, 2001.
15. Sayyid Ahmad Khan, *Maqalat-i Sir Sayyid*, vol. 10, Ismail Panipati (ed.), Majlis-i Taraqi-e Adab, Lahore, 1984, pp. 114–122.
16. Nazir Ahmed, *The Repentance of Nussooh (Tauhat-al-Nasuh): A Tale of a Muslim Family a Hundred Years Ago*, C. M. Naim (ed.) and M. Kempson (trans.), Permanent Black, New Delhi, 2004, p. 61.
17. Whilst the love mysticism practised amongst the earliest Sufi teachers in the first and second centuries of Islam did not accept a human medium for their meditations upon the divine, by the twelfth century it was common for mystical thinkers and poets to focus upon the figure of an idealised and semi-mystical human beloved. Thus, the *ghazal*'s intense evocation of mystical love may have served, in some contexts, to reinforce the knowledge of God's divine unity (*tawhid*) and the transitory nature of worldly things. Annemarie Schimmel, *Mystical Dimensions of Islam*, University of North Carolina Press, Chapel Hill, 1975, p. 291.
18. Shamsur Rahman Faruqi, *Early Urdu Literary Culture and History*, Oxford University Press, Delhi, 2001, p. 156.

19. Although prohibited in Islamic legal discourses, the theme of drunkenness was conventionally employed by poets and Sufi mystics as an acceptable and efficacious metaphor for the dissolution of the human soul in the divine reality.
20. My translation. The couplet can be viewed online in the Urdu, Devanagri and English scripts at the website of Frances W. Pritchett, *A Desertful of Roses: The Urdu Ghazals of Mirza Asadullah Khan Ghalib*, <http://www.columbia.edu/itc/mealac/pritchett/00ghalib/index.html> (accessed 8 July 2011).
21. In this regard, there is a well known anecdote about the celebrated poet, Muhammad Mir Taqi (1723–1810), who purportedly spent years confined to a solitary room with the shutters closed. Upon being informed about the beautiful garden located just outside his window, Mir expressed surprise and, gesturing towards drafts of his *ghazals*, said: 'I'm so absorbed in attending to this garden, I'm not even aware of that one.' This anecdote is related by Azad. See Azad, *Ab-e Hayat: Shaping the Canon of Urdu Poetry*, p. 199.
22. Annemarie Schimmel, *A Two-Colored Brocade: The Imagery of Persian Poetry*, University of North Carolina Press, Chapel Hill, 1992, pp. 39 and 131. Scott Alan Kugle, 'Sultan Mahmud's makeover: Colonial homophobia and the Persian-Urdu literary tradition', *Queering India: Same-Sex Love and Eroticism in Indian Culture and Society*, Ruth Vanita (ed.), Routledge, New York, 2002, pp. 30–46.
23. Barbara A. Babcock, 'Introduction', *The Reversible World: Symbolic Inversion in Art and Society*, Barbara A. Babcock (ed.), Cornell University Press, Ithaca, 1978, pp. 1–36.
24. See Russell, *The Pursuit of Urdu Literature*, chapter 2. See also, Ralph Russell and Kurshidul Islam, *Three Mughal Poets: Mir, Sauda. Mir Hasan*, Oxford University Press, Delhi, 1998, chapter 4. Far more interesting is Julie Scott Meisami's conclusion, in her study of the Persian *ghazal* tradition, that the poet's conception of 'love' formed a kind of fictional, symbolic model for those ideals which the aristocratic and upper-middle classes valued in common. Thus, Persian poets gestured not towards the 'real' status of the beloved, but 'towards an understanding of the ideals of love and the *realia* of love's actuality'. Julie Scott Meisami, *Medieval Persian Court Poetry*, Princeton University Press, Princeton, 1987, p. 252.
25. Harbans Mukhia interprets the *ghazal*'s themes of mystically intoned love accompanying the abrogation of social norms and taboos as a nuanced discourse of 'protest' and 'dissent' against the prevailing social and religious orthodoxies of the eighteenth century. Harbans Mukhia, 'The celebration of failure as dissent in Urdu Ghazal', *Modern Asian Studies*, 33 (4), 1999, pp. 861–881.

26. According to Pritchett, 'the ghazal has always aspired to move not from nature to art, but from art to art', so that its real message in such cases is intertextual, or is contained within the boundaries of a discursive medium. Pritchett, *Nets of Awareness*, p. 163.
27. According to Faruqi, the literary theories of Urdu poeticians were original and local to their Indian environment and should not be over-compared to the Arab-Persian poetic tradition from which Urdu's formal genres and styles are derived. Faruqi, *Early Urdu Literary Culture*, chapter 7. See also Pritchett, *Nets of Awareness*, chapters 7 and 8.
28. Also deserving of mention is Shibli Nu'mani's *Persian Poetry (Sh'ir al-'Ajam)* which represents a fine attempt of this period (in the Urdu language) to apply a modern historical methodology to Persian poetry's sources and themes. Shibli Nu'mani, *Sh'ir al-'Ajam*, 2 vols, Al-Faisak, Lahore, 1999.
29. M. H. Abrams, *The Mirror and the Lamp: Romantic Theory and the Critical Tradition*, W.W. Norton, New York, 1958, p. 315.
30. See Abrams, *The Mirror and the Lamp*, pp. 300–301.
31. Hali, *Muqaddimah Sh'ir aur Sha'iri*, pp. 55–63. It should be noted that Hali had access to imperfect translations of English authors. See Pritchett, *Nets of Awareness*, chapter 10.
32. Hali, *Muqaddimah Sh'ir aur Sha'iri*, p. 109.
33. Azad does not begin the history of Urdu poetry with its earlier development in Gujarat and the southern Muslim kingdoms of the Deccan and his attempt to provide the outline of a historical chronology sits uneasily with the anecdotal and digressive format – loosely conforming to the *tazkirah* anthology, or private notebook – to which the work is indebted. See Annemarie Schimmel, *Classical Urdu Literature: From the Beginning to Iqbal*, Harrassowitz, Wiesbaden, 1975.
34. Azad, *Ab-e Hayat: Shaping the Canon*, pp. 100–106.
35. Ibid., p. 105.
36. For the theory of literary decadence in Victorian circles, see Linda Downing, *Language and Decadence in the Victorian Fin de Siecle*, Princeton University Press, Princeton, 1986.
37. Mrinalina Sinha, *Colonial Masculinity: The 'Manly Englishman' and the 'Effeminate Bengali' in the Late Nineteenth Century*, Manchester University Press, Manchester, 1995, p. 21.
38. In contrast to the feeble and effeminate *babu* of Thomas Babington Macaulay's imagination, British Orientalism typically depicted Indian Muslims, such as the Pathans of the North-West Frontier Province, as warrior-men or 'martial-races' not unlike the Sikh and Rajput clans of northern India. See van der Veer, *Imperial Encounters*, p. 95.

39. For the attitude of the nineteenth-century religious reformer, Ashraf 'Ali Thanawi, to the everyday use of 'women's language' (*begumati zuban*) in northern India, see chapter 3 of this book.
40. Carla Petievitch, '*Rekhti*: Impersonating the feminine in Urdu poetry', *South Asia*, 24, 2001, p. 87.
41. See C. M. Naim, *Urdu Texts and Contexts: The Selected Essays of C. M. Naim*, Permanent Black, New Delhi, 2004, chapter 3.
42. Ruth Vanita, '"Married among their companions": Female homoerotic relations in nineteenth-century Urdu *rekhti* poetry in India', *Journal of Women's History*, 16 (1), 2004, pp. 12–13.
43. Azad, *Ab-e Hayat: Shaping the Canon*, pp. 232–233.
44. Ibid., p. 207.
45. Abdul Halim Sharar, *Lucknow: The Last Phase of an Oriental Culture*, E. S. Harcourt and Fakhir Hussain (trans. and ed.), Oxford University Press, New Delhi, 2000, pp. 87–88.
46. Quoted in Pritchett, *Nets of Awareness*, p. 177.
47. Hali, *Muqaddimah Sh'ir aur Sha'iri*, p. 105.
48. Quoted in Pritchett, *Nets of Awareness*, p. 177.
49. Michel Foucault, *The History of Sexuality*, vol. 1, Robert Hurley (trans.), Harmondsworth [England], Penguin, 1984.
50. Quoted in Pritchett, *Nets of Awareness*, p. 181.
51. Hali, *Muqaddimah Sh'ir aur Sha'iri*, p. 105.
52. Ibid., p. 106.
53. Pritchett, *Nets of Awareness*, p. 178.
54. Hali, *Muqaddimah Sh'ir aur Sha'iri*, pp. 104–105.
55. This is my translation of a part of the poem. Altaf Husain Hali 'Hubb-i watan', *Masterpieces of Patriotic Urdu Poetry*, C. K. Nanda (ed.), Sterling, New Delhi, 2005, pp. 82–87.
56. Hali, *Hali's Musaddas*, pp. 144–145. Here, I quote Shackle and Majeed's translation of Hali's poem. The two discuss other possible interpretations relating to Hali's use of the garden theme in their introduction to the work on pp. 59–65.
57. Guriqbal S. Sahota, 'A literature of the sublime in late colonial India: Romanticism and the epic form in modern Hindi and Urdu', PhD thesis, University of Chicago, 2006.
58. Hali, *Hali's Musaddas*, pp. 116–117.
59. Ibid. For Hali's use of time, see Shackle and Majeed's critical introduction to the poem, pp. 1–80.
60. That Hali's poem was so widely admired as to influence other religious and linguistic communities across northern India is commented on by Shackle and Majeed, ibid.

NOTES TO PAGES 96–102   249

61. Altaf Husain Hali, *Hayat-i Javid*, Saleem Akhtar (ed.), Sang-i Meel, Lahore, 1993.
62. Shamsur Rahman Faruqi, 'From antiquary to social revolutionary: Sayyid Ahmad Khan and the colonial experience', is available at Francis W. Pritchett's website, http://www.columbia.edu/itc/mealac/pritchett/00fwp/srf/index.html (accessed 8 July 2011).
63. Ibid.
64. Muhammad Iqbal, *Iqbal: A Selection of the Urdu Verse*, D. J. Mathews (trans.), Heritage Publishers, New Delhi, 1993, pp. 40–41 (my translation).
65. Ibid.

Chapter 3. Education and the Status of Women

1. Learning institutions which were then available to women included missionary and locally organised girls' schools, as well as training colleges for female nurses and other professions deemed acceptable for women at the time.
2. See Judith Tucker, *Women in Nineteenth-Century Egypt*, Cambridge University Press, Cambridge, 1985.
3. Leila Ahmed, *Women and Gender in Islam*, Yale University Press, New Haven, 1992.
4. Quoted in ibid., p. 153. Ahmed points out that under Cromer's authority, women's access to education and opportunities for employment as nurses and teachers were significantly reduced. The contradictory results of British colonial policy towards women's education in Egypt are also noted in Tucker, *Women in Nineteenth-Century Egypt*, pp. 129–130.
5. This does not mean that colonial discourses towards the position of Muslim women were all cut from the same cloth. There were always significant differences of viewpoint, according to the social status, political position or gender of the protagonist. In many cases, the fascination with Muslim women's customs of seclusion tell us more about European male sexual fantasies and social aspirations than about the Arab Muslim societies that are their subject. In this context, such texts are as much a reflection of the desire to escape the stifling social conventions and mores of the home society as a justification for the moral authority of the European coloniser. See Ruth Bernard Yeazell, *Harems of the Mind: Passages of Western Art and Literature*, Yale University Press, New Haven, 2000; and Edward Said, *Orientalism: Western Conceptions of the Orient*, Penguin, London, 1995.
6. See Earl of Cromer, *Modern Egypt*, vol. 2, Macmillan, London, 1908, p. 134, f.n. 4.
7. Quoted in Charles C. Adams, *Islam and Modernism in Egypt*, Oxford University Press, London, 1933, p. 152.

8. Altaf Husain Hali, *Voices of Silence: English Translation of Altaf Hussain Hali's Majalis un-Nissa and Chupp ki Dad*, Gail Minault (trans.), Chanakya Publications, Delhi, 1986, pp. 141–142.
9. See Ali Altaf Mian and Nancy Nyquist Potter, 'Invoking Islamic rights in British India, Maulana Ashraf 'Ali Thanawi's *Huquq al-Islam*', *Muslim World*, 99, 2009, p. 314. Mian and Potter point out that Thanawi adopted a reformist interpretation of Indian Sufism which was stricter in its practices than that of his mentor, Hajji Imdad Allah.
10. In particular, Amin's second publication on the subject of women's reform, *The New Woman (al-Mara'ah al-Jadidah)*, ignores the subject of religion altogether. Instead he argues that women's education is necessary for the good of national development alone, for which his paradigmatic example is modern France.
11. Qasim Amin, *The Liberation of Women and The New Woman*, Samina Sidhom Peterson (trans.), American University in Cairo Press, Cairo, 2001, p. 3.
12. For a closer examination of this discourse as it was employed by Qasim Amin and the Egyptian reformers of his time, see Omnia Shakry, 'Schooled mothers and structured play: Child rearing in turn-of-the-century Egypt', *Remaking Women: Feminism and Modernity in the Middle East*, Lila Abu-Lughod (ed.), Princeton University Press, Princeton, 1998, pp. 126–170.
13. Anne McClintock, *Imperial Leather: Race, Class and Gender in the Colonial Contest*, Routledge, New York, 1995, p. 51.
14. On the emerging disparities of social class in Egyptian society, see also Juan Ricardo Cole, 'Feminism, class and Islam in turn-of-the-century Egypt', *International Journal of Middle Eastern Studies*, 13, 1981, pp. 387–407.
15. Amin, *The Liberation of Women and The New Woman*, pp. 22–23.
16. Ibid., pp. 113 and 80.
17. Ibid., pp. 45–61.
18. Ibid., p. 60.
19. Ibid., p. 33.
20. Ahmed, *Women and Gender in Islam*, p. 157.
21. Lila Abu-Lughod, 'The marriage of feminism and Islamism in Egypt: Selective repudiation as a dynamic of postcolonial cultural politics', *Remaking Women: Feminism and Modernity in the Middle East*, Lila Abu-Lughod (ed.), Princeton University Press, Princeton, 1998, p. 256.
22. Timothy Mitchell, *Colonizing Egypt*, University of California Press, Berkeley, 1991.
23. Talal Asad, *Formations of the Secular: Christianity, Islam, Modernity*, Stanford University Press, Stanford, 2003, pp. 231–232. Asad correctly observes that the nineteenth-century focus on the family (*'ailah*) represented the articulation of a kinship unit whose valency to Arab society was increasing

NOTES TO PAGES 109–115   251

in modernizing urban centres at the expense of other networks, including the extended family and tribe.

24. Francis Robinson, 'Technology and religious change: Islam and the impact of print', *Modern Asian Studies*, 27 (1), 1993, pp. 229–251.
25. For two excellent studies on the Deoband movement in northern India, see Barbara Metcalf, *Islamic Revival in British India: Deoband, 1860–1900*, Princeton University Press, Princeton, 1982; and Muhammad Qasim Zaman, *The Ulama in Contemporary Islam*, Princeton University Press, Princeton, 2002.
26. Gail Minault, 'Other voices, other rooms: The view from the *zenana*', *Women as Subjects: South Asian Histories*, Anita Kumar (ed.), University Press of Virginia, London, 1994, pp. 180–124. For a study of the ritual songs and vernacular proverbs used amongst women in Northern India, see Gloria Goodwin Raheja, 'Women's speech genres, kinship and contradiction', in the same volume, pp. 49–80.
27. Concerning the emergence of high Urdu as a literary language in the Mughal courts of the eighteenth century, see David Lelyveld, '*Zuban-e Urdu-e mu'alla* and the idol of linguistic origins', *Annual of Urdu Studies*, 9, 1994, pp. 57–67.
28. Ashraf 'Ali Thanawi, *Perfecting Women: Maulana Ashraf 'Ali Thanawi's Bihishti Zewar*, Barbara Metcalf (trans.), University of California Press, Berkeley, 1990, pp. 110–111.
29. Ibid., p. 112.
30. Ibid., p. 59.
31. The absence of male reformist interest in the culture and performance of rural peasant and working-class women must be explained by the fact that they fell outside the constructed urban culture and identity of the former aristocracy and service gentry of India's metropolitan centres.
32. Thanawi, *Perfecting Women*, p. 372.
33. Ibid., p. 61.
34. Generally speaking, these women did not depart from the message provided by their male counterparts, although this is not to deny the potential of such women to voice their own discursive agendas. See Gail Minault, *Secluded Scholars: Woman's Education and Muslim Social Reform in Colonial India*, Oxford University Press, Delhi, 1999. Minault points out that whilst the proliferation of didactic, educational guides coincided with the expansion of such publications in the West, this may be more indicative of a parallel process of embourgeoisement, and of the need amongst educated men for learned wives, than of Indian reformers transplanting Western cultural prototypes to their own society.
35. Quoted in ibid., pp. 18–19.
36. Carole Pateman, *The Sexual Contract*, Polity Press, Oxford, 1988, p. 11.

37. Thanawi, *Perfecting Women*, p. 253.
38. Akbar Allahabadi, *Kulliyat-i Akbar*, vol. 1, Maktabah Sh'ir o Adab, Lahore, n.d., p. 298.

Chapter 4. Muhammad Iqbal, Islam and Modern Nationalism

1. Muhammad Iqbal, *Tulip in the Desert: A Selection of the Poetry of Muhammad Iqbal*, Mustansir Mir (ed. and trans.), Hurst, London, 2000, p. 126.
2. Gayanendra Pandey, *Remembering Partition: Violence, Nationalism and History in India*, Cambridge University Press, New Delhi, 2001.
3. Anuradha Dingwaney Needham and Rajeswari Sunder Rajan, 'Introduction', *The Crisis of Secularism in India*, Anuradha Dingwaney Needham and Rajeswari Sunder Rajan (eds.), Duke University Press, London, 2007, pp. 1–42.
4. Gyan Prakash, 'Secular nationalism, Hindutva and the minority', *The Crisis of Secularism in India*, Anuradha Dingwaney Needham and Rajeswari Sunder Rajan (eds), Duke University Press, London, 2007, pp. 177–188. Ayesha Jalal asserts that the term 'communal' has been used arbitrarily in the case of India's Muslim community and too frequently in the service of an essentialised 'Muslim identity' which supposedly cannot adapt to the demands of a broader Indian nationalism. See Ayesha Jalal, 'Exploding communalism: The politics of Muslim identity in South Asia', *Nationalism, Democracy and Development: State and Politics in India*, Sugata Bose and Ayesha Jalal (eds), Oxford University Press, Delhi, 1997, pp. 76–103.
5. Benedict Anderson, *Imagined Communities: Reflections on the Origins and Spread of Nationalism*, Verso, London, 1991.
6. Gyanendra Pandey, *The Construction of Communalism in Colonial North India*, Oxford University Press, New Delhi, 2006.
7. See Romila Thapar, 'Imagined religious communities? Ancient history and the modern search for a Hindu identity', *Modern Asian Studies*, 23 (2), 1989, pp. 209–231. Richard M. Eaton, 'Temple desecration and Indo-Muslim states', and other contributions to *Beyond Turk and Hindu: Rethinking Religious Identities in Islamicate South Asia*, David Gilmartin and Bruce B. Lawrence (eds), India Research Press, New Delhi, 2002, pp. 246–81. Shahid Amin, 'On retelling the Muslim conquest of north India', *History and The Present*, Partha Chatterjee and Anjan Ghosh (eds), Permanent Black, New Delhi, 2002, pp. 24–43.
8. This is an uncontested point amongst historians, who have shown how indigenous claims to social, religious or cultural uniqueness were largely drawn from colonial sociology. Here, I am indebted to historians and anthropologists associated with what is generally termed a constructivist view of Indian

institutions and traditions during the colonial and postcolonial periods. A small selection of fine examples include Bernard Cohn, *An Anthropologist Among the Historians and Other Essays*, Oxford University Press, New Delhi, 1987; Gauri Viswanathan, *Outside the Fold: Conversion, Modernity, and Belief*, Oxford University Press, New Delhi, 1998; Peter van der Veer, *Imperial Encounters: Religion and Modernity in India and Britain*, Princeton University Press, Princeton, 2001; Nicholas B. Dirks, *Castes of Mind: Colonialism and the Making of Modern India*, Permanent Black, New Delhi, 2004; and Gyanendra Pandey, *The Construction of Communalism in Colonial North India*, Oxford University Press, New Delhi, 2006.

9. Partha Chatterjee, *The Nation and its Fragments: Colonial and Post Colonial Histories*, Oxford University Press, Delhi, 1995.
10. For examples of this, see Saleem Qureshi, 'Iqbal and Jinnah: Personalities, perceptions and politics', *Iqbal, Jinnah and Pakistan: The Vision and the Reality*, C. M. Naim (ed.), Syracuse University, New York, 1979, pp. 11–39; and S. A. Vahid, *Introduction to Iqbal*, Pakistan Publication, Karachi, n.d., chapter 4.
11. Manzooruddin Ahmed, 'Iqbal and Jinnah on the two-nations theory', *Iqbal, Jinnah and Pakistan: The Vision and the Reality*, C. M. Naim (ed.), Syracuse University, New York, 1979, pp. 41–76.
12. Muhammad Iqbal, *Speeches, Writings and Statements of Iqbal*, Latif Ahmad Sherwani (ed.), Adam Publishers, New Delhi, 2006, p. 11.
13. Ibid., p. 26.
14. Quoted in *Letters and Writings of Iqbal*, B. A. Dar (ed.), Iqbal Academy, Karachi, 1967, pp. 117–118.
15. Ibid., pp. 119–120.
16. For a summary of Iqbal's political thought that leans towards his status as a founder of the contemporary Islamic revival, see John L. Esposito, 'Muhammad Iqbal and the Islamic state', *Makers of Contemporary Islam*, John L. Esposito and John O. Voll (eds), Oxford University Press, New York, 2001, pp. 175–190.
17. Sayyid Ali Khamenei, 'Iqbal: The poet-philosopher of Islamic resurgence', *Iqbal: Manifestation of the Islamic Spirit*, Mahliqa Qara'i and Laleh Bakhtiar (trans.), Open Press, Ontario, 1991, p. 24.
18. See Francis Robinson, 'Kawmiyya', *Encyclopaedia of Islam*, (2nd edn).
19. Sayyid Ahmad Khan, *Writings and Speeches of Sir Syed Ahmed Khan*, Shan Muhammad (ed.), Nachiketa Publications, Bombay, 1972, p. 266.
20. Quoted in Christian W. Troll, *Syed Ahmed Khan: A Reinterpretation of Muslim Theology*, Vikas Publishing House, New Delhi, 1978, p. 30. See also David Lelyveld, *Aligarh's First Generation: Muslim Solidarity in British India*, Princeton University Press, Princeton, 1978.
21. Quoted in Peter Hardy, *The Muslims of British India*, Cambridge University Press, Cambridge, 1972, p. 243. Maulana Hussain Ahmad Madani, *Composite*

Nationalism and Islam (Muttahida Qaumiyyah aur Islam), Mohammad Anwer Hussain Hasan Imam (trans.), Manohar, New Delhi, 2005.
22. Muhammad Iqbal, *Stray Reflections: A Note-book of Allama Iqbal*, Javid Iqbal (ed.), Taj Company, Delhi, 1985.
23. Iqbal, *Speeches, Writings and Statements*, pp. 123 and 302.
24. Muhammad Ali Jinnah, *Jinnah: Speeches and Statements 1947–1948*, Oxford University Press, Oxford, 2000, p. 29.
25. Such concerns precede the eventual separation of East Pakistan (now Bangladesh) in 1974, and continuing grievances amongst people of the regions of Baluchistan and Sindh, who include *muhajirun* (refugees) from India. To add to this, there is the state's reluctance, or inability, to extend its sovereignty into the tribal areas of the north-western frontier.
26. Ayesha Jalal, *The Sole Spokesman: Jinnah, the Muslim League, and the Demand for Pakistan*, Cambridge University Press, Cambridge, 1985.
27. Iqbal, *Thoughts and Reflections*, p. 35.
28. Ibid., p. 244.
29. Iqbal's relationship with three of the early twentieth century's finest Orientalist scholars, Thomas Arnold (1864–1930), R. A. Nicholson (1868–1945) and A. J. Arbery (1905–1969) greatly enriched the development of his thought. For Thomas Arnold's work in the area of Muslim ideological reform and political revival, see Katherine Watt, 'Thomas Walker Arnold and the re-evaluation of Islam, 1864–1930', *Modern Asian Studies*, 36 (1), 2002, pp. 1–98.
30. For the details of Iqbal's life, see Iqbal Singh, *The Ardent Pilgrim: An Introduction to the Life and Work of Mohammed Iqbal*, Oxford University Press, Delhi, 1997.
31. Henry E. Allison, 'Kant on freedom of the will', *The Cambridge Companion to Kant and Modern Philosophy*, Paul Guyer (ed.), Cambridge University Press, Cambridge, 2006, pp. 399–403.
32. J. G. Fichte, *Introductions to the Wissenschaftslehre and Other Writings*, Daniel Breazeale (trans. and ed.), Hackett, Indianapolis, 1994.
33. As Wayne Martin argues, this does not mean that Fichte denied the reality of mind-independent objects. Fichte maintained instead that just as the object of the mind's enquiries cannot be ascertained in and of itself, nor can it exist only as an object of the mind's representations. According to Martin, '*If* a thing exists for something then it must exist for an intellect', which points to the 'pervasive reflexivity' of consciousness – as consciousness exists 'for itself' – in Fichte's thought. Wayne M. Martin, *Idealism and Objectivity: Understanding Fichte's Jena Project*, Stanford University Press, Stanford, 1997, p. 47.
34. Iqbal, *The Reconstruction of Religious Thought in Islam*, p. 93.
35. Ibid., p. 35.

NOTES TO PAGES 129–133

36. I am using Reynold A. Nicholson's translation of Iqbal's Persian original. Not only does it capture something of the timbre of that era, but it was very popular with Iqbal himself who admitted having wept upon reading it. Muhammad Iqbal, *The Secrets of the Self*, Reynold A. Nicholson (trans.), Kitab Bhavan, New Delhi, 2004, p. 12.
37. Ibid., p. 15.
38. Annemarie Schimmel points out that Iqbal's dynamic and regenerating notion of self drew its inspiration from the archetype of the Prophet Muhammad's 'night journey', in which the Prophet ascended to the heavens and stood in God's presence without being annihilated. Annemarie Schimmel, *Gabriel's Wing*, Iqbal Academy, Lahore, 2000, pp. 120–121.
39. Iqbal, *The Reconstruction of Religious Thought in Islam*, p. 106.
40. Iqbal, *Iqbal: A Selection of the Urdu Verse*, p. 63.
41. Iqbal, *The Reconstruction of Religious Thought in Islam*, pp. 58–59.
42. For an explanation of the conventions of love in the Indian *ghazal* tradition, and its reconceptualisation at the hands of nineteenth-century modernist reformers, see chapter 2 of this book.
43. Quoted in Nicholson's 'Introduction' to Iqbal, *The Secrets of the Self*, p. xix.
44. Iqbal, *Thoughts and Reflections*, p. 244.
45. Iqbal, *The Reconstruction of Religious Thought in Islam*, pp. 24–25
46. Written shortly after the Italian seizure of Tripoli from the Turks, Iqbal's 'Complaint' (*Shikwah*) expressed much of the political anguish and uncertainty experienced by Indian Muslims leading up to World War II. Whilst this poem owes a large debt to the format and lachrymal theme of Hali's *The Flow and Ebb of Islam*, and was composed before the theme of selfhood is explicitly developed in Iqbal's *Secrets of the Self*, it nonetheless conveys those notions of self-assertion and audacity (before God) which are a distinguishing feature of his mature philosophy. Iqbal, *Iqbal: A Selection of the Urdu Verse*, pp. 30–42.
47. Muhammad Iqbal, *Kuliyyat-i Iqbal: Urdu*, Ittiqad, Delhi, 1491 h., p. 347.
48. Quoted in Syed Abdul Vahid, *Iqbal: His Art and Thought*, John Murray, London, 1959, p. 112.
49. As Annemarie Schimmel points out, Iqbal's complex notion of Satan (*Iblis*) embraced the theological conception of an evil seducer, alongside the mystically inspired notion of Satan as a pure monotheist, whose refusal to bow before Adam stemmed from his uncompromising love of God. Annemarie Schimmel, *Mystical Dimensions of Islam*, University of North Carolina Press, Chapel Hill, 1975, pp. 193–197.
50. Iqbal, *Speeches Writings and Statements*, p. 3.
51. Iqbal, *Stray Reflections: A Note-book of Allama Iqbal*, Javid Iqbal (ed.), Taj Company, Delhi, 1985.

52. For Iqbal's description of Wahhabism as the 'first throb of life in modern Islam', see *Speeches, Writings and Statements*, p. 229. For his thoughts on Aurengzeb as the 'ideal...Muslim type of character', see p. 127 of the same volume. And for a reference to the 'light' of Atatürk's 'Islamic conscience... illuminating the zone of his action' (after he disempowered the traditional '*ulama*) go to p. 234. See also Fazlur Rahman, 'Muhammad Iqbal and Atatürk's reforms', *Journal of Near Eastern Studies*, 43 (2), 1984, pp. 157–162.
53. Iqbal, *The Reconstruction of Religious Thought in Islam*, chapter 5.
54. Ibid., p. 113.
55. Ibid., p. 114.
56. Ibid., p. 123.
57. Ibid., pp. 114–119.
58. My source for understanding German historicism is George G. Iggers, *The German Conception of History: The National Tradition of German Thought from Herder to the Present*, Wesleyan University Press, Middletown, 1988.
59. Quoted in John Farrenkopf, *The Prophet of Decline: Spengler on World History and Politics*, Louisiana State University Press, Baton Rouge, 2001, p. 78.
60. Iqbal, *Thoughts and Reflections*, pp. 376–379.
61. The reciprocal relationship between individual and community, which is a theme of Iqbal's Persian poem *Rumuz-i Bekhudi (Mysteries of Selflessness)*, is discussed in Javed Majeed, *Muhammad Iqbal: Islam, Aesthetics and Postcolonialism*, Routledge, London, 2009, pp. 48–53.
62. Max Müller (1823–1900) stated: 'It is...a problem worth considering whether, as there is in nature a North and a South, so there are not two hemispheres in human nature...the active, combative and political on one side, the passive, meditative and philosophical on the other.' The former he attributed to the European civilisation of the 'Northern Aryans', whereas the latter were exemplified by those 'Southern Aryans' who, according to nineteenth-century race theory, migrated into Iran and India and became its ruling classes. Max Müller, 'India – What can it teach us?', *Historical Thinking in South Asia*, Michael Gottlob (ed.), Oxford University Press, New Delhi, 2003, p. 107. See also Richard King, *Orientalism and Religion: Postcolonial Theory, India and 'The Mystic East'*, Routledge, London, 1999; and Romila Thapar, 'The theory of Aryan race and India: History and politics', *Social Scientist*, 24 (1/3), 1996, pp. 3–29.
63. For the important work of German Indologists and Enlightenment philosophers within the Romantic critique of European thought, see Wilhelm Halbfass, *India and Europe: An Essay in Understanding*, State University of New York Press, New York, 1988.
64. Ian Almond, *The New Orientalists: Postmodern Representations of Islam from Foucault to Baudrillard*, I.B.Tauris, London, 2007, chapter 1.

65. The articulation of a 'mystical East' amongst the indigenous elites of India, China and Japan in the early twentieth century is explored in Stephen M. Hay, *Asian Ideas of East and West: Tagore and his Critics in Japan, China and India*, Harvard University Press, Cambridge Mass., 1970.
66. Iqbal, *Speeches, Writings and Statements*, p. 301.
67. Ibid., pp. 301–302.
68. Ibid., p. 303.
69. Iqbal, *Thoughts and Reflections*, p. 51.
70. Iqbal, *Speeches, Writings and Statements*, p. 157.
71. Whilst the term is derived from the Persian Magi, Iqbal's notion of Magianism differs considerably from that of Oswald Spengler. Spengler thought of Magianism as a culture defined more by the religious community than by the modern nation, and saw Islam (from its inception to the decline of the Ottoman Empire) as a quintessentially Magian religion. For Iqbal, on the other hand, Magianism was a foreign, ideological encrustation upon the face of Islam, whose renunciatory doctrine of endless prophesizing could not be reconciled with the latter's more dynamic, this-worldly message.
72. See Iqbal, *Speeches, Writings and Statements*, pp. 197–241.
73. Quoted in Singh, *The Ardent Pilgrim*, p. 50.
74. Iqbal in a letter to Sirajuddin Pal, 1916. Quoted in Ashgar Ali Engineer, 'Iqbal's "Reconstruction of Religious Thought in Islam": A critical appraisal', *Social Scientist*, 8 (8), 1980, p. 53. Whilst a disparaging evaluation of Persian mystical influences was familiar to Urdu literary reformers affiliated with modernist thought since the late nineteenth century, Iqbal nonetheless identifies with the work of the canonical Sufi poet, Jalal al-Din Rumi. In Rumi, Iqbal found an artist whose play upon the themes of mystical intoxication and worldly love was tailored to a conception of eternal life, and union with the divine, as a process of self-individuation. Indeed, Iqbal's conception of Rumi's Sufism overlaps with that of his friend, and one of the twentieth century's pre-eminent translators of the poet, Reynold A. Nicholson. A striking congruence between Iqbal's theory of self and Nicholson's interpretation of Sufism can be found in the latter's lecture, titled 'Personality in Sufism', in which Sufism is described as: 'a profound religious sentiment which seeks its final satisfaction, not in *denying* its own existence, but in *affirming* that it lives, moves and has its being in the eternally active Will of Allah'. See William Stoddart and R. A. Nicholson, *Sufism: The Mystical Doctrines and Idea of Personality*, Aryan Books, New Delhi, 2002, p. 76. The italics are Nicholson's.
75. Michael Banton, *Racial Theories*, Cambridge University Press, Cambridge, 1998, p. 92.

76. Iqbal, *Thoughts and reflections*, p. 48.
77. Iqbal, *Speeches, Writings and Statements*, p. 236. Keith Arthur's work pioneered an approach to race based on genetic process and upheld 'deracialisation' as that which would counter the destructive effects of 'race building'. Keith Arthur, *Ethnos, or, The Problem of Race Considered from a New Point of View*, K. Paul, London, 1931.
78. Iqbal, *Speeches, Writings and Statements*, p. 208.
79. Iqbal, *The Reconstruction of Religious Thought in Islam*, p. 85.
80. Ibid.
81. Iqbal, *Speeches, Writings and Statements*, p. 237.
82. Referring to racism's historical formation in Europe during the Age of Discovery and the Renaissance, and its continued existence in the present, Fredrickson points out that: 'It is uniquely in the West that we find the dialectical interaction between a premise of equality and an intense prejudice towards certain groups that would seem to be a precondition for the full flowering of racism as an ideology or worldview.' George M. Fredrickson, *Racism: A Short History*, Princeton University Press, Princeton, 2002, pp. 11–12.
83. Iqbal, *Speeches, Writings and Statements*, p. 6.
84. Alam Khundmiri's philosophically appreciative reading of Iqbal's attempt to resolve the problem of free will and predestination is presented in part III of *Secularism, Islam and Modernity: Selected Essays of Alam Khundmiri*, M. T. Ansari (ed.), Sage, New Delhi, 2001.
85. Iqbal, *The Reconstruction of Religious Thought in Islam*, p. 84.
86. Javed Majeed, 'Putting God in His place: Bradley, McTaggart and Muhammad Iqbal', *Journal of Islamic Studies*, 4 (2), pp. 208–236.
87. Faiz Ahmed Faiz, *Culture and Identity: Selected Writings of Faiz*, Sheema Majeed (ed.), Oxford University Press, Oxford, 2005, p. 176.
88. Iqbal, *Tulip in the Desert*, p. 136.
89. An important progressive Muslim reformer to cite Iqbal's influence is Fazlur Rahman, whose work I discuss in chapter 7 of this book.
90. Homi Bhabha, *The Location of Culture*, Routledge, London, 1994, pp. 219–220.
91. Singh, *The Ardent Pilgrim*, pp. 95–96.

Chapter 5. The Theory of Divine Sovereignty

1. Francis Fukuyama, 'Has history started again?', *Policy*, 18, 2002, pp. 5–7.
2. Bassam Tibi, *The Challenge of Fundamentalism: Political Islam and the New World Disorder*, University of California Press, Berkeley, 1998, p. 18.
3. Ibid.

NOTES TO PAGES 150–153   259

4. John Gray, *Black Mass: Apocalyptic Religion and the Death of Utopia*, Penguin, London, 2008, p. 1. This notion echoes Carl Schmitt's celebrated maxim: 'All significant concepts of the modern theory of the state are secularized theological concepts.' Carl Schmitt, *Political Theologies: Four Chapters on the Concept of Sovereignty*, MIT Press, Cambridge Mass., 1981, p. 36.
5. Talal Asad, *Formations of the Secular: Christianity, Islam, Modernity*, Stanford University Press, Stanford, 2003, p. 200.
6. The following biographical information about Maududi's life is based on Seyyed Vali Reza Nasr, *Maududi and the Making of Islamic Revivalism*, Oxford University Press, Oxford, 1996.
7. Gail Minault, *The Khilafat Movement: Religious Symbolism and Political Mobilization in India*, Columbia University Press, New York, 1982.
8. Sayyid Abul A'la Maududi, *The Islamic Law and Constitution* (first published 1955), Islamic Publications, Lahore, 2000, p. 145.
9. Sayyid Abul A'la Maududi, *Islami Riyasat* (*The Islamic State*, first published 1967), Islamic Publications, Lahore, 2000, p. 388. See also Sayyid Abul A'la Maududi, *Four Basic Qur'anic Terms*, Islamic Publications, Lahore, 1979, p. 29.
10. Quoted in Syed Asad Gilani, *Maududi: Thought and Movement*, Islamic Publications, Lahore, 1984, pp. 330–331. Whilst the Qur'an does not contain the term *hakimiyyah*, it does emphasise that *hukm* (command, judgment, decision) belongs to God alone. Theologically, this was understood to refer to God's power over the universe, and that God is the sole adjudicator amongst human beings on the day of judgment. Thus, when the Qur'an refers to God as the 'the best of judges' (*khair al-hakimin*, 7:87) and proclaims that 'judgment belongs to God' (*al-hukmu ilahi*, 40:12), this was interpreted in the context of ultimate judgment. See Bustami Khir, 'Sovereignty', *Encyclopaedia of the Qur'an*, Jane Dammen McAuliffe (ed.), Brill, Leiden, 2005. For the occurrences in the Qur'an of the term *hukm* and its derivations, see Muhammad Fouad Abd al-Baqi, *Al-Mujam al-Mufahras li Alfaz al-Qur'an al-Karim*, Dar wa Matab'a al-Sh'ab, n.d., pp. 214–215.
11. Maududi, *Islamic Law and Constitution*, p. 146.
12. Maududi, *Four Basic Quranic Terms*, p. 94. For Maududi, 'religion', 'way of life', and 'system of belief and action' are often rendered in attempts to translate the word *din*.
13. See L. Gardet, 'Din', *Encyclopaedia of Islam* (2nd edn). For an overview of the complex etymological uses of the words, *din*, *islam* and *iman* in the seventh century, see Wilfred Cantwell Smith, *The Meaning and End of Religion*, Harper & Row, New York, 1978, pp. 98–102 and 109–113.
14. Sayyid Abul A'la Maududi, *Let Us Be Muslims* (first published 1940), Khurram Murad (ed.), The Islamic Foundation, Kuala Lumpur, 1985,

pp. 295–296. See also, Christian W. Troll, 'The meaning of *din*: Recent views of three eminent Indian ulama', *Islam in India: Studies and Commentaries*, Christian W. Troll (ed.), Vikas, Delhi, 1982, pp. 168–177.
15. Maududi, *Four Basic Quranic Terms*, pp. 96 and 102.
16. Despite the emphasis in Maududi's early writings on the need to bring about an 'Islamic revolution' (*Islami inqilab*) in societies where the state was based on immoral and atheistic precepts, his sense of the term denoted a social revolution from the ground up. Furthermore, as Leonard Binder points out, the Jama'at-i Islami's embroilment in Pakistan's domestic politics led to Maududi adopting a softer line on the need for social change by working with the contemporary state as the basis for building a future Islamic society in Pakistan. See Leonard Binder, *Religion and Politics in Pakistan*, University of California Press, Berkeley, 1961, pp. 96–97.
17. Mumtaz Ahmad, 'Islamic fundamentalism in South Asia', *Fundamentalisms Observed*, Martin E. Marty and R. Scott Appleby (eds), University of Chicago Press, Chicago, 1994, p. 509. Seyyed Vali Reza Nasr, 'Democracy and Islamic revivalism', *Political Science Quarterly*, 110 (2), 1995, pp. 261–285.
18. Maududi, *The Islamic Law and Constitution*, p. 147.
19. For the implications of this regarding constructions of gender and the status of women, see chapter 6 of this book.
20. See 'Djahilliya', *Encyclopaedia of Islam* (2nd edn).
21. See Sayyid Abul A'la Maududi, *Human Rights in Islam* (first published 1976), Islamic Foundation, London, 1980.
22. Under Maududi's proposals, the non-Muslim citizens of an Islamic state are required to pay a poll-tax incumbent upon their recognition as a protected religious minority. Moreover they are barred from running for political office and exempt from military service. For Maududi's conception of the role of women under an Islamic state, see Maududi, *Islamic Law and Constitution*, pp. 139–140.
23. Nasr, *Maududi and the Making of Islamic Revivalism*, p. 96.
24. Maududi, *Islamic Law and Constitution*, p. 101.
25. Wilfred Cantwell Smith, *Islam in Modern History*, Princeton University Press, Princeton, 1957, p. 238.
26. Jacques Derrida, 'Force of law: The mystical foundation of authority', *Deconstruction and the Possibility of Justice*, Drucilla Cornell, Michel Rosenfeld and David Gray Carlson (eds), Routledge, New York, 1992, pp. 3–67.
27. Here, I am not interested in Derrida's focus upon the relationship between the idea of justice and the enforcement of law as one which allows for their deconstruction, so that deconstruction is associated by Derrida with justice itself. Rather, my interest is in how the aporia between justice and law

informs our thinking about the impossibility of their final actualisation, which is pertinent to discussions about the paradox within Islamist proposals for a religious state.

28. For the biographical details of Qutb's life, see Ahmad S. Moussalli, *Radical Islamic Fundamentalism: The Ideological and Political Discourse of Sayyid Qutb*, American University of Beirut, Beirut, 1992.

29. For Aqqad's conception of the role of poetry, and contribution to the Diwan school of modernist literary theory in Egypt during the early decades of the twentieth century, see M. M. Badawi, *A Critical Introduction to Modern Arabic Poetry*, Cambridge University Press, Cambridge, 1975, pp. 84–114; and A. M. K. al-Zubaida, 'The Diwan school', *Journal of Arabic Literature*, 1, 1970, pp. 36–48.

30. A. Musallam, 'Sayyid Qutb's literary and spiritual orientation (1931–1938)', *Muslim World*, 30 (3), 1990, pp. 176–189; Ibrahim Abu-Rabi, *Intellectual Origins of Islamic Resurgence in the Modern Arab World*, State University of New York Press, Albany, 1996, p. 98.

31. Moussalli, *Radical Islamic Fundamentalism*, p. 25.

32. For the details of Qutb's American journey, see John Calvert, 'The world is an undutiful boy! Sayyid Qutb's American experience', *Islam and Christian-Muslim Relations*, 11 (1), 2000, pp. 87–103.

33. Sayyid Qutb, *al-'Adalah al-Ijtima'iyyah fi al-Islam* (*Social Justice in Islam*, first published 1949), Dar al-Shuruq, Cairo, 2002; and Sayyid Qutb, *Sayyid Qutb and Islamic Activism: A Translation and Critical Analysis of Social Justice in Islam*, William E. Shepard (trans.), E.J. Brill, Leiden, 1996.

34. For the details of this, see Richard P. Mitchell, *The Society of the Muslim Brothers*, Oxford University Press, London, 1969.

35. In particular, Qutb's observers in the Egyptian government feared he would substitute the ideology of Arab nationalism (*al-qaumiyyah al-'Arabiyyah*) with a new sort of Islamic nationalism (*al-qaumiyyah al-Islamiyyah*). See Sayyid Qutb, *Ma'alim fi al-Tariq* (*Signposts on the Way*, first published 1964), Dar al-Shuruq, Cairo, 1983, pp. 136–148; and Sayed Khatab, 'Arabism and Islamism in Sayyid Qutb's thoughts on nationalism', *Muslim World*, 94, 2004, p. 221.

36. Across the numerous editions of *Social Justice in Islam* which were published after 1949, William Shepard discerns an increased emphasis on the doctrine of divine sovereignty (*hakimiyyah*) which corresponded to the development and strengthening of this theme in Qutb's writings during the 1950s. William E. Shepard, 'Introduction', *Sayyid Qutb and Islamic Activism*. See also, William E. Shepard, 'Islam as a "system" in the later writings of Sayyid Qutb', *Middle Eastern Studies*, 25 (1), 1989, pp. 31–50.

37. After Hasan al-Banna's assassination in 1949, the youth of Egypt's Muslim Brothers became influenced by Maududi's writings, which were translated into Arabic in the early 1950s. See Fathi Osman, 'Mawdudi's contribution to the development of modern Islamic thinking in the Arabic-speaking world', *Muslim World*, 93, 2003, pp. 465–485.
38. Abul Hasan 'Ali Nadwi, *Islam and the World: Madha Khasira al-'Alam bi-Inhitat al-Muslimin*, Muhammad Asif Kidwai (trans.), International Islamic Federation of Students Organizations, Riyadh, 2006.
39. Nadwi, *Islam and the World*, p. 13.
40. William E. Shepard, 'Sayyid Qutb's doctrine of *jahiliyya*', *International Journal of Middle Eastern Studies*, 35, 2003, pp. 521–545.
41. Qutb, *Ma'alim fi al-Tariq*, p. 8.
42. A recent study to link Sayyid Qutb's Islamism to the ideology of totalitarianism, and to terrorist violence, is Paul Berman, *Terror and Liberalism*, W.W. Norton, New York, 2004, pp. 103–120.
43. Qutb, *Ma'alim fi al-Tariq*, p. 78.
44. For an interesting discussion of the secular tendencies in modern Arab thought, including that of Sayyid Qutb, see Ahmad Shboul, 'Between rhetoric and reality: Islam and politics in the Arab world', *Islam in World Politics*, Nelly Lahoud and Anthony H. Johns (eds), Routledge, London, 2005, pp. 170–191.
45. Sayyid Qutb, *al-Taswir al-Fanni fi al-Qur'an* (Aesthetic Portrayal in the Qur'an, first published 1945), Dar al-Shuruq, Cairo, 2003, p. 36. Quoted in Issa J. Boullata, 'Sayyid Qutb's literary appreciation of the Qur'an', *Literary Structures of Religious Meaning in the Qur'an*, Issa J. Boullata (ed.), Curzon, London, 2000, p. 356.
46. Qutb, *al-Taswir al-Fanni fi al-Qur'an*, p. 7. Details of Qutb's village childhood are given in his autobiography, *Tifl min al-Qaryah* (A Child from the Village, first published in 1945–46), which takes after the style of *al-Ayyam* (The Days) by Egypt's prominent man of letters, Taha Hussain (1889–1973). See Sayyid Qutb, *A Child from the Village*, John Calvert and William E. Shepard (eds and trans), Syracuse University Press, New York, 2004.
47. Sayyid Qutb, *Basic Principles of the Islamic Worldview*, Rami David (trans.), Islamic Publications International, New Jersey, 2006. The main characteristics of the Islamic conception, as Qutb describes it, are: Islam's notion of divinity, permanence, comprehensiveness, balance, positive articulation, realism, and principle of the oneness of God.
48. Ibid., p. 11.
49. Ibid., p. 3.
50. Ibid., p. 12.
51. Ibid., p. 14.
52. Qutb, *al-Taswir al-Fanni fi al-Qur'an*, pp. 226–238.

53. Qutb, *Basic Principles of the Islamic Worldview*, p. 186.
54. Qutb, *al-'Adalah al-Ijtima'iyyah fi al-Islam*, p. 31; and Ronald A. T. Judy, 'Sayyid Qutb's *fiqh al-waqi'i* or new realist science', *Boundary 2, 31* (2), 2004, pp. 113–148.
55. Binder, *Islamic Liberalism*, p. 200.
56. Qutb, *Basic Principles of the Islamic Worldview*, pp. 157–159 and 183–185; and Shepard, *Sayyid Qutb and Islamic Activism*, pp. 25 and 333.
57. For an interesting comparison of Qutb's critique of modern rationalism with such movements in the history of Western philosophy and political thought see Roxanne L. Euben, *Enemy in the Mirror: Islamic Fundamentalism and the Limits of Modern Rationalism*, Princeton University Press, Princeton, 1990.
58. Qutb, *Basic Principles of the Islamic Worldview*, p. 45.
59. Qutb, *Ma'alim fi al-Tariq*, p. 33.
60. Hamid Algar, 'Preface' in Qutb, *Basic Principles of the Islamic Worldview*, p. xi.
61. Ibid., p. 55.
62. Alexis Carrel, *Man, The Unknown*, Hamish Hamilton, Melbourne, 1946, pp. 261, 296 and 298.
63. For the influence of Carrel on Qutb's theory of social decline and subsequent need for a vanguard, see Youssef M. Choueiri, *Islamic Fundamentalism*, Twayne, Boston, 1990, pp. 140–149.
64. Carrel, *Man, The Unknown*, p. 17; and Qutb, *Basic Principles of the Islamic Worldview*, p. 54.
65. Carrel, *Man, The Unknown*, pp. 19–23.
66. Ibid., pp. 21 and 23; and Qutb, *Basic Principles of the Islamic Worldview*, pp. 54–58.
67. Choueiri, *Islamic Fundamentalism*, pp. 146–147.
68. Derrida, 'The mystical foundations of authority', p. 27.
69. See footnote 18 above; and Nasr, *Maududi and the Making of Islamic Revivalism*, pp. 102–103.
70. Maududi, *Islamic Law and Constitution*, p. 52.
71. Maududi's rejection of the traditional religious scholars of Islam for neglecting the social and political needs of the modern age is discussed in Nasr, *Maududi and the Making of Islamic Revivalism*, pp. 115–125.
72. See Joseph Schacht, *Islamic Law: An Introduction*, Oxford University Press, Oxford, 1962, p. 92; and Avi Rubin, 'Legal borrowing and its impact on Ottoman legal culture in the late nineteenth century', *Continuity and Change*, 22 (2), 2007, pp. 279–303.
73. For the contribution of modernist reforms to the etatisation of certain aspects of *shari'ah* law within the civil law codes of Egypt during the late nineteenth and early twentieth centuries, see Malcolm H. Kerr, *Islamic Reform: The*

Political and Legal Theories of Muhammad 'Abduh and Rashid Rida, University of California Press, Berkeley, 1966, pp. 215–219.

74. Of course, this is a historical generalisation and I have bypassed (for purposes of brevity) the important and sophisticated legal reforms of such Arab Middle Eastern scholars of the twentieth century as 'Abd al-Razzaq al-Sanhuri of Egypt (1895–1971) and Mustafa al-Zarqa of Syria (1904–1999).
75. Bernard Cohn, *Colonialism and its Forms of Knowledge*, Princeton University Press, Princeton, 1996, chapter 3.
76. However, as Lauren Benton points out, the eventual incorporation of indigenous law into a modern legal code in British India, as in other modern colonies, was replete with jurisdictional tensions and inconsistencies. See Lauren Benton, 'Colonial law and cultural difference: Jurisdictional politics and the formation of the colonial state', *Comparative Studies in Society and History*, 41 (3), 1999, pp. 563–588.
77. As Scott Alan Kugle points out, by the end of the nineteenth century 'British jurisprudence had defined Islam as a rarefied and monolithic identity', which Indian Muslims accepted 'as a vehicle to agitate for political rights and nationalist agendas'. Scott Alan Kugle, 'Framed, blamed and renamed: The recasting of Islamic jurisprudence in colonial South Asia', *Modern Asian Studies*, 35 (2), 2001, p. 303.
78. N. Calder argues that the notion of *shari'ah* as an ideology of social justice 'is characteristically deprived of detail, of complexity, and of association with the intellectual tradition of *fiqh*. It functions instead as a constitutive element in a demand for loyalty, unity, and commitment; it represents an ideal (unreal) governmental system.' See N. Calder, 'Shari'a', *Encyclopaedia of Islam* (2nd edn).
79. The following biographical information is indebted to Yogindar Sikand, 'Peace, dialogue and *da'wa*: An analysis of the writings of Maulana Wahiduddin Khan', *Islam and Christian-Muslim Relations*, 14 (1), 2003, pp. 33–49; and Irfan A. Omar, 'Rethinking Islam: A study of the thought and mission of Maulana Wahiduddin Khan', PhD thesis, Temple University, 2001.
80. See Wahiduddin Khan, *T'abir ki Ghalti (The Interpretive Error,* first published 1963), Dar al-Tazkir, Lahore, 2002.
81. Ibid., pp. 25–26.
82. Ibid., p. 38. This is a reference to Qur'an 2:165.
83. Ibid., p. 27.
84. Wahiduddin Khan, *Islam Rediscovered: Discovering Islam from the Original Sources*, Goodword, New Delhi, 2001, pp. 151–152.
85. Ibid., pp. 148 and 147.
86. Some critical responses to Islamism, present in recent progressive and feminist reformist discourses, will be explored in chapter 7 of this book.

Chapter 6. Maududi and the Gendering of Muslim Identity

1. *Correspondence between Abi-l-A'ala Al-Maudoodi and Maryam Jameelah*, Abul-Qasim Publishing House, Jaddah, 1413 h., <http:/www.islamunveiled.org/eng/ebooks/maryamj/maryamj.htm> (accessed 8 July 2011).
2. Ibid.
3. Ibid.
4. Maryam Jamila, *Islam and Western Society: A Refutation of the Modern Way of Life*, Adam Publishers, New Delhi, 1982, p. 105.
5. N. Tomiche, 'al-Mar'a', *Encyclopaedia of Islam* (2nd edn).
6. Saba Mahmoud, *Politics of Piety: The Islamic Revival and the Feminist Subject*, Princeton University Press, Princeton, 2005, chapter 1.
7. Joan W. Scott, 'Experience', *Feminists Theorize the Political*, Judith Butler and Joan W. Scott (eds.), Routledge, New York, 1992, pp. 22–40.
8. David C. Lamberth, 'Intimations of the finite: Thinking pragmatically at the end of modernity', *Harvard Theological Review*, 90 (2), 1997, p. 209.
9. Maududi, *Correspondence between Abi-l-A'ala Al-Maudoodi and Maryam Jameelah*.
10. My source for what follows is Maududi's *Purdah* (later translated into Arabic as *Al-Hijab*) which was based on a series of articles written during the 1930s, and was collectively revised and published in 1939. Sayyid Abul A'la Maududi, *Purdah*, Islamic Publications, Lahore, 2002.
11. Quoted in Amina Wudud, *Qur'an and Woman: Rereading the Sacred Text from a Woman's Perspective*, Oxford University Press, New York, 1999, p. 35.
12. Maududi, *Purdah*, pp. 156–159.
13. Ibid., pp. 134–138.
14. See Fatima Mernissi, *Beyond the Veil: Male-Female Dynamics in a Modern Muslim Society*, Indiana University Press, Indianapolis, 1985, pp. xv-xvi and 34–41; and Fatima Mernissi, *The Veil and the Male Elite: A Feminist Interpretation of Woman's Rights in Islam*, Perseus Books, Cambridge, 1992.
15. Maududi, *Purdah*, pp. 221–222.
16. Ibid., p. 223.
17. Whilst the term *haya* appears nowhere in the Qur'an, Maududi draws support from the following *ahadith* (sayings of the Prophet) of Bayhaqi, 'Every religion has a morality and the morality of Islam is *haya*'; and of Bukhari, Abu Dawud and Ibn Baja, 'When you do not have *haya*, you may do whatever you please'.
18. Qur'an 33:32.
19. Maududi, *Purdah*, p. 226.
20. Ibid., p. 225. The abovementioned description of the social dangers that a woman poses, by the presence of her figure, her smell, the sound of her voice and so forth, are drawn from legal texts of the pre-modern period which had always upheld patriarchal juristic norms. For more on this, see Barbara

Freyer Stowasser, *Women in the Qur'an, Traditions, and Interpretation*, Oxford University Press, New York, 1994, chapter 9.
21. Maududi, *Purdah*, p. 229.
22. Ibid., p. 223.
23. Ibid., pp. 225–226.
24. This historicising approach is subtly exemplified in Michel Foucault's, *The Care of the Self: The History of Sexuality*, vol. 3, Robert Hurley (trans.), Penguin, London, 1990. See also Nikolas Rose, *Inventing Ourselves: Psychology, Power and Personhood*, Cambridge University Press, Cambridge, 1998.
25. Gabriele Taylor, *Pride, Shame and Guilt*, Clarendon Press, Oxford, 1985. According to the psychoanalyst Gerhart Piers, it is 'the all-seeing, all-knowing eye which is feared in the condition of shame, God's eye which reveals all [of the] shortcomings of mankind.' Gerhart Piers, *Guilt and Shame: A Psychoanalytic and Cultural Study*, Thomas Books, New York, 1953, p. 17.
26. Taylor, *Pride, Shame and Guilt*, p. 67.
27. Ibid., p. 131.
28. Maududi, *Purdah*, p. 222. My italics.
29. Ibid., p. 255.
30. Ibid., p. 226. The Qur'anic verse in question urges the Prophet's wives to 'stay at home and do not flaunt your finery as in the pagan past' (33:33). This directly follows that verse (cited above) enjoining seclusion to the Prophet's wives by way of a response to the difficult social and political conditions then prevailing in the city of Medina. See page 203, above.
31. Ibid., p. 225.
32. John Berger, *Ways of Seeing*, Penguin, London, 1986, pp. 47 and 46.
33. Taylor, *Pride, Shame and Guilt*, p. 133.
34. See Jennifer C. Manion, 'Girls blush, sometimes: Gender, moral agency, and the problem of shame', *Hypatia*, 18 (3), 2003, pp. 21–41; and Ullalina Lehtinen, 'How does one know what shame is? Epistemology, emotions and forms of life in juxtaposition', *Hypatia*, 13 (1), 1998, pp. 56–77.
35. Manion, 'Girls blush, sometimes'.
36. Maududi, *Purdah*, pp. 119–120.
37. Ibid., p. 122.
38. Ibid.
39. See Helene Deutsch, *The Psychology of Women: A Psychoanalytic Interpretation*, Grune & Stratton, New York, 1944; and 'Abdul Majid Daryabadi, *Tafsir-ul-Qur'an*, vol. 1, Darul Ishaat, Karachi, 1991, pp. 327–328. For the relevance of Deutsch's view of female sexuality and other Freudian-based psychoanalytic theories in minimizing the conceptualisation of rape in Western Europe and the USA in the twentieth century, see Joanna Burke, *Rape: Sex, Violence, History*, Shoemaker Hoard, Berkeley CA, 2007, pp. 67–76.

40. For a good analysis of the thought of Malik Bennabi (1905–1973), which includes the theme of 'colonisability', see Phillip Chiviges Naylor, 'The formative influence of French colonialism on the life and thought of Malik Bennabi (Malik bn Nabi)', *French Colonial History*, 7, 2006, pp. 129–142.
41. Maryam Jamila, *Islam and Western Society*, pp. 105 and 108.
42. In places, Maududi quotes such authors verbatim to bolster his assertion that an Islamic social system is best suited to natural human dispositions and needs. In other instances, the works of these authors were inserted into footnotes added by Maududi's friend, editor and translator, al-Ash'ari, in his English translation of *Purdah*. See, Sayyid Abul A'la Maududi, *Purdah and the Status of Women in Islam*, Al-Ash'ari (trans. and ed.), Islamic Publications, Lahore, 2002, pp. 50–71.
43. Maududi, *Purdah*, pp. 53 and 80–84.
44. Ibid., p. 95.
45. Here, Maududi quotes Scott's *History of Prostitution*. Ibid., pp. 97–99.
46. Ibid., p. 140.
47. Ibid., p. 106.
48. Quoted in Farhat Haq, 'Women, Islam and the state in Pakistan', *Muslim World*, 86 (2), 1996, pp. 158–175.

Chapter 7. Progressive Islam: The Hermeneutical Turn

1. Fazlur Rahman, *Islam and Modernity: Transformation of an Intellectual Tradition*, University of Chicago Press, Chicago, 1982, p. 4.
2. Nasr Abu-Zayd, 'The dilemma of the literary approach to the Qur'an', *Alif: Journal of Comparative Poetics*, 23, 2003, p. 34.
3. For a description and anthology of liberal Muslim thought, see *Liberal Islam: A Source Book*, Charles Kurzman (ed.), Oxford University Press, New York, 1998.
4. This definition serves a heuristic purpose, and is similar to that presented in Omid Safi, 'Introduction: The times they are a-changin' – a Muslim quest for justice, gender equality and pluralism', *Progressive Muslims: On Gender, Justice and Pluralism*, Omid Safi (ed.), Oneworld, Oxford, 2003, pp. 1–29.
5. Sayyid Ahmad Khan, *Tafsir al-Qur'an*, Dost Association, Lahore, 2004, p. 35.
6. Ibid.
7. For an analysis of the Islamist assault upon pre-modern traditions of jurisprudence and theology, see Khaled Abou El Fadl, *The Great Theft: Wrestling Islam from the Extremists*, HarperSanFrancisco, New York, 2005; and Tamara Albertini, 'The seductiveness of certainty: The destruction of Islam's intellectual legacy by the fundamentalists', *Philosophy East and West*, 53 (4), 2003, pp. 455–470.
8. Olivier Roy, *Secularism Confronts Islam*, George Holoch (trans.), Columbia University Press, New York, 2007.

9. For my analysis of Qutb's theory, see chapter 5 of this book.
10. Roxanne L. Euben, *Enemy in the Mirror: Islamic Fundamentalism and the Limits of Modern Rationalism*, Princeton University Press, Princeton, 1990, p. 88.
11. See Ebrahim Moosa, 'The poetics and politics of law after empire', *UCLA Journal of Islamic and Near Eastern Law*, 1 (1), 2001, pp. 1–36.
12. John O. Voll, 'Renewal and reform in Islamic history: *Taqdid* and *islah*', *Voices of Resurgent Islam*, John L. Esposito (ed.), Oxford University Press, New York, 1983, pp. 32–47. Two influential eighteenth-century revivalists to act within the *islahi* tradition (although they were responding to essentially internal pre-modern social, cultural and political conditions) were Shah Wali Allah (1703–1762) of Delhi, and Muhammad ibn 'Abdul Wahhab (1703–1787), of Najd in the Arabian peninsula.
13. Paul Ricoeur, *The Conflict of Interpretation*, Northwestern University Press, Evanston, 1974, pp. 6–7. Drawing on poststructuralist and semiotic theory, Ricoeur argued that real knowledge should not be concerned with how one interprets this or that being, but instead depends upon an analysis of the language through which the act of interpretation and understanding takes place. This is not to embed oneself in a totalizing interpretative position but to view 'the conjunction of the work of interpretation and the interpreted being' (p. 23).
14. Biographical details of Rahman's career are derived from 'Abdullah Saeed, 'Fazlur Rahman: A framework for interpreting the ethico-legal content of the Qur'an', *Modern Muslim Intellectuals and the Qur'an*, Suha Taji-Farouki (ed.), Oxford University Press, Oxford, 2004, pp. 37–66; and Rahman's *Islam and Modernity*.
15. Rahman, *Islam and Modernity*, p. 125.
16. Fazlur Rahman, *Major Themes of the Qur'an*, Bibliotheca Islamica, Chicago, 1980, p. xxii.
17. Rahman, *Islam and Modernity*, p. 3.
18. Rahman, *Major Themes of the Qur'an*, p. xxii.
19. See Rahman, *Major Themes of the Qur'an*, pp. xv–xvi; and Rahman, *Islam and Modernity*, pp. 145–147.
20. Rahman, *Islam and Modernity*, p. 143.
21. Fazlur Rahman, *Islam* (2nd edn), University of Chicago Press, Chicago, 1979, p. 33.
22. Ibid., p. 31.
23. Ibid., pp. 39–40.
24. Because of this criticism of the role of past Muslim exegetes, and due to a misunderstanding over what he meant when he wrote that the Qur'an was both the word of God and 'the word of Muhammad', Rahman was roundly condemned by the conservative Muslim scholars of Pakistan in the late 1960s.
25. Rahman, *Islam*, p. 85.

26. Rahman, *Islam and Modernity*, p. 5.
27. Abu-Zayd, 'The dilemma of the literary approach to the Qur'an', pp. 38–39.
28. Ibid.
29. Khaled Abou El Fadl, *Islam and the Challenge of Democracy*, Princeton University Press, Princeton, 2004, pp. 31 and 34.
30. Ibid., pp. 30–34.
31. Abu-Zayd, 'The dilemma of the literary approach to the Qur'an', p. 39.
32. Whilst the label 'feminist' is sometimes rejected by Muslim reformers because of its imbrication in the political struggles of Western women over the last few decades, I have retained it as a heuristic label for the designation of those who critically engage with traditional hermeneutical and contemporary thought for the purpose of defending religious principles of gender equality. Hereafter, the term will not be placed in quotation marks.
33. See Fatima Mernissi, *The Veil and the Male Elite: A Feminist Interpretation of Woman's Rights in Islam*, Perseus Books, Cambridge, 1992; Leila Ahmed, *Woman and Gender in Islam*, Yale University Press, New Haven, 1992; Asma Barlas, *Believing Women in Islam: Unreading Patriarchal Interpretations of the Qur'an*, Sama, Karachi, 2004; Barbara Freyer Stowasser, *Women in the Qur'an, Traditions, and Interpretation*, Oxford University Press, New York, 1994; and Amina Wadud, *Qur'an and Woman: Rereading the Sacred Text from a Woman's Perspective*, Oxford University Press, New York, 1999.
34. See Barlas, *Believing Women in Islam*.
35. See Asma Barlas, 'Amina Wadud's hermeneutics of the Qur'an', *Modern Muslim Intellectuals and the Qur'an*, Suha Taji-Farouki (ed.), Oxford University Press, Oxford, 2004, pp. 97–123.
36. Amina Wadud, *Inside the Gender Jihad: Women's Reform in Islam*, Oneworld, Oxford, 2006, chapters 1 and 3.
37. Wadud, *Qur'an and Woman*, p. 2.
38. Ibid., p. 6.
39. Ibid.
40. Ibid., p. 40.
41. Ibid., p. 74.
42. Ibid., p. 7.
43. The following summary of Soroush's life is based on 'Abdolkarim Soroush, *Reason, Freedom and Democracy in Islam: Essential Writings of 'Abdolkarim Soroush*, Mahmoud Sadri and Ahmad Sadri (trans. and eds), Oxford University Press, Oxford, 2000.
44. An account of this post-revolutionary ideological contest is given in Mehrzad Boroujerdi, *Iranian Intellectuals and the West: The Tormented Triumph of Nativism*, Syracuse University Press, New York, 1996, pp. 159–165. As Boroujerdi points out, Soroush was critical of the historicist methodology adopted by

his ideological opponents, such as Reza Davari-Ardakani (b.1933). At an epistemological level, however, he had no objection to the historicist presumption that human knowledge is essentially relative to time and place, for this is a fundamental assumption of his own thought (p. 174).

45. This is elucidated in Soroush's important theoretical essay, 'Islamic revival and reform'. See Soroush, *Reason, Freedom and Democracy in Islam*, p. 31.
46. The paradigm is also as relevant to those notions of finality which are imposed over the domain of theology (*kalam*), jurisprudence (*fiqh*) and mystical knowledge (*irfan*). Ibid., p. 34.
47. Ibid.
48. Ibid., chapter 4.
49. For Soroush's dept to the Mu'tazilah's use of reason-based argument, alongside revelation, on questions of morality, see 'I'm a neo-Mu'tazilite: An interview with Abdulkarim Soroush', Matin Ghaffarian, Nilou Mobasser (trans.), http://www.drsoroush.com/English/Interviews/E-INT-Neo-Mutazilite_July2008.html (accessed 8 July 2011). For an overview of the ethical system developed amongst thinkers associated with the Mu'tazilah movement, see George F. Hourani, 'Islamic and non-Islamic origins of Mu'tazilite ethical rationalism', *International Journal of Middle Eastern Studies*, 7, 1976, pp. 59–87.
50. Soroush, *Reason, Freedom and Democracy in Islam*, pp. 132–133.
51. Mohammed Arkoun, 'Contemporary critical practice and the Qur'an', *Encyclopaedia of the Qur'an*, Jane Dammen McAuliffe (ed.), Brill, Leiden, 2005.
52. For an exposition of this which analyses a theological treatise of the tenth-century scholar Abul Hasan al-'Amiri, see Mohammed Arkoun, *Islam: To Reform or to Subvert?*, Saqi, London, 2006, chapter 3.
53. The historiographical paradigm of the 'Mediterranean space' was first developed by the Annales historian, Fernand Braudel. See Fernand Braudel, *The Mediterranean and the Mediterranean World in the Age of Phillip II*, Sian Reynolds (trans.), Harper & Row, New York, 1972.
54. Mohammed Arkoun, *Rethinking Islam: Common Questions, Uncommon Answers*, Robert D. Lee (trans. and ed.), Westview Press, Boulder, 1994, p. 8.
55. Arkoun's argument is no doubt supported, indirectly, by Dimitri Gutas' conclusions about the failure of Orientalist and European historians of Arabic philosophy over the last century to draw meaningful parallels between developments in the intellectual history of the Middle East and that of Latin medieval philosophy, despite the commensurable age of these scholarly fields. See Dimitri Gutas, 'The study of Arabic philosophy in the twentieth century: An essay on the historiography of Arabic philosophy', *British Journal of Middle Eastern Studies*, 29 (1), 2002, pp. 5–25.

56. Arkoun derives this theme from Marxist theories of the 1960s and 1970s, especially Constantin Castoriadus' *The Imaginary Institution of Society*. See Arkoun, *Rethinking Islam: Common Questions, Uncommon Answers*, pp. 6–13.
57. Arkoun, *Islam: To Reform or to Subvert?*, chapter 6.
58. Mohammed Arkoun, 'Rethinking Islam today', *Annals, AAPSS*, 588, 2003, p. 27. The emphasis is Arkoun's.
59. Arkoun, *Islam: To Reform or to Subvert?*, pp. 49–50. Contemporary Muslims often hold to the doctrine of the eternal and uncreated Qur'an despite knowing of the imperfect process by which it was collected and standardised as a physical, commonly used book (*mushaf*). See also Mohammed Arkoun, 'The notion of revelation: From *ahl al-kitab* to the societies of the book', *Die Welt des Islams*, 28 (1/4), 1988, pp. 62–89.
60. Arkoun, 'Rethinking Islam Today', p. 31.
61. Jacques Derrida, *Of Grammatology*, Gayatri Chakravorti Spivak (trans.), Johns Hopkins University Press, Baltimore, 1976, p. 163.
62. Arkoun, *Islam: To Reform or to Subvert?*, pp. 10–11.
63. Arkoun, *Rethinking Islam: Common Questions, Uncommon Answers*, pp. 74–78.
64. Arkoun, *Islam: To Reform or to Subvert?*, p. 344.
65. Ibid., p. 35.
66. Ibid.
67. Ibid., p. 33.
68. For an interesting evaluation of the contribution of postmodern thought and the 'end of metaphysics' to Christian theological thinking, see Merold Westphal, *Overcoming Onto-Theology: Towards a Postmodern Christian Faith*, Fordham University Press, New York, 2001.
69. Wadud, *Inside the Gender Jihad*, p. 6.
70. Ibid.

BIBLIOGRAPHY

Abd al-Baqi, Muhammad Fouad, *Al-Mujam al-Mufahras li Alfaz al-Qur'an al-Karim*, Dar wa Matab'a al-Sh'ab, n.d.
Abdel-Malek, Anouar, 'Orientalism in crisis', *Diogenes*, 11, 1963, pp. 103–140.
'Abduh, Muhammad, *Risalah at-Tawhid: The Theology of Unity*, Ishaq Musa'ad and Kenneth Cragg (trans.), Islamic Book Trust, Kuala Lumpur, 2004.
———, *Risalah al-Tawhid* (1st edn), Majlis Idarah al-Azhar, 1345 h.
Abrams, M. H., *The Mirror and the Lamp: Romantic Theory and the Critical Tradition*, W.W. Norton, New York, 1958.
Abu-Deeb, K, *Al-Jurjani's Theory of Poetic Imagery*, Aris & Phillips, Surrey, 1979.
Abu-Lughod, Lila, 'The marriage of feminism and Islamism in Egypt: Selective repudiation as a dynamic of postcolonial cultural politics', *Remaking Women: Feminism and Modernity in the Middle East*, Lila Abu-Lughod (ed.), Princeton University Press, Princeton, 1998, pp. 243–269.
———, 'Anthropology's orient: The boundaries of theory on the Arab World', *Theory, Politics and the Arab world: Critical Responses*, Hisham Sharabi (ed.), Routledge, 1990, pp. 81–131.
Abu-Rabi, Ibrahim, *Intellectual Origins of Islamic Resurgence in the Modern Arab World*, State University of New York Press, Albany, 1996.
Abu-Zayd, Nasr, 'The dilemma of the literary approach to the Qur'an', *Alif: Journal of Comparative Poetics*, 23, 2003, pp. 8–47.
Adams, Charles C., *Islam and Modernism in Egypt*, Oxford University Press, London, 1933.
Adorno, Theodore and Max Horkheimer, *Dialectic of Enlightenment*, Verso, London, 1979.
Ahmad, Aziz, *Muslim Modernism in India and Pakistan: 1857–1964*, Oxford University Press, London, 1967.
Ahmad, Mumtaz, 'Islamic fundamentalism in South Asia', *Fundamentalisms Observed*, Martin E. Marty and R. Scott Appleby (eds), University of Chicago Press, Chicago, 1994, pp. 457–530.

BIBLIOGRAPHY 273

Ahmed, Leila, *Woman and Gender in Islam*, Yale University Press, New Haven, 1992.

Ahmed, Manzooruddin, 'Iqbal and Jinnah on the two-nations theory', *Iqbal, Jinnah and Pakistan: The Vision and the Reality*, C. M. Naim (ed.), Syracuse University, New York, 1979, pp. 41–76.

Ahmed, Nazir, *The Repentance of Nussooh (Tauhat-al-Nasuh): A Tale of a Muslim Family a Hundred Years Ago*, C. M. Naim (ed.) and M. Kempson (trans.), Permanent Black, New Delhi, 2004.

Ajami, Fouad, *The Arab Predicament: Arab Political Thought and Practice since 1967*, Cambridge University Press, Cambridge, 1992.

Alam, Mazaffar, *The Languages of Political Islam: India 1200–1800*, University of Chicago Press, Chicago, 2004.

Alatas, Sayyid Hussain, 'The captive mind in development studies', *International Social Science Journal*, 24 (1), 1972, pp. 9–25.

Albertini, Tamara, 'The seductiveness of certainty: The destruction of Islam's intellectual legacy by the fundamentalists', *Philosophy East and West*, 53 (4), 2003, pp. 455–470.

'Ali, Sayyid Amir, *Memoirs and Other Writings of Syed Ameer Ali*, People's Publishing House, Lahore, 1978.

Allahabadi, Akbar, *Kulliyat-i Akbar*, vol. 1, Maktabah Sh'ir o Adab, Lahore, n.d.

Allison, Henry E., 'Kant on freedom of the will', *The Cambridge Companion to Kant and Modern Philosophy*, Paul Guyer (ed.), Cambridge University Press, Cambridge, 2006, pp. 381–415.

Almond, Ian, *The New Orientalists: Postmodern Representations of Islam from Foucault to Baudrillard*, I.B.Tauris, London, 2007.

Amin, Qasim, *The Liberation of Women and The New Woman*, Samina Sidhom Peterson (trans.), American University in Cairo Press, Cairo, 2001.

Amin, Samir, *The Arab Nation: Nationalism and Class Struggle*, Zed Press, London, 1978.

Amin, Shahid, 'On retelling the Muslim conquest of North India', *History and The Present*, Partha Chatterjee and Anjan Ghosh (eds), Permanent Black, New Delhi, 2002, pp. 24–43.

Anderson, Benedict, *Imagined Communities: Reflections on the Origins and Spread of Nationalism*, Verso, London, 1991.

Anderson, Lisa, 'Policy making and theory building: American political science and the Arab Middle East', *Theory, Politics and the Arab World: Critical Responses*, Hisham Sharabi (ed.), Routledge, 1990, pp. 52–80.

Appadurai, Arjun, *Modernity at Large: Cultural Dimensions of Globalization*, University of Minnesota Press, Minneapolis, 1996.

Arberry, A. J., *Reason and Revelation in Islam*, Allen & Unwin, London, 1957.

Arkoun, Mohammed, *Islam: To Reform or to Subvert?*, Saqi, London, 2006.

———, 'Contemporary critical practice and the Qur'an', *Encyclopaedia of the Qur'an*, Jane Dammen McAuliffe (ed.), Brill, Leiden, 2005, pp. 412–431.

———, 'Rethinking Islam today', *Annals, AAPSS*, 588, 2003, pp. 18–39.
———, *Rethinking Islam: Common Questions, Uncommon Answers*, Robert D. Lee (trans. and ed.), Westview Press, Boulder, 1994.
———, 'The notion of revelation: From *ahl al-kitab* to the societies of the book', *Die Welt des Islams*, 28 (1/4), 1988, pp. 62–89.
Arthur, Keith, *Ethnos, or, The Problem of Race Considered from a New Point of View*, K. Paul, London, 1931.
Asad, Talal, *Formations of the Secular: Christianity, Islam, Modernity*, Stanford University Press, Stanford, 2003.
———, *Genealogies of Religion: Discipline and Reasons of Power in Christianity and Islam*, Johns Hopkins University Press, Baltimore, 1993.
———, *Anthropology and the Colonial Encounter*, Talal Asad (ed.), Ithaca, London, 1973.
Azad, Muhammad Husain, *Ab-e Hayat: Shaping the Canon of Urdu Poetry, Muhammad Husain Azad*, Francis W. Pritchett (trans. and ed.) in association with Shamsur Rahman Faruqi, Oxford University Press, New Delhi, 2001.
Al-Azmeh, Aziz, *Islams and Modernities*, Verso, London, 1996.
Babcock, Barbara A., 'Introduction', *The Reversible World: Symbolic Inversion in Art and Society*, Barbara A. Babcock (ed.), Cornell University Press, Ithaca, 1978, pp. 1–36.
Badawi, M. M., *A Critical Introduction to Modern Arabic Poetry*, Cambridge University Press, Cambridge, 1975.
Badiou, Alain, *Infinite Thought*, London, Continuum, 2003.
Ballantyne, Tony, *Orientalism and Race: Aryanism in the British Empire*, Palgrave, New York, 2002.
Banton, Michael, *Racial Theories*, Cambridge University Press, Cambridge, 1998.
Barakat, Halim, *The Arab World: Society, Culture and State*, University of California Press, Berkeley, 1993.
Barlas, Asma, *Believing Women in Islam: Unreading Patriarchal Interpretations of the Qur'an*, Sama, Karachi, 2004.
———, 'Amina Wadud's hermeneutics of the Qur'an', *Modern Muslim Intellectuals and the Qur'an*, Suha Taji-Farouki (ed.), Oxford University Press, Oxford, 2004, pp. 97–123.
Beinin, Joel, 'Bernard Lewis' anti-Semites', *Middle Eastern Report*, 147, 1987, pp. 43–45.
Benhabib, Seyla, *Situating the Self: Gender, Community and Postmodernism in Contemporary Ethics*, Polity Press, Oxford, 1992.
Benton, Lauren, 'Colonial law and cultural difference: Jurisdictional politics and the formation of the colonial state', *Comparative Studies in Society and History*, 41 (3), 1999, pp. 563–588.
Berger, John, *Ways of Seeing*, Penguin, London, 1986.
Berlin, Isaiah, *The Crooked Timber: Chapters in the History of Ideas*, Henry Hardy (ed.), John Murray, London, 1990.
Berman, Paul, *Terror and Liberalism*, W.W. Norton, New York, 2004.

Bibliography

Bhabha, Homi, *The Location of Culture*, Routledge, London, 1994.

Binder, Leonard, *Islamic Liberalism: A Critique of Development Ideologies*, University of Chicago Press, Chicago, 1989.

———, *Religion and Politics in Pakistan*, University of California Press, Berkeley, 1961.

Boroujerdi, Mehrzad, *Iranian Intellectuals and the West: The Tormented Triumph of Nativism*, Syracuse University Press, New York, 1996.

Boullata, Issa J., *Trends and Issues in Contemporary Arab Thought*, State University Press, New York, 1990.

———, 'Sayyid Qutb's literary appreciation of the Qur'an', *Literary Structures of Religious Meaning in the Qur'an*, Issa J. Boullata (ed.), Curzon, London, 2000, pp. 354–371.

Braudel, Fernand, *The Mediterranean and the Mediterranean World in the Age of Phillip II*, Sian Reynolds (trans.), Harper & Row, New York, 1972.

Brook, John Hedley, *Religion and Science: Some Historical Perspectives*, Cambridge University Press, Cambridge, 1991.

Burke, Joanna, *Rape: Sex, Violence, History*, Shoemaker Hoard, Berkeley CA, 2007.

Bush, George W., 'Address to a joint session of Congress and the American people' (20 September 2001), http://www.washingtonpost.com/wp-srv/nation/specials/attacked/transcripts/bushaddress_092001.html (accessed 8 July 2011).

Byrne, Peter, *Natural Religion and the Religion of Nature: The Legacy of Deism*, Routledge, London, 1989.

Calvert, John, 'The world is an undutiful boy! Sayyid Qutb's American experience', *Islam and Christian-Muslim Relations*, 11 (1), 2000, pp. 87–103.

Carrel, Alexis, *Man, The Unknown*, Hamish Hamilton, Melbourne, 1946.

Chakrabarty, Dipesh, *Provincializing Europe: Postcolonial Thought and Historical Difference*, Princeton University Press, Princeton, 2000.

Chatterjee, Partha, *The Nation and its Fragments: Colonial and Post Colonial Histories*, Oxford University Press, Delhi, 1995.

Choueiri, Youssef M., *Islamic Fundamentalism*, Twayne, Boston, 1990.

Cohn, Bernard, *Colonialism and its Forms of Knowledge*, Princeton University Press, Princeton, 1996.

———, *An Anthropologist Among the Historians and Other Essays*, Oxford University Press, New Delhi, 1987.

Cole, Juan Ricardo, 'Feminism, class and Islam in turn-of-the-century Egypt', *International Journal of Middle Eastern Studies*, 13, 1981, pp. 387–407.

Connolly, William E., *Why I Am Not a Secularist*, University of Minnesota Press, Minneapolis, 1999.

Coulson, N. J., *A History of Islamic Law*, Edinburgh University Press, Edinburgh, 1964.

Cromer, Evelyn Baring (Earl of Cromer), *Modern Egypt*, 2 vols, Macmillan, London, 1908.

Dallal, Ahmad, 'Science and the Qur'an', *Encyclopaedia of the Qur'an*, Jane Dammen McAuliffe (ed.), Brill, Leiden, 2005.

———, 'Appropriating the past: Twentieth century reconstructions of pre-modern Islamic thought', *Islamic Law and Society*, 7 (3), 2000, pp. 325–358.

———, 'Science, medicine and technology: The making of a scientific culture', *The Oxford History of Islam*, John Esposito (ed.), Oxford University Press, Oxford, 1999, pp. 155–213.

Daryabadi, 'Abdul Majid, *Tafsir-ul-Qur'an*, 4 vols, Darul Ishaat, Karachi, 1991.

Derrida, Jacques, 'Force of law: The mystical foundation of authority', *Deconstruction and the Possibility of Justice*, Drucilla Cornell, Michel Rosenfeld and David Gray Carlson (eds), Routledge, New York, 1992, pp. 3–67.

———, *Of Grammatology*, Gayatri Chakravorti Spivak (trans.), Johns Hopkins University Press, Baltimore, 1976.

Deutsch, Helene, *The Psychology of Women: A Psychoanalytic Interpretation*, Grune and Stratton, New York, 1944.

Devji, Faisal, *Landscapes of the Jihad: Militancy, Morality, Modernity*, Hurst, London, 2005.

De Vries, Hent, 'Before, around and beyond the theologico-political', *Political Theologies: Public Religions in a Post-Secular World*, Hent De Vries and Lawrence E. Sullivan (eds), Fordham University Press, New York, 2006, pp. 1–89.

———, *Minimal Theologies: Critiques of Secular Reason in Adorno and Levinas*, Geoffrey Hale (trans.), Johns Hopkins University Press, Baltimore, 2005.

Dhanani, Alnoor, 'Islam', *Science and Religion: A Historical Introduction*, Gary B. Ferngren (ed), Johns Hopkins University Press, Baltimore, 2002, pp. 73–92.

Dharwadker, Vinay, 'Orientalism and the study of Indian literatures', Orientalism and the Postcolonial Predicament: Perspectives on South Asia, Carol A. Breckenridge and Peter Van der Veer (eds), University of Pennsylvania Press, Philadelphia, 1993, pp. 158–185.

Dirks, Nicholas B., *Castes of Mind: Colonialism and the Making of Modern India*, Permanent Black, New Delhi, 2004.

Downing, Linda, *Language and Decadence in the Victorian Fin de Siecle*, Princeton University Press, Princeton, 1986.

Eaton, Richard M., 'Temple desecration and Indo-Muslim states', *Beyond Turk and Hindu: Rethinking Religious Identities in Islamicate South Asia*, David Gilmartin and Bruce B. Lawrence (eds), India Research Press, New Delhi, 2002, pp. 246–281.

Eickelman, Dale and James Piscatori, *Muslim Politics*, Princeton University Press, Princeton, 1996.

Eisenstadt, S. N., 'Multiple modernities in an age of globalization', *Canadian Journal of Sociology*, 24 (2), 1999, pp. 283–295.

Enayat, Hamid, *Modern Islamic Political Thought*, I.B.Tauris, London, 2004.

Engineer, Ashgar Ali, 'Iqbal's "Reconstruction of Religious Thought in Islam": A critical appraisal', *Social Scientist*, 8 (8), 1980, pp. 52–63.

Esposito, John L., 'Muhammad Iqbal and the Islamic state', *Makers of Contemporary Islam*, John L. Esposito (ed.), Oxford University Press, Oxford, 2001, pp. 175–190.

Euben, Roxanne L., *Enemy in the Mirror: Islamic Fundamentalism and the Limits of Modern Rationalism*, Princeton University Press, Princeton, 1990.

El Fadl, Khaled Abou, *The Great Theft: Wrestling Islam from the Extremists*, HarperSanFrancisco, New York, 2005.

———, *Islam and the Challenge of Democracy*, Princeton University Press, Princeton, 2004.

Faiz, Faiz Ahmed, *Culture and Identity: Selected Writings of Faiz*, Sheema Majeed (ed.), Oxford University Press, Oxford, 2005.

Fakhry, Majid, *A History of Islamic Philosophy* (2nd edn), Columbia University Press, New York, 1983.

Fanon, Frantz, *The Wretched of the Earth*, Constance Farrington (trans.), Penguin Books, London, 2001.

Farrenkopf, John, *The Prophet of Decline: Spengler on World History and Politics*, Louisiana State University Press, Baton Rouge, 2001.

Faruqi, Shamsur Rahman, *Early Urdu Literary Culture and History*, Oxford University Press, Delhi, 2001.

———, 'From antiquary to social revolutionary: Sayyid Ahmad Khan and the colonial experience', <http://www.columbia.edu/itc/mealac/pritchett/00fwp/srf/index.html> (accessed 8 July 2011).

Fichte, J. G., *Introductions to the Wissenschaftslehre and Other Writings*, Daniel Breazeale (trans. and ed.), Hackett, Indianapolis, 1994.

Forward, Martin, *The Failure of Islamic Modernism? Syed Ameer Ali's Interpretation of Islam*, Peter Lang, Bern, 1999.

Foucault, Michel, *The Order of Things: An Archaeology of the Human Sciences*, Vintage, New York, 1994.

———, *The Care of the Self: The History of Sexuality*, vol. 3, Robert Hurley (trans.), Penguin, London, 1990.

———, *The will to knowledge: The History of Sexuality*, vol. 1, Robert Hurley (trans.), Penguin, London, 1984.

———, *The Foucault Reader*, Paul Rabinow (ed.), Pantheon, New York, 1984.

Fredrickson, George M., *Racism: A Short History*, Princeton University Press, Princeton, 2002.

Friedman, Thomas L., *The Lexus and the Olive Tree*, Harper Collins, London, 1999.

Fukuyama, Francis, 'Has history started again?', *Policy*, 18 (2), 2002, pp. 3–7.

———, *The End of History and the Last Man*, Avon Books, New York, 1993.

Gardet, L., 'Din', *Encyclopaedia of Islam* (2nd edn).

Gerber, Haim, *The Social Origins of the Modern Middle East*, Mansell, London, 1987.

Ghalib, Mirza Asadullah Khan, *Divan-i Ghalib*, Liberty Art Press, Delhi, 1969.

al-Ghazali, Abu Hamid Muhammad, *The Niche of Lights*, David Buchman (trans.), Brigham Young University Press, Utah, 1998.

Gilani, Asad, *Maududi: Thought and Movement*, Islamic Publications, Lahore, 1984.

Gilman, Nils, *Mandarins of the Future: Modernization Theory in Cold War America*, Johns Hopkins University Press, Baltimore, 2003.

Goldziher, Ignaz, 'The attitude of orthodox Islam towards the 'ancient sciences'', *Studies in Islam*, M. Schwartz (ed.), Oxford University Press, Oxford, 1975, pp. 185–215.

Gole, Nulifer, 'Snapshots of Islamic modernities', *Daedalus*, 129 (1), pp. 91–117.

Gray, John, *Black Mass: Apocalyptic Religion and the Death of Utopia*, Penguin, London, 2008.

Grunebaum, G. E. von, *Modern Islam: The Search for Cultural Identity*, University of California Press, Berkeley, 1962.

Guha, Ranajit, *History at the Limits of World-History*, Columbia University Press, New York, 2002.

———, 'Dominance without hegemony and its historiography', *Subaltern Studies: Writing on South Asian History and Society*, vol. 4, Ranajit Guha (ed.), Oxford University Press, Delhi, 1985, pp. 210–309.

Gutas, Dimitri, 'The study of Arabic philosophy in the twentieth century: An essay on the historiography of Arabic philosophy', *British Journal of Middle Eastern Studies*, 29 (1), 2002, pp. 5–25.

———, *Greek Thought, Arabic Culture: The Graeco-Arabic Translation Movement in Baghdad and Early 'Abbasid Society (2nd – 4th/8th –10th centuries)*, Routledge, New York, 1999.

Habermas, Jurgen, *The Philosophical Discourses of Modernity*, Frederick Lawrence (trans.), MIT Cambridge Mass., 1990.

Halbfass, Wilhelm, *India and Europe: An Essay in Understanding*, State University of New York Press, New York, 1988.

Hali, Altaf Husain, 'Hubb-i watan', *Masterpieces of Patriotic Urdu Poetry*, C. K. Nanda (ed.), Sterling, New Delhi, 2005, pp. 82–87.

———, *Hali's Musaddas: The Flow and Ebb of Islam*, Christopher Shackle and Javed Majeed (trans), Oxford University Press, Delhi, 1997.

———, *Voices of Silence: English Translation of Altaf Hussain Hali's Majalis un-Nissa and Chupp ki Dad*, Gail Minault (trans.), Chanakya Publications, Delhi, 1986.

———, *Muqaddimah Sh'ir aur Sha'iri*, Khazinah 'Ilm-o Adab, Lahore, 2001.

———, *Hayat-i Javid*, Saleem Akhtar (ed.), Sang-i Meel, Lahore, 1993.

Hallaq, Wael B., *The Origins and Evolution of Islamic Law*, Cambridge University Press, Cambridge, 2005.

Hansen, Thomas Blom, *The Saffron Wave: Democracy and Hindu Nationalism in Modern India*, Oxford University Press, New Delhi, 2001.

Haq, Farhat, 'Women, Islam and the state in Pakistan', *Muslim World*, 86 (2), 1996, pp. 158–175.

Hardy, Peter, *The Muslims of British India*, Cambridge University Press, Cambridge, 1972.

Harris, Lee, *The Suicide of Reason: Radical Islam's Threat to the Enlightenment*, Basic Books, New York, 2007.

Hay, Stephen M., *Asian Ideas of East and West: Tagore and his Critics in Japan, China and India*, Harvard University Press, Cambridge Mass., 1970.

Herder, Johann Gottfreid, *On the Origin of Language: Two Essays*, Alexander Gode (trans.), University of Chicago Press, Chicago, 1966, pp. 85–176.

Hodgson, Marshall G. S., *The Venture of Islam: Conscience and History in a World Civilization*, 3 vols, University of Chicago Press, Chicago, 1977.

Hourani, Albert, *Arabic Thought in the Liberal Age, 1798–1939* (2nd edn), Cambridge University Press, Cambridge, 1983.

Hourani, George F., 'Islamic and non-Islamic origins of Mu'tazilite ethical rationalism', *International Journal of Middle Eastern Studies*, 7, 1976, pp. 59–87.

Huntington, Samuel, *The Clash of Civilizations and the Remaking of World Order*, Touchstone Books, London, 1997.

Iggers, George G., *The German Conception of History: The National Tradition of German Thought from Herder to the Present*, Wesleyan University Press, Middletown, 1988.

Ikram, Sheikh Muhammad, *Mauj-i Kausar*, Idarah-i Thaqafat-i Islamiyyah, Lahore, 2000.

Inalcik, Halil, *The Ottoman Empire: The Classical Age 1300–1600*, Phoenix, London, 1994.

Inayat, Hamid, *Modern Islamic Political Thought*, University of Texas Press, Austin, 1982.

Iqbal, Muhammad, *Speeches, Writings and Statements of Iqbal*, Latif Ahmad Sherwani (ed.), Adam Publishers, New Delhi, 2006.

———, *The Secrets of the Self*, Reynold A. Nicholson (trans.), Kitab Bhavan, New Delhi, 2004.

———, *Tulip in the Desert: A Selection of the Poetry of Muhammad Iqbal*, Mustansir Mir (ed. and trans.), Hurst, London, 2000.

The Reconstruction of Religious Thought in Islam, Sang-e-Meel Publications, Lahore, 1996.

———, *Iqbal: A Section of the Urdu Verse*, D. J. Mathews (trans.), Heritage Publishers, New Delhi, 1993.

———, *Stray Reflections: A Note-book of Allama Iqbal*, Javid Iqbal (ed.), Taj Company, Delhi, 1985.

———, *Letters and Writings of Iqbal*, B. A. Dar (ed.), Iqbal Academy, Karachi, 1967.

———, *Thoughts and Reflections of Iqbal*, Syed Abdul Vahid (ed.), Muhammad Ashraf, Lahore, 1964.

Jalal, Ayesha, 'Exploding communalism: The politics of Muslim identity in South Asia', *Nationalism, Democracy and Development: State and Politics in India*, Sugata Bose and Ayesha Jalal (eds), Oxford University Press, Delhi, 1997, pp. 76–103.

———, *The Sole Spokesman: Jinnah, the Muslim League, and the Demand for Pakistan*, Cambridge University Press, Cambridge, 1985.

Jamila, Maryam, *Islam and Western Society: A Refutation of the Modern Way of Life*, Adam Publishers, New Delhi, 1982.

Jayawardena, Kumari, *Feminism and Nationalism in the Third World*, Zed Books, London, 1986.
Jinnah, Muhammad Ali, *Jinnah: Speeches and Statements 1947–1948*, Oxford University Press, Oxford, 2000.
Judy, Ronald A. T., 'Sayyid Qutb's *fiqh al-waqi'i* or new realist science', *Boundary 2*, 31 (2), 2004, pp. 113–148.
Kamali, A. H., 'The heritage of Islamic thought', *Iqbal: Poet Philosopher of Pakistan*, Malik Hafeez (ed.), Columbia University Press, New York, 1971.
Keddie, Nikki R., *An Islamic Response to Imperialism: Political and Religious Writings of Sayyid Jamal ad-Din 'al-Afghani'*, University of California Press, Berkeley, 1968.
Kedourie, Elie, *Afghani and 'Abduh: An Essay on Religious Belief and Political Activism in Modern Islam*, Frank Cass, London, 1966.
Kerr, Malcolm H., *Islamic Reform: The Political and Legal Theories of Muhammad 'Abduh and Rashid Rida*, University of California Press, Berkeley, 1966.
Khalidi, Rashid, *Resurrecting Empire: Western Footprints and America's Perilous Path in the Middle East*, I.B.Tauris, London, 2004.
Khamenei, Sayyid Ali, 'Iqbal: The poet-philosopher of Islamic Resurgence', *Iqbal: Manifestation of the Islamic Spirit*, Mahliqa Qara'i and Laleh Bakhtiar (trans.), Open Press, Ontario, 1991, pp. 5–26.
Khan, Sayyid Ahmed, *Tafsir al-Qur'an*, Dost Association, Lahore, 2004.
———, *Maqalat-i Sir Sayyid*, 16 vols, Ismail Panipati (ed.), Majlis-i Taraqi-e Adab, Lahore, 1984.
———, *Writings and Speeches of Sir Syed Ahmed Khan*, Shan Muhammad (ed.), Nachiketa Publications, Bombay, 1972.
———, 'Sir Sayyid Ahmad Khan's principles of exegesis translated from his *Tahrir fi Usul al-Tafsir*', *Muslim World*, 46, Muhammad Daud Rahbar (trans.), 1956, pp. 104–112 and 324–335.
Khan, Wahiduddin, *T'abir ki Ghalti*, Dar al-Tazkir, Lahore, 2002.
———, *Islam Rediscovered: Discovering Islam from the Original Sources*, Goodword, New Delhi, 2001.
Khatab, Sayed, 'Arabism and Islamism in Sayyid Qutb's thoughts on nationalism', *Muslim World*, 94, 2004, pp. 217–244.
Khir, Bustami, 'Sovereignty', *Encyclopaedia of the Qur'an*, Jane Dammen McAuliffe (ed.), Brill, Leiden, 2005.
Khundmiri, Alam, *Secularism, Islam and Modernity: Selected Essays of Alam Khundmiri*, M. T. Ansari (ed.), Sage, New Delhi, 2001.
King, Richard, *Orientalism and Religion: Postcolonial Theory, India and 'The Mystic East'*, Routledge, London, 1999.
Kolakowski, Leszek, *Modernity on Endless Trial*, University of Chicago, Chicago, 1990.
Kolb, David, *The Critique of Pure Modernity: Hegel, Heidegger, and After*, University of Chicago Press, Chicago, 1986.
Kugelgen, Anke von, 'Muhammad 'Abduh', *Encyclopaedia of Islam* (3rd edn).

BIBLIOGRAPHY

Kugle, Scott Alan, 'Sultan Mahmud's makeover: Colonial homophobia and the Persian-Urdu literary tradition', *Queering India: Same-Sex Love and Eroticism in Indian Culture and Society*, Ruth Vanita (ed.), Routledge, New York, 2002, pp. 30–46.

———, 'Framed, blamed and renamed: The recasting of Islamic jurisprudence in colonial South Asia', *Modern Asian Studies*, 35 (2), 2001, pp. 257–313.

Kurzman, Charles, 'Liberal Islam and its Islamic context', *Liberal Islam: A Source Book*, Charles Kurzman (ed.), Oxford University Press, New York, 1998, pp. 3–27.

Lamberth, David C., 'Intimations of the finite: Thinking pragmatically at the end of modernity', *Harvard Theological Review*, 90 (2), 1997, pp. 205–223.

Landau, Jacob M., *The Politics of Pan-Islam: Ideology and Organization*, Clarendon Press, Oxford, 1990.

Lapidus, Ira M., 'The separation of state and religion in the development of early Islamic societies', *International Journal of Middle Eastern Studies*, 6 (4), 1975, pp. 363–385.

Laroui, Abdallah, *The Crisis of the Arab Intellectual: Traditionalism or Historicism?*, Diarmid Cammell (trans.), University of California Press, Berkeley, 1976.

Leaman, Oliver, *An Introduction to Classical Islamic Philosophy* (2nd edn), Cambridge University Press, Cambridge, 2002.

Lehtinen, Ullalina, 'How does one know what shame is? Epistemology, emotions and forms of life in juxtaposition', *Hypatia*, 13 (1), 1998, pp. 56–77.

Lelyveld, David, '*Zuban-e Urdu-e Mu'alla* and the idol of linguistic origins', *Annual of Urdu Studies*, 9, 1994, pp. 57–67.

———, *Aligarh's First Generation: Muslim Solidarity in British India*, Princeton University Press, Princeton, 1978.

Lerner, Daniel, *The Passing of a Traditional Society: Modernizing the Middle East*, Free Press, New York, 1964.

Lewis, Bernard, 'Does Iran have something in store?', http://www.metransparent.com/old/texts/bernard_lewis_does_iran_have_something_in_store.htm (accessed 8 July 2011).

———, *From Babel to Dragomans: Interpreting the Middle East*, Phoenix, London, 2004.

———, *What Went Wrong? Western Impact and Middle Eastern Response*, Oxford University Press, Oxford, 2002.

———, *Semites and Anti-Semites: An Inquiry into Conflict and Prejudice*, W.W. Norton, New York, 1999.

———, *Islam and the West*, Oxford University Press, New York, 1993.

———, 'Islam and liberal democracy', *Atlantic Monthly*, 271 (2), 1993, pp. 89–98.

———, 'The roots of Muslim rage', *Atlantic Monthly*, 266 (3), 1990, pp. 47–60.

Macaulay, Thomas Babington, *Selected Writings*, John Clive and Thomas Pinney (eds), University of Chicago Press, Chicago, 1972, pp. 237–251.

MacIntyre, Alasdair, *After Virtue: A Study in Moral Theory* (3rd edn), Duckworth, London, 2007.

Madani, Maulana Hussain Ahmad, *Composite Nationalism and Islam (Muttahidah Qaumiyyah aur Islam)*, Mohammad Anwer Hussain Hasan Imam (trans.), Manohar, New Delhi, 2005.

Mahmoud, Saba, *Politics of Piety: The Islamic Revival and the Feminist Subject*, Princeton University Press, Princeton, 2005.

Majeed, J., *Muhammad Iqbal: Islam, Aesthetics and Postcolonialism*, Routledge, London, 2009.

———, 'Putting God in his place: Bradley, McTaggart and Muhammad Iqbal', *Journal of Islamic Studies*, 4 (2), pp. 208–236.

Makdisi, Saree, *Romantic Imperialism: Universal Empire and the Culture of Modernity*, Cambridge University Press, Cambridge, 1998.

Malik, Ghulam Rasool, *Iqbal and the English Romantics*, Atlantic Publishers, New Delhi, 1988.

Malik, Hafeez, 'The man of thought and the man of action', *Iqbal: Poet Philosopher of Pakistan*, Malik Hafeez (ed.), Columbia University Press, New York, 1971.

Mamdani, Mahmood, *Good Muslim, Bad Muslim: America, the Cold War, and the Roots of Terror*, Doubleday, New York, 2005.

Manion, Jennifer C., 'Girls blush, sometimes: Gender, moral agency, and the problem of shame', *Hypatia*, 18 (3), 2003, pp. 21–41.

Marcotte, Roxanne D., 'Identity, power and the Islamist discourse on women: an exploration of Islamism and gender issues in Egypt', *Islam in World Politics*, Nelly Lahoud and Anthony H. Johns (eds), Routledge, London, 2005, pp. 67–92.

Marmura, Michael E., 'Ghazali and demonstrative science', *Journal of the History of Philosophy*, 3 (2), 1965, pp. 83–209.

———, 'Ghazali and Asharism revisited', *Arabic Sciences and Philosophy*, 12 (1), 2002, pp. 91–110.

Martin, Craig, 'Rethinking Renaissance Averroism', *Intellectual History Review*, 17 (1), 2007, pp. 3–19.

Martin, Richard C., 'The role of the Basrah Muʻtazilah in formulating the doctrine of the apologetic miracle', *Journal of Near Eastern Studies*, 39 (3), 1980, pp. 175–189.

Martin, Wayne M., *Idealism and Objectivity: Understanding Fichte's Jena Project*, Stanford University Press, Stanford, 1997.

Masuzawa, Tomoko, *The Invention of World Religions Or, How European Universalism was Preserved in the Language of Pluralism*, University of Chicago Press, Chicago, 2005.

Maududi, Sayyid Abul Aʻla, *Purdah*, Islamic Publications, Lahore, 2002.

———, *Purdah and the Status of Women in Islam*, Al-Ashʻari (trans. and ed.), Islamic Publications, Lahore, 2002.

———, *Al-Jihad fi al-Islam*, Idarah Tarjuman al-Qurʼan, Lahore, 2002.

———, *Islami Riyasat*, Islamic Publications, Lahore, 2000.

———, *Islamic Law and Constitution*, Islamic Publications, Lahore, 2000.

———, *Tafhimat*, 5 vols, Idarah Tarjuman al-Qur'an, Lahore, 1996.
———, *Let Us Be Muslims*, Khurram Murad (ed.), Islamic Foundation, Kuala Lumpur, 1985.
———, *Human Rights in Islam,* Islamic Foundation, London, 1980.
———, *Four Basic Qur'anic Terms,* Abu Asad (trans.), Islamic Publications, Lahore, 1979.
Mazarr, Michael J., *Unmodern Men in the Modern World: Radical Islam, Terrorism, and the War on Modernity*, Cambridge University Press, New York, 2007.
McClintock, Anne, *Imperial Leather: Race, Class and Gender in the Colonial Contest*, Routledge, New York, 1995.
Mehta, Uday Singh, *Liberalism and Empire: A Study in Nineteenth-Century British Liberal Thought*, University of Chicago Press, Chicago, 1999.
Meisami, Julie Scott, *Medieval Persian Court Poetry*, Princeton University Press, Princeton, 1987.
Mernissi, Fatima, *Beyond the Veil: Male-Female Dynamics in a Modern Muslim Society*, Indiana University Press, Indianapolis, 1985.
———, *The Veil and the Male Elite: A Feminist Interpretation of Woman's Rights in Islam*, Perseus Books, Cambridge, 1992.
Metcalf, Barbara, *Islamic Revival in British India: Deoband, 1860–1900*, Princeton University Press, Princeton, 1982.
Metcalf, Thomas R., *Ideologies of the Raj*, Cambridge University Press, Berkeley, 1995.
Mian, Ali Altaf and Nancy Nyquist Potter, 'Invoking Islamic rights in British India, Maulana Ashraf 'Ali Thanawi's *Huquq al-Islam*', *Muslim World*, 99, 2009, pp. 312–334.
Mill, James, *The History of British India (to 1834)* (5th edn), Horace H. Wilson (ed.), James Madden, London, 1858.
Mill, John Stuart, *On Liberty and Other Essays*, John Gray (ed.), Oxford University Press, Oxford, 1998.
Minault, Gail, *Secluded Scholars: Woman's Education and Muslim Social Reform in Colonial India*, Oxford University Press, Delhi, 1999.
———, 'Other voices, other rooms: The view from the *zenana*', *Woman as Subjects: South Asian Histories*, Nita Kumar (ed.), University Press of Virginia, Charlottesville, 1994, pp. 108–124.
———, *The Khilafat Movement: Religious Symbolism and Political Mobilization in India*, Columbia University Press, New York, 1982.
Mitchell, Richard P., *The Society of the Muslim Brothers*, Oxford University Press, London, 1969.
Mitchell, Timothy, *Colonizing Egypt*, University of California Press, Berkeley, 1991.
Moosa, Ebrahim, 'The poetics and politics of law after empire', *UCLA Journal of Islamic and Near Eastern Law*, 1 (1), 2001, pp. 1–46.
Moussalli, Ahmad S., *Radical Islamic Fundamentalism: The Ideological and Political Discourse of Sayyid Qutb*, American University of Beirut, Beirut, 1992.
Mukhia, Harbans, 'The celebration of failure as dissent in Urdu Ghazal', *Modern Asian Studies*, 33 (4), 1999, pp. 861–881.

Mukherjee, S. N., *William Jones: A Study in Eighteenth-Century British Attitudes to India*, Cambridge University Press, Cambridge, 1968.

Müller, Max, 'India – What can it teach us?', *Historical Thinking in South Asia*, Michael Gottlob (ed.), Oxford University Press, New Delhi, 2003.

Murad, Mehr Afroz, *Intellectual Modernism of Shibli Nu'mani: An Exposition of His Religious and Political Ideas*, Kitab Bhavan, New Delhi, 1996.

Musallam, A., 'Sayyid Qutb's literary and spiritual orientation (1931–1938)', *Muslim World*, 30 (3–4), 1990, pp. 176–189.

Nadwi, Abul Hasan 'Ali, *Islam and the World: Madha Khasira al-'Alam bi-Inhitat al-Muslimin*, Muhammad Asif Kidwai (trans.), International Islamic Federation of Students Organizations, Riyadh, 2006.

Nagel, Thomas, *The View From Nowhere*, Oxford University Press, New York, 1986.

Naim, C. M., *Urdu Texts and Contexts: The Selected Essays of C. M. Naim*, Permanent Black, New Delhi, 2004.

Nasr, Seyyed Vali Reza, *Maududi and the Making of Islamic Revivalism*, Oxford University Press, Oxford, 1996.

———, 'Democracy and Islamic revivalism', *Political Science Quarterly*, 110 (2), 1995, pp. 261–285.

Naylor, Phillip Chiviges, 'The formative influence of French colonialism on the life and thought of Malik Bennabi (Malik bn Nabi)', *French Colonial History*, 7, 2006, pp. 129–142.

Needham, Anuradha Dingwaney and Rajeswari Sunder Rajan, 'Introduction', *The Crisis of Secularism in India*, Anuradha Dingwaney Needham and Rajeswari Sunder Rajan (eds), Duke University Press, London, 2007, pp. 1–42.

Nu'mani, Shibli, *Sh'ir al-'Ajam*, 2 vols, Al-Faisak, Lahore, 1999.

———, *'Ilm al-Kalam aur al-Kalam*, Nafis Academy, Karachi, 1979.

Olender, Maurice, *The Languages of Paradise: Race, Religion and Philology in the Nineteenth Century*, Harvard University Press, London, 1992.

Omar, Ifran A., 'Rethinking Islam: A study of the thought and mission of Maulana Wahiduddin Khan', PhD thesis, Temple University, 2001.

Osman, Fathi, 'Mawdudi's contribution to the development of modern Islamic thinking in the Arabic-speaking world', *Muslim World*, 93, 2003, pp. 465–485.

Owen, Roger, *The Middle East in the World Economy: 1800–1914*, Methuen, London, 1981.

Pandey, Gyanendra, 'The secular state and the limits of dialogue', *The Crisis of Secularism in India*, Anuradha Dingwaney Needham and Rajeswari Sunder Rajan (eds), Duke University Press, London, 2007, pp. 157–176.

———, *The Construction of Communalism in Colonial North India*, Oxford University Press, New Delhi, 2006.

———, *Remembering Partition: Violence, Nationalism and History in India*, Cambridge University Press, New Delhi, 2001.

Pateman, Carole, *The Sexual Contract*, Polity Press, Oxford, 1988.

Petievitch, Carla, 'Rekhti: Impersonating the feminine in Urdu poetry', *South Asia*, 24, 2001, pp. 75–90.

Piers, Gerhart, *Guilt and Shame: A Psychoanalytic and Cultural Study*, Thomas Books, New York, 1953.

Pomeranz, Kenneth, *The Great Divergence: Europe, China, and the Making of the Modern World Economy*, Princeton University Press, Princeton, 2000.

Prakash, Gyan, 'Secular nationalism, Hindutva and the minority', *The Crisis of Secularism in India*, Anuradha Dingwaney Needham and Rajeswari Sunder Rajan (eds), Duke University Press, London, 2007, pp. 177–188.

———, *Another Reason: Science and the Imagination of Modern India*, Oxford University Press, New Delhi, 1999.

———, 'Introduction', *After Colonialism: Imperial Histories and Postcolonial Displacements*, Gyan Prakash (ed.), Princeton University Press, Princeton, 1995, pp. 3–19.

Pritchett, Francis W., *Nets of Awareness: Urdu Poetry and its Critics*, University of California Press, Berkeley, 1994.

Qureshi, Saleem M., 'Iqbal and Jinnah: Personalities, perceptions and politics', *Iqbal, Jinnah and Pakistan: The Vision and the Reality*, C. M. Naim (ed.), Syracuse University, New York, 1979.

Qutb, Sayyid, *Basic Principles of the Islamic Worldview*, David Rami (trans.), Islamic Publications International, New Jersey, 2006.

———, *A Child from the Village*, John Calvert and William E. Shepard (eds and trans.), Syracuse University Press, New York, 2004.

———, *al-Taswir al-Fanni fi al-Qur'an* (*Aesthetic Portrayal in the Qur'an*), Dar al-Shuruq, Cairo, 2003.

———, *al-'Adalah al-Ijtima'iyyah fi al-Islam* (*Social Justice in Islam*), Dar al-Shuruq, Cairo, 2002.

———, *Sayyid Qutb and Islamic Activism: A Translation and Critical Analysis of Social Justice in Islam*, William E. Shepard (trans.), E.J. Brill, Leiden, 1996.

———, *Ma'alim fi al-Tariq* (*Signposts on the Way*), Dar al-Shuruq, Cairo, 1983.

———, *Milestones* (English trans. of *Ma'alim fi al-Tariq*), The Mother Mosque Foundation, n.d.

Raheja, Gloria Goodwin, 'Women's speech genres, kinship and contradiction', *Women as Subjects: South Asian Histories*, Anita Kumar (ed.), University Press of Virginia, London, 1994, pp. 49–80.

Rahman, Fazlur, *Revival and Reform in Islam: A Study of Islamic Fundamentalism*, Ebrahim Moosa (ed.), Oneworld, Oxford, 2000.

———, 'Muhammad Iqbal and Atatürk's reforms', *Journal of Near Eastern Studies*, 43 (2), 1984, pp. 157–162.

———, *Islam and Modernity: Transformation of an Intellectual Tradition*, University of Chicago Press, Chicago, 1982.

———, *Major Themes of the Qur'an*, Bibliotheca Islamica, Chicago, 1980.

———, *Islam* (2nd edn), University of Chicago Press, Chicago, 1979.

Raymond, Andre, 'Islamic city, Arab city: Orientalist myths and recent views', *British Journal of Middle Eastern Studies*, 21 (1), 1994, pp. 3–18.

Renan, Ernst, *The Poetry of the Celtic Races and Other Studies by Ernst Renan*, Kennikat Press, William G. Hutchinson (trans.), New York, 1978.

———, *Studies of Religious History and Criticism*, O. B. Frothingham (trans.), Carleton, New York, 1864.

Ricoeur, Paul, *The Conflict of Interpretation*, Northwestern University Press, Evanston, 1974.

Robinson, Francis, 'Technology and religious change: Islam and the impact of print', *Modern Asian Studies*, 27 (1), 1993, pp. 229–251.

Rose, Nikolas, *Inventing Ourselves: Psychology, Power and Personhood*, Cambridge University Press, Cambridge, 1996.

el-Rouayheb, Khaled, 'Sunni Muslim scholars on the status of logic, 1500–1800', *Islamic Law and Society*, 11 (2), 2004, pp. 214–232.

Roy, Oliver, *Secularism Confronts Islam*, George Holoch (trans.), Columbia University Press, New York, 2007.

———, *Globalised Islam: The Search for a New Ummah*, Hurst, London, 2004.

Rubin, Avi, 'Legal borrowing and its impact on Ottoman legal culture in the late nineteenth century', *Continuity and Change*, 22 (2), 2007, pp. 279–303.

Russell, Colin A., 'The conflict of science and religion', *Science and Religion: A Historical Introduction*, Gary B. Ferngren (ed.), Johns Hopkins University Press, Baltimore, 2002, pp. 3–12.

Russell, Ralph and Kurshidul Islam, *Three Mughal Poets: Mir, Sauda, Mir Hasan*, Oxford University Press, New Delhi, 1998.

Russell, Ralph, *The Pursuit of Urdu Literature*, Zed Books, London, 1992.

Saeed, 'Abdullah, 'Fazlur Rahman: A framework for interpreting the ethico-legal content of the Qur'an', *Modern Muslim Intellectuals and the Qur'an*, Suha Taji-Farouki (ed.), Oxford University Press, Oxford, 2004, pp. 37–66.

Safi, Omid, 'Introduction: The times they are a-changin' – a Muslim quest for justice, gender equality and pluralism', *Progressive Muslims: On Gender, Justice and Pluralism*, Omid Safi (ed.), Oneworld, Oxford, 2003, pp. 1–29.

Sahota, Guriqbal S., 'A literature of the sublime in late colonial India: Romanticism and the epic form in modern Hindi and Urdu', PhD thesis, University of Chicago, 2006.

Said, Edward, *Orientalism: Western Conceptions of the Orient*, Penguin, London, 1995.

———, *Culture and Imperialism*, Vintage, New York, 1994.

———, *The World, The Text, and The Critic*, Harvard University Press, Cambridge Mass., 1983.

Salame, Ghassan, 'Introduction: Where are the democrats?', *Democracy Without Democrats: The Renewal of Politics in the Muslim World*, Ghassan Salame (ed.), I.B.Tauris, London, 1994, pp.1–20.

Salvatore, Armando, *Islam and the Political Discourses of Modernity*, Ithaca, Beirut, 1997.

Sands, Kristin Zahra, *Sufi Commentaries on the Qur'an in Classical Islam*, Routledge, New York, 2005.

Schacht, Joseph, *Islamic Law: An Introduction*, Oxford University Press, Oxford, 1962.

Scharbrodt, Oliver, 'The Salafiyya and Sufism: Muhammad 'Abduh and his *risalat al-waridat* (treatise on mystical inspirations)', *Bulletin of SOAS*, 70 (1), 2007, pp. 88–115.

Schimmel, Annemarie, *Gabriel's Wing*, Iqbal Academy, Lahore, 2000.

———, *A Two-Colored Brocade: The Imagery of Persian Poetry*, University of North Carolina Press, Chapel Hill, 1992.

———, *Mystical Dimensions of Islam*, University of North Carolina Press, Chapel Hill, 1975.

———, *Classical Urdu Literature: From the Beginning to Iqbal*, Harrassowitz, Wiesbaden, 1975.

Schmitt, Carl, *Political Theologies: Four Chapters on the Concept of Sovereignty*, MIT Press, Cambridge Mass., 1981.

Scott, Joan Wallach, *The Politics of the Veil*, Princeton University Press, Princeton, 2007.

———, 'Experience', *Feminists Theorize the Political*, Judith Butler and Joan W. Scott (eds), Routledge, New York, 1992, pp. 22–40.

———, *Gender and the Politics of History*, Columbia University Press, New York, 1988.

Scruton, Roger, *The West and the Rest: Globalization and the Terrorist Threat*, Continuum, London, 2002.

Shakry, Omnia, 'Schooled mothers and structured play: Child rearing in turn-of-the-century Egypt', *Remaking Women: Feminism and Modernity in the Middle East*, Lila Abu-Lughod (ed.), Princeton University Press, Princeton, 1998, pp. 126–170.

Sharabi, Hisham, *Neopatriarchy: A Theory of Distorted Change in Arab Society*, Oxford University Press, New York, 1988.

Sharar, Abdul Halim, *Lucknow: The Last Phase of an Oriental Culture*, E. S. Harcourt and Fakhir Hussain (eds and trans.), Oxford University Press, New Delhi, 2000.

Sharpe, Jenny, *Allegories of Empire: The Figure of Woman in the Colonial Text*, University of Minnesota Press, Minneapolis, 1993.

Shboul, Ahmad, 'Between rhetoric and reality: Islam and politics in the Arab world', *Islam in World Politics*, Nelly Lahoud and Anthony H. Johns (eds), Routledge, London, 2005, pp. 170–191.

Shepard, William E., 'Sayyid Qutb's doctrine of *jahiliyya*', *International Journal of Middle Eastern Studies*, 35, 2003, pp. 521–545.

———, 'Islam as a 'system' in the later writings of Sayyid Qutb', *Middle Eastern Studies*, 25 (1), 1989, pp. 31–50.

Sikand, Yoginder, 'Peace, dialogue and *da'wa*: An analysis of the writings of Maulana Wahiduddin Khan', *Islam and Christian-Muslim Relations*, 14 (1), 2003, pp. 33–49.

Singh, Iqbal, *The Ardent Pilgrim: An Introduction to the Life and Work of Mohammed Iqbal*, Oxford University Press, Delhi, 1997.

Sinha, Mrinalina, *Colonial Masculinity: The 'Manly Englishman' and the 'Effeminate Bengali' in the late Nineteenth Century*, Manchester University Press, Manchester, 1995.

Sivan, Emmanuel, *Radical Islam: Medieval Theology and Modern Politics*, Yale University Press, New Haven, 1985.

Smith, Charles, '"The crisis of orientation": The shift of Egyptian intellectuals to Islamic subjects in the 1930s', *International Journal of Middle Eastern Studies*, 4, 1973, pp. 382–410.

Smith, Jonathan Z., 'Religion, religions, religious', *Critical Terms for Religious Studies*, Mark C. Taylor (ed.), University of Chicago Press, Chicago, 1998, pp. 269–284.

———, *Relating Religion: Essays in the Study of Religion*, University of Chicago, Chicago, 2004.

Smith, Wilfred Cantwell, *The Meaning and End of Religion*, Harper & Row, New York, 1978.

———, *Islam in Modern History*, Princeton University Press, Princeton, 1957.

Soroush, 'Abdolkarim, 'I'm a neo-Mu'tazilite: An interview with Abdulkarim Soroush', by Matin Ghaffarian, Nilou Mobasser (trans.), <http://www.drsoroush.com/English/Interviews/E-INT-Neo-Mutazilite_July2008.html> (accessed 8 July 2011).

———, *Reason, Freedom and Democracy in Islam: Essential Writings of 'Abdolkarim Soroush*, Mahmoud Sadri and Ahmad Sadri (trans and eds), Oxford University Press, Oxford, 2000.

Spengler, Oswald, *The Decline of the West*, 2 vols, Charles Francis Atkinson (trans.), Allen & Unwin, London, 1980.

Steele, Laurel, 'Hali and his muqaddamah: The creation of a literary attitude in nineteenth century India', *Annual of Urdu Studies*, 1, 1981, pp. 1–45, Digital South Asia Library,
http://dsal.uchicago.edu/books/annualofurdustudies/toc.html?volume=1 (accessed 8 July 2011).

Stoddart, William and R. A. Nicholson, *Sufism: The Mystical Doctrines and Idea of Personality*, Aryan Books, New Delhi, 2002.

Stowasser, Barbara Freyer, *Women in the Qur'an, Traditions, and Interpretation*, Oxford University Press, New York, 1994.

Strum, Arthur, 'What Enlightenment is', *New German Critique*, 70, 2000, pp. 106–136.

Taylor, Gabriele, *Pride, Shame and Guilt*, Clarendon Press, Oxford, 1985.

Thanawi, Ashraf 'Ali, *Perfecting Women: Maulana Ashraf 'Ali Thanawi's Bihishti Zewar*, Barbara Metcalf (trans.), University of California Press, Berkeley, 1990.

Thapar, Romila, 'The theory of Aryan race and India: History and politics', *Social Scientist*, 24 (1/3), 1996, pp. 3–29.

———, 'Imagined religious communities? Ancient history and the modern search for a Hindu identity', *Modern Asian Studies*, 23 (2), 1989, pp. 209–231.

Tibi, Bassam, 'Culture and knowledge: The politics of Islamization of knowledge as a postmodern project? The fundamentalist claim to de-Westernization', *Theory, Culture and Society*, 12, 1995, pp. 1–25.

———, 'The worldview of Sunni Arab fundamentalists: Attitudes towards modern science and technology', *The Fundamentalism Project*, vol. 2, Martin E. Marty and R. Scott Appleby (eds), University of Chicago Press, Chicago, 1991–95, pp. 73–102.

———, *The Challenge of Fundamentalism: Political Islam and the New World Disorder*, University of California Press, Berkeley, 1998.

———, 'Islamic law/shari'ah, human rights, universal morality and international relations', *Human Rights Quarterly*, 16 (2), 1994, pp. 277–299.

Todorov, Tzvetan, *On Human Diversity: Nationalism, Racism and Exoticism in French Thought*, Catherine Porter (trans.), Harvard University Press, Cambridge Mass., 1993.

———, *Theories of the Symbol*, Catherine Porter (trans.), Cornell University, Ithaca, 1982.

Tomiche, N., 'al-Mar'a', *Encyclopaedia of Islam* (2nd edn).

Troll, Christian W., *Sayyid Ahmed Khan: A Reinterpretation of Muslim Theology*, Vikas Publishing House, Delhi, 1978.

———, 'The meaning of *din*: Recent views of three eminent Indian ulama', *Islam in India: Studies and Commentaries*, Christian W. Troll (ed.), Vikas Publishing House, Delhi, 1982, pp. 168–177.

Tucker, Judith, *Women in Nineteenth-Century Egypt*, Cambridge University Press, Cambridge, 1985.

Turner, Brian S., 'Sovereignty and emergency: Political theology, Islam and American conservatism', *Theory, Culture and Society*, 19 (4), 2002, pp. 103–119.

———, *Marx and the End of Orientalism*, George Allen & Unwin, London, 1978.

———, *Weber and Islam: A Critical Study*, Routledge, London, 1974.

———, 'Islam, capitalism and the Weber thesis', *The British Journal of Sociology*, 25 (2), 1974, pp. 230–243.

Vahid, S. A., *Introduction to Iqbal*, Pakistan Publication, Karachi, n.d.

———, *Iqbal: His Art and Thought*, John Murray, London, 1959.

Van der Veer, Peter, Imperial Encounters: Religion and Modernity in India and Britain, Princeton University Press, Princeton, 2001.

———, 'Pym Fortuyn, Theo Van Gogh, and the politics of tolerance in the Netherlands', *Political Theologies: Public Religions in a Post-Secular World*, Hent De Vries and Lawrence Sullivan (eds), Fordham University Press, New York, 2006, pp. 527–538.

Vanita, Ruth, "Married among their companions': Female homoerotic relations in nineteenth-century Urdu *rekhti* poetry in India', *Journal of Woman's History*, 16 (1), 2004, pp. 12–53.

Viswanathan, Gauri, *Outside the Fold: Conversion, Modernity, and Belief*, Oxford University Press, New Delhi, 1998.

―――, *Masks of Conquest: Literary Study and British Rule in India*, Columbia University Press, New York, 1989.
Voll, John O., 'Renewal and reform in Islamic history: *Tajdid* and *islah*', *Voices of Resurgent Islam*, John L Esposito (ed.), Oxford University Press, New York, 1983, pp. 32–47.
―――, *Islam: Continuity and Change in the Modern World*, Longman, Essex, 1982.
Wadud, Amina, *Inside the Gender Jihad: Women's Reform in Islam*, Oneworld, Oxford, 2006.
―――, *Qur'an and Woman: Rereading the Sacred Text from a Woman's Perspective*, Oxford University Press, New York, 1999.
Wali Allah, Shah, *The Conclusive Argument from God: Shah Wali Allah of Delhi's Hujjat Allah al-Balighah*, Marcia K. Hermansen (trans.), Islamic Research Institute, Islamabad, 2003.
Wallace, Walter L., 'Rationality, human nature, and society in Weber's theory', *Theory and Society*, 19 (2), 1990, pp. 199–223.
Walzer, R., 'Al-Farabi's theory of prophecy and divination', *The Journal of Hellenic Studies*, 77 (1), 1957, pp. 142–148.
Watt, Katherine, 'Thomas Walker Arnold and the re-evaluation of Islam, 1864–1930', *Modern Asian Studies*, 36 (1), 2002, pp. 1–98.
Watt, W. Montgomery, *The Formative Period of Islamic Thought*, Edinburgh University Press, Edinburgh, 1973.
Weber, Max, *The Protestant Ethic and the Spirit of Capitalism*, T. Parsons (trans.), Allen & Unwin, London, 1930.
Westphal, Merold, *Overcoming Onto-Theology: Towards a Postmodern Christian Faith*, Fordham University Press, New York, 2001.
Wilson, David B., 'The historiography of science and religion', *Science and Religion: A Historical Introduction*, Gary B. Ferngren (ed.), Johns Hopkins University Press, Baltimore, 2002, pp. 13–29.
Yeazell, Ruth Bernard, *Harems of the Mind: Passages of Western Art and Literature*, Yale University Press, New Haven, 2000.
Young, Robert J. C., *White Mythologies: Writing History and the West*, Routledge, New York, 2004.
Zaman, Muhammad Qasim, *The Ulama in Contemporary Islam*, Princeton University Press, Princeton, 2002.
Zebiri, Kate, *Mahmud Shaltut and Islamic Modernism*, Clarendon, Oxford, 1993.
al-Zubaida, A. M. K., 'The Diwan school', *Journal of Arabic Literature*, 1, 1970, pp. 36–48.
Zubaida, Sami, *Law and Power in the Islamic World*, I.B.Tauris, London, 2005.

INDEX

'Abduh, Muhammad, 38, 45, 49, 56–57, 74, 103, 163, 169, 225, 240n37
  democracy, attitude towards, 73, 243n74
  family, notion of, 109
  rationalist theology, 57–60
  women in Islam, status of, 102
Abou El Fadl, Khaled, 207–208
Abu-Lughod, Lila, 108
Abu-Zayd, Nasr, 200, 207, 208
Al-Afghani, Jamal al-Din, 23, 38, 45, 48–49, 74, 103, 225, 240n37, 243n76
  Khan, Sayyid Ahmad, criticism of, 71–72
  reformist views, 52–56
  Renan, debate with, 51–54, 56
agency, considerations of, 179–182
Ahmed, Leila, 101, 249n4
Ahmed, Nazeer, 80
Ajami, Fouad, 25–26
'alam al-mithal (imaginal world), 66–67
Algar, Hamid, 165
Aligarh reform movement, 39
  literary reform, movement for, 76–81, 98–99
Aligarh University, 61, 77, 114–115
'Ali, Muhammad (Pasha of Egypt), 101
'Ali, Sayyid Amir, 5–6
Allah, Shah Wali, 62–63, 268n12

Allahabadi, Akbar, 78, 84, 117–118
  poem on women's education, 118
Amin, Qasim, 39, 103, 119, 250n10
  conjugal love, notion of, 107–109
  reformist views, 105–109
Amin, Samir, 14–15
Anderson, Benedict, 21, 121–122
Arberry, A. J., 44
Aristotelian thought, 44, 58, 66, 134, 164, 216
Arkoun, Mohammed, 41, 215, 222
  Islamic history, notion of, 216–219, 270n55
  'thought and unthought', 219–221
Arnold, Thomas, 128, 254n29
Arthur, Keith, 258n77
Asad, Talal, 28, 37, 109, 150, 250–251n23
'Ashari theology, 58–59, 205
Azad, Muhammad Husain, 76, 79, 85–90, 247n33
Al-Azmeh, Aziz, 243n76

Badiou, Alain, 2
Beinin, Joel, 233n58
Benhabib, Seyla, 36, 237n98
Bennabi, Malik, 195
Bentham, Jeremy, 4, 86
Berger, John, 190

Bergson, Henri, 128
Berman, Paul, 34–35, 262n42
Bhabha, Homi, 5–6, 146

capitalism, 8, 12–13, 19, 101, 219
Carrel, Alexis, 165–167
civilization,
    'clash of civilisations', 22, 24–26, 30–35
    Eisenstadt's theory of, 15
    Europe as model of, 4–6
    Lewis, on, 18–21
    Tibi, on, 235–236n79
colonialism, 8–10, 18–19, 25, 37
    discourse of, 3–8, 9, 28–29
communalism, 121–122, 124, 252n4
Comte, Auguste, 67–68
Connolly, William, 37–38
Cromer, Lord, 74, 101–102, 249n4
'cultural modernity', 32
culture,
    Iqbal's, concept of, 135, 142
    Islamic modernist notions of, 75–76
    Orientalist theories of, 16–17, 20–22, 25–27, 29–30, 47, 223n58
    Tibi's, definition of, 32, 236n79

Daryabadi, 'Abdul Majid, 194.
Deism, 43, 67
democracy, 2, 19, 36
    Iqbal, on, 123–124, 138–139
    Maududi, on, 154
    and modernisation, 13
    Scruton, on, 35
'dependency theory', 14–15
Derrida, Jacques, 156–157, 167, 218, 260–261n27
Deutsch, Helen, 194, 266n39
Devji, Faisal, 233 fn53
De Vries, Hent, 36, 67
Draper, John William, 43

Eaton, Richard, 122
East/West binary, 136–138, 140–141, 217–218, 256n62, 257n65

Eisenstadt, S. N., 15
Enlightenment, 1, 2, 3–5, 7–8, 50, 227
Europe, as the subject of history (see also history), 1–2, 7, 10–11, 38, 136–137, 224

Faiz, Faiz Ahmed, 145
Fanon, Frantz, 6
al-Farabi, Abu Nasr, 54
Faruqi, Shamsur Rahman, 84–85, 96–97, 247n27
fatwa (legal opinion), 57, 170
feminism (see also Islamic feminism), 101, 178–182, 185, 191–192, 198–199, 209–210, 269n32
Fichte, J.G., 128–129, 254n33
fiqh (jurisprudence), 48, 169, 264n78
fitrah (human nature), 183, 189, 192, 199
Foucault, Michel, 28–29, 91, 188, 266n24
Fredrickson, George M., 143–144, 258n82
Fukuyama, Francis, 2, 149, 224

Ghalib, Mirza Asadullah Khan, 82–83, 94
al-Ghazali, Abu Hamid, 44, 66
globalisation, 8, 10, 15, 29, 41, 202
Goldziher, Ignaz, 44
Gray, John, 149–150
Grunebaum, Gustave von, 16–17
Guha, Ranajit, 78

Habermas, Jurgen, 32
Hali, Altaf Husain, 76, 85–96, 97–99, 102–103, 247n31
    literary romanticism of, 98–99
    'natural poetry', theory of, 86–87, 92–94, 99
Hanafi, Hasan, 73
Hegel, G.W.F., 128, 135
Herder, Johann Gottfried, 7, 46–47, 135, 239n16

heteronormativity, 88–91, 97
history, 7–8, 29, 38, 121, 227–228
   Arkoun's reading of, 216–220
   decline, Muslim theories of, 71–72, 75–76, 87–88, 90, 95, 131, 140, 154–155, 159–160, 172–173, 195
   Eurocentrism of, 10–11, 38, 136–137, 224
   Iqbal's notion of, 132–141, 145–146
   teleological theories of, 3–4 8, 12–13, 224–225, 228
homosexuality/homoeroticism, discourses towards, 89–91
Howard, John, 29–30.
hubb al-watan/wataniyyah (patriotism), 93–94, 125
human rights, 2, 10, 27, 32–34, 38, 149, 155, 228
Humbolt, William von, 135, 136
Hume, David, 3
Huntington, Samuel, 26, 234 fn60–61

ijtihad (independent reasoning), 24, 169, 205
Insha, Allah Khan, 90
Iqbal, Muhammad, 39–40, 98, 226, 254n29, 255n46, 255n49, 256n52
   historicism of, 132–138
   nationalism, concept of, 39–40, 123–127, 138–144
   philosophy of, 127–132, 145–147, 255n38, 257n71
   race, views on, 141–144
   Sufism, concept of, 130–131, 140, 257n74
Ishaq, Adib, 49
'ishq (love), 81–84, 92, 130–131
Islam,
   essentialisation/reification of, 39, 45, 57–58, 70, 72–73, 75, 144, 225, 226
   and modernity, 1–3, 10–11, 74, 119, 222–228
   and modernization, 17
   and science, 44–45, 50–53

   singular definition of, 16–17
   theocentrism of, 19–20, 31, 33–35
Islamic feminism, 209–211, 222, 269n32
Islamic law, 20, 23, 111, 116, 207–208, 227, 264n78
   etatisation of, 24, 168–171, 202, 263n73
Islamic modernism, 38–39, 45–74, 201, 225, 238n10, 243–244n78, 244n79
Islamism, 73, 148, 153, 155, 225
   aporia of, 156–157, 167–168, 174–175
   and totalitarianism, 2, 148–150, 160–161, 262n42
   women, essentialisation of, 182, 198–199

Jalal, Ayesha, 252n4
Jamila, Maryam, 176–180, 182, 183, 195
jihad, 23, 30
Jinnah, Muhammad Ali, 124, 127
Jones, William, 47
Al-Jurjani, 'Abd al-Qahir, 64
justice, 36
   Derrida's theory of, 156–157, 167, 260–260n27
   and Maududi, 198
   and *shari'ah*, 264n78
   Soroush's notion of, 214

Kant, Immanuel, 3, 128
Keddie, Nikki, 71
Khamenei, Sayyid Ali, 125
Khan, Sayyid Ahmad, 38, 45, 60–72, 74, 201–202, 225, 241n48
   literary reform, efforts towards, 76–77, 79, 96–97
   patriotism, notion of, 125–126
   theology of, 62–70, 242n60, 242n68
   on women's education, 114–115
Khan, Wahiduddin, 225
   Maududi, criticism of, 171–175

Kolakowski, Leszek, 34–35
Kugle, Scott Alan, 264n77

Lamberth, David, 182
Lane-Pool, Stanley, 101–102
Laroui, Abdallah, 7
Lelyveld, David, 77–78
Lerner, Daniel, 13–14, 16
Lewis, Bernard, 17–23, 25, 27, 30–32, 41, 225, 232n42, 233n58, 234n65

Macaulay, Thomas Babington, 4, 5, 76, 244n4, 247n38
MacIntyre, Alasdair, 41–42
Madani, Husain Ahmad, 126
Mahmoud, Saba, 179–180
Manion, Jennifer, 192
Marcus, Margaret, *see* Jamila, Maryam
Maududi, Sayyid Abul A'la, 24, 40, 150–152, 160–161, 171–174, 202, 225, 260n16
   divine sovereignty, theory of, 152–153
   haya (shame), notion of, 177, 186–187, 189–191, 192–193, 199
   Islamic law, concept of, 153, 168–169
   Islamic state, theory of an, 153–157, 167–168, 233n55, 260n22
   male sexuality, views on, 193–194
   women, discourse towards, 176–177, 182–186, 194–199
McClintock, Anne, 105–106
McTaggart, John, 128
Meisami, Julie Scott, 246n24
Mernissi, Fatima, 184–186, 209
Michaelis, J. D., 46
Mill, James, 4
Mill, John Stuart, 4, 85, 229 fn5
Minault, Gail, 251n34
   on *begumati zaban* (women's language), 111
minorities, 31–32, 35–36, 121, 227–228, 260n22
Mir, Mir Taqi, 94, 246n21

modernity, 1–7, 224
   and colonialism, 8–9
   dialectical conception of, 7–8, 34–35;
   and Islam, 1–3, 10–11, 74, 119, 222–228
   and Islamism, 150, 168, 174–175
   'multiple modernities', 15
modernization, 11–14, 17
   and 'rationalisation', 12
Moosa, Ebrahim, 203
Muhammad (Prophet), 55–56, 62–64, 95, 116–117, 185, 186–187, 206, 255n38, 266n30
Muir, William, 61
Müller, Max, 67, 136–137, 256n62
Muslim women,
   discourses towards education of, 100–119, 249n4, 250n10, 251n34
   in France 36
   symbolic status of, 39, 40, 100–104, 109–110, 114–119, 176–199, 211, 249n5
Mu'tazilah theology, 58–59, 214, 270n49

al-Nabhani, Taqi al-Din, 73
Nadwi, Abul Hasan 'Ali, 160
Nagel, Thomas, 36
Naim, C. M., 89
nationalism,
   Anderson's theory of, 21, 121
   constructivist approach to, 121–123, 252–253n8
   in India and Pakistan, 120–123, 146, 252–253n8
   Iqbal's theory of, 39–40, 123–127, 138–144
Nicholson, R. A., 257n74
Nietzsche, Friedrich, 128, 137, 138–139
Nu'mani, Shibli, 44–45, 242n69, 247n28

Orientalism 16–17, 27–29, 79, 101, 122, 136–137, 235n72, 247n38, 249n5, 270n55
   Said's criticism of, 28–29
Ottoman Empire, 18–21, 169, 232n41

Index

Pandey, Gyanendra, 35–36, 122
Pasha, Ismail (Khedive of Egypt), 48
Pateman, Carole, 115–116
Phillips, Melanie, 227
Piers, Gerhart, 188, 266n25
Pipes, Daniel, 227
poetry, *see* Urdu literature
political totalitarianism, 25–26, 148–149
Prakash, Gyan, 47
Pritchett, Francis, 84, 91–92, 247n26
progressive Islam, 40–41, 200–201, 225
   hermeneutical approaches of, 40–41, 201, 208–209, 220, 222–223
prophecy, theories of, 62–67, 133–134, 139–140, 206

qaum/qaumiyyah (nation/nationalism), 87–88, 123, 125–127, 142–143, 159
Qur'an, hermeneutical approaches to, 62–64, 202–204, 218, 241n53, 259n10
Qutb, Sayyid, 24, 40, 73, 157–159, 202, 225, 261n36, 262n46
   Carrel, influence of, 165–167
   Islamic conception of, 161–165, 262n47
   jahilliya, theory of, 160–161
   literary aesthetic notions of, 161–165, 174–175

race 47, 49–50
Rahman, Fazlur, 41, 66, 200, 204, 209, 211, 218, 222, 268n24
   hermeneutical approach of, 204–207
Rangin, Yar Khan, 89, 90
rape, 194, 266n39
reason, 36, 37–38, 60, 227, 237n98
   Arkoun's theory of, 216–217, 219–221
   colonial/orientalist discourses towards, 43, 45, 47–48, 50–52, 70–74, 224–225
   and Enlightenment, 4, 5, 50
   Iqbal's attitude towards, 133–134

Islamic modernist discourse towards, 51–74, 242n69
   Qutb's view towards, 163–165
   in secular discourses, 12, 32, 33–34
   and Soroush, 214–215
Reisman, David, 13
religion,
   deontological theory of, 220–221, 222, 271n68
   dichotomy with science, 43–45
   modern reification of, 39, 45, 73, 95
   and philology, 45–47
religious nationalism, 14, 122–123, 148–150, 213–214
Renan, Ernst, 47, 49–53, 56, 74, 239n21, 239–240n26
Ricoeur, Paul, 203, 268n13
Rida, Muhammad Rashid, 73, 240n37, 243n77
Romanticism, 8, 45–46, 93–96, 97–99, 135, 137, 243n79
Rose, Nikolas, 188
Roy, Olivier, 202
Russell, Colin, 43
Russell, Ralph, 84

Said, Edward (*see also* Orientalism), 28–29, 235 fn72
as-salaf as-salih/salafiyyah, 23, 55, 57, 73
Schimmel, Annemarie, 255n38, 255n49
Scott, George Riley, 196–197
Scott, Joan, 36, 181
Scruton, Roger, 35
secularism, 2, 29, 32, 34–38
secular time, 9, 19–22
secularity, 37–38
shame, 177, 185–186, 188–194, 199, 266n25
Sharabi, Hisham, 231n33
Sharar, Abdul Halim, 90
shari'ah (*see also* Islamic law), 109, 111, 116–117, 126, 153, 156, 168–171, 173, 207–208, 227, 264n78
Singh, Iqbal, 147
Sinha, Mrinalina, 88

Smith, Wilfred Cantwell, 156, 238n11
Soroush, 'Abdolkarim, 41, 211–212, 222, 270n49
   epistemology, theory of, 212–213, 269–270n44
   secularism, advocacy of, 214–215
Spencer, Herbert, 67–68
Spengler, Oswald, 51, 135, 139, 257n71
Strum, Arthur, 7–8
subjectivity, notions of, 32, 182, 188, 288
sufism, 68, 83, 92–93, 130–132, 140, 240n37, 245n17, 246n19, 250n9, 257n74
sunnah (tradition of the Prophet), 57, 116, 170

Taylor, Gabriele,
   shame, notion of, 188–189, 191–193
Ibn Taymiyyah, 55, 134
terrorism, 2, 22, 27, 29–30, 227
Thanawi, Ashraf 'Ali, 39, 103–104, 110–111, 119
   Muslim women's reform, views on, 111–113, 116–117
   women's language, 111–112
Thapar, Romila, 122
Thompson, Edward, 124
Tibi, Bassam, 32–34, 36, 149, 235–236n79, 236n84
Todorov, Tzetan, 50, 239n21
Tomiche, N., 179

Urdu literature, 39, 247n27, 251n34
   ghazal, conventions of, 81–85, 97, 245n17, 246n25, 247n26
   rekhti, 88–91
   Romantic themes in, 93–96, 97–99
   Victorian literary influence on, 79–80, 85–88

van der Veer, Peter, 9
Vanita, Ruth, 89
Vico, Giambattista, 7
Viswanathan, Gauri, 78, 245n9

Wadud, Amina, 41, 209–210, 221
   hermeneutical approach of, 210–211
Wahhab, Muhammad ibn 'Abdul, 55, 256n52, 268n12
Wallace, Walter L., 231n23
'war against terrorism', 18, 27
Ward, James, 128
Weber, Max, 11–12, 34, 231n23
women, agency of (*see also* Muslim women), 179–182
women's rights, 102, 105, 179, 182, 198–199

Young, Robert, 8

Zaghlul, Sa'd, 49
Zamakshari, Abu al-Qasim, 183
Zubaida, Sami, 24